JAPAN'S ECONOMY:

A Bibliography of its Past and Present

JAPAN'S ECONOMY:

A Bibliography of its Past and Present

WILLIAM D. WRAY
University of British Columbia

Markus Wiener Publishing
New York

For information write to:
Markus Wiener Publishing, Inc.
225 Lafayette Street, New York, NY 10012

Library of Congress Catologing-in-Publication Data

Wray, William D., 1943–

   Japan's economy.

   1. Japan—Economic conditions—To 1868—Bibliography.
2. Japan—Economic conditions—1868–   —Bibliography.
I. Title.
Z7165.J3W7   1989   [HC462]   016.330952   89-5845

ISBN 0-910129-79-7

Printed in the United States of America

CONTENTS

PREFACE

Once, while working in the stacks of Harvard's Widener Library in the late 1960s, I dropped a large rectangular file box containing bibliographical cards. As users of that library will know, beneath the book shelves there is nothing, just empty space above the shelves of the level below. Unable to catch my cards before they fell through the floor, I rushed to the nearby stairway with visions of them floating downward through several levels until they reached the basement. Fortunately, I found all of them (I think) on the floor below. But not having the technology to learn from my experience, I continued to collect cards, and the boxes kept piling up. This, of course, disproves John Dower's contention (in his *Japanese History & Culture From Ancient To Modern Times: Seven Basic Bibliographies*, Markus Wiener Publishing, 1986, p. vi) that his would be the last of the survey bibliographies on Japanese history to emanate from file cards (if this present book can be regarded as a survey bibliography). In truth, probably more than half of my entries were entered directly into my made-in-Britain-with-Japanese-parts Apricot computer. Certainly, I would never have had the patience to record on file cards all the works listed here on "Japanese-style management."

The file cards in boxes constitute the origins of the present bibliography. However, its organization owes more to the needs of the classroom and how they have governed the bibliography's evolution. For the first three years after I began teaching Japanese history in the mid-1970s I never taught the same course twice. Each time I began a new course, whether in intellectual or business history, I prepared a new and separate bibliography. Eventually this became tiresome, and it seemed more efficient to have one single, large bibliography that could cover the needs of various course offerings. Shortly after I prepared this new unified bibliography, my teaching responsibilities finally stabilized and were divided into two main courses: one, a survey of modern Japan, starting in the Tokugawa era but with only brief coverage of the post-Occupation period, and the other, a specialized offering in economic and business history, over a third of which dealt with the postwar years. My unified bibliography could not meet the needs of this latter course without creating an imbalance through disproportionate emphasis on economics. Thus my "grand unified" list lasted only a year or so, and I spun off a second bibliography on economics (or more precisely, industry and business). The postwar section of the present bibliography derives its organization from this second list, while the coverage of pre-World War II periods is largely an expansion of the economic portions of the earlier, unified bibliography.

In size, as opposed to organization, this book is much more than an amalgamation of the two earlier lists. Indeed, the continued expansion in the number of entries, especially for the postwar period, has taken far more time than I originally anticipated in undertaking this project. The effort, I would hope, has made the work as useful for the concerns of contemporary policy issues of the Japanese economy as for the needs of the history classroom. Nevertheless, the result cannot be called a fully comprehensive bibliography. Certain periods, such as the Occupation, I have treated lightly, since good references are already available for them. Most important, I have omitted a whole class of magazines, newspapers, and popular periodicals which provide only short articles. Though they are important, inclusion of these short pieces would not only have taken an excessive amount of time, but would also have created an unwieldy product. I have listed these articles in exceptional cases—such as those about the distribution system under the section on "Market Access," the coverage of which has not been commensurate with its importance. Otherwise, I have simply listed the journals which fall into this category in my opening explanations. More generally, my survey covers material through 1988 and some works slated for publication in early 1989.

Two particular issues of substance also require explanation. The first relates to subject matter and the second to periodization. Though this is a bibliography of the economy, it contains substantial material on thought, politics, and society. In determining whether to include items from these and other fields, my principal criterion has been their relevance to economics. Thus, I have generally omitted works on political background that deal only passingly with economic issues as well as publications on labor that are primarily oriented toward politics. Works of this nature can easily be found in the Dower bibliography. Second, I have begun the bibliography in the early Tokugawa period—that is, around 1600. My rationale for this is that with a few exceptions there is still not enough writing in English on earlier periods which draws sufficient distinction between, say, commerce and politics or between land, economics, and military power to make criteria for selection reasonably clear. Furthermore, pre-1600 material can be found, again, in the Dower bibliography.

Each chapter of the bibliography is divided into sections and, in most cases, into sub-sections as well. (See the Detailed Contents for these). Usually, the order of individual entries follows the year of publication. This makes it possible to gain a fairly quick impression of how the historiography of a particular topic has evolved (at least from the titles, if the reader is unfamiliar with the authors). In certain cases I have found it more convenient to list entries by the chronology of the subject, or alternatively, by topical sequence.

Bibliographies with a large number of topical headings present both advantages and frustrations for the reader. On the one hand, they provide convenient mini-bibliographies on a great many specific issues. On the other hand, the entries under a specific heading sometimes seem insufficient, since they cannot include everything that is relevant. Extensive cross-referencing can partially overcome this, but it can also make a bibliography more awkward to use. Instead of cross-referencing I have followed a policy of repeating individual entries under different topics if their subject matter warrants it. In doing so, I have tried almost entirely to avoid the use of abbreviations, even within the same section, when the title of, say, a composite volume is repeated. This eliminates the need for extensive coding systems and saves the reader the trouble of looking elsewhere for full bibliographic information. I confess also that with a computer it is faster to repeat full titles than to use multiple abbreviations. Similarly, with a few exceptions listed below, I have maintained full titles for periodicals as well.

Two recent trends among periodicals on Japan are worth mentioning. First, until the 1980s most of the English-language journals on economics issued by Japanese universities served a fairly broad audience and published a relatively small number of technical papers. Except for journals specializing in business and management, this has changed in the past decade. Increasingly technical articles have appeared in the economic periodicals, making them more valuable to Western economists but less accessible to non-mathematical historians and political scientists. Among Western publications, perhaps the most noteworthy development is the growing volume of well-researched Japanese-language based articles appearing in professional law journals.

Finally, we might ask, what is the next stage in the bibliographical coverage of Japan? One might expect it to be the appearance of a fully comprehensive computer-based list of works. I am not so sure. I have always had a sense of the law of diminishing returns about large comprehensive bibliographies. Boredom sets in before one reaches all the interesting parts. I hope that the present work achieves a happy medium between compactness and comprehensiveness that makes it easy to use. Among specialists, more useful than the fully comprehensive bibliography in English would be topical bibliographies of Japanese works for the benefit of Western scholars. The market for such references may still be too small in the West to follow the conventional publishing route, but the spread of Japanese kanji-based laptop computers and word processors among Westerners will reduce the publishing cost. The next step, therefore, may be a bibliography of Japanese works in economic and business history. The obstacle to that will be less the cost than the time involved in surveying the immense amount of material available, especially since a great deal of work published by younger Japanese scholars remains in relatively inaccessible or poorly distributed periodicals issued by university faculties and institutes. For the time being, the best bibliographical source on Japanese works in this field is the Annual Reports section of the *Japanese Yearbook on Business History* published in English by the Japan Business History Institute.

For help in raising this project above the level of the classroom, I am especially grateful to Hyung Gu Lynn who invested not only his considerable talents but also his physical resources in hauling books up to my office. I would also like to thank Nina Raj and Susan Schmidt of the University of Tokyo Press for some last-minute checking and several scholars for sending me lists of their publications. Future arrangements may be made to provide updates on this project. I would thus be grateful to anyone who brought to my attention any errors of recording or serious omissions. I would like to thank Frank Shulman for sending me an advance copy of one of his dissertation bibliographies, and I am grateful to the Japan Foundation in that part of the work for this bibliography was completed while I was on a grant from the Foundation for another project.

Finally, I input most of the bibliography with SuperWriter, a British program akin to WordStar. This produces clear macrons (marks over Japanese long vowels) but only with such a cumberous process that I decided against using them. I later converted everything to WordPerfect, but too late to change my macron policy. Names in this work appear in Western order with family name last.

Vancouver,
January 1989

ABBREVIATIONS & JOURNALS

1. Abbreviations

Although I have tried to keep abbreviations to a minimum, the constant repetition of some titles would have left a messy appearance. I have used the following abbreviations not just because the periodicals concerned appear frequently but because they often appear sequentially within the same section.

CJ   *Contemporary Japan*

DE   *Developing Economies*

JES   *Japanese Economic Studies*

Yearbook   *Japanese Yearbook on Business History*

2. Journals not Surveyed

With a few exceptions I have not listed individual articles, mainly because they are very short, from the following selected journals. Publications of this type, however, are essential for covering Japan's economy through English sources.

Asiaweek

Asian Wall Street Journal

Aviation Week & Space Technology

Business Japan

Business Tokyo

Business Week

Dataquest (on the electronics industry)

Economic Eye

Far Eastern Economic Review

Fortune

Japan Echo

Japan Economic Journal

Japan Times

Japan Quarterly

Journal of Japanese Trade & Industry

Oriental Economist (title changed to *Tokyo Business Today* in 1986)

Speaking of Japan

Tokyo Business Today (successor to *Oriental Economist*)

Wall Street Journal

DETAILED CONTENTS

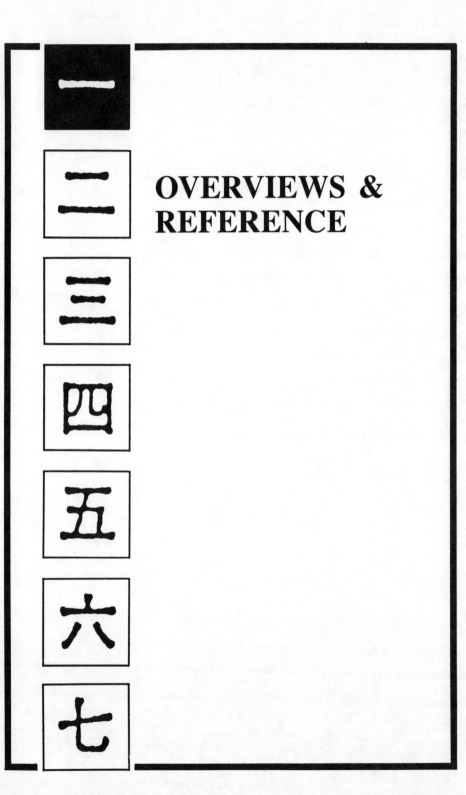

OVERVIEWS & REFERENCE

A. REFERENCE

Encyclopedias & Dictionaries

Kodansha Encyclopedia of Japan, 8 vols., plus index, Kodansha, 1983.

Encyclopedia of Asian History, 4 vols., New York, Macmillan, 1988.

Janet E. Hunter, *Concise Dictionary of Modern Japanese History*, University of California Press, 1984.

Seiichi Iwao, ed. *Biographical Dictionary of Japanese History*, Kodansha, 1978.

Bibliographies

Bernard S. Silberman, *Japan and Korea: A Critical Bibliography*, University of Arizona Press, 1962.

John W. Dower, *Japanese History & Culture from Ancient to Modern Times: Seven Basic Bibliographies*, New York, Markus Wiener Publishing, 1986.

Bibliography of Asian Studies, Association of Asian Studies, annual. (This is still useful as a guide to past publications, but since it is now roughly five years behind, it has limited value as a reference to current research).

Frank J. Shulman, comp. & ed. *Doctoral Dissertations on Japan and Korea, 1969-1979: An Annotated Bibliography of Studies in Western Languages*, University of Washington Press, 1982.

Frank J. Shulman, *Doctoral Dissertations on Asia*, periodic publication (recently annual) for the Association for Asian Studies, University Microfilms. (This is probably the most valuable bibliography for ongoing research).

"Complete Index to Volumes I (1926)—L (1980)," *Kyoto University Economic Review* 50:1-2 (Apr-Oct 1980), 50-68.

Data

Bank of Japan, *Hundred-Year Statistics of the Japanese Economy*, Statistics Department, Bank of Japan, 1966 (Japanese title: *Meiji iko hompo shuyo keizai tokei*).

Historiography

Hisao Otsuka, "Modernization Reconsidered—with Special Reference to Industrialization," *DE* 3:4 (Dec 1965), 387-403.

Kozo Yamamura, "Recent Research in Japanese Economic History," in Robert Gallman, ed. *Recent Developments in the Study of Business and Economic History*, Greenwich, Conn., Greenwood Press, 1977, 221-46.

Kozo Yamamura, "Introduction," to quantitative studies in *Explorations in Economic History* 15:1 (Jan 1978), 1-10.

Kozo Yamamura, "Introduction to Part Four [Rural Economy and Material Conditions]," in *Marius Jansen and Gilbert Rozman, eds. Japan in Transition: From Tokugawa to Meiji*, Princeton University Press, 1986, 377-81.

Shin'ichi Yonekawa, "Recent Writing on Japanese Economic and Social History," *Economic History Review* 38:1 (Feb 1985), 107-23.

B. GENERAL

(Covers material which overlaps the three periods surveyed in the bibliography: Tokugawa, Modern, and Postwar).

Surveys

John Whitney Hall, "Aspects of Japanese Economic Development," in Hall & Richard K. Beardsley, *Twelve Doors to Japan*, New York, McGraw-Hill, 1965, 538-86.

Johannes Hirschmeier & Tsunehiko Yui, *The Development of Japanese Business, l600-1980*, 2nd ed., London, Allen & Unwin, 1981.

Ryoshin Minami, *The Economic Development of Japan: A Quantitative Study*, London, Macmillan, 1986.

Kazuo Sato, *Economic Development of Japan*, London, Basil Blackwell, 1987.

Case Studies in Political Economy: Japan, 1854-1977, Harvard Business School, (Intercollegiate Case Clearing House), n.d.

Mikio Sumiya & Koji Taira, eds. *An Outline of Japanese Economic History, 1603-1940: Major Works and Research Findings*, University of Tokyo Press, 1979.

Regional

The History of Kanagawa, Kanagawa Prefectural Government, 1985.

Angus Maddison, *Economic Growth in Japan and the USSR*, New York, W. W. Norton, 1969.

C. COMPARATIVE ACCOUNTS

(Works are listed here only if they do not appear elsewhere in this bibliography).

Norman Jacobs, *The Origins of Modern Capitalism and Eastern Asia*, Hong Kong University Press, 1958.

David S. Landes, "Japan and Europe: Contrasts in Industrialization," in William W. Lockwood, ed. *The State and Economic Enterprise in Japan*, Princeton University Press, 1965, 93-182.

Lloyd D. Musolf, "Mixed Enterprise in a Developmental Perspective: France, Italy, and Japan," *Journal of Comparative Administration* 3:2 (Aug 1971), 131-68.

Frank B. Tipton, Jr., "Government Policy and Economic Development in Germany and Japan: A Skeptical Reevaluation," *Journal of Economic History* 41:1 (March 1981), 139-50.

B. R. Tomlinson, "Writing History Sideways: Lessons for Indian Economic Historians from Meiji Japan," *Modern Asian Studies* 19:3 (July 1985), 669-98.

Walter Goldfrank, "Silk and Steel: Italy and Japan Between the Two World Wars," in Edmund Burke, III, *Global Crises and Social Movements: Artisans, Peasants, Populists, and the World Economy*, Boulder, Westview Press, 1988, 218-40.

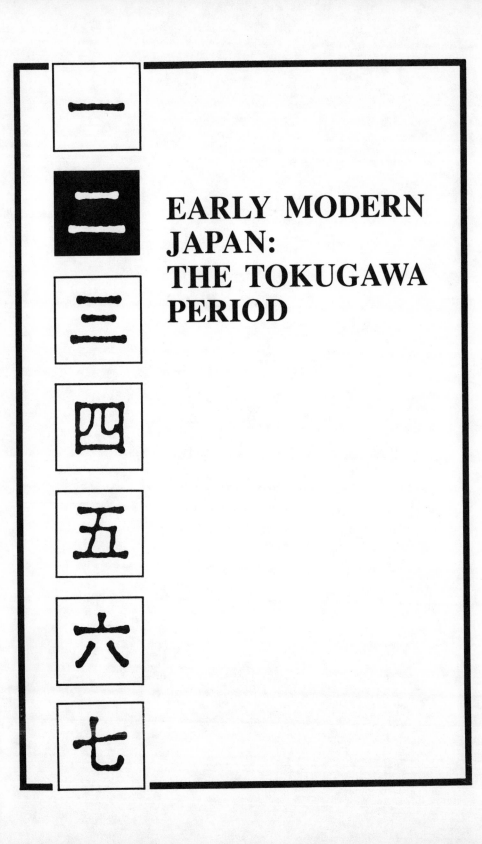

EARLY MODERN JAPAN: THE TOKUGAWA PERIOD

1. GENERAL

A. SURVEYS, COMPOSITE WORKS

George Sansom, *A History of Japan, 1615-1867*, Stanford University Press, 1963.

Neil Skene Smith, ed. *Materials on Japanese Social and Economic History: Tokugawa Japan*, London, P.S. King & Sons, 1937.

John W. Hall and Marius B. Jansen, eds. *Studies in the Institutional History of Early Modern Japan*, Princeton University Press, 1968.

Seymour Broadbridge, "Economic and Social Trends in Tokugawa Japan," *Modern Asian Studies* 8:3 (1974), 347-72.

Kozo Yamamura, "Returns on Unification: Economic Growth in Japan, 1550-1650," in John Whitney Hall et al., eds. *Japan Before Tokugawa: Political Consolidation and Economic Growth, 1500 to 1650*, Princeton University Press, 1981, 327-72.

Akira Hayami, "A Great Transformation: Social and Economic Changes in Sixteenth and Seventeenth Century Japan," in Erich Pauer, ed. *Silkworms, Oil, and Chips . . . Proceedings of the Economics and Economic History Section of the Fourth International Conference on Japanese Studies*, Japan Seminar, University of Bonn, 1986, 3-13.

William A. Spurr, "Business Cycles in Japan before 1853," *Journal of Political Economy* 46 (Oct 1938), 653-87.

Daniel L. Spencer, "Japan's Pre-Perry Preparation for Economic Growth," *American Journal of Economics and Scoiology* 17 (1958), 195-216.

E.S. Crawcour, "The Premodern Economy," in Arthur Tiedemann, ed. *An Introduction to Japanese Civilization*, Columbia University Press, 1973, 461-86.

E.S. Crawcour, "The Tokugawa Period and Japan's Preparation for Modern Economic Growth," *Journal of Japanese Studies* 1:1 (Aut 1974), 113-25.

E.L. Jones, *Growth Recurring: Economic Change in World History*, Oxford University Press, 1988, chapter on "Japan," 149-67.

B. REFERENCE & HISTORIOGRAPHICAL ACCOUNTS

Sydney Crawcour, "Documentary Sources of Tokugawa Economic and Social History," *Journal of Asian Studies* 20:3 (May 1961), 343-51.

Susan Hanley & Kozo Yamamura, "A Quiet Transformation in Tokugawa Economic History," 30:2 *Journal of Asian Studies* (Feb 1971), 373-84.

2. GOVERNMENTAL AUTHORITY, THE ECONOMY & FINANCIAL POLICY

A. GOVERNMENT POLICY

John W. Hall, "The Tokugawa Bakufu and the Merchant Class," *Occasional Papers*, University of Michigan, Center for Japanese Studies, 1 (1951), 26-33.

John Whitney Hall, *Tanuma Okitsugu (1719-1788): Forerunner of Modern Japan*, Harvard University Press, 1955.

Keiji Nagahara, "The Historical Premise for the Modernization of Japan: On the Structure of the Tokugawa Shogunate," *Hitotsubashi Journal of Economics* 3:1 (Oct 1962), 61-72.

Junnosuke Sasaki, "Some Remarks on the Economic Foundation of Military Service under the Tokugawa Shogunate System," *Hitotsubashi Journal of Social Studies* 2:1 (1964), 36-53.

Donald Shively, "Sumptuary Regulations and Status in Early Tokugawa Japan," *Harvard Journal of Asiatic Studies* 25 (1964-65), 123-64.

Dan F. Henderson, *Conciliation and Japanese Law*, 2 vols., University of Washington Press, 1965.

Toshio Tsukahira, *Feudal Control in Tokugawa Japan: The Sankin Kotai System*, Harvard University Press, 1966.

Harold Bolitho, *Treasures Among Men: The Fudai Daimyo in Tokugawa Japan*, Yale University Press, 1974.

William H. Coaldrake, "Edo Architecture and Tokugawa Law," *Monumenta Nipponica* 36:3 (Aut 1981), 235-84.

William B. Hauser, "Osaka Castle and Tokugawa Authority in Western Japan," in Jeffrey P. Mass and Hauser, eds. *The Bakufu in Japanese History*, Stanford University Press, 1986.

Kate Wildman Nakai, *Shogunal Politics: Arai Hakuseki and the Premises of Tokugawa Rule*, Harvard University Press, 1987.

Harold Bolitho, "The Tempo Crisis," in Marius Jansen, ed. *The Cambridge History of Japan*, vol. V, *The Nineteenth Century*, Cambridge University Press, 1989.

Albert M. Craig, *Choshu in the Meiji Restoration*, Harvard University Press, 1961, 9-25, "Choshu and the Tokugawa Polity."

B. FINANCIAL POLICY

George Sansom, *A History of Japan, 1615-1867*, Stanford University Press, 1963, esp. 154-98.

Sho Sawada, "Financial Difficulties of the Edo Bakufu," *Harvard Journal of Asiatic Studies* 1 (1936), 308-26.

John Whitney Hall, *Tanuma Okitsugu (1719-1788): Forerunner of Modern Japan*, Harvard University Press, 1955, 57-83.

Isao Soranaka, "The Kansei Reforms—Success or Failure?" *Monumenta Nipponica* 33:2 (Sum 1978), 151-64.

Albert M. Craig, *Choshu in the Meiji Restoration*, Harvard University Press, 1961, 26-50, "Choshu Finances and the Tokugawa Economy."

C. CURRENCY AND MONETARY POLICY

Tetsuo Kamiki, "The Circulation of Commodities and the Use of Money in Early Medieval Japan," *Kobe University Economic Review* 12 (1966), 117-28.

Kozo Yamamura & Tetsuo Kamiki, "Silver Mines and Sung Coins: A Monetary History of Medieval and Modern Japan in International Perspective," in J.F. Richards, ed. *Precious Metals in the Later Medieval and Early Modern Worlds*, Durham, Carolina Academic Press, 1983, 329-62.

Kozo Yamamura, "From Coins to Rice: Hypotheses on the *Kandaka* and *Kokudaka* Systems," *Journal of Japanese Studies* 14:2 (Sum 1988), 341-67.

A. Kobata, "The Production and Uses of Gold and Silver in Sixteenth and Seventeenth Century Japan," *Economic History Review* 18:2 (Aug 1965), 245-66.

Special Issue: "Studies in the History of Japanese Currency Systems," *Acta Asiatica* 39 (1980), including the following articles:
Takeo Takizawa, "Early Currency Policies of the Tokugawas, 1563-1608," 21-41.
Soji Enomoto, "Domain Coins in the Early Edo Period," 42-60.
Yotaro Sakudo, "Domain Paper Currencies and Money Merchants in the Tokugawa Period," 6l-77.

Matsuyo Takizawa, *The Penetration of Money Economy in Japan and its Effects upon Social and Political Institutions*, New York, Columbia University, 1927.

Kokichi Miyashita, " 'Money Economy' in the Tokugawa Era," *Kobe University Economic Review* 8 (1962), 1-19.

E.S. Crawcour & Kozo Yamamura, "The Tokugawa Monetary System, 1787-1868," *Economic Development and Cultural Change* 18:4.Pt. 1 (July 1970), 489-518.

Takehiko Ohkura & Hiroshi Shimbo, "The Tokugawa Monetary Policy in the Eighteenth and Nineteenth Centuries," *Explorations in Economic History* 15:1 (Jan 1978), 101-24.

Erich Pauer, "Iron Versus Copper Coinage in Pre-Modern Japan," *Asian Monetary Monitor* 9:2 (March-Apr 1985), 23-38.

3. SOCIAL HISTORY, LABOR & THE RURAL ECONOMY

A. GENERAL

Yasukichi Yasuba, "The Tokugawa Legacy: A Survey," *Economic Studies Quarterly* 38:4 (Dec 1987), 290-308.

Thomas C. Smith, *Native Sources of Japanese Industrialization, 1750-1920*, University of California Press, 1988 (collected essays).

B. SOCIAL LIFE & THE VILLAGE

Thomas C. Smith, "The Japanese Village in the Seventeenth Century," in John W. Hall and Marius B. Jansen, eds. *Studies in the Institutional History of Early Modern Japan*, Princeton University Press, 1968, 263-82, reprinted from *Journal of Economic History* 12:1 (Win 1952).

Dan F. Henderson, " 'Contracts' in Tokugawa Villages," *Journal of Japanese Studies* 1:1 (Aut 1974), 51-90.

Special Issue: "The Family in Japanese History," *Journal of Family History* 8:1 (Spr 1983), including the following articles:
Akira Hayami, "The Myth of Primogeniture and Impartible Inheritance in Tokugawa Japan," 3-29.
L. L. Cornell, "Retirement, Inheritance, and Intergenerational Conflict in Preindustrial Japan," 55-69.

Laurel L. Cornell, "Life Cycle Service, Age at Marriage, and Household Formation in the Industrialization of Japan," in Akira Hayami, ed. Pre-Conditions to Industrialization in Japan, Papers from Ninth International Economic History Congress, Bern, 1986.

Anne Walthall, "Village Networks: Sōdai and the Sale of Edo Nightsoil," *Monumenta Nipponica* 43:3 (Aut 1988), 279-303.

C. AGRICULTURE & COMMERCE

Agriculture, Forestry & Whaling

Thomas C. Smith, "Okura Nagatsune and the Technologists," in Albert Craig & Donald Shively, eds. *Personality in Japanese History*, University of California Press, 1970, 127-54.

William W. Kelly, *Water Control in Tokugawa Japan: Irrigation Organization in a Japanese River Basin, 1600-1870*, Cornell University, East Asia Papers, No. 31, 1982.

Ann Waswo, "Innovation and Growth in Japanese Agriculture, 1600-1868," in Akira Hayami, ed. Pre-Conditions to Industrialization in Japan, Papers from Ninth International Economic History Congress, Bern, 1986.

Conrad Totman, "Forestry in Early Modern Japan, 1650-1850: A Preliminary Survey," *Agricultural History* 56:2 (1982), 415-25.

Conrad Totman, "Land-Use Patterns and Afforestation in the Edo Period," *Monumenta Nipponica* 93:1 (Spr 1984), 1-10.

Conrad Totman, *The Origins of Japan's Modern Forests*, University Press of Hawaii, 1984.

Conrad Totman, "Plantation Forestry in Early Modern Japan: Economic Aspects of its Emergence," *Agricultural History* 60 (Sum 1986), 23-51.

Conrad Totman, "Lumber Provisioning in Early Modern Japan, 1580-1850," *Journal of Forestry History* 31 (Apr 1987), 56-70.

Conrad Totman, *Green Archipelago*, University of California Press, 1988.

Arne Kalland, "Pre-Modern Whaling in Northern Kyushu," in Erich Pauer, ed. *Silkworms, Oil, and Chips . . . Proceedings of the Economics and Economic History Section of the Fourth International Conference on Japanese Studies*, Japan Seminar, University of Bonn, 1986, 29-50.

Taxation

Thomas C. Smith, "The Land Tax in the Tokugawa Period," in John W. Hall and Marius B. Jansen, eds. *Studies in the Institutional History of Early Modern Japan*, Princeton University Press, 1968, 283-99, reprinted from *Journal of Asian Studies* 18:1 (Nov 1958).

Constantine N. Vaporis, "Post Station and Assisting Villages: Corvee Labor and Peasant Contention," *Monumenta Nipponica* 41:4 (Win 1986), 377-414.

Philip C. Brown, "The Mismeasure of Land: Land Surveying in the Tokugawa Period," *Monumenta Nipponica* 42:2 (Sum 1987), 115-55.

Philip C. Brown, " 'Feudal Remnants' and Tenant Power: The Case of Niigata, Japan, in the Nineteenth and early Twentieth Centuries," *Peasant Studies* 15:1 (Fall 1987), 5-26.

Kozo Yamamura, "From Coins to Rice: Hypotheses on the *Kandaka* and *Kokudaka* Systems," *Journal of Japanese Studies* 14:2 (Sum 1988), 341-67.

Philip C. Brown, "Practical Constraints on Early Tokugawa Land Taxation: Annual Versus Fixed Assessments in Kaga Domain," *Journal of Japanese Studies* 14:2 (Sum 1988), 369-401.

Rural Commerce

Thomas C. Smith, "Landlords and Rural Capitalists in the Modernization of Japan," *Journal of Economic History* 16:2 (June 1956), 165-81.

Thomas C. Smith, *The Agrarian Origins of Modern Japan*, Stanford University Press, 1959.

Thomas C. Smith, "Farm Family By-Employments in Preindustrial Japan," *Journal of Economic History* 29:4 (Dec 1969), 687-715.

Kozo Yamamura, "Economic Responsiveness in Japanese Industrialization," in L.P. Cain & P. Uselding, eds. *Business Enterprises and Economic Change*, Kent State University Press, 1973, 173-97.

Thomas C. Smith, "Pre-modern Economic Growth: Japan and the West," *Past & Present* 60 (Aug 1973), 127-60.

Arne Kalland, "Rural Credit Institutions in Tokugawa Japan," in Akira Hayami, ed. Pre-Conditions to Industrialization in Japan, Papers from Ninth International Economic History Congress, Bern, 1986.

Shunsaku Nishikawa, "The Economy of Choshu on the Eve of Industrialization," *Economic Studies Quarterly* 38:4 (Dec 1987), 323-37.

D. POPULATION & ECONOMIC CHANGE

Population, Demography & Living Standards

Garrett Droppers, "The Population of Japan in the Tokugawa Period," *Transactions, Asiatic Society of Japan* 22:2 (1894), 253-84.

Akira Hayami, "The Population at the Beginning of the Tokugawa Period: An Introduction to the Historical Demography of Pre-industrial Japan," *Keio Economic Studies* 4 (1966-67), 1-28.

Akira Hayami, "The Demographic Analysis of a Village in Tokugawa Japan: Kando-Shinden of Owari Province, 1778-1871," *Keio Economic Studies* 5 (1968), 50-88.

Akira Hayami, "Demographic Aspects of a Village in Tokugawa Japan," in Paul Deprez, ed. *Population and Economics*, Winnipeg, University of Manitoba Press, 1970, 109-25.

Kozo Yamamura, *A Study of Samurai Income and Entrepreneurship*, Harvard University Press, 1974.

Robert Eng & Thomas Smith, "Peasant Families and Population Control in Eighteenth Century Japan," *Journal of Interdisciplinary History* 6:3 (Win 1976), 417-45.

Susan Hanley & Kozo Yamamura, *Economic and Demographic Change in Preindustrial Japan, 1600-1868*, Princeton University Press, 1977.

Thomas C. Smith, *Nakahara: Family Farming and Population in a Japanese Village, 1717-1830*, Stanford University Press, 1977.

Akira Hayami, "Thank You Francisco Xavier: An Essay in the Use of Micro-Data for Historical Demography of Tokugawa Japan," *Keio Economic Studies* 16:1-2 (1979), 65-81.

Akira Hayami, "Class Differences in Marriage and Fertility among Tokugawa Villagers in Mino Province," *Keio Economic Studies* 17:1 (1980), 1-16.

James I. Nakamura & Matao Miyamoto, "Social Structure and Population Change: A Comparative Study of Tokugawa Japan and Ch'ing China," *Economic Development and Cultural Change* 30:2 (Jan 1982), 229-69.

Osamu Saito, "Population and the Peasant Economy in Proto-Industrial Japan," *Journal of Family History* 8:1 (Spr 1983), 30-54.

Susan Hanley, "Economic Growth and Population Control in Preindustrial Japan," in George Dalton, ed. *Research in Economic Anthropology*, vol. 5, 1983, 185-223.

Arne Kalland & Jon Pedersen, "Famine and Population in Fukuoka Domain During the Tokugawa Period,"*Journal of Japanese Studies* 10:1 (Win 1984), 31-72.

Susan B. Hanley and Arthur P. Wolf, eds. *Family and Population in East Asian History*, Stanford University Press, 1985.

Ann Bowman Jannetta, *Epidemics and Mortality in Early Modern Japan*, Princeton University Press, 1987.

Susan Hanley, "How Well Did the Japanese Live in the Tokugawa Period? A Historian's Reappraisal," *Economic Studies Quarterly* 38:4 (Dec 1987), 309-22.

Migration

Keio Economic Studies 10:2 (1973), the following articles:
Akira Hayami, "Labor Migrants in a Pre-Industrial Society: A Study Tracing the Life Histories of the Inhabitants of a Village," 1-17.
Susan B. Hanley, "Migration and Economic Change in Okayama during the Tokugawa Period," 19-36.
W. Mark Fruin, "Farm Family Migration: The Case of Echizen in the Nineteenth Century," 37-46.

W. Mark Fruin, "A Social Geography of Preindustrial Labor Migration in Japan: Tajima and Kurome Villages in the 19th Century," *The Journal of Historical Geography* 4:2 (Win 1978).

W. Mark Fruin, "Peasant Migrants in the Economic Development of Nineteenth-Century Japan," *Agricultural History* 54:2 (Apr 1980), 261-77.

Osamu Saito, "Changing Structure of Urban Employment and its Effects on Migration Patterns in Eighteenth- and Nineteenth-Century Japan," in Akira Hayami, ed. Pre-Conditions to Industrialization in Japan, Papers from Ninth International Economic History Congress, Bern, 1986.

Labor Market

Osamu Saito, "Labor Market in Tokugawa Japan: Wage Differentials and Real Wage Level, 1727-1830," *Explorations in Economic History* 15 (January 1978), 84-100.

James I. Nakamura, "Human Capital Accumulation in Premodern Rural Japan," *Journal of Economic History* 41:2 (June 1981), 263-81.

Landholding

Kozo Yamamura, "Pre-Industrial Landholding Patterns in Japan and England," in Albert M. Craig, ed. *Japan: A Comparative View*, Princeton University Press, 1979, 276-323.

E. SOCIAL UNREST

Hugh Borton, *Peasant Uprisings in Japan of the Tokugawa Period*, New York, Paragon, 1968, originally published in *Transactions of the Asiatic Society in Japan* 2nd series, 16 (1938).

W. Donald Burton, "Peasant Struggle in Japan, 1590-1760," *Journal of Peasant Studies* 5:2 (Jan 1978), 135-71.

M. Hashimoto, "The Social Background of Peasant Uprisings in Tokugawa Japan," in Tetsuo Najita & J. Victor Koschmann, eds. *Conflict in Modern Japanese History: The Neglected Tradition*, Princeton University Press, 1982, 145-63.

Anne Walthall, *Social Protest and Popular Culture in Eighteenth-Century Japan*, University of Arizona Press, 1986.

Stephen Vlastos, *Peasant Protests and Uprisings in Tokugawa Japan*, University of California Press, 1986.

Herbert P. Bix, *Peasant Protest in Japan, 1590-1884*, Yale University Press, 1986.

Conrad Totman, "Tokugawa Peasants: Win, Lose, or Draw?" *Monumenta Nipponica* 41:4 (Win 1986), 457-76.

4. COMMERCE

A. URBAN HISTORY & COMMERCE

General

John Whitney Hall, "The Castle Town and Japan's Modern Urbanization," in John W. Hall and Marius B. Jansen, eds. *Studies in the Institutional History of Early Modern Japan*, Princeton University Press, 1968, 169-88, reprinted from *Far Eastern Quarterly* 15:1 (Nov 1955).

Thomas C. Smith, "Pre-modern Economic Growth: Japan and the West," *Past & Present* 60 (Aug 1973), 127-60.

Gilbert Rozman, *Urban Networks in Ch'ing China and Tokugawa Japan*, Princeton University Press, 1974.

Gilbert Rozman, "The Tokugawa Urban Network: A Foundation for Modernization," in Akira Hayami, ed. Pre-Conditions to Industrialization in Japan, Papers from Ninth International Economic History Congress, Bern, 1986.

Specific Cities

Hyojiro Kuroha, "Commerce of Osaka in the Tokugawa Era," *Bulletin of the University of Osaka Prefecture*, ser. D: Sciences of Economy, Commerce & Law 9 (1965), 1-15.

William B. Hauser, "Osaka: A Commercial City in Tokugawa Japan," *Urbanism Past & Present* 5 (Win 1977-78), 23-36.

Gilbert Rozman, "Edo's Importance in the Changing Tokugawa Society," *Journal of Japanese Studies* 1:1 (Aut 1974), 91-112.

Social Issues

Robert J. Smith, "Town and City in 'Pre-Modern' Japan," in Peter Laslett, ed. *Household and Family in Past Time*, Cambridge University Press, 1972, 429-71.

Robert J. Smith, "The Domestic Cycle in Selected Commoner Families in Urban Japan, 1757-1858," *Journal of Family History* 3:3 (Fall 1978), 219-35.

Susan B. Hanley, "Urban Sanitation in Preindustrial Japan," *Journal of Interdisciplinary History* 18:1 (Sum 1987), 1-26.

B. COMMERCIAL ENTERPRISE

Commercial Systems

E. Sydney Crawcour, "The Development of a Credit System in Seventeenth-Century Japan," *Journal of Economic History* 21:3 (Sept 1961), 342-60.

Shinichiro Kurimoto, "Silent Trade in Japan," in George Dalton, ed. *Research in Economic Anthropology* 3 (1980), 97-108. (See theoretical articles on "silent trade" in this issue).

Matao Miyamoto, "Emergence of National Market and Commercial Activities in Tokugawa Japan: With Special Reference to the Development of the Rice Market," in Akira Hayami, ed. Pre-Conditions to Industrialization in Japan, Papers from Ninth International Economic History Congress, Bern, 1986.

Surveys of Commerce

Takeshi Toyoda, "Japanese Guilds," *Annals of the Hitotsubashi Academy* 5:1 (Oct 1954), 72-85.

Charles Sheldon, *The Rise of the Merchant Class in Tokugawa Japan, 1600-1868*, Locust Valley, N.Y., J.J. Augustin, 1958.

E.S. Crawcour, "Changes in Commerce in the Tokugawa Period," in John W. Hall and Marius B. Jansen, eds. *Studies in the Institutional History of Early Modern Japan*, Princeton University Press, 1968, 189-202, reprinted from *Journal of Asian Studies* 22:4 (Aug 1963).

Takeshi Toyoda, *A History of Pre-Meiji Commerce in Japan*, Tokyo, Kokusai Bunka Shinkokai, 1969.

Merchants: Characteristics

Takafusa Mitsui, "Chonin's Life under Feudalism," *Cultural Nippon* 8 (June 1940), 65-96.

E.S. Crawcour, "Some Observations on Merchants: A Translation of Mitsui Takafusa's *Chonin koken roku* with an Introduction and Notes," *Transactions, Asiatic Society of Japan*, 3rd ser. 8 (Dec 1961), 1-139.

Charles D. Sheldon, " 'Pre-Modern' Merchants and Modernization in Japan," *Modern Asian Studies* 5:3 (July 1971), 193-206.

Charles D. Sheldon, "Merchants and Society in Tokugawa Japan," *Modern Asian Studies* 17:3 (July 1983), 477-88.

Merchant Firms

J. Mark Ramseyer, "Thrift and Diligence: House Codes of Tokugawa Merchant Families," *Monumenta Nipponica* 34:2 (Sum 1979), 209-30.

Yotaro Sakudo, "Traditional Labor Management in Japan, 1710-1990," in *Labor and Management*, vol. 4 of *International Conference on Business History*, ed. by Keiichiro Nakagawa, University of Tokyo Press, 1979, 127-40.

W. Mark Fruin, "The Firm as Family and the Family as Firm in Japan," *The Journal of Family History* 5:4 (Win 1980), 432-49.

·Shigeaki Yasuoka, "The Early History of Japanese Companies," in *Yearbook* 3, 1986, 1-25.

Mataji Miyamoto, "The Merchants of Osaka II," *Osaka Economic Papers* 15:28 (Nov 1966), 11-32.

Yasuhiro Mori, "Loans to Daimyos by the Osaka Money Changers," *Osaka Economic Papers* 15:29 (March 1967), 19-28.

Mataji Miyamoto, *Onogumi no kenkyu* [A study of the Onogumi], 4 vols., Tokyo, Ohara Shinseisha, 1970 (contains English summaries).

Sadao Takatera and Noboru Nishikawa, "Genesis of Divisional Management and Accounting Systems in the House of Mitsui, 1710-1730," *The Accounting Historians Journal* 11:1 (Spr 1984), 141-49.

Hiroshi Irie, "Apprenticeship Training in Tokugawa Japan," *Acta Asiatica* 54 (1988), 1-23.

Shipping

E.S. Crawcour, "Kawamura Zuiken: A Seventeenth Century Entrepreneur," *Transactions, Asiatic Society of Japan* 9 (May 1966), 28-50.

E. Sydney Crawcour, "Notes on Shipping and Trade in Japan and the Ryukyus," *Journal of Asian Studies* 23:3 (May 1964), 377-81.

Robert G. Flershem, "Some Aspects of Japan Sea Trade in the Tokugawa Period," *Journal of Asian Studies* 23:3 (May 1964), 405-16.

Ryoichi Furuta & Yoshikazu Hirai, *A Short History of Japanese Merchant Shipping*, trans. by Duncan MacFarlane, Tokyo News Service, 1967.

Charles D. Sheldon, "Some Economic Reasons for the Marked Contrast in Japanese and Chinese Modernization, as Seen in Examples from 'Pre-Modern' Shipping and Trading by Water," *Kyoto University Economic Review* 23:2 (Oct 1953), 30-60.

C. EARLY INDUSTRY & TECHNOLOGY

Nagatsune Okura, *Seiyu roku: On Oil Manufacturing*, ed. by Carter Litchfield and trans. by Eiko Ariga, New Brunswick, NJ, Olearius Editions, 1974.

William B. Hauser, "The Diffusion of Cotton Processing and Trade in the Kinai Region in Tokugawa Japan," *Journal of Asian Studies* 33:4 (Aug 1974), 633-49.

William Hauser, *Economic Institutional Change in Tokugawa Japan: Osaka and the Kinai Cotton Trade*, Cambridge University Press, 1974.

Shunsaku Nishikawa, "Protoindustrialisation in the Domain of Choshu in the Eighteenth and Nineteenth Centuries," *Keio Economic Studies* 18:2 (1981), 13-26.

W. Mark Fruin, *Kikkoman: Company, Clan, and Community*, Harvard University Press, 1983, 12-52.

Keiji Nagahara and Kozo Yamamura, "Shaping the Process of Unification: Technological Progress in Sixteenth- and Seventeenth-Century Japan," *Journal of Japanese Studies* 14:1 (Win 1988), 77-109.

5. THOUGHT, CULTURE, AND ECONOMIC ACTIVITY

A. ECONOMIC THOUGHT

N. Skene Smith, "An Introduction to Some Japanese Economic Writings of the 18th Century," *Transactions, Asiatic Society of Japan*, 2nd ser. 11 (1934), 32-165.

Eijiro Honjo, *Economic Theory and History of Japan in the Tokugawa Period*, Tokyo, Maruzen, 1943.

Tatsunosuke Ueda, "Saikaku's 'Economic Man'," *Annals of the Hitotsubashi Academy* 7:1 (Oct 1956), 10-32.

Ivan I. Morris, "Economic Realism in the Later Works of Ihara Saikaku, with Special Reference to Seken Munesanyo," *Transactions, Asiatic Society of Japan* 7 (Nov 1959), 1-30.

R. Tsunoda et al., eds. *Sources of Japanese Tradition*, 2 vols., Columbia University Press, 1965 (paperback), including:
vol. 1, Kaiho Seiryo and the Law of Economics, 488-93.
vol. 2, Honda Toshiaki, 48-56; Ninomiya Sontoku, 73-83.

Takao Shimazaki, "Introduction to the Economic Thought of Japan," *Keio Economic Studies* 5 (1968), 11-34.

Donald Keene, *The Japanese Discovery of Europe, 1720-1830*, expanded ed. Stanford University Press, 1969.

Tetsuo Najita, "Political Economism in the Thought of Dazai Shundai (1680-1747)," *Journal of Asian Studies* 31:4 (Aug 1972), 821-39.

B. CULTURE & COMMERCE

Robert N. Bellah, *Tokugawa Religion: The Values of Pre-Industrial Japan*, Glencoe, Illinois, The Free Press, 1957.

Hajime Nakamura, "Suzuki Shosan (1579-1655) and the Spirit of Capitalism in Japanese Buddhism," *Monumenta Nipponica* 22:1&2 (1967), 1-14.

Jennifer Robertson, "Rooting the Pine: Shingaku Methods of Organization," *Monumenta Nipponica* 34:3 (Aut 1979), 311-22.

Tetsuo Najita, *Visions of Virtue in Tokugawa Japan: The Kaitokudo Merchant Academy of Osaka*, University of Chicago Press, 1987.

6. JAPAN IN THE WORLD ECONOMY

A. GENERAL

General Works & Surveys of Trade

Yoshi S. Kuno, *Japanese Expansion on the Asiatic Continent*, vol. 1, University of California Press, 1940 (1967 reprint, Port Washington, New York, Kennikat Press).

Special Issue: Early Modern Foreign Trade, *Acta Asiatica* 30 (1976), including: Seiichi Iwao, "Japanese Foreign Trade in the 16th and 17th Centuries," 1-18.

Robert L. Innes, "The Door Ajar: Japan's Foreign Trade in the Seventeenth Century," Ph.D. diss., University of Michigan, 1980.

Currency Issues & Economic Change

Kazui Tashiro, "Foreign Relations during the Edo Period: Sakoku Reexamined," *Journal of Japanese Studies* 8:2 (Sum 1982), 283-306.

A. Kobata, "The Production and Uses of Gold and Silver in Sixteenth and Seventeenth Century Japan," *Economic History Review* 18:2 (Aug 1965), 245-66.

William S. Atwell, "Some Observations on the 'Seventeenth Century Crisis' in China and Japan," *Journal of Asian Studies* 45:2 (Feb 1986), 223-244.

Diplomacy & Thought

Horst Menderhausen & Nancy V. Meyer, *The Concept of Hostile Trade and a Case Study of Seventeenth Century Japan*, Santa Monica, The Rand Corporation, 1965 [RM-4433-PR].

Ronald Toby, *State and Diplomacy in Early Modern Japan: Asia in the Development of the Tokugawa Bakufu*, Princeton University Press, 1984.

Donald Keene, *The Japanese Discovery of Europe, 1720-1830*, expanded ed. Stanford University Press, 1969.

B. EARLY TOKUGAWA & THE WEST

General

Leonard Blussé, "Japanese Historiography and European Sources," in P.C. Emmer and H.L. Wesseling, eds. *Reappraisals in Overseas History*, Leyden University Press, 1979, esp. 193-222.

Charles R. Boxer, *Christian Century in Japan, 1549-1650*, University of California Press, 1951.

Portuguese & the Jesuits

C.R. Boxer, *The Great Ship from Amacon: Annals of Macao and the Old Japan Trade, 1555-1640*, Lisbon, Centro de Estudos Historicos Ultramarinos, 1960.

Michael Cooper, "The Mechanics of the Macao-Nagasaki Silk Trade," *Monumenta Nipponica* 27:4 (Win 1972), 423-33 (includes document).

Koichiro Takase, "Unauthorized Commercial Activities by Jesuit Missionaries in Japan," *Acta Asiatica* 30 (1976), 19-33.

Spanish

W.L. Schurz, *The Manila Galleon*, New York, 1939.

Lothar G. Knauth, "Pacific Confrontation: Japan Encounters the Spanish Overseas Empire, 1542-1639," Ph.D. dissertation, Harvard University, 1970.

James K. Irikura, "Trade and Diplomacy Between the Philippines and Japan, 1585-1623," Ph.D. dissertation, Yale University, 1958.

English

Ludwig Reiss, "History of the English Factory at Hirado," *Transactions, Asiatic Society of Japan* 26 (1898), 1-114, 163-218.

Dutch

Yoko Nagazumi, "Japan's Isolationist Policy as Seen through Dutch Source Materials," *Acta Asiatica* 22 (1972), 18-35.

Eiichi Kato, "Development of Japanese Studies on *Sakoku* (Closing the Country): A Survey," *Acta Asiatica* 22 (1972), 84-103.

Eiichi Kato, "The Japanese-Dutch Trade in the Formative Period of the Seclusion Policy: Particularly on the Raw Silk Trade by the Dutch Factory at Hirado, 1620-1640," *Acta Asiatica* 30 (1976), 34-84.

Eiichi Kato, "Unification and Adaptation: The Early Shogunate and Dutch Trade Policies," in Leonard Blusse & Femme Gaastra, eds. *Companies and Trade: Essays on Overseas Trading Companies during the Ancien Regime*, Leiden University Press, 1981, 207-29.

Charles R. Boxer, *Jan Compagnie in Japan, 1600-1850*, 2nd rev. ed., The Hague, Martinus Nijhoff, 1950.

Charles R. Boxer, "Jan Compagnie in Japan, 1672-1674; or, Anglo-Dutch Rivalry in Japan and Formosa," in *Papers on Portuguese, Dutch, and Jesuit Influences in 16th- and 17th-Century Japan: Writings of Charles Ralph Boxer*, comp. by Michael Moscato, reprint edition, Washington, University Publications of America, 1979, 147-211 [from *Transactions, Asiatic Society of Japan* 7 (1930)].

M.E. van Opstall, "Dutchmen and Japanese in the Eighteenth Century," in J. van Goor, ed. *Trading Companies in Asia, 1600-1830*, Utrecht, HES Uitgevers, 1986, 107-26.

M.P.H. Roessingh, *The Archive of the Dutch Factory in Japan*, The Hague, 1964.

C. THE DUTCH & INTRA-ASIAN TRADE

Kristof Glamann, "The Dutch East India Company's Trade in Japanese Copper, 1645-1736," *Scandinavian Economic History Review* 1:1 (1953), 41-79.

Kristof Glamann, *Dutch-Asiatic Trade, 1620-1740*, Copenhagen, Martinus Nijhoff, 1958, 2nd edition, 1981.

Kristof Glamann, "Japanese Copper on the European Market in the 17th Century," in Herman Kellenbenz, ed. *Schwerpunkte der Kuperproduktion und des Kupferhandels in Europa, 1500-1650*, Hrsg. von Hermann Koln, Bohlau, 1977, 280-89.

Om Prakash, *The Dutch East India Company and the Economy of Bengal, 1630-1720*, Princeton University Press, 1985, esp. 118-141.

D. TRADE WITH ASIA

China

John W. Hall, "Notes on the Early Ch'ing Copper Trade with Japan," *Harvard Journal of Asiatic Studies* 12 (1949), 444-61.

Teijiro Yamawaki, "The Great Trading Merchants, Cocksinja and His Son," *Acta Asiatica* 30 (1976), 106-16.

John Whitney Hall, *Tanuma Okitsugu (1719-1788): Forerunner of Modern Japan*, Harvard University Press, 1955, 83-86.

Korea

Kazui Tashiro, "Tsushima han's Korean Trade, 1684-1710," *Acta Asiatica* 30 (1976), 85-105.

Kazui Tashiro, "Foreign Relations during the Edo Period: Sakoku Reexamined," *Journal of Japanese Studies* 8:2 (Sum 1982), 283-306.

Kazui Tashiro, "Coinage and Exports of Silver during the Tokugawa Era," in Akira Hayami, ed. Pre-Conditions to Industrialization in Japan, Papers from Ninth International Economic History Congress, Bern, 1986.

Southeast Asia

Seiichi Iwao, "Reopening of the Diplomatic and Commercial Relations Between Japan and Siam During the Tokugawa Period," *Acta Asiatica* 4 (1963), 1-31.

Sarasin Viraphol, *Tribute and Profit: Sino-Siamese Trade, 1652-1853*, Harvard University Press, 1977, 7-17, 58-69.

Seiichi Iwao, "Japanese Emigrants in Batavia During the 17th Century," *Acta Asiatica* 18 (1970), 1-25.

Ryukyus

E. Sydney Crawcour, "Notes on Shipping and Trade in Japan and the Ryukyus," *Journal of Asian Studies* 23:3 (May 1964), 377-81.

Robert S. Sakai, "The Satsuma-Ryukyu Trade and the Tokugawa Seclusion Policy," *Journal of Asian Studies* 23:3 (May 1964), 391-403.

Robert K. Sakai, "The Ryukyu (Liu-Ch'iu) Islands as a Fief of Satsuma," in John K. Fairbank, ed. *The Chinese World Order*, Harvard University Press, 1968, 112-34.

Mitsugu Sakihara, "Ryukyu's Tribute-tax to Satsuma During the Tokugawa Period," *Modern Asian Studies* 6:3 (1972), 329-35.

E. LATE TOKUGAWA

John Whitney Hall, *Tanuma Okitsugu (1719-1788): Forerunner of Modern Japan*, Harvard University Press, 1955, 83-105.

Madoka Kanai, "Salem and Nagasaki: Their Encounter, 1797-1807," *CJ* 29:1 (Sept 1968), 82-102.

Sir Stamford Raffles, *Report on Japan to the Secret Committee of the English East India Company, 1812-1816*, Kobe, 1929. (New Edition, London, Curzon Press, 1971).

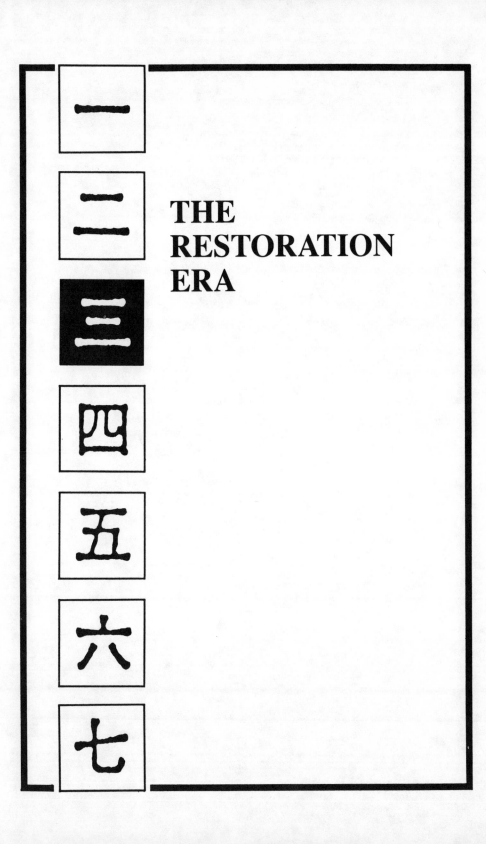

一
二
三
四
五
六
七

THE
RESTORATION
ERA

A. GOVERNMENT POLICIES

W.G. Beasley, "Feudal Revenue in Japan at the Time of the Meiji Restoration," *Journal of Asian Studies* 19:3 (May 1960), 255-72.

Albert M. Craig, *Choshu in the Meiji Restoration*, Harvard University Press, 1961, esp. 51-84, "Choshu and the Tempo Reform."

Conrad Totman, *The Collapse of the Tokugawa Bakufu, 1862-1868*, University Press of Hawaii, 1980.

B. THE ECONOMY IN TRANSITION

General

Kazuo Yamaguchi, "Opening of Japan at the End of the Shogunate and its Effects," in Keizo Shibusawa, ed. *Japanese Society in the Meiji Era*, Tokyo, Obunsha, 1958, 1-46.

Everitt E. Hagen, "How Economic Growth Begins: A General Theory Applied to Japan," *Public Opinion Quarterly* 22 (1958), 373-90.

Richard Nelson, "Growth Models and the Escape from the Low-level Equilibrium Trap: The Case of Japan," *Economic Development and Cultural Change* 8:4-l (1960), 378-88.

E.S. Crawcour, "The Tokugawa Heritage," in William W. Lockwood, ed. *The State and Economic Enterprise in Japan*, Princeton University Press, 1965, 17-44.

Mataji Miyamoto et al, "Economic Development in Pre-Industrial Japan, 1859-1894," *Journal of Economic History* 25:4 (Dec 1965), 541-64.

Satoru Nakamura, "The Historical Preconditions of the Formations of Capitalism in Japan," *Kyoto University Economic Review* 43:1-2 (Apr-Oct 1973), 30-44.

Hiroya Akimoto, "Capital Formation and Economic Growth in mid-19th Century Japan," *Explorations in Economic History* 18:1 (Jan 1981), 40-59 (mostly on agriculture in Choshu).

E.S. Crawcour, "Aspects of Economic Transition in Japan, 1840-1906," *Papers on Far Eastern History* 24 (Sept 1981), 39-61.

Shunsaku Nishikawa & Osamu Saito, "The Economic History of the Restoration Period," in Michio Nagai & Miguel Urrutia, eds. *Meiji Ishin: Restoration and Revolution*, Tokyo, United Nations University, 1985, 175-9l.

Osamu Saito, "Scenes of Japan's Economic Development and the 'Longue Dure'," in Erich Pauer, ed. *Silkworms, Oil, and Chips . . . Proceedings of the Economics and Economic History Section of the Fourth International Conference on Japanese Studies*, Japan Seminar, University of Bonn, 1986, 15-27.

Akira Hayami, ed. Pre-Conditions to Industrialization in Japan, Papers from Ninth International Economic History Congress, Bern, 1986.

James L. McClain, "Failed Expectations: Kaga Domain on the Eve of the Meiji Restoration," *Journal of Japanese Studies* 14:2 (Sum 1988), 403-47.

Thomas C. Smith, *Native Sources of Japanese Industrialization, 1750-1920*, University of California Press, 1988 (collected essays).

E.S. Crawcour, "Economic Change in the Nineteenth Century," in Marius B. Jansen, ed. *The Cambridge History of Japan*, vol. V, *The Nineteenth Century*, Cambridge University Press, forthcoming.

Money & Currency

John McMaster, "The Japanese Gold Rush of 1859," *Journal of Asian Studies* 19:3 (May 1960), 273-87.

Peter Frost, *The Bakumatsu Currency Crisis*, Harvard University Press, 1970.

Takehiko Ohkura & Hiroshi Shimbo, "The Tokugawa Monetary Policy in the Eighteenth and Nineteenth Centuries," *Explorations in Economic History* 15:1 (Jan 1978), 101-24.

Commerce

Marius B. Jansen, *Sakamoto Ryoma and the Meiji Restoration*, Princeton University Press, 1961 (re: Tosa enterprise and the origins of Mitsubishi, passim).

William D. Wray, "Shipping: From Sail to Steam," in Marius Jansen and Gilbert Rozman, eds. *Japan in Transition: From Tokugawa to Meiji*, Princeton University Press, 1986, 248-70.

Industry & Communications

Ian Nish, ed. *Bakumatsu and Meiji: Studies in Japan's Economic and Social History*, in *International Studies* (1981/2), London School of Economics and Political Science, including:

Janet Hunter, "The Bakumatsu Textile Industry: Continuity and Change," 18-38.

Jean-Pierre Lehman, "The Silk Trade in the Bakumatsu Era and Patterns of Japanese Economic Development," 39-55.

Stephen W. McCallion, "Silk Reeling in Meiji Japan: The Limits to Change," Ph.D. diss., Ohio State University, 1983.

Takaharu Mitsui, "The System of Communications at the Time of the Meiji Restoration," *Monumenta Nipponica* 4:1 (Jan 1941), 88-101.

Mitsukuni Yoshida, "The Restoration and the History of Technology," in Michio Nagai & Miguel Urrutia, eds. *Meiji Ishin: Restoration and Revolution*, Tokyo, United Nations University, 1985, 192-204.

Tetsuo Kamiki, "Progress in Western Technology At the Yokosuka Shipbuilding Works, 1865-1887," *Papers on Far Eastern History* 37 (March 1988), 105-23.

The Foreign Presence

Eijiro Honjo, *Economic Theory and History of Japan in the Tokugawa Period*, Tokyo, Maruzen, 1943.

Mark D. Ericson, "The Bakufu Looks Abroad: The 1865 Mission to France," *Monumenta Nipponica* 34:4 (Win 1979), 383-407.

Shinya Sugiyama, "Thomas B. Glover: A British Merchant in Japan, 1861-70," *Business History* 26:2 (July 1984), 115-38.

Shinya Sugiyama, "The Impact of the Opening of the Ports on Domestic Japanese Industry: The Case of Silk and Cotton," *Economic Studies Quarterly* 38:4 (Dec 1987), 338-53.

Context of International Trade

Frances V. Moulder, *Japan, China and the Modern World Economy: Toward A Reinterpretation of East Asian Development, ca. 1600 to 1918*, Cambridge University Press, 1977.

Heita Kawakatsu, "International Competition in Cotton Goods in the Late 19th Century: Britain vs. India & East Asia," in *The Emergence of a World Economy, 1500-1914, Papers of the IX. International Congress of Economic History*, ed. Wolfram Fischer et al., Stuttgart, Franz Steiner Verlag Wiesbaden GmbH, 1986, 619-43.

Claudio Zanier, "Japan and the 'Pebrine' Crisis of European Sericulture During the 1860s," in Erich Pauer, ed. *Silkworms, Oil, and Chips . . . Proceedings of the Economics and Economic History Section of the Fourth International Conference on Japanese Studies*, Japan Seminar, University of Bonn, 1986, 51-63.

Shinya Sugiyama, *Japan's Industrialization in the World Economy, 1859-1899: Export Trade and Overseas Competition*, London, The Athlone Press, 1988.

J. Richard Huber, "Effects on Price of Japan's Entry into World Commerce after 1858," *Journal of Political Economy* 79:3 (May/June 1971), 614-29.

3. SOCIAL TRANSITION

The Local Economy

William J. Chambliss, *Chiaraijima Village, Land Tenure, Taxation, and Local Trade 1818-1884*, Tucson, University of Arizona, 1965.

Shunsaku Nishikawa, "Productivity, Subsistence, and By-Employments in the Mid-Nineteenth Century Choshu," *Explorations in Economic History* 15:1 (Jan 1978), 69-83.

Shunsaku Nishikawa, "Grain Consumption: The Case of Choshu," in Marius Jansen and Gilbert Rozman, eds. *Japan in Transition: From Tokugawa to Meiji*, Princeton University Press, 1986, 421-46.

Social Conditions

Robert J. Smith, "Aspects of Mobility in Pre-Industrial Japanese Cities," *Comparative Studies in Society and History* 5 (July 1963), 416-23

Akira Hayami, "Population Changes," in Marius Jansen and Gilbert Rozman, eds. *Japan in Transition: From Tokugawa to Meiji*, Princeton University Press, 1986, 280-317.

Susan B. Hanley, "A High Standard of Living in Nineteenth-Century Japan: Fact or Fantasy?" *Journal of Economic History* 43:1 (March 1983), 183-92.

Yasukichi Yasuba, "Standard of Living in Japan Before Industrialization: From What Level Did Japan Begin? A Comment," *Journal of Economic History* 46:1 (March 1986) 217-24. (reply by Susan Hanley, 225-26).

Social Class

Thomas C. Smith, "Landlords and Rural Capitalists in the Modernization of Japan," *Journal of Economic History* 16:2 (1956), 165-81.

Thomas C. Smith, "Peasant Time and Factory Time in Japan," *Past & Present* 111 (May 1986), 165-97.

Social Unrest

Patricia Sippel, "Popular Protest in Early Modern Japan: The Bushu Outburst," *Harvard Journal of Asiatic Studies* 37:2 (Dec 1977), 273-322.

Herbert Bix, "Miura Meisuke; or Peasant Rebellion Under the Banner of 'Distress'," *Bulletin of Concerned Asian Scholars* (Apr-June 1978), 18-26.

William W. Kelly, *Deference and Defiance in Nineteenth-Century Japan*, Princeton University Press, 1985.

Stephen Vlastos, *Peasant Protests and Uprisings in Tokugawa Japan*, University of California Press, 1986.

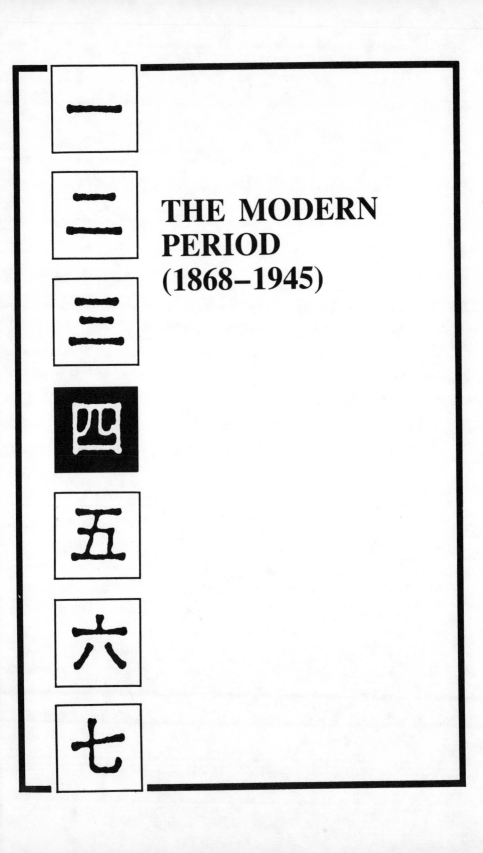

THE MODERN
PERIOD
(1868–1945)

1. GENERAL WORKS

A. SURVEYS & COMPOSITE WORKS

Historical Surveys

William W. Lockwood, *The Economic Development of Japan: Growth and Structural Change, 1868-1938*, Princeton University Press, 1954.

G.C. Allen, *A Short Economic History of Modern Japan*, 2nd rev. ed., London, Allen & Unwin, 1962.

Yasuzo Horie, "The Transformation of the National Economy: A Chapter in Japan's Economic History," *DE* 3:4 (Dec 1965), 404-26.

Masao Takahashi, *Modern Japanese Economy since 1868*, Tokyo, Kokusai Bunka Shinkokai, 1968.

Kamekichi Takahashi, *The Rise and Development of Japan's Modern Economy*, Tokyo, Jiji Tsushinsha, 1969.

E.S. Crawcour, "The Modern Economy," in Arthur Tiedemann, ed. *An Introduction to Japanese Civilization*, Columbia University Press, 1973, 487-513.

Yasuzo Horie, "Japan's Economic Development and Inflation since the Meiji Restoration," *KSU Economic and Business Review* (Kyoto Sangyo University) 1 (May 1974), 1-23.

Jon Halliday, *A Political History of Japanese Capitalism*, Pantheon, 1975.

Takafusa Nakamura, *Economic Growth in Prewar Japan*, Yale University Press, 1983.

Takafusa Nakamura, *Economic Development of Modern Japan*, Ministry of Foreign Affairs, Japan, 1985.

Kunio Yoshihara, *Japanese Economic Development: A Short Introduction*, Tokyo, Oxford University Press, 2nd ed., 1986.

W.J. Macpherson, *The Economic Development of Japan c.1868-1941*, London, Macmillan, 1987.

"Lessons" & "Models"

M. Bronfenbrenner, "Some Lessons of Japan's Economic Development, 1853-1938," *Pacific Affairs* 34:1 (Spr 1961), 7-27.

Allen Kelley & Jeffrey Williamson, *Lessons from Japanese Development: An Analytical Economic History*, University of Chicago Press, 1974.

Michio Morishima, *Why has Japan 'Succeeded'? Western Technology and the Japanese Ethos*, Cambridge University Press, 1982.

Economic Growth

Yuzo Yamada, "The Income Growth and the Rate of Saving in Japan," *Annals of the Hitotsubashi Academy* 4:2 (Apr 1954), 79-97.

Simon S. Kuznets, Wilber E. Moore, & Joseph J. Spengler, *Economic Growth: Brazil, India, Japan*, Durham, Duke University Press, 1955.

Miyohei Shinohara, "An Estimate of Capital Formation in Japan by 'Commodity Flow' Method," *Annals of the Hitotsubashi Academy* 5:2 (Apr 1955), 116-39.

Kazushi Ohkawa, *The Growth Rate of the Japanese Economy since 1878*, Tokyo, Kinokuniya, 1957.

Gustav Ranis, "Factor Proportions in Japanese Economic Development," *American Economic Review* 47:5 (Sept 1957), 594-607.

Koichi Emi, "Capital Formation in Residential Real Estate in Japan, 1887-1940," *Annals of the Hitotsubashi Academy* 9:2 (Apr 1959), 233-43.

Miyohei Shinohara, "Growth and the Long Swing in the Japanese Economy," *Hitotsubashi Journal of Economics* 1:1 (Oct 1960), 59-83.

Henry Rosovsky, *Capital Formation in Japan, 1868-1940*, New York, The Free Press, 1961.

L.R. Klein, "A Model of Japanese Economic Growth, 1878-1937," *Econometrica* 29:3 (July 1961), 277-92.

Hollis B. Chenery, Shuntaro Shishido & Tsunehiko Watanabe, "The Pattern of Japanese Growth: 1914-1954," *Econometrica* 30:1 (Jan 1962), 98-139.

Kazushi Ohkawa & Henry Rosovsky, "Economic Fluctuations in Prewar Japan: A Preliminary Analysis of Cycles and Long Swings," *Hitotsubashi Journal of Economics* 3:1 (Oct 1962), 10-33.

Koichi Emi, *Government Fiscal Activity and Economic Growth in Japan, 1868-1960*, Tokyo, Kinokuniya, 1963.

T. Ishimitsu, "Energy Inputs and the Economic Growth in Japan, 1875-1962," *Kobe University Economic Review* 10 (1964), 29-62.

Henry Rosovsky, "Capital Formation in Pre-War Japan: Current Findings and Future Problems," in C.D. Cowan, ed. *The Economic Development of China and Japan*, London, Allen & Unwin, 1964, 205-19.

William W. Lockwood, ed. *The State and Economic Enterprise in Japan*, Princeton University Press, 1965, including:
Kazushi Ohkawa & Henry Rosovsky, "A Century of Japanese Economic Growth," 47-92.
Alan H. Gleason, "Economic Growth and Consumption in Japan," 391-444.

Minoru Tachi & Yoichi Okazaki, "Economic Development and Population Growth," *DE* 3:4 (Dec 1965), 497-515.

Miyohei Shinohara, "Long-Term Changes of Consumption Expenditures in Japan, 1874-1940," *DE* 5:2 (June 1967), 217-46.

Koichi Emi, "Long-Term Movement of Capital Formation: The Japanese Case, 1868-1940," *DE* 5:2 (June 1967), 247-73.

William V. Rapp, "Theory of Changing Trade Patterns Under Economic Growth: Tested for Japan," *Yale Economic Essays* 7:2 (Fall 1967), 69-135.

Lawrence Klein & Kazushi Ohkawa, eds. *Economic Growth: The Japanese Experience since the Meiji Era*, Yale Economic Growth Series, Homewood, Ill., Richard D. Irwin, 1968.

Miyohei Shinohara, *Structural Changes in Japan's Economic Development*, Tokyo, Kinokuniya, 1970.

Nobuko Nosse, "Japanese Economic Growth since the Meiji Restoration: A Social Accounting Approach," *Kobe Economic and Business Review* 17 (1970), 9-34.

Takafusa Nakamura, "A Long-Term Survey of Japan's Prewar Growth Process," *JES* 1:1 (Fall 1972), 49-98.

Kazushi Ohkawa & Henry Rosovsky, *Japanese Economic Growth: Trend Acceleration in the Twentieth Century*, Stanford University Press, 1973.

Kazuo Sato, "Growth and Technical Change in Japan's Nonprimary Economy, 1930-1967," *JES* 1 (Sum 1973), 63-103.

Kazushi Ohkawa, "Past Economic Growth of Japan in Comparison with the Western Case: Trend Acceleration and Differential Structure," in Shigeto

Tsuru, ed. *Growth and Resources Problems Related to Japan*: Proceedings of Session VI of the Fifth Congress of the International Economic Association, Tokyo, Asahi Evening News, 1978, 3-15.

K. Ohkawa & H. Rosovsky, "Capital Formation in Japan," in Peter Mathias & M.M. Postan, eds. *The Cambridge Economic History of Europe*, Cambridge University Press, 1978, vol. vii, part 2, 134-214.

Kazushi Ohkawa & Miyohei Shinohara, eds. *Patterns of Japanese Economic Developments: A Quantitative Appraisal*, Yale University, Economic Growth Centre and Council on East Asian Studies, 1979.

Naohiro Ogawa & Daniel B. Suits, "Lessons on Population and Economic Change from the Japanese Meiji Experience," *DE* 20:2 (June 1982), 196-219.

Harry T. Oshima, *Economic Growth in Monsoon Asia: A Comparative Survey*, University of Tokyo Press, 1987, esp. 101-36, "Contrasting the Economic Growth of Prewar and Postwar Japan."

Composite Works

Elizabeth B. Schumpeter, ed. *The Industrialization of Japan and Manchukuo, 1930-1940: Population, Raw Materials and Industry*, New York, Macmillan, 1940.

William W. Lockwood, ed. *The State and Economic Enterprise in Japan*, Princeton University Press, 1965.

Seiichi Tobata, ed. *The Modernization of Japan*, Tokyo, The Institute of Asian Economic Affairs, 1966.

Hugh Patrick, ed. *Japanese Industrialization and its Social Consequences*, University of California Press, 1973.

Erich Pauer, ed. *Silkworms, Oil, and Chips . . . Proceedings of the Economics and Economic History Section of the Fourth International Conference on Japanese Studies*, Japan Seminar, University of Bonn, 1986.

B. ANALYSES BY PERIOD

Meiji

John Dower, ed. *Origins of the Modern Japanese State: Selected Writings of E.H. Norman*, Pantheon, 1975.

E. Sydney Crawcour, "Industrialization and Technological Change, 1885-1918," in Peter Duus, ed. *The Cambridge History of Japan*, vol. VI, *The Twentieth Century*, Cambridge University Press, 1989.

Mataji Miyamoto et al, "Economic Development in Pre-Industrial Japan, 1859-1894," *Journal of Economic History* 25:4 (Dec 1965), 541-64.

Keizo Shibusawa, ed. *Japanese Society in the Meiji Era*, Tokyo, Obunsha, 1958 (misleading title—mostly about economics).

Henry Rosovsky, "Japan's Transition to Modern Economic Growth, 1868-1885," in Rosovsky, ed. *Industrialization in Two Systems*, New York, Wiley, 1966, 91-139.

Koichi Emi, "The Growth of the Japanese Economy in the First Half of the Meiji Period: In Terms of the Problems of Underdeveloped Nations," *Hitotsubashi Journal of Economics* 3:2 (June 1963), 6-15.

Jintaro Fujii, ed. *Outline of Japanese History in the Meiji Era*, Tokyo, Obunsha, 1958, 507-535, "Developments in Agriculture and Industry."

Chotaro Takahashi, "Capital Accumulation in Early Meiji Era," *Asian Affairs* 1 (1956), 130-48.

Shozaburo Fujino, "Business Cycles in Japan, 1868-1962," *Hitotsubashi Journal of Economics* 7:1 (June 1966), 56-79.

Yasuzo Horie, "The Transformation of the National Economy: A Chapter in Japan's Economic History," in Seiichi Tobata, ed. *The Modernization of Japan*, Tokyo, The Institute of Asian Economic Affairs, 1966, 67-89.

Shigeto Tsuru, "The Take-Off of Japan, 1868-1900," in his *Essays on Economic Development*, Tokyo, Kinokuniya, 1968, 105-22.

Allen Kelley & Jeffrey Williamson, "Writing History Backwards: Meiji Japan Revisited," *Journal of Economic History* 31:4 (1971), 729-76.

Shigeto Tsuru, "Economic Fluctuations in Japan, 1868-1893," *Review of Economic Statistics* 23 (Nov 1941), 176-89.

General View of Commerce & Industry in the Empire of Japan, Tokyo, Bureau of Commerce and Industry, Department of Agriculture and Commerce, 1893.

Japan in the Beginning of the 20th Century by the Department of Agriculture and Commerce, Tokyo, 1904.

Interwar

Takafusa Nakamura, "Depression, Recovery, and War, 1918-1945," in Peter Duus, ed. *The Cambridge History of Japan*, vol. VI, *The Twentieth Century*, Cambridge University Press, 1989.

Yasukichi Yasuba, "Salient Features of Japanese Economic Growth in the post-Meiji Era," in Hongladarom Chira & Medhi Kronkaew, eds. *Comparative Development: Japan and Thailand*, Bangkok, Thammasat University Press, 1981, 33-70.

Kozo Yamamura, "The Japanese Economy, 1911-1930: Concentration, Conflicts, and Crises," in Bernard Silberman & Harry Harootunian, eds. *Japan in Crisis: Essays on Taisho Democracy*, Princeton University Press, 1974, 299-328.

Kozo Yamamura, "Then Came the Great Depression: Japan's Interwar Years," in Herman van der Wee, ed. *The Great Depression Revisited*, The Hague, Martinus Nijhoff, 1972, 182-211.

Hugh Patrick, "The Economic Muddle of the 1920s," in James Morley, ed. *Dilemmas of Growth in Prewar Japan*, Princeton University Press, 1971, 211-66.

John E. Orchard, Japan's Economic Position, New York, Whittlesey House, 1930.

Harold G. Moulton, *Japan: An Economic and Financial Appraisal*, Washington, Brookings Institution, 1931 (reprint, 1944).

Yasushi Taji, "Our Industrial Reformation," *CJ* 3:1 (June 1934), 96-104.

Yukio Cho, "From the Showa Economic Crisis to Military Economy: With Special Reference to the Inoue and Takahashi Financial Policies," *DE* 5:4 (Dec 1967), 568-96.

Ronald Dore & Radha Sinha, eds. *Japan and the World Depression, Then and Now: Essays in Memory of E.F. Penrose*, London, Macmillan, 1987, including:
Takafusa Nakamura, "The Japanese Economy in the Interwar Period: A Brief Summary," 52-67.
Tuvia Blumenthal, "Depressions in Japan: The 1930s and the 1970s," 68-82.

E.F. Penrose, "Japan, 1920-1936," in Elizabeth B. Schumpeter, ed. *The Industrialization of Japan and Manchukuo, 1930-1940: Population, Raw Materials and Industry*, New York, Macmillan, 1940, 80-270 (focuses on population, agriculture, and raw materials).

Kaoru Sugihara, "Japan's Industrial Recovery, 1931-1936," in Ian Brown, ed. *Economies of Africa and Asia during the Inter-war Depression*, London, Croom Helm, 1988.

Mitsubishi Economic Research Bureau, *Japanese Trade and Industry: Present and Future*, London, Macmillan, 1936.

Emil Lederer, "Japan in World Economics," *Social Research* 4:1 (Feb 1937), 1-32.

G.C. Allen, *Japan: The Hungry Guest*, London, Allen & Unwin, 1938.

Shigeto Tsuru, *Essays on Japanese Economy*, Tokyo, Kinokuniya, 1958.

G.C. Allen, "Japanese Industry: Its Organization and Development to 1937," in Elizabeth B. Schumpeter, ed. *The Industrialization of Japan and Manchukuo, 1930-1940: Population, Raw Materials and Industry*, New York, Macmillan, 1940, 477-786.

Kusuo Fushiki, "The Strength of Japan's Economy," *CJ* 7:3 (Dec 1938), 469-77.

Juichi Tsushima, "Japan's Economic & Financial Position," *CJ* 8:4 (June 1939), 443-54.

G.C. Allen, *Japanese Industry: Its Recent Development and Present Condition*, New York, Institute of Pacific Relations, 1940.

Shintaro Ryu, "Economic Development of Modern Japan," in Hiro Sassa & Shintaro Ryu, *Recent Political and Economic Developments in Japan*, Tokyo, Japan Council, Institute of Pacific Relations, 1941, 59-95.

Walter Goldfrank, "Silk and Steel: Italy and Japan Between the Two World Wars," in Edmund Burke, III, *Global Crises and Social Movements: Artisans, Peasants, Populists, and the World Economy*, Boulder, Westview Press, 1988, 218-40.

C. MODERN WARS (pre-1937)

Kenneth E. Boulding & Alan Gleason, "War as an Investment: The Strange Case of Japan," *Peace Research Society Papers* 3 (1965), 1-17 (reprinted in Kenneth E. Boulding & Tapan Mukerjee, eds. *Economic Imperialism: A Book of Readings*, University of Michigan Press, 1972.

Giichi Ono, *Expenditures of the Sino-Japanese War*, New York, Oxford University Press, 1922.

Uchisaburo Kobayashi, *War and Armament Loans of Japan*, Oxford University Press, 1922.

Uchisaburo Kobayashi, *War and Armament Taxes of Japan*, Oxford University Press, 1922.

Ushisaburo Kobayashi, *The Basic Industries and Social History of Japan, 1914-1918*, Yale University Press, 1930.

D. BIBLIOGRAPHY & HISTORIOGRAPHY

Yoshitaka Komatsu, "The Birth, Development and Recent Trends of Economic History in Japan: An Outline with Special Reference to Waseda University," *Waseda Economic Papers* 2 (1958), 15-27.

Kozo Yamamura & Henry Rosovsky, "Entrepreneurial Studies in Japan: An Introduction," *Business History Review* 44:1 (Spr 1970), 1-12.

Juro Teranishi, "A Survey of Economic Studies on Prewar Japan," *JES* 1:2 (Win 1972-73), 47-98.

Ian Inkster, "Meiji Economic Development in Perspective: Revisionist Comments upon the Industrial Revolution in Japan," *DE* 17 (1979), 45-68.

Leon Hollerman, "A Sampling of Japanese Economic Issues—A Review Article," *Journal of Asian Studies* 40:4 (Aug 1981), 735-43.

Shin'ichi Yonekawa, "The Development of Chinese and Japanese Business in an International Perspective—a Bibliographical Introduction," *Business History Review* 56:2 (Sum 1982), 155-67.

Mariko Tatsuki, "Business Archives and Research for Business History in Japan," in Keiichiro Nakagawa & Tsunehiko Yui, eds. *Organization and Management, 1900-1930*: Proceedings of the Japan-Germany Conference on Business History, Japan Business History Institute, 1983, 194-99.

Mitoshi Yamaguchi, "Some Critical Analyses of Japanese Economic Development," *Kobe University Economic Review* 32 (1986), 41-68.

William D. Wray, "Afterword: The Writing of Japanese Business History," in Wray, ed. *Managing Industrial Enterprise: Cases from Japan's Prewar Experience*, Harvard University Press, 1989.

"Reports," in *Yearbook* (Annual).

E. REFERENCE

Financial and Economic Annual of Japan, The Department of Finance, Japan, Government Printing Oﬁce, Annual. (prewar).

Bank of Japan, *Hundred-Year Statistics of the Japanese Economy*, Statistics Department, Bank of Japan, 1966 (Japanese title: *Meiji iko hompo shuyo keizai tokei*).

Kazushi Ohkawa, Miyohei Shinohara & Mataji Umemura, eds. *Long-Term Economic Statistics of Japan*, 14 vols. Tokyo, Toyo Keizai Shimposha, 1965ff., (in Japanese with some English column titles), including: 1: *National Income*; 2: *Population and Labor Force*; 3: *Capital Stock*; 4: *Capital Formation*; 6: *Personal Consumption Expenditures*; 7: *Government Expenditure*; 8: *Prices*; 9: *Agriculture and Forestry*; 10: *Mining and Manufacturing*; 11: *Textiles*; 12: *Railways and Electricity*; 13: *Regional Economic Statistics*; 14: *Foreign Trade and Balance of Payments*.

2. ECONOMIC THOUGHT

A. GENERAL

Tessa Morris-Suzuki, *A History of Japanese Economic Thought*, New York, Routledge, 1988.

William Braisted, ed. *Meiroku Zasshi: Journal of the Japanese Enlightenment*, Harvard University Press, 1976, especially essays by Kanda Kohei.

Gianni Fodella, "The Economic Ideas of Fukuzawa Yukichi," *Transactions of the International Congress of Orientalists in Japan* 15 (1970), 22-33.

Toyoji Kotake, "Yukichi Fukuzawa's Views of Stock-Exchange Speculation and Investment," *Keio Economic Studies* 5 (1968), 1-10.

Chuhei Sugiyama, "The Development of Economic Thought in Meiji Japan," *Modern Asian Studies* 2:4 (1968), 325-41.

Chuhei Sugiyama & Hiroshi Mizuta, eds. *Enlightenment and Beyond: Political Economy Comes to Japan*, University of Tokyo Press, 1988, including:
Chuhei Sugiyama, "Fukuzawa Yukichi," 37-57, and "Nishi Amane and Tsuda

Mamichi," 59-72, as well as articles on "The Institutionalization of Political Economy in Higher Education," and "Political Economy Outside Educational Institutions." (This is more of a reference book than an analysis of thought).

Akiteru Kubota, "Three Economists of Waseda University, 1886-1920," *Waseda Economic Papers* 2 (1958), 1-14.

Yoshitaka Komatsu, "The Birth, Development and Recent Trends of Economic History in Japan: An Outline with Special Reference to Waseda University," *Waseda Economic Papers* 2 (1958), 15-27.

Hisao Otsuka, "Modernization Reconsidered—with Special Reference to Industrialization," *DE* 3:4 (Dec 1965), 387-403.

Eiji Ohno, "Theory of Economic Policy by Young Kawakami," *Kyoto University Economic Review* 55:2 (Oct 1985), 1-31 (on Kawakami Hajime).

N.S. Siddharthan, "The Non-Neoclassical Paradigm: Buddhism and Economic Development," *Japanese Journal of Religious Studies* 11:4 (Dec 1984), 351-69.

B. MARXISM

Prewar Issues

Nobutake Ike, "The Development of Capitalism in Japan," *Pacific Affairs* 22:2 (June 1949), 185-90.

Kojiro Niino, "The Formation of the Japanese Finance Capital and its Characteristics," *Kobe University Economic Review* 2 (1956), 53-68.

Kazuo Shibagaki, "The Logic of Japanese Imperialism," *Annals of the Institute of Social Science* 14 (1973), 70-87.

Yasukichi Yasuba, "Anatomy of the Debate on Japanese Capitalism," *Journal of Japanese Studies* 2:1 (Aug 1975), 63-82.

Germaine A. Hoston, *Marxism and the Crisis of Development in Prewar Japan*, Princeton University Press, 1986.

Joshua A. Fogel, "The Debates over the Asiatic Mode of Production in Soviet Russia, China, and Japan," *American Historical Review* 93:1 (Feb 1988), 56-79.

Kaoru Sugihara, "The Japanese Capitalism Debate, 1927-1937," *Journal of Peasant Studies* (1989), forthcoming.

Postwar Developments

Yoshitomo Takeuchi, "The Role of Marxism in Japan," *DE* 5:4 (1967), 727-47.

Thomas T. Sekine, "Uno-riron: A Japanese Contribution to Marxist Political Economy," *Journal of Economic Literature* 13:3 (Sept 1975), 847-77.

Makoto Itoh, *Value and Crisis: Essays on Marxian Economics in Japan*, New York, Monthly Review Press, 1980.

Hiroji Baba, "Contemporary Capitalism or State Monopoly Capitalism: A Review," *Annals of the Institute of Social Science* 21 (1980), 106-29.

Tsutomu Ouchi, "Notes on the Theory of State Monopoly Capitalism," *Annals of the Institute of Social Science* 23 (1982), 1-21.

Shohken Mawatari, "The Uno School: A Marxian Approach in Japan," *History of Political Economy* 17:3 (Fall 1985), 403-18.

Hiroji Baba, "Changing the Paradigms of Japanese Marx Economics," *Annals of the Institute of Social Science* 27 (1985), 26-53.

Robert Albritton, *A Japanese Reconstruction of Marxist Theory*, London, Macmillan, 1986.

C. ECONOMIC EXPANSION

Akira Iriye, "The Failure of Economic Expansion, 1918-1931," in Bernard Silberman & Harry Harootunian, eds. *Japan in Crisis: Essays on Taisho Democracy*, Princeton University Press, 1974, 237-69.

Germaine A. Hoston, "Marxism and Japanese Expansionism: Takahashi Kamekichi and the Theory of 'Petty Imperialism'," *Journal of Japanese Studies* 10:1 (Win 1984), 1-30.

3. INDUSTRIAL DEVELOPMENT

A. GENERAL

General Works

Miyohei Shinohara, "The Production Function for Manufacturing in Japan," *Annals of the Hitotsubashi Academy* 2:1 (Oct 1951), 37-55.

Ryuziro Ishida, "The Industrialization of Japan: A Geographical Analysis," *Annals of the Hitotsubashi Academy* 7:1 (Oct 1956), 61-80.

Keishi Ohara, ed. *Japanese Trade and Industry in the Meiji-Taisho Era*, Tokyo, Obunsha, 1957.

Misao Sekiguchi, "The Backgrounds of Business Creed in Japan," *Keio Business Review* 2 (1963), 95-124.

Takafusa Nakamura, "The Modern Industries and the Traditional Industries—at the Early Stage of the Japanese Economy," *DE* 4:4 (Dec 1966), 567-93.

The History of Kanagawa, Kanagawa Prefectural Government, 1985.

Yukihiko Kiyokawa & Shigeru Ishikawa, "The Significance of Standardization in the Development of the Machine-Tool Industry: The Cases of Japan and China," *Hitotsubashi Journal of Economics* (1) 28:2 (Dec 1987), 123-54.

Toshiyuki Kako, "Development of the Farm Machinery Industry in Japan: A Case Study of the Walking Type Tractor," *Hitotsubashi Journal of Economics* 28:2 (Dec 1987), 155-71.

William D. Wray, ed. *Managing Industrial Enterprise: Cases from Japan's Prewar Experience*, Harvard University Press, 1989.

Minoru Sawai, "The Development of Machine-Building Industries and the Evolution of Production & Labor Management: Cases of Rolling Stock, Spinning & Weaving Machines, Machine Tools and Electric Machineries," in *Japanese Management in Historical Perspective*, vol. 15 of *International Conference on Business History*, ed. by Keiichiro Nakagawa & Tsunehiko Yui, University of Tokyo Press, 1989.

Industrial Structure & Industrial Organization

Miyohei Shinohara, *Structural Changes in Japan's Economic Development*, Tokyo, Kinokuniya, 1970.

Kazuo Shibagaki, "The Logic of Japanese Imperialism," *Annals of the Institute of Social Science* 14 (1973), 70-87.

Keiichiro Nakagawa, "The Structure and Motives of Investment by Private Enterprises in Japan before the Second World War," in Herman Daems & Herman van der Wee, eds. *The Rise of Managerial Capitalism*, Louvain, Leuven University Press, 1974, 197-212.

Keiichiro Nakagawa, "Business Strategy and Industrial Structure in Pre-World War II Japan," in *Strategy and Structure of Big Business*, vol. 1 of *Interna-*

tional Conference on Business History, ed. by Keiichiro Nakagawa, University of Tokyo Press, 1976, 3-38.

Kozo Yamamura, "The Japanese Economy, 1911-1930: Concentration, Conflicts, and Crises," in Bernard Silberman & Harry Harootunian, eds. *Japan in Crisis: Essays on Taisho Democracy*, Princeton University Press, 1974, 299-328.

Trade Associations in Business History, vol. 14 of *International Conference on Business History*, ed. by Hiroaki Yamazaki & Matao Miyamoto, University of Tokyo Press, 1988, including:
Takeo Kikkawa, "Functions of Japanese Trade Associations Before World War II: The Case of Cartel Organizations," 53-83.

Teiichiro Fujita, "Local Trade Associations (Dogyo Kumiai) in Prewar Japan," 87-113.

Technology

Erich Pauer, "Traditional Technology and its Impact on Japan's Industry during the Early Period of the Industrial Revolution," *Economic Studies Quarterly* 38:4 (Dec 1987), 354-71.

Masaru Saito, "Introduction of Foreign Technology in the Industrialization Process: Japanese Experience since the Meiji Restoration (1868)," *DE* 13:2 (June 1975), 168-86.

Special Issue: "Technology Transfer and Adaptation: The Japanese Experience," *DE* 17 (1979), 373-528, including:
Takeshi Hayashi, "Introduction," 373-97.
Asim Sen, "Followers' Strategy for Technological Development," 506-28.

Akio Okochi, "A Comparison of Choice of Technology Among Three Nations: Great Britain, United States and Japan," in *Strategy and Structure of Big Business*, vol. 1 of *International Conference on Business History*, ed. by Keiichiro Nakagawa, University of Tokyo Press, 1976, 153-70.

Keiichiro Nakagawa, "The 'Learning Industrial Revolution' and Business Management in Japan," in *Japanese Management in Historical Perspective*, vol. 15 of *International Conference on Business History*, ed. by Nakagawa & Tsunehiko Yui, University of Tokyo Press, 1989.

Science & Education

Masatoshi Ohkochi, "Applied Science as a Natural Resource," *CJ* 10:3 (March 1941), 295-309.

Tetu Hirosige, "The Role of the Government in the Development of Science," *Journal of World History* 9:2 (1965), 320-39.

Kamatani Chikayoshi, "The Role Played by the Industrial World in the Progress of Japanese Science and Technology," *Journal of World History* 9:2 (1965), 400-21.

Japanese National Commission for Unesco, *Technological Development in Japan*, vol. 1 of Case Studies on Technological Development, Paris, Unesco, 1981.

Kiyonobu Itakura & Eri Yagi, "The Japanese Research System and the Establishment of the Institute of Physical and Chemical Research," in Shigeru Nakayama, ed. *Science and Society in Modern Japan*, MIT Press, 1974.

Ryoichi Iwauchi, "The Growth of White Collar Employment in Modern Japan," *Japanese Management in Historical Perspective*, vol. 15 of *International Conference on Business History*, ed. by Keiichiro Nakagawa & Tsunehiko Yui, University of Tokyo Press, 1989.

B. TEXTILES

General

Mitsuhaya Kajinishi, "Development of Light Industry," in Keizo Shibusawa, ed. *Japanese Society in the Meiji Era*, Tokyo, Obunsha, 1958, 237-303.

Keiichiro Nakagawa & Henry Rosovsky, "The Case of the Dying Kimono: The Influence of Changing Fashions on the Development of the Japanese Woolen Industry," *Business History Review* 37:1&2 (Spr-Sum 1963), 59-80.

Hiroshi Shimbo, "An Aspect of Industrialization in Japan: In its Formative Stage," *Kobe University Economic Review* 13 (1967), 19-42.

Shinya Sugiyama, *Japan's Industrialization in the World Economy, 1859-1899: Export Trade and Overseas Competition*, London, The Athlone Press, 1988 (covers silk, tea, and coal).

Silk

Iwajiro Honda, *The Silk Industry of Japan*, Tokyo, 1909.

Sakuzo Kawada, "Rayon in the Land of Silk," *CJ* 2:1 (June 1933), 76-82.

Richard F. Hough, "Impact of the Decline in Raw Silk on the Suwa Basin of Japan," *Economic Geography* 44:2 (Apr 1968), 95-116.

Stephen W. McCallion, "Silk Reeling in Meiji Japan: The Limits to Change," Ph.D. diss., Ohio State University, 1983.

Yukihiko Kiyokawa, "Entrepreneurship in Japan: An Implication of the Experience of Technological Development in the Textile Industry," *DE* 22:3 (1984), 211-36.

Yukihiko Kiyokawa, "The Diffusion of New Technologies in the Japanese Sericulture Industry: The Case of the Hybrid Silkworm," *Hitotsubashi Journal of Economics* 25:1 (June 1984), 31-59.

Akira Ono, "Technical Progress in Silk Industry in Prewar Japan: The Types of Borrowed Technology," *Hitotsubashi Journal of Economics* 27:1 (June 1986), 1-10.

Yukihiko Kiyokawa, "Transplantation of the European Factory System and Adaptations in Japan: The Experience of the Tomioka Model Filature," *Hitotsubashi Journal of Economics* 28:1 (June 1987), 27-39.

Stephen W. McCallion, "Trial and Error: The Model Filature at Tomioka," in William D. Wray, ed. *Managing Industrial Enterprise: Cases from Japan's Prewar Experience*, Harvard University Press, 1989.

Cotton

Sanji Muto, "Cotton: Past, Present & Future," *CJ* 1:2 (Sept 1932), 224-34.

Keijiro Ishiyama, "Our Staple Fibre Industry," *CJ* 5:3 (Dec 1936), 400-06.

Jae Koh Sung, *Stages of Industrial Development in Asia: A Comparative History of the Cotton Industry in Japan, India, China, and Korea*, University of Pennsylvania Press, 1966.

Gary Saxonhouse, "A Tale of Japanese Technological Diffusion in the Meiji Period," *Journal of Economic History* 34:1 (March 1974), 149-65.

Moriaki Tsuchiya, "Management Organization of Vertically Integrated Non-zaibatsu Business," in *Strategy and Structure of Big Business*, vol. 1 of *International Conference on Business History*, ed. by Keiichiro Nakagawa, University of Tokyo Press, 1976, 65-78.

Kang Chao, *The Development of Cotton Textile Production in China*, Harvard University Press, 1977.

Kazuo Sugiyama, "Trade Credit and the Development of the Cotton Spinning Industry," in *Marketing and Finance in the Course of Industrialization*, vol.

3 of *International Conference on Business History*, ed. by Keiichiro Nakagawa, University of Tokyo Press, 1978, 59-82.

Takeo Izumi, "The Cotton Industry," *DE* 17 (1979), 398-420.

Shin'ichi Yonekawa, "The Growth of Cotton Spinning Firms and Vertical Integration: A Comparative Study of U.K., U.S.A., India and Japan," *Hitotsubashi Journal of Commerce and Management* 14:1 (Oct 1979), 1-14.

The Textile Industry and its Business Climate, vol. 8 of *International Conference on Business History*, ed. by Akio Okochi & Shin'ichi Yonekawa, University of Tokyo Press, 1982, including the following articles:
Tetsuya Kuwahara, "The Business Strategy of Japanese Cotton Spinners: Overseas Operations, 1890 to 1931," 139-66.
Naosuke Takamura, "Japanese Cotton Spinning Industry during the Pre-World War I Period," 277-85.

Naosuke Takamura, "Japanese Cotton Spinning Industry during the pre-World War I Period: Its Growth and Essential Conditions," in Hans Pohl, ed. *Innovation, Know How, Rationalization and Investment in the German and Japanese Economies, 1868/1871-1930/1980*, Wiesbaden, Franz Steiner Verlag, 1982, 207-30.

Tetsuya Kuwahara, "The Establishment of Oligopoly in the Japanese Cotton-Spinning Industry and the Business Strategies of Latecomers: The Case of Naigaiwata & Co., Ltd.," in *Yearbook* 3, 1986, 103-34.

Tadao Kiyonari, "The Development of Middle and Small Business in Japan: A Case Study of the Textile Industry," in Keiichiro Nakagawa & Tsunehiko Yui, eds. *Organization and Management, 1900-1930*: Proceedings of the Japan-Germany Conference on Business History, Japan Business History Institute, 1983, 158-76.

Ryoshin Minami & Fumiko Makino, "Choice of Technology: A Case Study of the Japanese Cotton Weaving Industry, 1902-1938," *Hitotsubashi Journal of Economics* 27:2 (Dec 1986), 111-32.

Shin'ichi Yonekawa, "Flotation Booms in the Cotton Spinning Industry, 1870-1890: A Comparative Study," *Business History Review* 61:4 (Win 1987), 551-81.

C. FOOD PROCESSING

Joseph Laker, "Entrepreneurship and the Development of the Japanese Beer Industry, 1872-1937," Ph.D. diss., University of Indiana, 1975.

Tsunehiko Yui, "The Traditional System of Middlemen and Marketing Policies of Food Manufacturers," in *Strategy and Structure of Big Business*, vol. 1 of *International Conference on Business History*, ed. by Keiichiro Nakagawa, University of Tokyo Press, 1976, 105-114.

W. Mark Fruin, *Kikkoman: Company, Clan, and Community*, Harvard University Press, 1983.

D. MINING

Yoshio Ando, "Development of Mining Industry," in Keizo Shibusawa, ed. *Japanese Society in the Meiji Era*, Tokyo, Obunsha, 1958, 347-67.

Coal

Olive & Sydney Checkland, "British and Japanese Economic Interaction under the Early Meiji: The Takashima Coal Mine, 1868-88," *Business History* 26:2 (July 1984), 139-55.

Nisaburo Murakami, "Coal Mining," *DE* 17 (1979), 461-83.

Yukio Yamashita, "The Inside Contract System in Japan: With Particular Reference to the Coal Mining Industry," *Yearbook* 4, 1987, 1-25.

Metal

Fumio Yoshiki, "Metal Mining and Foreign Employees," *DE* 17 (1979), 484-505.

Symposium: "The Ashio Copper Mine Pollution Incident," *Journal of Japanese Studies* 1:2 (Spr 1975), including:
Fred G. Notehelfer, "Japan's First Pollution Incident," 351-83.
Alan Stone, "The Japanese Muckrakers," 385-407.

Yoshiro Hoshino, "Technological and Managerial Development of Japanese Mining: The Case of the Ashio Copper Mine," *DE* 20:2 (June 1982), 220-39.

E. TRANSPORT & SERVICE

Mitsuhaya Kajinishi, "Development of Transportation and Communication Systems," in Keizo Shibusawa, ed. *Japanese Society in the Meiji Era*, Tokyo, Obunsha, 1958, 369-400.

Shipping

Renpei Kondo, "Japanese Communications: The Mercantile Marine," in Shigenobu Okuma, ed. *Fifty Years of New Japan*, vol. 1, 1910 (Reprint: New York, Kraus, 1970), 447-64.

Sadaki Fukumoto, "On Shipping & Its Outlook," *CJ* 3:4 (March 1935), 584-95.

Ryutaro Fukao, "Shozo Murata: Shipping Magnate," *CJ* 9:1 (Jan 1940), 16-24.

Ryoichi Furuta & Yoshikazu Hirai, *A Short History of Japanese Merchant Shipping*, trans. by Duncan MacFarlane, Tokyo News Service, 1967.

Seiji Sasaki, "The Early Development of Kobe Port," *Kobe University Economic Review* 15 (1968), 17-28.

Hiromi Masuda, "Japan's Industrial Development Policy and the Construction of Nobiru Port: The Case Study of a Failure," *DE* 18:3 (Sept 1980), 333-63.

Takeaki Teratani, "Japanese Business and Government in the Takeoff Stage," in *Government and Business*, vol. 5 of *International Conference on Business History*, ed. by Keiichiro Nakagawa, University of Tokyo Press, 1980, 57-78.

William D. Wray, *Mitsubishi and the N.Y.K., 1870-1914: Business Strategy in the Japanese Shipping Industry*, Harvard University Press, 1984.

Business History of Shipping: Strategy and Structure, vol. 11 of *International Conference on Business History*, ed. by Tsunehiko Yui & Keiichiro Nakagawa, University of Tokyo Press, 1985, including the following:
Keiichiro Nakagawa, "Japanese Shipping in the Nineteenth and Twentieth Centuries: Strategy and Organization," 1-33.
Ryoichi Miwa, "Maritime Policy in Japan: 1868-1937," 123-56.
Kazuo Sugiyama, "Shipbuilding Finance of the *Shasen* Shipping Firms, 1920s-1930s," 255-72.
William D. Wray, "NYK and the Commercial Diplomacy of the Far Eastern Freight Conference, 1896-1956," 279-311.

The First Century of Mitsui O.S.K. Lines Ltd. ed. Japan Business History Institute, Tokyo, 1985.

Shin Goto, "The Progress of Shipping Operators Belonging to Trading Companies: The Scheduled Services to North America of the Shipping Division of Mitsui Trading Company between the Two World Wars," in *Yearbook* 3, 1986, 52-81.

William D. Wray, "Kagami Kenkichi and the N.Y.K., 1929-1935: Vertical Control, Horizontal Strategy, and Company Autonomy," in Wray, ed. *Managing*

Industrial Enterprise: Cases from Japan's Prewar Experience, Harvard University Press, 1989.

Railways

Tokihiko Tanaka, "Meiji Government and the Introduction of Railways," *CJ* 28:3 (May 1966), 567-88 and 28:4 (May 1967), 750-88.

Masaho Noda, "Corporate Finance of Railroad Companies in Meiji Japan," in *Marketing and Finance in the Course of Industrialization*, vol. 3 of *International Conference on Business History*, ed. by Keiichiro Nakagawa, University of Tokyo Press, 1978, 87-101.

Yoshinobu Oikawa, "Market Structure and the Construction of Rural Railways during the Formative Period of Industrial Capitalism in Japan," *Journal of Transport History* 5:2 (Sept 1984), 34-46.

Takenori Inoki, "Railway Nationalization and the Expansion of the Money Supply—The Case of Ohtsu City in Japan: 1880-1894," in Akira Hayami, ed. Pre-Conditions to Industrialization in Japan, Papers from Ninth International Economic History Congress, Bern, 1986.

Steven J. Ericson, "Railways in Crisis: The Financing and Management of Japanese Railway Companies during the Panic of 1890," in William D. Wray, ed. *Managing Industrial Enterprise: Cases from Japan's Prewar Experience*, Harvard University Press, 1989.

Steven J. Ericson, "The Professionalization of Private Railroad Management in Meiji Japan," in *Japanese Management in Historical Perspective*, vol. 15 of *International Conference on Business History*, ed. by Keiichiro Nakagawa & Tsunehiko Yui, University of Tokyo Press, 1989.

Toshiharu Watarai, *Nationalization of Railways in Japan*, Columbia University, 1915.

Takeshi Yuzawa, "The Introduction of Electric Railways in Britain and Japan," *Journal of Transport History* 6:1 (March 1985), 1-22.

Shoji Yasuda, "Ichizo Kobayashi: Versatile Businessman," *CJ* 9:4 (Apr 1940), 396-404.

Service, Distribution, & Communications

The Tokio Marine & Fire Insurance: The First Century, 1879-1979, ed. Japan Business History Institute, Tokyo, 1980.

Kyutaro Ota, "Department Stores," *CJ* 1:1 (June 1932), 95-100.

Giichi Fukami, "Department Store Business in Japan," *Annals of the Hitotsubashi Academy* 3:1 (Oct 1952), 114-28.

Yutaka Arase, "Mass Communications between the Two World Wars," *DE* 5:4 (Dec 1967), 748-66.

F. HEAVY INDUSTRY

General

Uchisaburo Kobayashi, *Military Industries of Japan*, New York, Oxford University Press, 1922.

Yoshio Ando, "Development of Heavy Industry," in Keizo Shibusawa, ed. *Japanese Society in the Meiji Era*, Tokyo, Obunsha, 1958, 305-46.

Yoshio Ando, "The Formation of Heavy Industry: One of the Processes of Industrialization in the Meiji Period," in Seiichi Tobata, ed. *The Modernization of Japan*, Tokyo, The Institute of Asian Economic Affairs, 1966, 115-35.

Steel

Reisaku Wakai, "Japan's Greatest Iron Enterprise," *CJ* 5:1 (June 1936), 57-63.

Ippei Yamazawa, "Industry Growth and Foreign Trade: A Study of Japan's Steel Industry, *Hitotsubashi Journal of Economics* 12:2 (Feb 1972), 41-59.

Ken'ichi Iida, "The Iron and Steel Industry," *DE* 17 (1979), 444-60.

Masaru Udagawa & Seishi Nakamura, "Japanese Business and the Industrial Rationalization Movement," in *Government and Business*, vol. 5 of *International Conference on Business History*, ed. by Keiichiro Nakagawa, University of Tokyo Press, 1980, 83-100.

Akira Ono, "Borrowed Technology in the Iron and Steel Industry: A Comparison between Brazil, India and Japan," *Hitotsubashi Journal of Economics* 21:2 (Feb 1981), 1-18.

Hidemasa Morikawa, "The Zaibatsu in the Japanese Iron and Steel Industry," in Hans Pohl, ed. *Innovation, Know How, Rationalization and Investment in the German and Japanese Economies, 1868/1871-1930/1980*, Wiesbaden, Franz Steiner Verlag, 1982, 134-45.

Tatsuji Okazaki, "The Japanese Iron and Steel Industry, 1929-33, and the Establishment of Nippon Steel Co.," *Yearbook* 4, 1987, 126-51.

Shipbuilding

Tuvia Blumenthal, "The Japanese Shipbuilding Industry," in Hugh Patrick, ed. *Japanese Industrialization and its Social Consequences*, University of California Press, 1973, 129-60.

Seymour Broadbridge, "Shipbuilding and the State in Japan Since the 1880s," *Modern Asian Studies* 11:4 (Oct 1977), 601-13.

Takao Shiba, "Succeeding Against Odds, Courting Collapse: How Mitsubishi and Kawasaki Dockyard Managed the Post-WWI Slump," in *Yearbook* 2, 1985, 100-18.

Takao Shiba, "A Comparative Study of the Managerial Structure of Two Japanese Shipbuilding Firms: Mitsubishi Shipbuilding and Engineering Co. and Kawasaki Dockyard Co., 1896-1927," in *Development of Managerial Enterprise*, vol. 12 of *International Conference on Business History*, ed. by Kesaji Kobayashi & Hidemasa Morikawa, University of Tokyo Press, 1986, 211-33.

Yukiko Fukasaku, "Technology Imports and R&D at Mitsubishi Nagasaki Shipyard in the Pre-War Period," in Erich Pauer, ed. *Silkworms, Oil, and Chips . . . Proceedings of the Economics and Economic History Section of the Fourth International Conference on Japanese Studies*, Japan Seminar, University of Bonn, 1986, 77-90.

Tetsuo Kamiki, "Progress in Western Technology At the Yokosuka Shipbuilding Works, 1865-1887," *Papers on Far Eastern History* 37 (March 1988), 105-23.

G. "NEW" INDUSTRIES

Electrical

Development and Diffusion of Technology: Electrical and Chemical Industries, vol. 6 of *The International Conference on Business History*, ed. by Akio Okochi & Hoshimi Uchida, University of Tokyo Press, 1980, including:
Kenji Imazu, "Modern Technology and Japanese Electrical Engineers," 125-41.
Hoshimi Uchida, "Western Big Business and the Adoption of New Technology in Japan: The Electrical Equipment and Chemical Industries, 1890-1920," 145-72.

Helmut Wilhelms, "The German Electrical Industry and Japan: A Historical Sketch," in Hans Pohl, ed. *Innovation, Know How, Rationalization and Investment in the German and Japanese Economies, 1868/1871-1930/1980*, Wiesbaden, Franz Steiner Verlag, 1982, 59-71.

Yoshikatsu Hayashi, "The Introduction of American Technology into the Japanese Electrical Industry: Another Aspect of Japanese-American Relations at the Turn of the Century," Ph.D. diss., University of California, Santa Barbara, 1986.

Masaki Yoshida, "An Observation on the Foundation of Hitachi Seisakusho: Prehistory of the Hitachi Trust," *Keio Business Review* 14 (1977), 97-119.

Hisashi Watanabe, "A History of the Process Leading to the Formation of Fuji Electric," in *Yearbook* 1, 1984, 47-71.

Kozo Yamamura, "Japan's Deus ex Machina: Western Technology in the 1920s," *Journal of Japanese Studies* 12:1 (Winter 1986), 65-94.

Toshiaki Chokki, "Modernization of Technology and Labor in Pre-War Japanese Electrical Machinery Enterprises," *Yearbook* 4, 1987, 26-49.

NEC Corporation: The First 80 Years, NEC Corporation, 1984.

Shin Hasegawa, "The Development of Yasukawa Electric Co. and its Entrepreneurial Activities," *Yearbook* 4, 1987, 77-102.

Konosuke Matsushita, *Quest for Prosperity: The Life of a Japanese Industrialist*, Kyoto, PHP Institute, 1988.

Richard B. Rice, "Hitachi: Japanese Industry in an Era of Militarism, 1937-1945," Ph.D. dissertation, Harvard University, 1974 [Archives call no. HU 90/10838/10].

Chemical

Robert D. Walton, "Individualism and Self-Aggrandisement in Prewar Japanese Entrepreneurship: Noguchi Jun and the Rising Entrepreneurs," *Papers on Far Eastern History* 24 (Sept 1981), 1-38.

The following articles from *Development and Diffusion of Technology: Electrical and Chemical Industries*, vol. 6 of *The International Conference on Business History*, ed. by Akio Okochi & Hoshimi Uchida, University of Tokyo Press, 1980:
Eisuke Daito, "The Development of the Ammonia-Soda Process in Japan, 1917-1932," 177-92.
Atsufumi Mikami, "Old and New Zaibatsu in the History of Japan's Chemical Industry: With Special Reference to the Sumitomo Chemical Co. and the Showa Denko Co.," 201-18.

Tsuneo Suzuki, "The Foundations and Amalgamation of Miike Nitrogen Industries Inc. and Toyo Koatsu Industries Inc.," *Yearbook* 4, 1987, 103-25.

Barbara Molony, "Noguchi Jun and Nitchitsu: Colonial Investment Strategy of a High Technology Enterprise," in William D. Wray, ed. *Managing Industrial Enterprise: Cases from Japan's Prewar Experience*, Harvard University Press, 1989.

Barbara Molony, "Innovation and Business Strategy in the Prewar Japanese Chemical Industry," in *Japanese Management in Historical Perspective*, vol. 15 of *International Conference on Business History*, ed. by Keiichiro Nakagawa & Tsunehiko Yui, University of Tokyo Press, 1989.

Barbara Molony, *Technology & Investment: The Prewar Japanese Chemical Industry*, Harvard University Press, 1989.

Automobile

Kikuo Kawauchi, "An Automobile Industry for Japan," *CJ* 1:4 (March 1933), 657-63.

Yukio Cho, "Keeping Step with the Military: The Beginning of the Automobile Age," *Japan Interpreter* 7:2 (1972), 168-78.

Masaru Udagawa & Seishi Nakamura, "Japanese Business and the Industrial Rationalization Movement," in *Government and Business*, vol. 5 of *International Conference on Business History*, ed. by Keiichiro Nakagawa, University of Tokyo Press, 1980, 83-100.

Development of Mass Marketing: The Automobile and Retailing Industries, vol. 7 of *International Conference on Business History*, ed. by Akio Okochi & Koichi Shimokawa, University of Tokyo Press, 1981.

Taizo Yakushiji, "The Government in a Spiral Dilemma: Dynamic Policy Interventions Vis-a-Vis Auto Firms, C.1900-C.1960," in Masahiko Aoki, ed. *The Economic Analysis of the Japanese Firm*, Amsterdam, North Holland, 1984, 265-310.

Michael A. Cusumano, *The Japanese Automobile Industry: Technology and Management at Nissan and Toyota*, Harvard University Press, 1985.

Masaru Udagawa, "The Prewar Japanese Automobile Industry and American Manufacturers,' in *Yearbook* 2, 1985, 81-99.

H. OTHERS (including small industry & dual structure)

Specific

Shigeru Fujii, "Characteristics and Modernization of Match Industry: A Case of Small Business in Japan," *Kobe University Economic Review* 9 (1963), 13-30.

Johzen Takeuchi, "Rural Relocation of the Shell Button Industry," *DE* 17 (1979), 421-43.

Hoshimi Uchida, *Osaka Watch Incorporated: History of the Japanese Clock and Watch Industry*, ed, Japan Business History Institute, Hattori Seiko, 1986.

Hoshimi Uchida, *Wall Clocks of Nagoya, 1885-1925*, vol. 2 of *History of the Japanese Clock and Watch Industry*, ed. Japan Business History Institute, Hattori Seiko, 1987.

Sen'ichi Shozui, "Our Fishing Industry," *CJ* 9:6 (June 1940), 698-705.

A.B. Jamieson, "Tokyo's Central Fish Market," *CJ* 9:7 (July 1940), 848-55.

Small Industry & Dual Structure

Teijiro Uyeda, *The Small Industries of Japan*, New York, Institute of Pacific Relations, 1938.

Tokutaro Yamanaka, "Japanese Small Industries during the Industrial Revolution," *Annals of the Hitotsubashi Academy* 2:1 (Oct 1951), 15-36.

John C. Pelzel, "The Small Industrialist in Japan," *Explorations in Entrepreneurial History* 7:2 (Dec 1954), 79-93.

Tsunehiko Watanabe, "Economic Aspects of Dualism in the Industrial Development of Japan," *Economic Development and Cultural Change* 13:3 (April 1965), 293-312.

Takafusa Nakamura, "The Modern Industries and the Traditional Industries—at the Early Stage of the Japanese Economy," *DE* 4:4 (Dec 1966), 567-93.

Shigeto Kawano, "Implementation of the Industrial Cooperative System in the Meiji Era," *DE* 15:4 (Dec 1977), 462-86.

Ryoshin Minami & Akira Ono, "Modeling Dualistic Development in Japan," *Hitotsubashi Journal of Economics* 18:2 (Feb 1978), 18-32.

I. ELECTRIC POWER

Toshiye Obama, "Our Electric Power Industry," *CJ* 9:5 (May 1940), 537-47.

Ryoshin Minami, "The Introduction of Electric Power and Its Impact on the Manufacturing Industries: With Special Reference to Smaller Scale Plants," in Hugh Patrick, ed. *Japanese Industrialization and its Social Consequences*, University of California Press, 1973, 299-325.

Ryoshin Minami, "Mechanical Power in the Industrialization of Japan," *Journal of Economic History* 37:4 (Dec 1977), 935-58.

Ryoshin Minami & Fumio Makino, "Conditions for Technological Diffusion: Case of Power Looms," *Hitotsubashi Journal of Economics* 23:2 (Feb 1983), 1-20.

Erich Pauer, "Synthetic Oil and Fuel Policy of Japan in the 1920s and 1930s," in Erich Pauer, ed. *Silkworms, Oil, and Chips . . . Proceedings of the Economics and Economic History Section of the Fourth International Conference on Japanese Studies*, Japan Seminar, University of Bonn, 1986, 105-124.

Takeo Kikkawa, "Management and Regulation of the Electric Power Industry (1923-1935)," in *Yearbook* 3, 1986, 82-102.

Ryoshin Minami, *Power Revolution in the Industrialization of Japan: 1885-1940*, Tokyo, Kinokuniya, 1987.

4. BUSINESS

A. GENERAL OVERVIEWS

Johannes Hirschmeier & Tsunehiko Yui, *The Development of Japanese Business, 1600-1980*, 2nd ed., London, Allen & Unwin, 1981.

William D. Wray, ed. *Managing Industrial Enterprise: Cases from Japan's Prewar Experience*, Harvard University Press, 1989.

B. ENTREPRENEURSHIP

General

Yeiichi Shibusawa, "Joint-Stock Enterprise in Japan," in Shigenobu Okuma, ed. *Fifty Years of New Japan*, vol. 1, 1910 (Reprint: New York, Kraus, 1970), 465-85.

Gustav Ranis, "The Community Centered Entrepreneur in Japanese Development," *Explorations in Entrepreneurial History* 8:2 (Dec 1955), 80-98.

Thomas C. Smith, "Landlords' Sons in the Business Elite," *Economic Development and Cultural Change* 9:1&2 (Oct 1960), 93-107.

Yasuzo Horie, "Modern Entrepreneurship in Meiji Japan," in William W. Lockwood, ed. *The State and Economic Enterprise in Japan*, Princeton University Press, 1965, 183-208.

Kazuo Yamaguchi, "The Leaders of Industrial and Economic Development in Modern Japan," *Cahiers d'histoire mondaile* 9:2 (1965), 234-53.

Johannes Hirschmeier, *The Origins of Entrepreneurship in Meiji Japan*, Harvard University Press, 1965.

Kozo Yamamura, *A Study of Samurai Income and Entrepreneurship*, Harvard University Press, 1974.

Yasuzo Horie, "The Tradition of *Ie* (House) and the Industrialization of Japan," in *Social Order and Entrepreneurship*, vol. 2 of *International Conference on Business History*, ed. by Keiichiro Nakagawa, University of Tokyo Press, 1977, 231-54.

Masaaki Kobayashi, " 'Political Merchants' in the Meiji Era," *Kanto Gakuin University Economic Review* 2 (1980), 62-71.

Specific Entrepreneurs

Kee-Il Choi, "Shibusawa Eiichi and His Contemporaries: A Study of Japanese Entrpreneurial History," Ph.D. dissertation, Harvard University, 1958 [call no. HU 90 7327.8].

Takao Tsuchiya, "Shibusawa Eiichi," *Japan Quarterly* 12 (Jan/Mar 1965), 99-108.

Johannes Hirschmeier, "Shibusawa Eiichi: Industrial Pioneer," in William W. Lockwood, ed. *The State and Economic Enterprise in Japan*, Princeton University Press, 1965, 209-47.

Kyugoro Obata, *An Interpretation of the Life of Viscount Shibusawa*, Tokyo, Shibusawa Seien o Kinenkai, 1937.

William D. Hoover, "Godai Tomoatsu (1836-1885): An Economic Statesman of Early Meiji Japan," Ph.D. dissertation, University of Michigan, 1973.

Robert D. Walton, "Individualism and Self-Aggrandisement in Prewar Japanese Entrepreneurship: Noguchi Jun and the Rising Entrepreneurs," *Papers on Far Eastern History* 24 (Sept 1981), 1-38.

Andrew Fraser, "Hachisuka Mochiaki (1846-1918): From Feudal Lord to Modern Businessman," in *Japanese Management in Historical Perspective*, vol. 15 of *International Conference on Business History*, ed. by Keiichiro

Nakagawa & Tsunehiko Yui, University of Tokyo Press, 1989. (See the similar article in *Papers on Far Eastern History* 37 (March 1988), 93-104).

C. MANAGEMENT

General

Japanese Yearbook on Business History, Japan Business History Institute 1984-. (abbreviated as *Yearbook*).

Kozo Yamamura, "Entrepreneurship, Ownership, and Management in Japan," in Peter Mathias & M.M. Postan, eds. *The Cambridge Economic History of Europe*, Cambridge University Press, 1978, vol. vii, part 2, 215-64.

W. Mark Fruin, *Kikkoman: Company, Clan, and Community*, Harvard University Press, 1983.

Strategy

Keiichiro Nakagawa, "Business Strategy and Industrial Structure in Pre-World War II Japan," in *Strategy and Structure of Big Business*, vol. 1 of *International Conference on Business History*, ed. by Keiichiro Nakagawa, University of Tokyo Press, 1976, 3-38.

Tsunehiko Yui, "Development, Organization, and International Competitiveness of Industrial Enterprises in Japan, 1880-1915," *Business and Economic History* 2nd ser. 17 (1988), 31-48.

Company Systems & Organization

Toshikazu Nakase, "The Introduction of Scientific Management in Japan and Its Characteristics: Case Studies of Companies in the Sumitomo Zaibatsu," in *Labor and Management*, vol. 4 of *International Conference on Business History*, ed. by Keiichiro Nakagawa, University of Tokyo Press, 1979, 171-202.

Satoshi Sasaki, "Scientific Management Movements in Pre-War Japan," *Yearbook* 4, 1987, 50-76.

W. Mark Fruin, "The Firm as Family and the Family as Firm in Japan," *The Journal of Family History* 5:4 (Win 1980), 432-49.

Keiichiro Nakagawa & Tsunehiko Yui, eds. *Organization and Management, 1900-1930*: Proceedings of the Japan-Germany Conference on Business History, Japan Business History Institute, 1983.

Family Business in the Era of Industrial Growth: Its Ownership and Management,
vol. 10 of *International Conference on Business History*, ed. by Akio
Okochi & Shigeaki Yasuoka, University of Tokyo Press, 1984, including:
Matao Miyamoto, "The Position and Role of Family Business in the Development
of the Japanese Company System," 39-91.

Tsunehiko Yui, "The Development of the Organizational Structure of Top Management in Meiji Japan," in *Yearbook* 1, 1984, 1-23.

Hisashi Masaki, "The Formation and Evolution of the Corporate Business System
in Japan," in *Yearbook* 3, 1986, 26-5l.

Management Personnel

Shin'ichi Yonekawa, "University Graduates in Japanese Enterprises Before the
Second World War," *Business History* 26:2 (July 1984), 193-281.

Keiichiro Nakagawa, "The 'Learning Industrial Revolution' and Business Management in Japan," in *Japanese Management in Historical Perspective*, vol. 15
of *International Conference on Business History*, ed. by Nakagawa &
Tsunehiko Yui, University of Tokyo Press, 1989.

The Role of Managers

Yoshitaka Suzuki, "The Formation of Management Structure in Japanese Indus-
trials, 1920-40," *Business History* 27:3 (Nov 1985), 259-82.

Development of Managerial Enterprise, vol. 12 of *International Conference on
Business History*, ed. by Kesaji Kobayashi & Hidemasa Morikawa, Univer-
sity of Tokyo Press, 1986, including:
Hidemasa Morikawa, "Prerequisites for the Development of Managerial Cap-
italism: Cases in Prewar Japan," 1-33.
Takao Shiba, "A Comparative Study of the Managerial Structure of Two Japanese
Shipbuilding Firms: Mitsubishi Shipbuilding and Engineering Co. and Ka-
wasaki Dockyard Co., 8196-1927," 211-33.

Takeo Kikkawa, "Management and Regulation of the Electric Power Industry
(1923-1935)," in *Yearbook* 3, 1986, 82-102.

Hidemasa Morikawa, "The Increasing Power of Salaried Managers in Japan's
Large Corporations," in William D. Wray, ed. *Managing Industrial Enterprise: Cases from Japan's Prewar Experience*, Harvard University Press,
1989.

Middle Management

Hidemasa Morikawa, "The Significance and Process of Development of Middle Management in Japanese Business, Mainly in the 20th Century," in Keiichiro Nakagawa & Tsunehiko Yui, eds. *Organization and Management, 1900-1930*: Proceedings of the Japan-Germany Conference on Business History, Japan Business History Institute, 1983, 132-40.

Eisuke Daito, "Recruitment and Training of Middle Managers in Japan, 1900-1930," in *Development of Managerial Enterprise*, vol. 12 of *International Conference on Business History*, ed. by Kesaji Kobayashi & Hidemasa Morikawa, University of Tokyo Press, 1986, 151-84. (mostly on Mitsubishi).

Ryoichi Iwauchi, "The Growth of White Collar Employment in Modern Japan," *Japanese Management in Historical Perspective*, vol. 15 of *International Conference on Business History*, ed. by Keiichiro Nakagawa & Tsunehiko Yui, University of Tokyo Press, 1989.

Comparative

Nobuo Noda, "How Japan Absorbed American Management Methods," in British Institute of Management, ed. *Modern Japanese Management*, 1970, 29-66.

A.D. Chandler, Jr. & H. Daems, "The Rise of Managerial Capitalism and its Impact on Investment Strategy in the Western World and Japan," in H. Daems and H. van der Wee, eds. *The Rise of Managerial Capitalism*, The Hague, 1974.

Mansel G. Blackford, *The Rise of Modern Business in Great Britain, the United States, and Japan*, Chapel Hill, The University of North Carolina Press, 1988.

D. ZAIBATSU

General

John K. Fairbank, Edwin O. Reischauer & Albert M. Craig, *East Asia: The Modern Transformation*, Boston, Houghton Mifflin, 1965, 505-13, "The Zaibatsu System."

Kazuo Shibagaki, "The Early History of the Zaibatsu," *DE* 4:4 (Dec 1966), 535-66.

Ownership

Shigeaki Yasuoka, "The Tradition of Family Business in the Strategic Decision Process and Management Structure of Zaibatsu Business," in *Strategy and Structure of Big Business*, vol. 1 of *International Conference on Business History*, ed. by Keiichiro Nakagawa, University of Tokyo Press, 1976, 81-101.

Family Business in the Era of Industrial Growth: Its Ownership and Management, vol. 10 of *International Conference on Business History*, ed. by Akio Okochi & Shigeaki Yasuoka, University of Tokyo Press, 1984, including:
Shigeaki Yasuoka, "Capital Ownership in Family Companies: Japanese Firms Compared with Those in Other Countries," 1-37.

Neil Skene Smith, "Japan's Business Families," *The Economist*, June 18, 1938, 651-56.

Management & Control

Hidemasa Morikawa, "The Organizational Structure of the Mitsubishi and Mitsui Zaibatsu, 1868-1922," *Business History Review* 44:1 (Spr 1970), 62-83.

Hidemasa Morikawa, "Management Structure and Control Devices for Diversified Zaibatsu Business," in *Strategy and Structure of Big Business*, vol. 1 of *International Conference on Business History*, ed. by Keiichiro Nakagawa, University of Tokyo Press, 1976, 45-60.

Tsunehiko Yui, "The Personality and Career of Hikojiro Nakamigawa, 1887-1901," *Business History Review* 44:1 (Spr 1970), 39-61.

Finance

Hisashi Masaki, "The Financial Characteristics of the Zaibatsu in Japan: The Old Zaibatsu and its Closed Finance," in *Marketing and Finance in the Course of Industrialization*, vol. 3 of *International Conference on Business History*, ed. by Keiichiro Nakagawa, University of Tokyo Press, 1978, 33-54.

Shoichi Asajima, "Flow-of-Funds Analysis of the Sumitomo Zaibatsu," in *Yearbook* 1, 1984, 72-103.

Shoichi Asajima, "Financing of the Japanese Zaibatsu: Sumitomo as a Case Study," in *Family Business in the Era of Industrial Growth: Its Ownership and Management*, vol. 10 of *International Conference on Business History*, ed. by Akio Okochi & Shigeaki Yasuoka, University of Tokyo Press, 1984, 95-117.

The following articles from Keiichiro Nakagawa & Tsunehiko Yui, eds. *Organization and Management, 1900-1930*: Proceedings of the Japan-Germany Conference on Business History, Japan Business History Institute, 1983:
Shoichi Asajima, "Industry and Finance in Japan: Financing of Large Enterprises in the 1910s and 1920s," 26-41.
Yasuo Mishima, "Family Business in Modern Japan," 96-107.

Individual Zaibatsu

Oland D. Russell, *The House of Mitsui*, 1939 (reprint: Westport, Greenwood Press, 1970).

John Roberts, *Mitsui: Three Centuries of Japanese Business*, Tokyo, Weatherhill, 1973.

Seiichiro Yonekura, "The Emergence of the Prototype of Enterprise Group Capitalism: The Case of Mitsui," *Hitotsubashi Journal of Commerce & Management* 20:1 (Dec 1985), 63-104.

William D. Wray, *Mitsubishi and the N.Y.K., 1870-1914: Business Strategy in the Japanese Shipping Industry*, Harvard University Press, 1984.

Eisuke Daito, "Recruitment and Training of Middle Managers in Japan, 1900-1930," in *Development of Managerial Enterprise*, vol. 12 of *International Conference on Business History*, ed. by Kesaji Kobayashi & Hidemasa Morikawa, University of Tokyo Press, 1986, 151-84.

William D. Wray, "Kagami Kenkichi and the N.Y.K., 1929-1935: Vertical Control, Horizontal Strategy, and Company Autonomy," in Wray, ed. *Managing Industrial Enterprise: Cases from Japan's Prewar Experience*, Harvard University Press, 1989.

Toshikazu Nakase, "The Introduction of Scientific Management in Japan and Its Characteristics: Case Studies of Companies in the Sumitomo Zaibatsu," in *Labor and Management*, vol. 4 of *International Conference on Business History*, ed. by Keiichiro Nakagawa, University of Tokyo Press, 1979, 171-202.

Masahiro Shimotani, "Formation of 'New Zaibatsu' in Prewar Japan," *Kyoto University Economic Review* 54:1 (Apr 1984), 40-59.

Masatoshi Ohkochi, "Building up Village Industries," *CJ* 4:2 (Sept 1935), 179-86.

Satoshi Saito, "The Formation of the Riken Industrial Group," in *Yearbook* 2, 1985, 119-40.

Michael A. Cusumano, " 'Scientific Industry': Strategy, Technology, and Management in the Riken Industrial Group, 1917 to 1945," in William D. Wray, ed. *Managing Industrial Enterprise: Cases from Japan's Prewar Experience*, Harvard University Press, 1989.

Zaibatsu & the Economy

G.C. Allen, "The Concentration of Economic Control in Japan," *The Economic Journal* 47 (June 1937), 271-86.

Kozo Yamamura, "The Japanese Economy, 1911-1930: Concentration, Conflicts, and Crises," in Bernard Silberman & Harry Harootunian, eds. *Japan in Crisis: Essays on Taisho Democracy*, Princeton University Press, 1974, 299-328.

Strategy and Structure of Big Business, vol. 1 of *International Conference on Business History*, ed. by Keiichiro Nakagawa, University of Tokyo Press, 1976.

E. BUSINESS FINANCE

General

Marketing and Finance in the Course of Industrialization, vol. 3 of *The International Conference on Business History*, ed. by Keiichiro Nakagawa, Tokyo University Press, 1978, including:
Ryushi Iwata, "A Comparative Analysis of the Ways that Limiting Factors were Overcome in Three Nations: The United States, Japan, and the United Kingdom, 3-29.

Toyoji Kotake, "A Comparative Study of the Securities Markets with Reference to the Structural Characteristics of Financial Capital," *Keio Business Review* 10 (1971), 25-37.

Kozo Yamamura, "Japan, 1868-1930: A Revised View," in Rondo Cameron, ed. *Banking and Economic Development*, Oxford University Press, 1972, 168-98.

Kazuo Sugiyama, "Business Finance in Japanese Business History," in *Yearbook* 1, 1984, 24-46.

Ken'ichiro Shoda, "Trade and Credit in a Local Industrial Area in the Early Years of the Meiji Era," *Waseda Economic Papers* 10 (1967), 47-76.

Takenori Inoki, "Railway Nationalization and the Expansion of the Money Supply—The Case of Ohtsu City in Japan: 1880-1894," in Akira Hayami, ed.

Pre-Conditions to Industrialization in Japan, Papers from Ninth International Economic History Congress, Bern, 1986.

Steven J. Ericson, "Railways in Crisis: The Financing and Management of Japanese Railway Companies during the Panic of 1890," in William D. Wray, ed. *Managing Industrial Enterprise: Cases from Japan's Prewar Experience*, Harvard University Press, 1989.

Specific Industries

Marketing and Finance in the Course of Industrialization, vol. 3 of *The International Conference on Business History*, ed. by Keiichiro Nakagawa, Tokyo University Press, 1978, including:
Kazuo Sugiyama, "Trade Credit and the Development of the Cotton Spinning Industry," 59-82.
Masaho Noda, "Corporate Finance of Railroad Companies in Meiji Japan," 87-101.

Takao Shiba, "Succeeding Against Odds, Courting Collapse: How Mitsubishi and Kawasaki Dockyard Managed the Post-WWI Slump," in *Yearbook* 2, 1985, 100-18.

Kazuo Sugiyama, "Shipbuilding Finance of the *Shasen* Shipping Firms, 1920s-1930s," in *Business History of Shipping: Strategy and Structure*, vol. 11 of *International Conference on Business History*, ed. by Tsunehiko Yui & Keiichiro Nakagawa, University of Tokyo Press, 1985, 255-72.

Thomas Richard Schalow, "Transforming Railroads into Steamships: Banking with the Matsukata Family at the 15th Bank," *Hitotsubashi Journal of Commerce and Management* 22:1 (Dec 1987), 55-67.

Corporate Accounting

Sadao Takatera, "Early Experiment of Depreciation Accounting in National Bank', 1875-1879," *Kyoto University Economic Review* 32:1 (Apr 1962), 50-67.

Kojiro Nishikawa, "The Introduction of Western Bookkeeping into Japan," *Accounting Historians Journal* 4:1 (Spr 1977), 25-36.

Sadao Takatera, "Introduction and Diffusion of Depreciation Accounting in Japan, 1875-1903," in *Marketing and Finance in the Course of Industrialization*, vol. 3 of *The International Conference on Business History*, ed. by Keiichiro Nakagawa, Tokyo University Press, 1978, 105-115.

Sadao Takatera, "Comparative Accounting History between the Old Japanese Bookkeeping Method and the Western Bookkeeping Method," *Kyoto University Economic Review* 50:1-2 (Apr-Oct 1980), 31-36.

F. BUSINESS, GOVERNMENT & POLITICS

General

Government and Business, vol. 5 of *International Conference on Business History*, ed. by Keiichiro Nakagawa, University of Tokyo Press, 1980, including:
Sakae Tsunoyama, "Government and Business: An Introductory Essay," 1-18.
Keiichiro Nakagawa, "Government and Business in Japan: A Comparative Approach," 213-32.

Business Organizations

H. Nakamura, "The Activities of the Japan Economic Federation," in Dorothy Borg & Shumpei Okamoto, eds. *Pearl Harbor as History: Japanese-American Relations, 1931-1941*, Columbia University Press, 1973, 411-20.

Matao Miyamoto, "The Development of Business Associations in Prewar Japan," in *Trade Associations in Business History*, vol. 14 of *International Conference on Business History*, ed. by Hiroaki Yamazaki & Matao Miyamoto, University of Tokyo Press, 1988, 1-45.

Politics

A. Morgan Young, *Japan in Recent Times, 1912-1926*, New York, William Morrow, 1929 (Greenwood reprint, 1973), re:scandals.

Yunosuke Kirimoto, "Business Leader in State Politics [re: Fujiwara Ginjiro]," *CJ* 9:3 (March 1940), 253-59.

Shoji Yasuda, "Ichizo Kobayashi: Versatile Businessman," *CJ* 9:4 (Apr 1940), 396-404.

Frank Langdon, "Japan," in Arnold Heidenheimer & Langdon, eds. *Business Associations and the Financing of Political Parties*, The Hague, Martinus Nijhoff, 1968, 140-205.

Arthur Tiedemann, "Big Business and Politics in Prewar Japan," in James W. Morley, ed. *Dilemmas of Growth in Prewar Japan*, Princeton University Press, 1971, 267-316.

Andrew Fraser, "Komuro Shinobu (1839-1898): A Meiji Politician and Businessman," *Papers on Far Eastern History* 3 (March 1971), 61-83.

G. IDEOLOGY

Yasuzo Horie, "The Role of the *Ie* (House) in the Economic Modernization of Japan," *Kyoto University Economic Review* 36:1 (Apr 1966), 1-16.

Byron K. Marshall, *Capitalism and Nationalism in Prewar Japan: The Ideology of the Business Elite, 1868-1941*, Stanford University Press, 1967.

Johannes Hirschmeier, "The Japanese Spirit of Enterprise, 1868-1970," *Business History Review* 44:1 (Spr 1970), 13-38.

Social Order and Entrepreneurship, vol. 2 of *International Conference on Business History*, ed. by Keiichiro Nakagawa, University of Tokyo Press, 1977, including the following articles:
Johannes Hirschmeier, "Entrepreneurs and the Social Order: America, Germany and Japan, 1870-1900," 3-41.
Hiroshi Hazama, "Industrialization and 'Groupism'," 199-223.
Yasuzo Horie, "The Tradition of *Ie* (House) and the Industrialization of Japan,", 231-54.
Mataji Miyamoto, "Local Culture and Business Behavior in Japan," 257-90.

W. Mark Fruin, "From Philanthropy to Paternalism in the Noda Soy Sauce Industry: Pre-Corporate and Corporate Charity in Japan," *Business History Review* 56:2 (Sum 1982), 168-91.

5. GOVERNMENT ECONOMIC POLICY

A. GENERAL OVERVIEWS

George Allen, *Japan's Economic Policy*, London, Macmillan, 1980.

B. FINANCIAL POLICY

General

Koichi Emi, *Government Fiscal Activity and Economic Growth in Japan, 1868-1960*, Tokyo, Kinokuniya, 1963.

Kengo Matsuno, "A Brief History of Japan's Public Finance," *Kobe University Economic Review* 9 (1963), 31-39.

Raymond W. Goldsmith, *The Financial Development of Japan, 1868-1977*, Yale University Press, 1983.

Meiji

Kazuaki Kato, "Financial Administration in the Early Meiji Era: The Processes of Establishment of the General Accounting Office in Japan," *Kwansei Gakuin University Annual Studies* 11 (1962), 125-54.

Motokazu Kimura, "Fiscal Policy: Fiscal and Industrialization in Japan, 1868-95," in Kenneth Berrill, ed. *Economic Development: With Special Reference to East Asia*, New York, St. Martin's Press, 1964, 273-86.

Harry T. Oshima, "Meiji Fiscal Policy and Economic Progress," in William W. Lockwood, ed. *The State and Economic Enterprise in Japan*, Princeton University Press, 1965, 353-89.

Takao Takeda, "The Financial Policy of the Meiji Government," in Seiichi Tobata, ed. *The Modernization of Japan*, Tokyo, The Institute of Asian Economic Affairs, 1966, 91-113. [also in *DE* 3:4 (Dec 1965), 427-49].

Giichi Ono, *Expenditures of the Sino-Japanese War*, New York, Oxford University Press, 1922 [real author: Keiichi Asada].

Hugh T. Patrick, "External Equilibrium and Internal Convertibility: Financial Policy in Meiji Japan," *Journal of Economic History* 25:2 (June 1965), 187-213.

Kenneth B. Pyle, "The Technology of Japanese Nationalism: The Local Improvement Movement, 1900-1918," *Journal of Asian Studies* 33:1 (Nov 1973), 51-65.

Interwar

Junnosuke Inouye, *Problems of the Japanese Exchange, 1914-1926*, London, Macmillan, 1931.

Nobuki Mochida, "The Role of Local Government Expenditures in Prewar Japan," *Annals of the Institute of Social Science* 26 (1984), 33-63.

Kozo Yamamura, "Then Came the Great Depression: Japan's Interwar Years," in Herman van der Wee, ed. *The Great Depression Revisited*, The Hague, Martinus Nijhoff, 1972, 182-211.

Hugh Patrick, "The Economic Muddle of the 1920s," in James Morley, ed. *Dilemmas of Growth in Prewar Japan*, Princeton University Press, 1971, 211-66.

Hyoye Ohuchi, "The Government's Financial Policy," *CJ* 1:3 (Dec 1932), 349-62.

Kenichi Abe, "The Emergency Budget and Inflation," *CJ* 1:4 (March 1933), 570-83.

Ippei Fukuda, "Takahashi Korekiyo: Japan's Sage of Finance," *CJ* 1:4 (March 1933), 610-18.

Sobun Yamamuro, "Japan's Economic Conditions since the Gold Embargo," *CJ* 2:2 (Sept 1933), 232-39.

Aiichi Nishinoiri, "The Budgetary Dilemma," *CJ* 2:3 (Dec 1933), 435-43.

Tetsuzo Watanabe, "Japan and World Recovery," *CJ* 2:3 (Dec 1933), 453-61.

Dick K. Nanto & Shinji Takagi, "Korekiyo Takahashi and Japan's Recovery from the Great Depression," *American Economic Review* 75:2 (May 1985), 369-74.

Eigo Fukai, "The Recent Monetary Policy of Japan," in A.D. Gayer, ed. *The Lessons of Monetary Experience: Essays in Honour of Irving Fisher*, London, Allen & Unwin, 1937, 379-95.

Yukio Cho, "From the Showa Economic Crisis to Military Economy—with Special Reference to the Inoue and Takahashi Financial Policies," *DE* 5:4 (Dec 1967), 568-96.

Kamekichi Takahashi, "Japan's Finances and Takahashi's Policies," *CJ* 4:4 (March 1936), 519-26.

Kamekichi Takahashi, "The Fiscal Policy of Finance Minister, Dr. Baba," *CJ* 5:1 (June 1936), 25-34.

Guenther Stein, "Japanese State Finance," *Pacific Affairs* 10 (1937), 393-406.

Terutomo Makino, "The 1938-39 Budget," *CJ* 6:4 (March 1938), 658-66.

Katsuro Yamamura, "The Role of the Finance Ministry," in Dorothy Borg & Shumpei Okamoto, eds. *Pearl Harbor as History: Japanese-American Relations, 1931-1941*, Columbia University Press, 1973, 287-302.

C. INDUSTRIAL PROMOTION

General

Herbert M. Bratter, "The Role of Subsidies in Japan's Economic Development," *Pacific Affairs* 4 (1931), 377-93.

Takao Tsuchiya, "Transition and Development of Economic Policy," in Keizo Shibusawa, ed. *Japanese Society in the Meiji Era*, Tokyo, Obunsha, 1958, 103-79.

Harry D. Harootunian, "The Economic Rehabilitation of the Samurai in the Early Meiji Period, *Journal of Asian Studies* 19:4 (Aug 1960), 433-44.

Ichiro Nakayama, "The Japanese Economy and the Role of the Government," *Hitotsubashi Journal of Economics* 1:1 (Oct 1960), 1-12.

Ippei Yamazawa, "Industrial Growth and Trade Policy in Prewar Japan," *DE* 13:1 (March 1975), 38-65.

Sidney D. Brown, "Okubo Toshimichi: His Political and Economic Policies in Early Meiji Japan," *Journal of Asian Studies* 21:2 (Feb 1962), 183-97.

Proposals of Okubo Toshimichi concerning the promotion of industry, in *Meiji Japan through Contemporary Sources*, vol. 3, 1969-1894, Tokyo, The Centre for East Asian Cultural Studies, 1972, 13-23.

Henry Rosovsky, "Japan's Transition to Modern Economic Growth, 1868-1885," in Rosovsky, ed. *Industrialization in Two Systems*, New York, Wiley, 1966.

Thomas C. Smith, *Political Change and Industrial Development in Japan: Government Enterprise, 1868-1880*, Stanford University Press, 1955.

Masaaki Kobayashi, "Policy of Encouraging Industry by the Meiji Government," *Kanto Gakuin University Economic Review* 1 (1978), 29-41.

Kesaji Kobayashi & Masaaki Kobayashi, "Government Promotion of Manufacturing as a Pre-condition for Industrialization," in *Government and Business*, vol. 5 of *International Conference on Business History*, ed. by Keiichiro Nakagawa, University of Tokyo Press, 1980, 25-53.

Masaaki Kobayashi, "Japan's Early Industrialization and the Transfer of Government Enterprises: Government and Business," in *Yearbook* 2, 1985, 54-80.

Frances V. Moulder, *Japan, China and the Modern World Economy: Toward A Reinterpretation of East Asian Development, ca. 1600 to 1918*, Cambridge University Press, 1977.

The Modern Period (1868–1945)

Arthur E. Tiedemann, "Japan's Economic Foreign Policies, 1868-1893," in James W. Morley, ed. *Japan's Foreign Policy, 1868-1941: A Research Guide*, New York, Columbia University Press, 1971, 118-52.

Yasuzo Horie, "Foreign Trade Policy in the Early Meiji Period," *Kyoto University Economic Review* 22:2 (Oct 1952), 1-21.

Kozo Yamamura, "Success Illgotten? The Role of Meiji Militarism in Japan's Technological Progress," *Journal of Economic History* 37:1 (March 1977), 113-35.

Gautam Sen, *The Military Origins of Industrialisation and International Trade Rivalry*, London, Frances Pinter, 1984, 125-35.

E.B. Schumpeter, "Government Policy and Recovery in Japan," in Elizabeth B. Schumpeter, ed. *The Industrialization of Japan and Manchukuo, 1930-1940: Population, Raw Materials and Industry*, New York, Macmillan, 1940, 3-37.

Specific Industries

Stephen W. McCallion, "Trial and Error: The Model Filature at Tomioka," in William D. Wray, ed. *Managing Industrial Enterprise: Cases from Japan's Prewar Experience*, Harvard University Press, 1989.

Hiromi Masuda, "Japan's Industrial Development Policy and the Construction of Nobiru Port: The Case Study of a Failure," *DE* 18:3 (Sept 1980), 333-63.

William D. Wray, *Mitsubishi and the N.Y.K., 1870-1914: Business Strategy in the Japanese Shipping Industry*, Harvard University Press, 1984.

Takeaki Teratani, "Japanese Business and Government in the Takeoff Stage," in *Government and Business*, vol. 5 of *International Conference on Business History*, ed. by Keiichiro Nakagawa, University of Tokyo Press, 1980, 57-78.

Ryoichi Miwa, "Maritime Policy in Japan: 1868-1937," in *Business History of Shipping: Strategy and Structure*, vol. 11 of *International Conference on Business History*, ed. by Tsunehiko Yui & Keiichiro Nakagawa, University of Tokyo Press, 1985, 123-56.

Atsumu Shigemitsu, "Renewing the Merchant Marine," *CJ* 4:4 (March 1936), 561-65.

Taizo Yakushiji, "The Government in a Spiral Dilemma: Dynamic Policy Interventions Vis-a-Vis Auto Firms, C.1900-C.1960," in Masahiko Aoki, ed. *The Economic Analysis of the Japanese Firm*, Amsterdam, North Holland, 1984, 265-310.

D. COMMERCIAL LAW

W. Silver Hall, *A Review of the Japanese Patent Law, Including Regulations Relating to Trade Marks and Designs*, London, Office of the Engineer, 1898, 31pp.

F. Schroeder, *Notes on the Commercial Code of Japan and the Law Concerning its Operation*, Yokohama, Eastern World, 1900.

Mataji Miyamoto, "Local Culture and Business Behavior in Japan," in *Social Order and Entrepreneurship*, vol. 2 of *International Conference on Business History*, ed. by Keiichiro Nakagawa, University of Tokyo Press, 1977, 257-90.

E. TAXATION

Kunio Niwa, "The Reform of the Land Tax and the Government Programme for the Encouragement of Industry," *DE* 4:4 (Dec 1966), 447-71.

Richard M. Bird, "Land Taxation and Economic Development: The Model of Meiji Japan," *The Journal of Development Studies* 13:2 (Jan 1977), 162-74.

Satoru Nakamura, "National Unification and Land Reform in the Modernization Process of Japan," *Kyoto University Economic Review* (1) 55:1 (Apr 1985), 20-40; (2) 55:2 (Oct 1985), 53-77.

Kozo Yamamura, "The Meiji Land Tax Reform and Its Effects," in Marius B. Jansen and Gilbert Rozman, eds. *Japan in Transition: From Tokugawa to Meiji*, Princeton University Press, 1986, 382-99.

Nobutaka Ike, "Taxation and Landownership in the Westernization of Japan," *Journal of Economic History* 27:2 (Nov 1947), 160-82.

Nobutaka Ike, *The Beginnings of Political Democracy in Japan*, Baltimore, Johns Hopkins University Press, 1950.

Kotaro Ikeda, "The Establishment of the Income Tax in Japan: A Historical and Sociological Study," *Public Finance* 12:2 (1957), 145-70.

Masazo Ohkawa, "The Armament Expansion Budgets and the Japanese Economy after the Russo-Japanese War," *Hitotsubashi Journal of Economics* 5:2 (Jan 1965), 68-83.

Gustav Ranis, "The Financing of Japanese Economic Development," *Economic History Review* 11:3 (Apr 1959), 440-54.

F. INDUSTRIAL POLICY, GOVERNMENT PLANNING & CONTROL

Ichirou Inukai & Arlon Tussing, "*Kogyo Iken*: Japan's Ten Year Plan, 1884," *Economic Development and Cultural Change* 16:1 (Oct 1967), 51-71.

Ichiro Inukai, "The Kogyo Iken: Japan's Ten Year Plan, 1884," *KSU Economic and Business Review* (Kyoto Sangyo University) 6 (May 1979), 1-100.

Chalmers Johnson, *MITI and the Japanese Miracle: The Growth of Industrial Policy, 1925-1975*, Stanford University Press, 1982, esp. 83-156.

Masaru Udagawa & Seishi Nakamura, "Japanese Business and the Industrial Rationalization Movement," in *Government and Business*, vol. 5 of *International Conference on Business History*, ed. by Keiichiro Nakagawa, University of Tokyo Press, 1980, 83-100.

Jotaro Yamamoto, "A Five-Year Plan for Japan," *CJ* 1:1 (June 1932), 45-51.

Chalmers Johnson, *Japan's Public Policy Companies*, Washington, American Enterprise Institute, 1978.

Peter Duus, "The Reaction of Japanese Big Business to a State-Controlled Economy in the 1930s," *Rivista Internazionale di Scienze Economiche e Commerciali* 31:9 (Sept 1984), 819-31.

M. Matsuo, "The Control of Industry in Japan," *Far Eastern Survey* 4:14 (July 17, 1935), 105-109.

Shigeichi Mayeda, "Control of Industry and Trade," *CJ* 4:2 (Sept 1935), 199-212.

Kozaburo Shiraishi, "The Problem of Oil Industry and Control," *CJ* 4:4 (March 1936), 535-44.

Mark Peattie, *Ishiwara Kanji and Japan's Confrontation with the West*, Princeton University Press, 1975, esp. 185-222.

Shinji Yoshino, "Our Planned Economy," *CJ* 6:3 (Dec 1937), 369-77.

6. MONEY AND BANKING

A. OVERVIEWS

Toyoji Kotake, "A Comparative Study of the Securities Markets with Reference to the Structural Characteristics of Financial Capital," *Keio Business Review* 10 (1971), 25-37.

Hugh Patrick, "Japanese Financial Development in Historical Perspective, 1868-1980," in Gustav Ranis et al., eds. *Comparative Development Perspectives*, Boulder, Col., Westview Press, 1984, 302-27.

B. CURRENCY & THE MONETARY SYSTEM

Hiroshi Shinjo, *History of the Yen*, Tokyo, Kinokuniya, 1962.

Shigeru Yamaguchi, "Interrelations between 'Ginme' Bar Silver, the Mexican Silver Dollar, and Foreign Exchange Rates during the Early Meiji Era," *Annals of the Hitotsubashi Academy* 3:2 (Apr 1953), 209-26.

Hirokichi Taya, "The Modernization of the Japanese Currency System," *Acta Asiatica* 39 (1980), 78-94.

Kikunosuke Ono, "Inflation in the Early Era of Meiji," *Kobe University Economic Review* 2 (1956), 79-102.

Toshihiko Kato, "Development of the Monetary System," in Keizo Shibusawa, ed. *Japanese Society in the Meiji Era*, Tokyo, Obunsha, 1958, 181-235.

David J. Ott, "The Financial Development of Japan, 1878-1958," *Journal of Political Economy* 69:1 (Feb 1961), 122-41.

The Currency of Japan (A Reprint of Articles, Letters and Official Reports; published by the *Japan Gazette*), 1882.

Erich Pauer, "Money Substitutes in the Japanese Coal Mining Industry," *Asian Monetary Monitor* 3:5 (Sept-Oct 1979), 36-41.

Masayoshi Takaki, *The History of Japanese Paper Currency (1868-1890)*, Baltimore, Johns Hopkins Press, 1903.

Takeshi Hamashita, "A History of the Japanese Silver Yen and the Hongkong and Shanghai Banking Corporation, 1871-1913," in Frank H. H. King, ed. *Eastern Banking: Essays in the History of The Hongkong and Shanghai Banking Corporation*, London, The Athlone Press, 1983, 321-49.

Hugh T. Patrick, "External Equilibrium and Internal Convertibility: Financial Policy in Meiji Japan," *Journal of Economic History* 25:2 (June 1965), 187-213.

Norio Tamaki, "Economists in Parliament: The Fall of Bimetallism in Japan," in Chuhei Sugiyama & Hiroshi Mizuta, eds. *Enlightenment and Beyond: Political Economy Comes to Japan*, University of Tokyo Press, 1988, 223-36.

Masayoshi Matsukata, *Report on the Adoption of the Gold Standard*, Tokyo, Government Press, 1899.

Junnosuke Inouye, *Problems of the Japanese Exchange, 1914-1926*, London, Macmillan, 1931.

C. BANKING

General

Herbert M. Bratter, *Japanese Banking*, U.S. Department of Commerce, Bureau of Foreign and Domestic Commerce, Trade Promotion Series, No. 116, Washington, Government Printing Office, 1931.

Phra Sarasas, *Money and Banking in Japan*, London, Heath Cranton, 1940.

Yasuo Noritake, "The Development of Monetary and Banking System in Japan, 1932-1945," *Kobe University Economic Review* 2 (1956), 69-77.

Fuji Bank, ed. *Banking in Modern Japan*, Fuji Bank Bulletin 11:4 (1961), Special Issue.

Kokichi Asakura, "The Characteristics of Finance in the Meiji Period (The Period of Take-Off)," *DE* 5:2 (June 1967), 274-300.

Hugh Patrick, "Japan, 1868-1914," in Rondo Cameron, ed. *Banking in the Early Stages of Industrialization*, Oxford University Press, 1967, 239-89.

Kozo Yamamura, "Japan, 1868-1930: A Revised View," in Rondo Cameron, ed. *Banking and Economic Development*, Oxford University Press, 1972, 168-98.

Yukio Cho, "Exposing the Incompetence of the Bourgeoisie: The Financial Panic of 1927," *Japan Interpreter* 8:4 (Win 1974), 492-501.

Toshiya Hanawa & Eiji Ogawa, "Taisho Era Controversies Over Currency and Banking Principles," *Hitotsubashi Journal of Commerce & Management* 20:1 (Dec 1985), 21-47.

H. Neuburger & H.H. Stokes, "German Banking and Japanese Banking: A Comparative Analysis," *Journal of Economic History* 35:1 (March 1975), 238-52.

Specific Banks

Toshihiko Yoshino, "The Creation of the Bank of Japan: Its Western Origin and Adaptation," *DE* 15:4 (Dec 1977), 381-401.

The Mitsui Bank: A Brief History, Tokyo, 1926.

The Mitsui Bank: A History of the First 100 Years, ed. Japan Business History Institute, Tokyo, 1976.

Matao Miyamoto & Kensuke Hiroyama, "The Retreat from Diversification and the Desire for Specialization in Konoike: Late Meiji to Early Showa," in *Yearbook* 1, 1984, 104-30.

7. INTERNATIONAL ECONOMIC RELATIONS

A. INTERNATIONAL FINANCE

Hiroshi Shinjo, *History of the Yen*, Tokyo, Kinokuniya, 1962.

Masayoshi Matsukata, *Report on the Adoption of the Gold Standard*, Tokyo, Government Press, 1899.

William Burke, "Japan's Entrance into the International Financial Community," *The American Journal of Economic and Sociology* 23:3 (July 1964), 325-35.

Gary D. Best, "Financial Diplomacy: The Takahashi Korekiyo Missions of 1904-05," *Asian Studies* 12 (April 1974), 52-76.

Gary D. Best, "Financing a Foreign War: Jacob Schiff and Japan, 1904-1905," *American Jewish Historical Quarterly* 61:4 (June 1972), 313-24.

Cyrus Adler, *Jacob H. Schiff: His Life and Letters*, 2 vols., New York, Doubleday, 1928.

Taichiro Mitani, "Japan's International Financiers and World Politics, 1904-1931," in John Chapman & Jean-Pierre Lehmann., eds. *Proceedings of the British Association for Japanese Studies*, Vol. 5: Part 1, 1980, *History and Interna-

tional Relations, University of Sheffield, Centre for Japanese Studies, 29-53.

William F. Spalding, *Eastern Exchange, Currency and Finance*, London, Pitman, 1917, esp. 126-69.

Junnosuke Inouye, *Problems of the Japanese Exchange, 1914-1926*, London, Macmillan, 1931.

Toshiya Hanawa & Eiji Ogawa, "Taisho Era Controversies Over Currency and Banking Principles," *Hitotsubashi Journal of Commerce & Management* 20:1 (Dec 1985), 21-47.

Sidney DeVere Brown, "Shidehara Kijuro: The Diplomacy of the Yen," in Richard Burns & E. Bennett, eds. *Diplomats in Crisis: United States-Chinese-Japanese Relations, 1919-1941*, Santa Barbara, Clio Press, 1974, 201-25.

Ann Trotter, *Britain and East Asia: 1933-1937*, Cambridge Uuniversity Press, 1975.

B. SHIPPING, TRADING ENTERPRISES, & COMMUNICATIONS

Shipping

Yasukichi Yasuba, "Freight Rates and Productivity in Ocean Transportation for Japan, 1875-1943," *Explorations in Economic History* 15:1 (Jan 1978), 11-39.

William D. Wray, *Mitsubishi and the N.Y.K., 1870-1914: Business Strategy in the Japanese Shipping Industry*, Harvard University Press, 1984.

Keiichiro Nakagawa, "Japanese Shipping in the Nineteenth and Twentieth Centuries: Strategy and Organization," *Business History of Shipping: Strategy and Structure*, vol. 11 of *International Conference on Business History*, ed. by Tsunehiko Yui & Keiichiro Nakagawa, University of Tokyo Press, 1985, 1-33.

The First Century of Mitsui O.S.K. Lines Ltd. ed. Japan Business History Institute, Tokyo, 1985.

Eric Jennings, *Cargoes: A Centenary Story of the Far Eastern Freight Conference*, Singapore, Meridian, 1980.

William D. Wray, "NYK and the Commercial Diplomacy of the Far Eastern Freight Conference, 1896-1956," in *Business History of Shipping: Strategy and Structure*, vol. 11 of *International Conference on Business History*, ed.

by Tsunehiko Yui & Keiichiro Nakagawa, University of Tokyo Press, 1985, 279-311.

Shin Goto, "The Progress of Shipping Operators Belonging to Trading Companies: The Scheduled Services to North America of the Shipping Division of Mitsui Trading Company between the Two World Wars," in *Yearbook 3*, 1986, 52-81.

W.A. Radius, *United States Shipping in Trans-Pacific Trade, 1922-1938*, Stanford University Press, 1944.

Tessa Morris-Suzuki, "The South Seas Empire of Ishihara Hiroichiro: A Case Study in Japan's Economic Relations with Southeast Asia, 1914-1941," in Alan Rix & Ross Mouer, eds. *Japan's Impact on the World*, Griffith University, Japanese Studies Association of Australia, 1984, 151-69.

Hiroshi Shimizu, "Dutch-Japanese Competition in the Shipping Trade on the Java-Japan Route in the Inter-war Period," *Southeast Asian Studies* (Kyoto University) 26:1 (June 1988), 3-23.

Trading

Stephanie Jones, "George Benjamin Dodwell: A Shipping Agent in the Far East, 1872-1908," *Journal of Transport History* 6:2 (March 1985), 23-40.

Shinya Sugiyama, "A British Trading Firm in the Far East: John Swire & Sons, 1867-1914," in *Business History of General Trading Companies*, vol. 13 of *International Conference on Business History*, ed. by Shin'ichi Yonekawa & Hideki Yoshihara, Univeristy of Tokyo Press, 1987, 171-202.

Keiichiro Nakagawa, "Organized Entrepreneurship in the Course of the Industrialization of Pre-War Japan," in H. Nagamine, ed. *Nation Building and Regional Development: The Japanese Experience*, Singapore, Maruzen Asia, 1981, 55-76.

Kozo Yamamura, "General Trading Companies in Japan: Their Origins and Growth," in Hugh Patrick, ed. *Japanese Industrialization and its Social Consequences*, University of California Press, 1973, 161-99.

Kunio Yoshihara, *Sogo Shosha: The Vanguard of the Japanese Economy*, Tokyo, Oxford University Press, 1982.

Kunio Yoshihara, "Sogo Shosha and Japanese Industrialization," in *Essays in Development Economics in Honor of Harry T. Oshima*, Manila, Philippine Institute for Development Studies, 1982, 459-81.

Shin'ichi Yonekawa, "The Formation of General Trading Companies: A Comparative Study," in *Yearbook* 2, 1985, 1-31.

Business History of General Trading Companies, vol. 13 of *International Conference on Business History*, ed. by Shin'ichi Yonekawa & Hideki Yoshihara, Univeristy of Tokyo Press, 1987, the following articles:
Hideki Yoshihara, "Some Questions on Japan's Sogo Shosha," 1-14.
Hideki Yoshihara, "The Business History of the Sogo Shosha in International Perspective," 337-53.
Hiroaki Yamazaki, "The Logic of the Formation of General Trading Companies in Japan," 21-64.
Nobuo Kawabe, "Development of Overseas Operations by General Trading Companies, 1868-1945," 71-103.

The 100 Year History of Mitsui & Co., Ltd., 1876-1976, ed. by the Japan Business History Institute, Tokyo, 1977.

Kumiko Terazawa, "Mitsui Bussan Kaisha: Its Growth and Effects on the Japanese Economy (1876-1930)," *Stone Lion Review* 3 (Spr 1979), 39-50. Harvard University, East Asian Graduate Students Colloquium.

Hiroaki Yamazaki. "A Note on the Commodity Transactions of Japanese General Trading Companies during the 1920s: The Case of Mitsui Bussan," *Annals of the Institute of Social Science* 25 (1983-84), 25-42.

Seiichiro Yonekura, "The Emergence of the Prototype of Enterprise Group Capitalism: The Case of Mitsui," *Hitotsubashi Journal of Commerce & Management* 20:1 (Dec 1985), 63-104.

Nobuo Kawabe, "Japanese Business in the United States before World War II: The Case of Mitsubishi Shoji Kaisha, The San Francisco and Seattle Branches," Ph.D. diss., Ohio State University, 1980.

Yoshi Katsura, "The Role of One *Sogoshosha* in Japanese Industrialization: Suzuki & Co., 1877-1927," *Proceedings of the Business History Conference*, Indiana University, 2nd series, 3 (1975), 32-61.

C. Itoh, *An Outline of C. Itoh & Co., Ltd.*, 1937.

Communications

Jorma Ahvenainen, *The Far Eastern Telegraphs: The History of Telegraphic Communications between the Far East, Europe and America before the First World War*, Helsinki, Suomalainen Tiedeakatemia, 1981.

C. TRADE & INDUSTRY

General Works

Nobutaro Kawashima, *Statistical Survey of Japanese Foreign Trade*, The Hokuseido Press, 1938.

Shinya Sugiyama, *Japan's Industrialization in the World Economy, 1859-1899: Export Trade and Overseas Competition*, London, The Athlone Press, 1988.

Keinosuke Baba, "Japanese Gains from Trade, 1878-1932," *Annals of the Hitotsubashi Academy* 8:2 (Apr 1958), 127-42.

Kiyoshi Kojima, "Japanese Foreign Trade and Economic Growth: With Special Reference to the Terms of Trade," *Annals of the Hitotsubashi Academy* 8:2 (Apr 1958), 143-68.

Masao Baba and Masahiro Tatemoto, "Foreign Trade and Economic Growth in Japan, 1858-1937," in Lawrence Klein & Kazushi Ohkawa, eds. *Economic Growth: The Japanese Experience since the Meiji Era*, Yale Economic Growth Series, Homewood, Ill., Richard D. Irwin, 1968, 162-96.

William V. Rapp, "Firm Size and Japan's Export Structure: A Microview of Japan's Changing Export Competitiveness since Meiji," in Hugh Patrick, ed. *Japanese Industrialization and its Social Consequences*, University of California Press, 1973, 201-48.

Miyohei Shinohara, "Economic Development and Foreign Trade in Pre-War Japan," in C.D. Cowan, ed. *The Economic Development of China and Japan*, London, Allen & Unwin, 1964, 220-48.

Ippei Yamazawa, "Industrial Growth and Trade Policy in Prewar Japan," *DE* 13:1 (March 1975), 38-65.

Keishi Ohara, ed. *Japanese Trade and Industry in the Meiji-Taisho Era*, Tokyo, Obunsha, 1957.

Accounts by Period

J. Richard Huber, "Effects on Price of Japan's Entry into World Commerce after 1858," *Journal of Political Economy* 79:3 (May/June 1971), 614-29.

Yukimasa Hattori, *The Foreign Commerce of Japan since the Restoration, 1869-1900*, Baltimore, Johns Hopkins Press, 1904.

The Modern Period (1868–1945)

Kaoru Sugihara, "Patterns of Asia's Integration into the World Economy, 1880-1913," in *The Emergence of a World Economy, 1500-1914, Papers of the IX. International Congress of Economic History*, ed. Wolfram Fischer et al., Stuttgart, Franz Steiner Verlag Wiesbaden GmbH, 1986, 709-28.

Toshihiko Kato, "Development of Foreign Trade," in Keizo Shibusawa, ed. *Japanese Society in the Meiji Era*, Tokyo, Obunsha, 1958, 473-509.

Arthur E. Tiedemann, "Japan's Economic Foreign Policies, 1868-1893," in James W. Morley, ed. *Japan's Foreign Policy, 1868-1941: A Research Guide*, New York, Columbia University Press, 1971, 118-52.

U.S. Department of State, *The Place of Foreign Trade in the Japanese Economy*, 2 vols., OIR Report, OCL-285 [re: 1930-1938].

Kamekichi Takahashi, "Japan's Trade and the World," *CJ* 3:1 (June 1934), 73-83.

Guenther Stein, *Made in Japan*, London, Methuen, 1935.

S. Uyehara, *The Industry and Trade of Japan*, London, P.S. King & Son, 2nd rev. ed., 1936.

Albert E. Hindmarsh, *The Basis of Japanese Foreign Policy*, Harvard University Press, 1936.

Jihei Inouye, "The Necessity of Foreign Trade Adjustment," *CJ* 5:2 (Sept 1936), 236-44.

Miriam S. Farley, *The Problem of Japanese Trade Expansion in the Post-War Situation*, New York, Institute of Pacific Relations, 1940.

Shintaro Ryu, "Economic Development of Modern Japan," in Hiro Sassa & Shintaro Ryu, *Recent Political and Economic Developments in Japan*, Tokyo, Japan Council, Institute of Pacific Relations, 1941, 96-119.

Margaret S. Gordon, "Japan's Balance of International Payments, 1904-1931," in Elizabeth B. Schumpeter, ed. *The Industrialization of Japan and Manchukuo, 1930-1940: Population, Raw Materials and Industry*, New York, Macmillan, 1940, 863-925.

The Foreign Trade of Japan: A Statistical Survey, Tokyo, Oriental Economist, 1935.

Kiyoshi Oshima, "The World Economic Crisis and Japan's Foreign Economic Policy," *DE* 5:4 (Dec 1967), 628-47.

Specific Industries

Haru Matsukata Reischauer, *Samurai and Silk: A Japanese and American Heritage*, Harvard University Press, 1986.

Lillian M. Li, "Silks by Sea: Trade, Technology, and Enterprise in China and Japan," *Business History Review* 56:2 (Sum 1982), 192-217.

Freda Utley, *Lancashire and the Far East*, London, Allen & Unwin, 1931.

Osamu Ishii, "Cotton-Textile Diplomacy: Japan, Great Britain and the United States, 1930-1936," Ph.D. diss., Rutgers University, 1977. (published in New York, Arno Press, 1981).

Resources

Yasukichi Yasuba, "Resources in Japan's Development," Shigeto Tsuru, ed. *Growth and Resources Problems Related to Japan*: Proceedings of Session VI of the Fifth Congress of the International Economic Association, Tokyo, Asahi Evening News, 1978, 229-53.

Robert Henriques, *Marcus Samuel: First Viscount Bearsted and Founder of the 'Shell' Transport and Trading Company, 1853-1927*, London, Barrie and Rockliff, 1960.

Erich Pauer, "Synthetic Oil and Fuel Policy of Japan in the 1920s and 1930s," in Erich Pauer, ed. *Silkworms, Oil, and Chips . . . Proceedings of the Economics and Economic History Section of the Fourth International Conference on Japanese Studies*, Japan Seminar, University of Bonn, 1986, 105-124.

Jamie W. Moore, "Economic Interests and American-Japanese Relations: The Petroleum Monopoly Controversy," *The Historian* 35:4 (Aug 1973), 551-67.

Thomas Breslin, "Trouble over Oil: America, Japan and the Oil Cartel, 1934-35," *Bulletin of Concerned Asian Scholars* 7:3 (July-Sept 1975), 41-50.

Yasushi Taji, "The Manchoukuo Oil Problem," *CJ* 3:4 (March 1935), 596-605.

Kozaburo Shiraishi, "The Problem of Oil Industry and Control," *CJ* 4:4 (March 1936), 535-44.

Irvine Anderson, *The Standard-Vacuum Oil Company and United States East Asian Policy, 1933-1941*, Princeton University Press, 1975.

D. FOREIGN INVESTMENT AND INFLUENCE

General

G.C. Allen & Audrey G. Donnithorne, *Western Enterprise in Far Eastern Economic Development: China and Japan*, London, Allen & Unwin, 1954.

Grace Fox, *Britain and Japan, 1858-1883*, Oxford University Press, 1969.

Noboru Umetani, *The Role of Foreign Employees in the Meiji Era in Japan*, Tokyo, Institute of Developing Economies, 1971.

Olive Checkland, "Scotland and Japan, 1860-19l4: A Study of Technical Transfer and Cultural Exchange," in Ian Nish, ed. *Bakumatsu and Meiji: Studies in Japan's Economic and Social History*, in *International Studies* (1981/2), London School of Economics and Political Science, 56-76.

Ardath W. Burks, ed. *The Modernizers: Overseas Students, Foreign Employees, and Meiji Japan*, Boulder, Westview, 1985.

Masaru Saito, "Introduction of Foreign Technology in the Industrialization Process: Japanese Experience since the Meiji Restoration (1868)," *DE* 13:2 (June 1975), 168-86.

Nurul Islam, *Foreign Capital and Economic Development in Japan, India, and Canada*, Tokyo, Tuttle, 1960.

Meiji: Specific Industries

John McMaster, "The Takashima Mine: British Capital and Japanese Industrialization," *Business History Review* 37:3 (Aut 1963), 217-39.

Olive & Sydney Checkland, "British and Japanese Economic Interaction under the Early Meiji: The Takashima Coal Mine, 1868-88," *Business History* 26:2 (July 1984), 139-55.

Fumio Yoshiki, "Metal Mining and Foreign Employees," *DE* 17 (1979), 484-505.

Tetsuo Kamiki, "Progress in Western Technology At the Yokosuka Shipbuilding Works, 1865-1887," *Papers on Far Eastern History* 37 (March 1988), 105-23.

Robert F. Durden, "Tar Heel Tobacconist in Tokyo, 1899-1904," *North Carolina Historical Review* 53:4 (October 1976), 347-63.

Sherman Cochran, *Big Business in China: Sino-Foreign Rivalry in the Cigarette Industry, 1890-1930*, Harvard University Press, 1980, 40ff.

Electrical Industry & Foreign Borrowing: 1890s-1930

Hoshimi Uchida, "Western Big Business and the Adoption of New Technology in Japan: The Electrical Equipment and Chemical Industries, 1890-1920," in *Development and Diffusion of Technology: Electrical and Chemical Industries*, vol. 6 of *The International Conference on Business History*, ed. by Akio Okochi & Uchida, University of Tokyo Press, 1980, 145-72.

Yoshikatsu Hayashi, "The Introduction of American Technology into the Japanese Electrical Industry: Another Aspect of Japanese-American Relations at the Turn of the Century," Ph.D. diss., University of California, Santa Barbara, 1986.

Mark Mason, "Foreign Direct Investment and Japanese Economic Development, 1899-1931," *Business and Economic History*, ed. by Jeremy Atack, 2nd series 16 (1987), 93-107.

Hisashi Watanabe, "A History of the Process Leading to the Formation of Fuji Electric," in *Yearbook* 1, 1984, 47-71.

Yasuzo Horie, "Foreign Capital and the Japanese Capitalism after the World War I," *Kyoto University Economic Review* 20:1 (Apr 1950), 38-59.

Nobuo Noda, "How Japan Absorbed American Management Methods," in British Institute of Management, ed. *Modern Japanese Management*, 1970, 29-66.

Kozo Yamamura, "Japan's Deus ex Machina: Western Technology in the 1920s," *Journal of Japanese Studies* 12:1 (Winter 1986), 65-94.

NEC Corporation: The First 80 Years, NEC Corporation, 1984.

Other Interwar Industries

Floyd J. Fithian, "Dollars Without the Flag: The Case of Sinclair and Sakhalin Oil [1920s]," *Pacific Historical Review* 39:2 (May 1970), 205-22.

Yukiko Fukasaku, "Technology Imports and R&D at Mitsubishi Nagasaki Shipyard in the Pre-War Period," in Erich Pauer, ed. *Silkworms, Oil, and Chips . . . Proceedings of the Economics and Economic History Section of the Fourth International Conference on Japanese Studies*, Japan Seminar, University of Bonn, 1986, 77-90.

Masaru Udagawa, "The Prewar Japanese Automobile Industry and American Manufacturers," in *Yearbook* 2, 1985, 81-99.

Japanese Business Abroad

Mira Wilkins, "American-Japanese Direct Foreign Investment Relationships, 1930-1952," *Business History Review* 56:4 (Win 1982), 497-518.

Nobuo Kawabe, "Japanese Business in the United States before World War II: The Case of Mitsubishi Shoji Kaisha, The San Francisco and Seattle Branches," Ph.D. diss., Ohio State University, 1980.

Mira Wilkins, "Japanese Multinational Enterprise before 1914," *Business History Review* 60:2 (Sum 1986), 199-231.

E. TRADE BY AREA

General

Francis E. Hyde, *Far Eastern Trade, 1860-1914*, London, A. & C. Black, 1973.

G.E. Hubbard, *Eastern Industrialization and its Effects on the West*, Oxford University Press, 1935.

Tetsujiro Shidachi, "Japan's Part at the World Economic Conference," *CJ* 2:1 (June 1933), 1-9.

Tokyo Association for Liberty of Trading, *The Trade Agreements Between Japan and Some Other Countries*, Tokyo Association Press, 1937.

The History of Kanagawa, Kanagawa Prefectural Government, 1985.

J. Arthur Lower, *Ocean of Destiny: A Concise History of the North Pacific, 1500-1978*, University of British Columbia Press, 1978.

Barbara Wertheim, "The Russo-Japanese Fisheries Controversy," *Pacific Affairs* 8:2 (June 1935), 185-198.

USA

Akira Iriye, *Pacific Estrangement: Japanese and American Expansion, 1897-1911*, Harvard University Press, 1972.

Alan T. Moriyama, *Imingaisha: Japanese Emigration Companies and Hawaii, 1894-1908*, University of Hawaii Press, 1985.

Jeffrey J. Safford, "Experiment in Containment: The United States Steel Embargo and Japan, 1917-1918," *Pacific Historical Review* 39:4 (Nov 1970), 439-451.

John P. Rossi, "A 'Silent Partnership'?: The U.S. Government, RCA, and Radio Communications with East Asia, 1919-1928," *Radical History Review* 33 (1985), 32-52.

Philip G. Wright, *The American Tariff and Oriental Trade*, University of Chicago Press, 1931.

William W. Lockwood, "Japanese Cotton Goods in the American Market," *Far Eastern Survey* 4:8 (April 24, 1935), 57-61.

Miriam S. Farley, "Japan as a Consumer of American Cotton," *Far Eastern Survey* 4:13 (July 3, 1935), 97-101.

Thomas Breslin, "Trouble over Oil: America, Japan and the Oil Cartel, 1934-35,"*Bulletin of Concerned Asian Scholars* 7:3 (July-Sept 1975), 41-50.

Irvine Anderson, *The Standard-Vacuum Oil Company and United States East Asian Policy, 1933-1941*, Princeton University Press, 1975.

Tokichi Tanaka, "Abrogation of the Japanese-American Commercial Treaty," *CJ* 8:7 (Sept 1939), 815-23.

Lloyd C. Gardner, *Economic Aspects of New Deal Diplomacy*, Boston, Beacon Press, 1971 (orig. pub., 1964), esp. 24-46, 64-85.

Peter C. Hoffer, "American Businessmen and the Japan Trade, 1931-1941: A Case Study of Attitude Formation," *Pacific Historical Review* 41:2 (May 1972), 189-205.

Joan Hoff Wilson, *American Business & Foreign Policy, 1920-1933*, Boston, Beacon Press, 1973 (orig. pub., 1971).

Dorothy Borg & Shumpei Okamoto, eds. *Pearl Harbor as History: Japanese-American Relations, 1931-1941*, Columbia University Press, 1973, including:
Katsuro Yamamura, "The Role of the Finance Ministry," 287-302.
Mira Wilkins, "The Role of U.S. Business," 341-76.

James R. Herzberg, *A Broken Bond: American Economic Policies Toward Japan, 1931-1941*, New York, Garland Publishing, 1988.

Britain

E. Hertslet, *Treaties and Tariffs Regulating the Trade Between Great Britain and Foreign Nations*, Vol. VI, Japan, London, 1879.

Peter Lowe, *Great Britain and Japan, 1911-1915: A Study of British Far Eastern Policy*, London, Macmillan, 1969.

Ian Nish, "Britain's View of the Japanese Economy in the Early Showa Period," in Ronald Dore & Radha Sinha, eds. *Japan and the World Depression, Then and Now: Essays in Memory of E.F. Penrose*, London, Macmillan, 1987, 135-48.

Barbara Wootton, "Some Implications of Anglo-Japanese Competition," *Pacific Affairs* 9:4 (Dec 1936), 524-31.

Stephen Lyon Endicott, *Diplomacy and Enterprise: British China Policy, 1933-37*, University of British Columbia Press, 1975, esp. 102-49.

Peter Lowe, *Great Britain and the Origins the Pacific War: A Study of British Policy in East Asia, 1937-1941*, Oxford University Press, 1977.

Canada & Australia

Robert J. Gowen, "Canada and the Myth of the Japan Market, 1896-1911," *Pacific Historical Review* 39:1 (Feb 1970), 63-83.

A.R.M. Lower, *Canada and the Far East*, New York, Institute of Pacific Relations, 1940.

D.C.S. Sissons, "Manchester v. Japan: The Imperial Background of the Australian Trade Diversion Dispute with Japan, 1936," *Australian Outlook* (December 1976), 480-502.

D.C.S. Sissons, "Private Diplomacy in the 1936 Trade Dispute with Japan," *Australian Journal of Political History* 27:2 (1981), 143-59.

Shigeyasu Ijima, "Japan, Wool and Australia," *CJ* 4:4 (March 1936), 566-71.

Europe

Kurt Bloch, *German Interests and Policies in the Far East*, New York, Institute of Pacific Relations, 1940.

Andrew Malozemoff, *Russian Far Eastern Policy, 1881-1904*, University of California, 1958.

South and Southeast Asia

Nalini Ranjan Chakravarti, *Hundred Years of Japan and India (1868-1968)*, Calcutta, Progressive Publishers, 1978.

Balmukund M. Agrawal, *Indo-Japanese Trade Relations: A Diagnosis*, Delhi, Aalekh Publishers, 1974.

Kumakichi Nakajima et al., "Japan's Trade with India: A Symposium," *CJ* 2:2 (Sept 1933), 218-26.

Kyung-Mo Huh, *Japan's Trade in Asia: Developments since 1926—Prospects for 1970*, New York, Praeger, 1970.

Tessa Morris-Suzuki, "The South Seas Empire of Ishihara Hiroichiro: A Case Study in Japan's Economic Relations with Southeast Asia, 1914-1941," in Alan Rix & Ross Mouer, eds. *Japan's Impact on the World*, Griffith University, Japanese Studies Association of Australia, 1984, 151-69.

William J. Ronan, "The Kra Canal: A Suez for Japan?" *Pacific Affairs* 9:3 (Sept 1936), 406-15.

Grant K. Goodman, "The Philippine Legislature Trade Mission to Japan, 1933," *Monumenta Nipponica* 25:3&4 (1970), 239-48.

Latin America

Nobuya Tsuchida, "The Japanese in Brazil, 1908-41," Ph.D. diss., UCLA, 1978.

Catherine Porter, "Japan's 'Penetration' of Latin America," *Far Eastern Survey* 4:10 (May 22, 1935), 72-78.

C. Harvey Gardiner, *The Japanese and Peru, 1873-1973*, Albuquerque, University of New Mexico Press, 1975.

F. RELATIONS WITH CHINA: TRADE AND IMPERIALISM

Reference Works & Composite Volumes

Akira Iriye, ed. *The Chinese and the Japanese: Essays in Political and Cultural Interactions*, Princeton University Press, 1980.

Peter Duus, Ramon H. Myers & Mark R. Peattie, eds. *Japan's Informal Empire in China, 1895-1937*, Princeton University Press, 1989.

John MacMurray, comp. *Treaties and Agreements with and Concerning China, 1894-1919*, 2 vols., New York, Oxford University Press, 1921.

Ting-yee Kuo, comp. *Sino-Japanese Relations, 1862-1927: A Checklist of the Chinese Foreign Minsitry Archives*, ed. by James W. Morley, Columbia University, 1965.

General: To 1930s

Noriko Kamachi, *Reform in China: Huang Tsun-hsien and the Japanese Model*, Harvard University Press, 1981, 67-75.

Michael H. Hunt, "Americans in the China Market: Economic Opportunities and Economic Nationalism, 1890s-1931," *Business History Review* 51:3 (Aut 1977), 277-307.

Madeleine Chi, *China Diplomacy, 1914-1918*, Harvard East Asian Monographs, 1970.

Madeleine Chi, "Bureaucratic Capitalists in Operation: Ts'ao Ju-lin and his New Communications Clique, 1916-1919," *Journal of Asian Studies* 34:3 (May 1975), 675-88.

Madeleine Chi, "Ts'ao Ju-lin (1876-1966): His Japanese Connections," in Akira Iriye, ed. *The Chinese and the Japanese: Essays in Political and Cultural Interactions*, Princeton University Press, 1980, 140-60.

Tien-yi Yang, "Foreign Business Activities and the Chinese Response, 1842-1937," in *Overseas Business Activities*, vol. 9 of *International* Conference on Business History, *ed. by Akio Okochi & Tadakatsu Inoue*, University of Tokyo Press, 1984, 215-57.

Peter Duus, Ramon H. Myers & Mark R. Peattie, eds. *Japan's Informal Empire in China, 1895-1937*, Princeton University Press, 1989, including:
Toshiyuki Mizoguchi, "The Changing Pattern of Sino-Japanese Trade, 1884-1937."
Mark R. Peattie, "The Japanese Treaty Port Settlements in China, 1895-1937: With Special Reference to Hankow, Tientsin, and Shanghai."
Junji Banno, "The Japanese (Industrialists and Merchants) and the Anti-Japanese Boycotts in China, 1919-1928."

Marius B. Jansen, *The Japanese and Sun Yat-sen*, Stanford University Press, 1970.

Shumpei Okamoto, "Ishibashi Tanzan and the Twenty-One Demands," in Akira Iriye, ed. *The Chinese and the Japanese: Essays in Political and Cultural Interactions*, Princeton University Press, 1980, 184-98.

A. Morgan Young, *Japan in Recent Times, 1912-1926*, New York, William Morrow, 1929 (Greenwood reprint, 1973), 97-103 & 188-99.

Charles F. Remer, *Foreign Investments in China*, New York, Macmillan, 1933, esp. 408-553. (reprint: New York, Howard Fertig, 1968).

Charles F. Remer, *A Study of Chinese Boycotts*, Johns Hopkins University Press, 1935.

Roy Hidemichi Akagi, "Japan's Economic Relations with China," *Pacific Affairs* 4 (1931), 488-510.

Banking & Currency

Maurice Collis, *Wayfoong: The Hongkong and Shanghai Banking Corporation*, London, Faber and Faber, 1965.

Takeshi Hamashita, "A History of the Japanese Silver Yen and the Hongkong and Shanghai Banking Corporation, 1871-1913," in Frank H. H. King, ed. *Eastern Banking: Essays in the History of The Hongkong and Shanghai Banking Corporation*, London, The Athlone Press, 1983, 321-49.

Frank H.H. King, *The History of the Hongkong and Shanghai Banking Corporation*, vol. 2, *The Hongkong Bank in the Period of Imperialism and War, 1895-1918: Wayfoong, the Focus of Wealth*, Cambridge University Press, 1988.

Ann Trotter, *Britain and East Asia: 1933-1937*, Cambridge University Press, 1975.

Toshihiko Shimada, "Designs on North China, 1933-1937," in James W. Morley, ed. *The China Quagmire: Japan's Expansion on the Asian Continent, 1933-1941*, Columbia University Press, 1983, 11-230, esp. 136-41, "Chinese Monetary Reform."

Chuzo Mitsuchi, "Future of the Yuan Currency," *CJ* 8:1 (March 1939), 39-47.

D.K. Lieu, "The Sino-Japanese Currency War," *Pacific Affairs* 12 (1939), 413-26.

Shigeyoshi Hijikata, "The Battle of Currencies in China," *CJ* 8:8 (Oct 1939), 962-73.

Industries

Marius B. Jansen, "Yawata, Hanyehping, and the Twenty-One Demands," *Pacific Historical Review* 23 (Feb 1954), 31-48.

Albert Feuerwerker, "China's Nineteenth-Century Industrialization: The Case of the Hanyehping Coal and Iron Company, Limited," in C.D. Cowan, ed. *The Economic Development of China and Japan*, London, Allen & Unwin, 1964, 70-110.

Tim Wright, "Sino-Japanese Business in China: The Luda Company, 1921-1937," *Journal of Asian Studies* 39:4 (Aug 1980), 711-27.

Ernest R. May & John K. Fairbank, eds. America's China Trade in Historical Perspective: The Chinese and American Performance, Harvard University Press, 1986, the following articles:
Lillian M. Li, "The Silk Export Trade and Economic Modernization in China and Japan," 77-99.
Kang Chao, "The Chinese-American Cotton-Textile Trade, 1830-1930," 103-27.
Bruce L. Reynolds, "The East Asian Textile Cluster' Trade, 1868-1973: A Comparative Advantage Interpretation," 129-50.
Sherman Cochran, "Commercial Penetration and Economic Imperialism in China: An American Cigarette Company's Entrance into the Market," 151-203.
Mira Wilkins, "The Impacts of American Multinational Enterprise on American-Chinese Economic Relations, 1786-1949," 259-92.

Kang Chao, *The Development of Cotton Textile Production in China*, Harvard University Press, 1977.

Tetsuya Kuwahara, "The Business Strategy of Japanese Cotton Spinners: Overseas Operations, 1890 to 1931," in *The Textile Industry and its Business Climate*, vol. 8 of *International Conference on Business History*, ed. by Akio Okochi & Shin'ichi Yonekawa, University of Tokyo Press, 1982, 139-66.

Peter Duus, "Zaikabo: Japanese Cotton Mills in China, 1895-1937," in Duus, Ramon H. Myers & Mark R. Peattie, eds. *Japan's Informal Empire in China, 1895-1937*, Princeton University Press, 1989.

William D. Wray, *Mitsubishi and the N.Y.K., 1870-1914: Business Strategy in the Japanese Shipping Industry*, Harvard University Press, 1984, esp. 332-400.

William D. Wray, "Japan's Big Three Service Enterprises in China, 1896-1936," in Peter Duus, Ramon H. Myers & Mark Peattie, eds. *Japan's Informal Empire in China, 1895-1937*, Princeton University Press, 1989.

General: 1930s

Christopher Howe, "Japan's Economic Experience in China before the Establishment of the People's Republic of China: A Retrospective Balance-sheet," in Ronald Dore & Radha Sinha, eds. *Japan and the World Depression, Then and Now: Essays in Memory of E.F. Penrose*, London, Macmillan, 1987, 155-77.

Parks M. Coble, Jr., *The Shanghai Capitalists and the Nationalist Government, 1927-1937*, Harvard University Press, 1980, esp. 124-60.

Stephen Lyon Endicott, *Diplomacy and Enterprise: British China Policy, 1933-37*, University of British Columbia Press, 1975, esp. 102-49.

Russell G. Shiman, "North China in a Japanese Trading Bloc," *Far Eastern Survey* 4:25 (Dec 18, 1935), 198-205.

Takafusa Nakamura, "Japan's Economic Thrust into North China, 1933-1938: Formation of the North China Development Corporation," in Akira Iriye, ed. *The Chinese and the Japanese: Essays in Political and Cultural Interactions*, Princeton University Press, 1980, 220-53.

Chuan-hua Lowe, *Japan's Economic Offensive in China*, London, Allen & Unwin, 1939.

Imperialism

Frances V. Moulder, *Japan, China and the Modern World Economy: Toward A Reinterpretation of East Asian Development, ca. 1600 to 1918*, Cambridge University Press, 1977.

Tim Wright, "Imperialism and the Chinese Economy: A Methodological Critique of the Debate," *Bulletin of Concerned Asian Scholars* 18:1 (Jan-Mar 1986), 36-45.

Albert Feuerwerker, "Japanese Imperialism in China: A Commentary," in Peter Duus, Ramon H. Myers & Mark R. Peattie, eds. *Japan's Informal Empire in China, 1895-1937*, Princeton University Press, 1989.

8. THE COLONIAL ECONOMY

A. GENERAL

W. G. Beasley, *Japanese Imperialism, 1894-1945*, Oxford University Press, 1987, 122-41.

Ramon H. Myers & Mark R. Peattie, eds. *The Japanese Colonial Empire, 1895-1945*, Princeton University Press, 1984, including the following articles:

Samuel Pao-San Ho, "Colonialism and Development: Korea, Taiwan, and Kwantung," 347-98.
Toshiyuki Mizoguchi & Yuzo Yamamoto, "Capital Formation in Taiwan and Korea," 399-419.
Ramon H. Myers & Saburo Yawada, "Agricultural Development in the Empire," 420-52.

Wolfgang J. Mommsen & Jurgen Osterhammel, eds. *Imperialism and After: Continuities and Discontinuities*, London, Allen & Unwin, 1986, including:
Bernd Martin, "The Politics of Expansion of the Japanese Empire: Imperialism or Pan-Asiatic Mission?" 63-82.

E.B. Schumpeter, "Japan, Korea and Manchukuo, 1936-1940," in Elizabeth B. Schumpeter, ed. *The Industrialization of Japan and Manchukuo, 1930-1940: Population, Raw Materials and Industry*, New York, Macmillan, 1940, 271-474.

James I. Nakamura, "Incentives, Productivity Gaps, and Agricultural Growth Rates in Prewar Japan, Taiwan, and Korea," in Bernard Silberman & Harry Harootunian, eds. *Japan in Crisis: Essays on Taisho Democracy*, Princeton University Press, 1974, 329-73.

Fumio Kaneko, "Prewar Japanese Investments in Colonial Taiwan, Korea, and Manchuria: A Quantitative Analysis," *Annals of the Institute of Social Science* 23 (1982), 32-64.

B. MANCHURIA

General

Baron Y. Sakatani, *Manchuria: A Survey of its Economic Development*, Garland Publishing, 1979 (orig. pub. for Carnegie Endowment for International Peace, 1932).

Kungtu C. Sun, *The Economic Development of Manchuria in the First Half of the Twentieth Century*, Harvard University Press, 1969.

Ramon H. Myers and Thomas R. Ulie, "Foreign Influence and Agricultural Development in Northeast China: A Case Study of the Liaotung Peninsula, 1906-1942," *Journal of Asian Studies* 31:2 (Feb 1972), 329-50.

Herbert P. Bix, "Japanese Imperialism and the Manchurian Economy, 1900-1931," *China Quarterly* 51 (July-Sept 1972), 425-43.
Response to above article:
Ramon Myers, "Economic Development in Manchuria under Japanese Imperialism: A Dissenting View," *China Quarterly* 55 (July-Sept 1973), 547-56, and "Herbert Bix replies," 556-59.

Ramon H. Myers, "Japanese Imperialism in Manchuria: The South Manchuria Railway Company, 1906-1933," in Peter Duus, Myers & Mark R. Peattie, eds. *Japan's Informal Empire in China, 1895-1937*, Princeton University Press, 1989.

Pre-World War I

E.W. Edwards, "Great Britain and the Manchurian Railway Question, 1909-1910," *English Historical Review* 81:321 (1966), 740-69.

Michael H. Hunt, *Frontier Defense and the Open Door: Manchuria in Chinese-American Relations, 1895-1911*, Yale University Press, 1973.

Cyrus Adler, *Jacob H. Schiff: His Life and Letters*, 2 vols., New York, Doubleday, 1928, esp. vol. 1, 246-59 re: Manchurian railways.

Post-1919

Edith E. Ware, *Business and Politics in the Far East*, Yale University Press, 1932.

C. Walter Young, *The International Relations of Manchuria*, University of Chicago Press, 1929.

C. Walter Young, *Japan's Special Position in Manchuria: Its Assertion, Legal Interpretation and Present Meaning*, New York, AMS Press, 1971 (orig pub. 1931).

Seiichi Kishi, "Japan-Manchukuo Economic Bloc," *CJ* 1:4 (March 1933), 467-74.

Kimmochi Ohkura, "Tapping Manchuria's Resources," *CJ* 1:4 (March 1933), 484-91.

Goro Hirata, "Manchoukuo's Foreign Trade," *CJ* 2:1 (June 1933), 51-60.

W.S.Y. Tinge, "Some Economic Achievements of Manchoukuo," *CJ* 2:3 (Dec 1933), 426-34.

Ayayoshi Takeuchi, "Manchoukuo Seen After Three Years," *CJ* 4:3 (Dec 1935), 365-74.

Walter R. Godard, *Japan's Manchurian Steel Economy*, New York Public Library, 1956.

Katsuji Nakagane, "Manchukuo: Government and Economic Development," in Peter Duus, Ramon H. Myers & Mark R. Peattie, eds. *Japan's Informal Empire in China, 1895-1937*, Princeton University Press, 1989.

John Young, *The Research Activities of the South Manchurian Railway Company, 1907-1945*, Columbia University, The East Asian Institute, 1966.

Joshua A. Fogel, *Life Along the South Manchurian Railway: The Memoirs of Ito Takeo*, Armonk, N.Y., M.E. Sharpe, 1988.

Yukio Cho, "An Inquiry into the Problem of Importing American Capital into Manchuria: A Note on Japanese-American Relations, 1931-1941," in Dorothy Borg & Shumpei Okamoto, eds. *Pearl Harbor as History: Japanese-American Relations, 1931-1941*, Columbia University Press, 1973, 377-410.

E. Wallace Moore, "The New Order in Manchoukuo," *CJ* 8:8 (Oct 1939), 982-90.

Kimmochi Ohkura, "Japan and Manchoukuo's Industrial Development," *CJ* 9:7 (July 1940), 848-55.

Edwin W. Pauley, *Report on Japanese Assets in Manchuria to the President of the United States*, Washington, D.C., 1946.

C. KOREA

From the "Opening" to Early Colonial Period

Martina Deuchler, *Confucian Gentlemen and Barbarian Envoys: The Opening of Korea, 1875-1885*, University of Washington Press, 1977, esp. 67-84 & 173-97.

Bonnie B. Oh, "Sino-Japanese Rivalry in Korea, 1876-1885," in Akira Iriye, ed. *The Chinese and the Japanese: Essays in Political and Cultural Interactions*, Princeton University Press, 1980, 37-57.

Hilary Conroy, *The Japanese Seizure of Korea, 1868-1910*, University of Pennsylvania Press, 1960, esp. 442-91.

Janet Hunter, "Japanese Government Policy, Business Opinion and the Seoul-Pusan Railway, 1894-1906," *Modern Asian Studies* 11:4 (1977), 573-99.

Peter Duus, "Economic Dimensions of Meiji Imperialism: The Case of Korea, 1895-1910," in Ramon H. Myers & Mark R. Peattie, eds. *The Japanese Colonial Empire, 1895-1945*, Princeton University Press, 1984, 128-171.

Karl Moskowitz, "The Creation of the Oriental Development Company: Japanese Illusions Meet Korean Reality," *Occasional Papers on Korea* 2 (1974), 73-121.

Post-1919: General

Annual Report on Administration of Chosen, (1910-1938), Keijo, Government-General of Chosen.

Wonmo Dong, "Japanese Colonial Policy and Practice in Korea, 1905-1945: A Study in Assimilation," Ph.D. diss., Georgetown University, 1965.

Andrew Nahm, ed., *Korea under Japanese Colonial Rule: Studies of the Policy and Techniques of Japanese Colonialism*, Western Michigan University, Center for Korean Studies, 1973, including the following articles:
Chul Won Kang, "An Analyis of Japanese Policy and Economic Change in Korea, 77-88.
Young-iob Ching, "Japanese Investment in Korea, 1904-1945," 89-98.
Kwan Suk Kim, "An Analysis of Economic Change in Korea," 99-112.
Daniel Sungil Juhn, "The Development of Korean Entrepreneurship," 113-34.

C.I. Eugene Kim & Doretha E. Mortimore, eds. *Korea's Response to Japan: The Colonial Period, 1920-1945*, Western Michigan University, Center for Korean Studies, 1977, including the following articles:
Young-iob Chung, "Korean Investment Under Japanese Rule," 15-41.
Daniel S. Juhn, "Nationalism and Korean Businessmen," 42-52.
Yun-shik Chang, "Planned Economic Transformation and Population Change," 53-84.
Kirk Y.K. Kim, "The Impact of Japanese Colonial Development on the Korean Economy," 85-100.

Sang-chul Suh, *Growth and Structural Changes in the Korean Economy, 1910-1940*, Harvard University Press, 1978.

Randall S. Jones, "The Economic Development of Colonial Korea," Ph.D. diss., University of Michigan, 1984.

Clive Hamilton, *Capitalist Industrialization in Korea*, Boulder, Westview Press, 1986, esp. 9-20 & 111-16.

Kenkichi Ishiyama, "Industrialization of Korea," *CJ* 10:9 (Sept 1941), 1160-65.

Toshiyuki Mizoguchi, "Economic Growth of Korea under the Japanese Occupation: Background of Industrialization of Korea, 1911-1940," *Hitotsubashi Journal of Economics* 20:1 (June 1979), 1-19.

Specific Industrial Studies

Mitsuhiko Kimura, "Financial Aspects of Korea's Economic Growth under Japanese Rule," *Modern Asian Studies* 20:4 (Oct 1986), 793-820.

Dennis I. McNamara, "Entrepreneurship in Colonial Korea: Kim Yon-su," *Modern Asian Studies* 22:1 (Feb 1988), 165-77.

Barbara Molony, "Noguchi Jun and Nitchitsu: Colonial Investment Strategy of a High Technology Enterprise," in William D. Wray, ed. *Managing Industrial Enterprise: Cases from Japan's Prewar Experience*, Harvard University Press, 1989.

Barbara Molony, "Japan's Strategic Investment in High Technology in Korea, 1925-1945," *Journal of Modern Korean Studies*, forthcoming.

Political Perspectives

Gregory Henderson, *Korea: The Politics of the Vortex*, Harvard University Press, 1968.

Shobei Shiota, "A 'Ravaged' People: The Koreans in World War II," *Japan Interpreter* 7:1 (Win 1971), 43-53.

Bruce Cumings, "The Legacy of Japanese Colonialism in Korea," in Ramon H. Myers & Mark R. Peattie, eds. *The Japanese Colonial Empire, 1895-1945*, Princeton University Press, 1984, 478-496.

Bruce Cumings, *The Origins of the Korean War: Liberation and the Emergence of Separate Regimes, 1945-1947*, Princeton University Press, 1981.

D. TAIWAN

Samuel P.S. Ho, "The Economic Development of Colonial Taiwan: Evidence and Interpretation," *Journal of Asian Studies* 34:2 (Feb 1975), 417-39.

Samuel Ho, *Economic Development of Taiwan, 1860-1970*, Yale University Press, 1978.

Han-yu Chang & Ramon H. Myers, "Japanese Colonial Development Policy in Taiwan, 1895-1906: A Case of Bureaucratic Entrepreneurship," *Journal of Asian Studies* 22:4 (Aug 1963), 433-49.

Ramon H. Myers & Adrienne Ching, "Agricultural Development in Taiwan under Japanese Colonial Rule," *Journal of Asian Studies* 23:4 (Aug 1964), 555-70.

George Barclay, *Colonial Development and Population in Taiwan*, Princeton University Press, 1954.

9. LABOR

A. LABOR MARKET & LABOR ECONOMICS

Yasoh Kusama, "Coping with Unemployment," *CJ* 1:2 (Sept 1932), 292-300.

Mataji Umemura, "Labor's Relative Share in the Japanese Manufacturing Industry since 1900," *Annals of the Hitotsubashi Academy* 8:2 (Apr 1958), 176-87.

Shunsaku Nishikawa, "Domestic Labor Migration in Japan," *Keio Business Review* 1 (1962), 79-99.

Koji Taira, "Characteristics of Japanese Labor Markets," *Economic Development and Cultural Change* 10:2-1 (1962), 150-68.

Minoru Tachi, "Labour: Population Trend and Economic Growth in Japan," in Kenneth Berrill, ed. *Economic Development: With Special Reference to East Asia*, New York, St. Martin's Press, 1964, 53-70.

Arlon Tussing, "The Labor Force in Meiji Economic Growth: A Quantitative Study of Yamanashi Prefecture," *Journal of Economic History* 26:1 (March 1966), 59-92.

Koji Taira, *Economic Development and the Labor Market in Japan*, Columbia University Press, 1970.

Osamu Saito, "Migration and the Labour Market in Japan, 1872-1920: A Regional Study," *Keio Economic Studies* 10:2 (1973), 47-60.

Robert E. Cole & Ken'ichi Tominaga, "Japan's Changing Occupational Structure and its Significance," in Hugh Patrick, ed. *Japanese Industrialization and its Social Consequences*, University of California Press, 1973, 53-95.

Ryoshin Minami, *The Turning Point in Economic Development: Japan's Experience*, Tokyo, Kinokuniya, 1973.

Gary R. Saxonhouse, "Productivity Change and Labor Absorption in Japanese Cotton Spinning, 1891-1935," *Quarterly Journal of Economics* 91:2 (May 1977), 195-219.

Gary R. Saxonhouse, "The Supply of Quality Workers and the Demand for Quality in Jobs in Japan's Early Industrialization," *Explorations in Economic History* 15:1 (Jan 1978), 40-68.

Taishiro Shirai & Haruo Shimada, "Japan," in John T. Dunlop & Walter Galenson, eds. *Labor in the Twentieth Century*, New York, Academic Press, 1978, 241-322.

Sanford Jacoby, "Origins of Internal Labor Markets in Japan," *Industrial Relations* 18:2 (Spr 1979), 184-96.

Ryoshin Minami & Akira Ono, "Behavior of Income Shares in a Labor Surplus Economy: Japan's Experience," *Economic Development and Cultural Change* 29:2 (Jan 1981), 309-24.

Ron Napier, "The Transformation of the Japanese Labor Market, 1894-1937," in Tetsuo Najita & J. Victor Koschmann, eds. *Conflict in Modern Japanese History: The Neglected Tradition*, Princeton University Press, 1982, 342-65.

Gary Saxonhouse and Y. Kiyokawa, "Supply and Demand for Quality Workers in Cotton Spinning in Japan and India," in Kazushi Ohkawa & Gustav Ranis, eds. *Japan and Developing Countries*, Oxford University Press, 1985, 177-211.

Koji Taira, "Economic Development, Labor Markets, and Industrial Relations in Japan, 1905-1955," in Peter Duus, ed. *The Cambridge History of Japan*, vol. VI, *The Twentieth Century*, Cambridge University Press, 1989.

B. LABOR RELATIONS

General

International Labour Office, *Industrial Labour in Japan*, Geneva, 1933.

Kazuo Okochi, *Labor in Modern Japan*, Tokyo, The Science Council of Japan, 1958.

Mikio Sumiya, *Social Impact of Industrialization in Japan*, Tokyo, Japanese National Commission for UNESCO, 1963.

Hisashi Kawada, *The Government, Industrial Relations and Economic Development in Japan*, Kobe University, Management and Labour Studies, English Series, No. ll, November 1964.

Mikio Sumiya, "The Development of Japanese Labour-Relations," *DE* 4:4 (Dec 1966), 499-515.

Vlasta Hilska & Zdenka Vasiljevova, *Problems of Modern Japanese Society*, Prague, Universita Karlova, 1971 [re: Industrial Patriotic Movement].

Reiko Okayama, "Industrial Relations in Great Britain and Japan, from the 1880s to the 1920s," in *Labor and Management*, vol. 4 of *International Conference on Business History*, ed. by Keiichiro Nakagawa, University of Tokyo Press, 1979, 207-37.

Mikio Sumiya, "The Japanese System of Industrial Relations," in Peter Doeringer, ed. *Industrial Relations in International Perspective: Essays on Research and Policy*, Holmes & Meier, 1981, 287-323.

Labor Management

Eitaro Kishimoto, "The Characteristics of Labor-Management Relations in Japan and Their Historical Formation," *Kyoto University Economic Review* 35:2 (1965), 33-55.

Robert Evans, Jr., "Evolution of the Japanese System of Employer-Employee Relations, 1868-1945," *Business History Review* 44:1 (Spr 1970), 110-25.

Hiroshi Hazama, "Formation of the Management System in Meiji Japan: Personnel Management in Large Corporations," *DE* 15:4 (Dec 1977), 402-19.

Essays on "The Japanese Employment System," *Journal of Japanese Studies* 4:2 (Sum 1978), as follows:
Sydney Crawcour, "The Japanese Employment System," 225-45.
Robert E. Cole, "The Late-Developer Hypothesis: An Evaluation of Its Relevance for Japanese Employment Patterns," 247-65.
W. Mark Fruin, "The Japanese Company Controversy: Ideology and Organization in a Historical Perspective," 267-300.
—and in response:
Ronald P. Dore, "More About Late Development," *Journal of Japanese Studies* 5:1 (Win 1979), 137-51.

Labor and Management, vol. 4 of *International Conference on Business History*, ed. by Keiichiro Nakagawa, University of Tokyo Press, 1979, including:
Eisuke Daito, "Management and Labor: The Evolution of Employer-Employee Relations in the Course of Industrial Development," 1-25.
Masumi Tsuda, "The Formation and Characteristics of the Work Group in Japan," 29-42.
Toshiaki Chokki, "Labor Management in the Cotton Spinning Industry," 145-67.
Toshikazu Nakase, "The Introduction of Scientific Management in Japan and Its Characteristics: Case Studies of Companies in the Sumitomo Zaibatsu," 171-202.

Eisuke Daito, "Industrial Training and Management in Japan, 1900-1930," in Keiichiro Nakagawa & Tsunehiko Yui, eds. *Organization and Manage-*

ment, 1900-1930: Proceedings of the Japan-Germany Conference on Business History, Japan Business History Institute, 1983, 59-71.

Akiko Chimoto, "Employment in the Meiji Period: From Tradition' to Modernity,'" in *Yearbook* 3, 1986, 135-59.

W. Mark Fruin, "Hands-On and Hands-Off Management: Internal Contracting and Industrial Management in Nineteenth Century Japan," in Akira Hayami, ed. Pre-Conditions to Industrialization in Japan, Papers from Ninth International Economic History Congress, Bern, 1986.

Japanese Management in Historical Perspective, vol. 15 of *International Conference on Business History*, ed. by Keiichiro Nakagawa & Tsunehiko Yui, University of Tokyo Press, 1989, including:
W. Mark Fruin, "Instead of Management: Internal Contracting and the Genesis of Modern Labor Relations in Japan."
Andrew Gordon, "Araki Toichiro and the Shaping of Japanese Labor Management."

Yukio Yamashita, "The Inside Contract System in Japan: With Particular Reference to the Coal Mining Industry," *Yearbook* 4, 1987, 1-25.

Toshiaki Chokki, "Modernization of Technology and Labor in Pre-War Japanese Electrical Machinery Enterprises," *Yearbook* 4, 1987, 26-49.

Satoshi Sasaki, "Scientific Management Movements in Pre-War Japan," *Yearbook* 4, 1987, 50-76.

Factory Labor

Ronald P. Dore, "The Modernizer as a Special Case: Japanese Factory Legislation, 1882-1911," *Comparative Studies in Society and History* 11:4 (Oct 1969), 433-50.

Koji Taira, "Factory Legislation and Management Modernization during Japan's Industrialization, 1868-1916," *Business History Review* 44:1 (Spr 1970), 84-109.

Ronald P. Dore, *British Factory-Japanese Factory, The Origins of National Diversity in Employment Relations*, University of California Press, 1973, 375-403.

Kanae Iida, "The Iron Worker's Union in the Earliest Stages of the Japanese Labor Movement: The Rise and Fall of a Craft Union," *Keio Economic Studies* 10:1 (1973), 39-59.

Koji Taira, "Factory Labour and the Industrial Revolution in Japan," *Cambridge Economic History of Europe*, Vol. 7, Part 2, Cambridge University Press, 1978, 166-214.

Andrew Gordon, *The Evolution of Labor Relations in Japan: Heavy Industry, 1853-1955*, Harvard University Press, 1985.

Minoru Sawai, "The Development of Machine-Building Industries and the Evolution of Production & Labor Management: Cases of Rolling Stock, Spinning & Weaving Machines, Machine Tools and Electric Machineries," in *Japanese Management in Historical Perspective*, vol. 15 of *International Conference on Business History*, ed. by Keiichiro Nakagawa & Tsunehiko Yui, University of Tokyo Press, 1989.

Disputes

A. Morgan Young, *Japan in Recent Times, 1912-1926*, New York, William Morrow, 1929 (Greenwood reprint, 1973), 230-39 (re: dockyard strikes of 1920).

Eitaro Kishimoto, "The Characteristics of Labour-Management Relations in Japan and Their Historical Formation," *Kyoto University Economic Review* (1) 35:2 (Oct 1965), 33-55; (2) 36:1 (Apr 1966), 17-38.

George O. Totten, "Collective Bargaining and Works Councils as Innovations in Industrial Relations in Japan during the 1920's," in Ronald Dore, ed. *Aspects of Social Change in Modern Japan*, Princeton University Press, 1967, 203-43.

George O. Totten, "Japanese Industrial Relations at the Crossroads: The Great Noda Strike of 1927-1928," in Bernard Silberman & Harry Harootunian, eds. *Japan in Crisis: Essays on Taisho Democracy*, Princeton University Press, 1974, 398-436.

W. Mark Fruin, *Kikkoman: Company, Clan, and Community*, Harvard University Press, 1983, 155-210.

Tomoyoshi Okada, "The State and Society in History as Seen from the History of the Japanese Labor Union Movement," *Annals of the Institute of Social Science* 25 (1983-84), 9-24.

Andrew Gordon, "Labor Disputes and the Emergence of the Working Class in Japan, 1897-1917," Working Papers in Asian/Pacific Studies, Duke University, 1985.

Ideology

Byron K. Marshall, *Capitalism and Nationalism in Prewar Japan: The Ideology of the Business Elite, 1868-1941*, Stanford University Press, 1967.

Hiroshi Hazama, "Japanese Labor-Management Relations and Uno Riemon," *Journal of Japanese Studies* 5:1 (Win 1979), 71-106.

Hiroshi Hazama, "Labor Management in Japan," in *Yearbook*, 2, 1985, 32-53.

Miscellaneous

Ryoichi Iwauchi, "Institutionalizing the Technical Manpower Formation in Meiji Japan," *DE* 15:4 (Dec 1977), 420-39.

Kenzo Yukizawa, "International Levels of Labor Productivity in Prewar Japanese Manufacturing Industry: Comparison of Japan, Britain, and the United States," *JES* 1:4 (Sum 1973), 33-47.

Shuichi Harada, *Labor Conditions in Japan*, Columbia University Press, 1928.

Takiji Kobayashi, *"The Factory Ship" and "The Absentee Landlord,"* University of Tokyo Press, 1973 (novels).

Mikiso Hane, *Peasants, Rebels, and Outcasts: The Underside of Modern Japan*, New York, Pantheon, 1982, 226-45, "The Coal Miners."

Fred G. Notehelfer, "Between Tradition and Modernity: Labor and the Ashio Copper Mine," *Monumenta Nipponica* 39:1 (Spr 1984), 11-24.

Paolo Calvetti, *The Ashio Copper Mine Revolt (1907): A Case Study on the Changes of the Labor Relations in Japan at the Beginning of the XX Century*, Naples, Istituto Universitario Orientale, Dipartimento di Studi Asiatici, Series Minor, 29, 1987.

K. Odaka, "History of Money Wages in the North Kyushu Industrial Area, 1898-1939," *Hitotsubashi Journal of Economics* 8:2 (Feb 1968), 71-100.

Hugh Patrick, ed. *Japanese Industrialization and its Social Consequences*, University of California Press, 1973, including:
Hiroshi Hazama, "Historical Changes in the Life Style of Industrial Workers," 21-51.
Yasukichi Yasuba, "The Evolution of Dualistic Wage Structure," 249-98.

Penelope Francks, "The Japanese Farmer and the Industrialisation Process: A Re-Appraisal," in Janet Hunter, ed. *Aspects of the Relationship between Agri-*

culture and Industrialization in Japan, in *International Studies* (1986/4), London, Suntory and Toyota International Centre, London School of Economics, 1-16.

Thomas C. Smith, "The Right to Benevolence: Dignity and Japanese Workers, 1890-1920," *Comparative Studies in Society and History* 26:4 (Oct 1984), 587-613.

C. THE STATE & LABOR

Mitsutoshi Azuma, "Labor Legislation in Japan," *Annals of the Hitotsubashi Academy* 1:2 (Apr 1951), 181-95.

Iwao F. Ayusawa, *A History of Labor in Modern Japan,* Honolulu, University of Hawaii, East-West Center Press, 1966.

Robert A. Scalapino, *The Early Japanese Labor Movement: Labor and Politics in a Developing Society,* University of California, 1984.

Sheldon Garon, "State Autonomy and Labor in Modern Japan," in Labor, Society and State in Twentieth Century China and Japan, Working Papers in Asian/Pacific Studies, Duke University, 1986, 3-21.

Sheldon Garon, *The State and Labor in Modern Japan,* University of California Press, 1987.

Andrew Gordon, "Business and the Corporate State: The Business Lobby and Bureaucrats on Labor, 1911-1941," in William D. Wray, ed. *Managing Industrial Enterprise: Cases from Japan's Prewar Experience,* Harvard University Press, 1989.

D. WOMEN WORKERS

Alice Mabel Bacon, *Japanese Girls & Women,* Boston, Houghton, Mifflin, rev. ed., 1902.

Sidney L. Gulick, *Working Women of Japan,* New York, Missionary Education Movement, 1915.

H. Matsuoka, Labor *Conditions of Women and Children in Japan,* Washington, U.S. Department of Labor, Bureau of Labor Statistics, Government Printing Office, 1931.

Baroness Shidzue Ishimoto, *Facing Two Ways: The Story of My Life,* New York, Farrar & Rinehart, 1935. (See Stanford University Press, 1984 paperback edited by Barbara Molony).

Kazuo Kusano, "Industrialization and the Status of Women in Japan," Ph.D. dissertation, University of Washington, 1973.

Gary Saxonhouse, "Country Girls and Communication Among Competitors in the Japanese Cotton-Spinning Industry," in Hugh Patrick, ed. *Japanese Industrialization and its Social Consequences*, University of California Press, 1973, 97-125.

Yasue Aoki Kidd, *Women Workers in the Japanese Cotton Mills: 1880-1920*, Cornell University, East Asia Papers, No. 20, 1979.

Mikiso Hane, *Peasants, Rebels, and Outcasts: The Underside of Modern Japan*, New York, Pantheon, 1982, 172-204, "The Textile Factory Workers."

Sharon Sievers, *Flowers in Salt: The Beginnings of Feminist Consciousness in Modern Japan*, Stanford University Press, 1983, esp. 54-86, "The Textile Workers."

Janet Hunter, "Recruitment in the Japanese Silk Reeling and Cotton Spinning Industries, 1870s-1930s," *Proceedings of the British Association for Japanese Studies* 9 (1984), 64-85.

Janet Hunter, "Labour in the Japanese Silk Industry in the 1870s: The *Tomioka Nikki* of Wada Ei," in Gordon Daniels, ed. *Europe Interprets Japan*, Tenterden, Kent, 1984.

E. Patricia Tsurumi, "Female Textile Workers and the Failure of Early Trade Unionism in Japan," *History Workshop* 18 (Aug 1984), 3-27.

E. Patricia Tsurumi, "Problem Consciousness and Modern Japanese History: Female Textile Workers of Meiji and Taisho," *Bulletin of Concerned Asian Scholars* 18:4 (Oct-Dec 1986), 41-48.

Kaoru Sugihara, "The Transformation of Social Values of Young Country Girls: Towards a Reinterpretation of the Japanese Migrant (Dekasegi) Industrial Labour Force," in Janet Hunter, ed. *Aspects of the Relationship between Agriculture and Industrialization in Japan*, in *International Studies* (1986/4), London, Suntory and Toyota International Centre, London School of Economics, 32-51.

E. Patricia Tsurumi, "Serving in Japan's Industrial Army: Female Textile Workers, 1868-1930," *Canadian Journal of History* 23:2 (Aug 1988), 155-76.

Janet Hunter, "Factory Legislation and Employer Resistance: The Abolition of Night Work in the Japanese Cotton Spinning Industry," in *Japanese Management in Historical Perspective*, vol. 15 of *International Conference on Business History*, ed. by Keiichiro Nakagawa & Tsunehiko Yui, University of Tokyo Press, 1989.

E. POVERTY, LIVING STANDARDS, & INCOME DISTRIBUTION

R.H.P. Mason, "The Debate on Poor Relief in the First Meiji Diet," *Oriental Society of Australia Journal* 3:1 (Jan 1965), 2-26.

Koji Taira, "Public Assistance in Japan," *Journal of Asian Studies* 27:1 (Nov 1967), 95-109.

Koji Taira, "Urban Poverty, Ragpickers, and the Ants Villa' in Tokyo," *Economic Development and Cultural Change* 17:2 (Jan 1969), 155-77.

Masayoshi Chubachi & Koji Taira, "Poverty in Modern Japan: Perceptions and Realities," in Hugh Patrick, ed. *Japanese Industrialization and its Social Consequences*, University of California Press, 1973, 391-437.

Iwao Ishizaka, "The Formation and Development of Welfare Work in Business: Its Japanese-Style Disposition," *Keio Business Review* 12 (1973), 71-98.

Toshiyuki Mizoguchi, "Laboring Poor of Japan in the Early Stages of Industrialization," in *Essays in Development Economics in Honor of Harry T. Oshima*, Manila, Philippine Institute for Development Studies, 1982, 315-33.

Kakichi Morimoto, *The Standard of Living in Japan*, Baltimore, 1918.

Alan H. Gleason, "Economic Growth and Consumption in Japan," in William W. Lockwood, ed. *The State and Economic Enterprise in Japan*, Princeton University Press, 1965, 391-444.

Susan B. Hanley, "The Material Culture: Stability in Transition," in Marius Jansen and Gilbert Rozman, eds. *Japan in Transition: From Tokugawa to Meiji*, Princeton University Press, 1986, 447-69.

Chotaro Takahashi, "Changes of Income Distribution in Japan," *Annals of the Hitotsubashi Academy* 6:1 (Oct 1955), 16-26.

Miyoji Hayakawa, "Distribution of Income in Japan, 1905-1956," *Waseda Economic Papers* 4 (1959), 19-35.

Akira Ono & Tsunehiko Watanabe, "Changes in Income Inequality in the Japanese Economy," in Hugh Patrick, ed. *Japanese Industrialization and its Social Consequences*, University of California Press, 1973, 363-89.

Mine Yasuzawa, "Changes in Lifestyle in Japan: Pattern and Structure of Modern Consumption," in Henri Baudet & Henk van der Meulen, eds. *Consumer*

Behaviour and Economic Growth in the Modern Economy, London, Croom Helm, 1982, 179-205.

Mitoshi Yamaguchi & George Kennedy, "Contribution of Population Growth to Per Capita Income and Sectoral Output Growth in Japan, 1880-1970," *DE* 22:3 (Sept 1984), 237-63.

F. POPULATION

Minoru Tachi & Yoichi Okazaki, "Economic Development and Population Growth," *DE* 3:4 (Dec 1965), 497-515.

Hiroshi Ohbuchi, "Demographic Transition in the Process of Japanese Industrialization," in Hugh Patrick, ed. *Japanese Industrialization and its Social Consequences*, University of California Press, 1973, 329-61.

Dennis P. Hogan & Takashi Mochizuki, "Demographic Transitions and the Life Course: Lessons from Japanese and American Comparisons," *Journal of Family History* 13:3 (1988), 291-305.

Ernest F. Penrose, *Population Theories and their Application, with Special Reference to Japan*, Stanford University Press, 1934.

Albert E. Hindmarsh, *The Basis of Japanese Foreign Policy*, Harvard University Press, 1936, 28-116.

Ryoichi Ishii, *Population Pressure and Economic Life in Japan*, London, King, 1937.

E.B. Schumpeter, "The Population of the Japanese Empire," in Elizabeth B. Schumpeter, ed. *The Industrialization of Japan and Manchukuo, 1930-1940: Population, Raw Materials and Industry*, New York, Macmillan, 1940, 41-79.

Allan B. Cole, "Japan's Population Problems in War and Peace," *Pacific Affairs* 16 (1943), 397-417.

Irene B. Taeuber, "Demographic Research in Japan," *Pacific Affairs* 22:4 (Dec 1949), 392-97.

Irene Taeuber, *The Population of Japan*, Princeton University Press, 1958.

Irene B. Taeuber, "Urbanization and Population Change in the Development of Modern Japan," *Economic Development and Cultural Change* 9:1.Pt. 2 (Oct 1960), 1-28.

Masaaki Yasukawa, "Estimates of Annual Births and the General Fertility Rates in Japan, 1890-1920," *KSU Economic and Business Review* (Kyoto Sangyo University) 1 (1963), 52-88.

Thomas O. Wilkinson, *The Urbanization of Japanese Labor, 1868-1955*, Amherst, 1965.

Masaaki Yasukawa & Keijiro Hirooka, "Estimates of the Population Size and of the Birth- and Death-Rates in Japan, 1865-1920," *Keio Economic Studies* 11:2 (1974), 41-75.

Yoshi Matsuda, "Formation of the Census System in Japan, 1871-1955: Development of the Statistical System in Japan Proper and her Colonies," *Hitotsubashi Journal of Economics* 21:2 (Feb 1981), 44-68.

Carl Mosk, "Demographic Transition in Japan," *Journal of Economic History* 37:3 (Sept 1977), 655-74.

Carl Mosk, "Fecundity, Infanticide, and Food Consumption in Japan," *Explorations in Economic History* 15:3 (July 1978), 269-89.

Carl Mosk, "The Evolution of the Pre-Modern Demographic Regime in Japan," *Population Studies* 35:1 (March 1981), 28-52.

Carl Mosk, "Fertility and Occupation: Mining Districts in Prewar Japan," *Social Science History* 5:3 (Sum 1981), 293-315.

Carl Mosk, *Patriarchy and Fertility: Japan and Sweden, 1880-1960*, New York, Academic Press, 1983.

S. Ryan Johansson & Carl Mosk, "Exposure, Resistance and Life Expectancy: Disease and Death during the Economic Development of Japan, 1900-1960," *Population Studies* 41 (July 1987), 207-35.

10. LAND: RURAL & URBAN SOCIETY

A. AGRICULTURE

Agricultural Growth

E.F. Penrose, *Food Supply and Raw Materials in Japan*, University of Chicago Press, 1930.

Bruce F. Johnston, "Agricultural Productivity and Economic Development in Japan," *Journal of Political Economy* 59:6 (Dec 1951), 498-415.

Kazuo Yamaguchi, "Development of Agricultural and Marine Industries," in Keizo Shibusawa, ed. *Japanese Society in the Meiji Era*, Tokyo, Obunsha, 1958, 401-72.

Tsutomu Noda, "Labor's Relative Share in the Japanese Agriculture since 1878," *Annals of the Hitotsubashi Academy* 9:2 (Apr 1959), 244-54.

Hideichi Horie, "The Agricultural Structure of Japan in the Period of Meiji Restoration," *Kyoto University Economic Review* (1) 31:2 (Oct 1961), 1-16; (2) 32:1 (Apr 1962), 1-23.

Takekazu Ogura, ed. *Agricultural Development in Modern Japan*, Tokyo, Japan FAO Association, 1963.

Kazushi Ohkawa & Henry Rosovsky, "The Role of Agriculture in Modern Japanese Economic Development," *Economic Development and Cultural Change* 9:1&2 (Oct 1960), 43-67.

Nobufumi Kayo, "The Characteristics of Heavy Applications of Fertilizers in Japanese Agriculture," *DE* 2:4 (Dec 1964), 373-96.

Kazushi Ohkawa, "Agricultural Policy: The Role of Agriculture in Early Economic Development: A Study of the Japanese Case," in Kenneth Berrill, ed. *Economic Development: With Special Reference to East Asia*, New York, St. Martin's Press, 1964, 322-35.

William W. Lockwood, ed. *The State and Economic Enterprise in Japan*, Princeton University Press, 1965, including:
James I. Nakamura, "Growth of Japanese Agriculture, 1875-1920," 249-324.
Shujiro Sawada, "Innovation in Japanese Agriculture, 1880-1935," 325-51.

James I. Nakamura, *Agricultural Production and the Economic Development of Japan, 1873-1922*, Princeton University Press, 1966.

Kazushi Ohkawa, "Agriculture and the Turning-points in Economic Growth," in Seiichi Tobata, ed. *The Modernization of Japan*, Tokyo, The Institute of Asian Economic Affairs, 1966, 137-53. [also in *DE* 3:4 (Dec 1965), 471-86].

Seymour Broadbridge, "The Economic Development of Japan, 1870-1920: A Review Article," *The Journal of Development Studies* 4:2 (Jan 1968), 268-87.

Henry Rosovsky, "Rumbles in the Ricefields: Professor Nakamura vs. the Official Statistics," *Journal of Asian Studies* 27:2 (Feb 1968), 347-60.

Kazushi Ohkawa, Bruce F. Johnston, & Hiromitsu Kaneda, *Agriculture and Economic Growth: Japan's Experience*, Princeton University Press, 1970.

Kee-Il Choi, "Technological Diffusion in Agriculture under the Bakuhan System," *Journal of Asian Studies* 30:4 (Aug 1971), 749-59.

Kazushi Ohkawa, *Deferential Structure and Agriculture: Essays on Dualistic Growth*, Kinokuniya, 1972.

James I. Nakamura, "Incentives, Productivity Gaps, and Agricultural Growth Rates in Prewar Japan, Taiwan, and Korea," in Bernard Silberman & Harry Harootunian, eds. *Japan in Crisis: Essays on Taisho Democracy*, Princeton University Press, 1974, 329-73.

Mitoshi Yamaguchi, "Population Growth, Agricultural and Economic Development of Japan since the Meiji Period," *Kobe University Economic Review* 20 (1974), 71-91.

Yujiro Hayami, *A Century of Agricultural Growth in Japan*, Minneapolis, University of Minnesota Press, 1975.

Kazumi Kobayashi, "Economic Development and Agriculture: In the Case of Japan," *KSU Economic and Business Review* (Kyoto Sangyo University) 2 (May 1975), 24-47.

Koji Taira, "Growth, Trends and Swings in Japanese Agriculture and Industry," *Economic Development and Cultural Change* 24:2 (Jan 1976), 423-36.

Sudipto Mundle & Kazushi Ohkawa, "Agricultural Surplus Flow in Japan, 1888-1937," *DE* 17:3 (Sept 1979), 247-65.

Masakatsu Akino, "Land Infrastructure Improvement in Agricultural Development: The Japanese Case, 1900-1965," *Economic Development and Cultural Change* 28:1 (Oct 1979), 97-117.

Radha Sinha, "Agriculture and Economic Development in Meiji Japan," *Development and Change* (The Hague) 10:4 (Oct 1979), 601-25.

Takekazu Ogura, *Can Japanese Agriculture Survive? A Historical and Comparative Approach*, Tokyo, Argicultural Research Center, 1980.

Yujiro Hayami, "Agricultural Development: The Japanese Experience," in J.D. Drilon, Jr. & G.P. Saquiquit, eds. *Accelerating Agricultural Development*, Laguna, Southeast Asian Regional Center, 1981, 278-317.

William W. Kelly, *Irrigation Management in Japan: A Critical Review of Japanese Social Science Research*, Cornell University, East Asia Papers, No. 30, 1981.

Yujiro Hayami, "The Role of Policy and Institutions in Agricultural Development in Japan," in Chi-ming Hou & Tzong-shian Yu, eds. *Agricultural Development in China, Japan, and Korea*, Taipei, Academia Sinica, 1982, 97-141.

Penelope Francks, *Technology and Agricultural Development in Pre-War Japan*. Yale University Press, 1984.

Richard Grabowski, "A Historical Reassessment of Early Japanese Development," *Development & Change* 16:2 (Apr 1985), 235-50.

Land Reform

Irving I. Kramer, "Land Reform and Industrial Development in Meiji Japan," *Land Economics* 29 (1953), 314-22.

Morris D. Morris, "The Problem of the Peasant Agriculturalist in Meiji Japan, 1873-1885," *Far Eastern Quarterly* 15:3 (Feb 1956), 357-70.

Ronald Dore, "The Meiji Landlord: Good or Bad?" *Journal of Asian Studies* 18:3 (May 1959), 343-55.

R.P. Dore, "Agricultural Improvements in Japan: 1870-1900," *Economic Development and Cultural Change* 9:1&2 (Oct 1960), 69-91.

R.P. Dore, "Land Reform and Japan's Economic Development," *DE* 3:4 (Dec 1965), 487-96.

James I. Nakamura, "Meiji Land Reform, Redistribution of Income, and Saving from Agriculture," *Economic Development and Cultural Change* 14:4 (July 1966), 428-39.

Ronald P. Dore, "Land Reform and Japan's Economic Development: A Reactionary Thesis," in Teodor Shanin, ed. *Peasants and Peasant Societies*, New York, 1971.

Tsutomu Takigawa, "Historical Background of Agricultural Land Reform in Japan," *DE* 10:3 (Sept 1972), 290-310.

Kozo Yamamura, "The Meiji Land Tax Reform and Its Effects," in Marius B. Jansen and Gilbert Rozman, eds. *Japan in Transition: From Tokugawa to Meiji*, Princeton University Press, 1986, 382-99.

Toshiyuki Kako, "Development of the Farm Machinery Industry in Japan: A Case Study of the Walking Type Tractor," *Hitotsubashi Journal of Economics* 28:2 (Dec 1987), 155-71.

Village Society

John Embree, *Suye Mura: A Japanese Village*, University of Chicago Press, 1939 (paperback, 1964).

Richard K. Beardsley, John W. Hall & Robert E. Ward, *Village Japan*, University of Chicago Press, 1959 (paperback, 1969).

Chie Nakane, *Kinship and Economic Organization in Rural Japan*, London, Athlone Press, 1967.

Tadashi Fukutake, *Japanese Rural Society*, Oxford University Press, 1967 (paperback: Cornell University Press, 1972).

Thomas Havens, *Farm and Nation in Modern Japan*, Agrarian Nationalism, 1870-1940, Princeton University Press, 1974.

Osamu Saito, "The Rural Economy: Commercial Agriculture, By-employment, and Wage Work," in Marius Jansen and Gilbert Rozman, eds. *Japan in Transition: From Tokugawa to Meiji*, Princeton University Press, 1986, 400-20.

Economic Distress & Depression

Shuzo Teruoka, "Japanese Capitalism and its Agricultural Problems—Culminating in the Rice Riots," *DE* 4:4 (Dec 1966), 472-98.

Shobei Shiota, "The Rice Riots and the Social Problems," *DE* 4:4 (Dec 1966), 516-34.

Tsutomu Ouchi, "Agricultural Depression and Japanese Villages," *DE* 5:4 (Dec 1967), 597-627.

Shigeichi Mayeda, "Our Stricken Agriculture," *CJ* 1:2 (Sept 1932), 266-75.

Michinosuke Hamada, "Coping with Agrarian Distress," *CJ* 5:1 (June 1936), 77-84.

B. LANDLORDS AND TENANTS

W. Ladejinsky, "Farm Tenancy and Japanese Agriculture," *Foreign Agriculture* (Bureau of Agricultural Economics, U.S. Department of Agriculture) 1:9 (Sept 1937), 425-46.

Seiyei Wakukawa, "The Japanese Farm-Tenancy System," in Douglas G. Haring, ed. *Japan's Prospect*, Harvard University Press, 115-73.

Nobutaka Ike, "Taxation and Landownership in the Westernization of Japan," *Journal of Economic H*story 27:2 *(Nov 1947), 160-82*.

Ronald P. Dore, *Land Reform in Japan*, Oxford University Press, 1959, 1-125.

Robert K. Sakai, "Landholding in Satsuma, 1868-1877," *Studies on Asia* 4 (1963), 55-68.

Barrington Moore, *Social Origins of Dictatorship and Democracy: Lord and Peasant in the Making of the Modern World*, Boston, Beacon Press, 1966, esp. 228-313.

Ronald Dore & Tsutomu Ouchi, "Rural Origins of Japanese Fascism," in Ronald Dore, ed. *Aspects of Social Change in Modern Japan*, Princeton University Press, 1967, 181-209.

Ann Waswo, "The Origins of Tenant Unrest," in Bernard Silberman & Harry Harootunian, eds. *Japan in Crisis: Essays on Taisho Democracy*, Princeton University Press, 1974, 374-97.

Ann Waswo, *Japanese Landlords: The Decline of a Rural Elite*, University of California Press, 1977.

Osamu Tanaka, "The Japanese Landlord-Tenant Tenure System in the Meiji Era," *Kobe University Economic Review* 27 (1981), 1-13.

Ann Waswo, "In Search of Equity: Japanese Tenant Unions in the 1920s," in Tetsuo Najita & J. Victor Koschmann, eds. *Conflict in Modern Japanese History: The Neglected Tradition*, Princeton University Press, 1982, 366-411.

Richard J. Smethurst, *Agricultural Development and Tenancy Disputes in Japan, 1870-1940*, Princeton University Press, 1986.

Janet Hunter, ed. *Aspects of the Relationship between Agriculture and Industrialization in Japan*, in *International Studies* (1986/4), London, Suntory and Toyota International Centre, London School of Economics, including:

Penelope Francks, "The Japanese Farmer and the Industrialisation Process: A Re-Appraisal," 1-16.

Hiroshi Watanabe, "The Agricultural Problem in Japan: Historical Perspective," 17-31.

Michael Lewis, "The 1918 Japanese Rural Rice Riots: Taxation Populaire and the Tenant-Landlord Riots," in Rural Social Protest in Twentieth Century China and Japan, Working Papers in Asian/Pacific Studies, Duke University, 1986, 30-58.

Philip C. Brown, "'Feudal Remnants' and Tenant Power: The Case of Niigata, Japan, in the Nineteenth and early Twentieth Centuries," *Peasant Studies* 15:1 (Fall 1987), 5-26.

Ann Waswo, "The Transformation of Rural Society, 1900-1950," in Peter Duus, ed. *The Cambridge History of Japan*, vol. VI, *The Twentieth Century*, Cambridge University Press, 1989.

C. URBAN HISTORY

The Reconstruction of Tokyo, Tokyo Municipal Office, 1933.

Shinobu Wada, "Osaka: The Nation's Manufacturing Centre," *CJ* 3:2 (Sept 1934), 259-65.

Robert B. Hall, "Tokaido: Road and Region," *The Geographical Review* 27:3 (July 1937), 353-77.

Special Issue: *City and Village in Japan*, ed. by Thomas C. Smith, *Economic Development and Cultural Change* 9:1.Part 2 (Oct 1960).

Takeo Yazaki, *Social Change and the City in Japan*, Tokyo, Japan Publications Trading, 1968.

Gary Allinson, *Japanese Urbanism: Industry and Politics in Kariya, 1872-1972*, University of California Press, 1975.

Robert August, "Urbanization and Local Government in Japan: A Study of Shibuya, 1889-1931," Ph.D. diss., University of Pittsburgh, 1975.

J. Douglas Downard, "Tokyo: The Depression Years, 1927-1933," Ph.D. diss., Indiana University 1976.

Nobuhiko Kosuge, "Development of Waterworks in Japan," *DE* 19:1 (March 1981), 69-94.

Hiromichi Ishizuka, "The Slum Dwellings and the Urban Renewal Scheme in Tokyo, 1868-1923," *DE* 19:2 (June 1981), 169-93.

John D. Eyre, *Nagoya: The Changing Geography of a Japanese Regional Metropolis*, University of North Carolina at Chapel Hill, Department of Geography, 1982.

Gilbert Rozman, "Castle Towns in Transition," in Marius Jansen and Gilbert Rozman, eds. *Japan in Transition: From Tokugawa to Meiji*, Princeton University Press, 1986, 318-46.

Henry D. Smith II, "The Edo-Tokyo Transition: In Search of Common Ground," in Marius Jansen and Gilbert Rozman, eds. *Japan in Transition: From Tokugawa to Meiji*, Princeton University Press, 1986, 347-74.

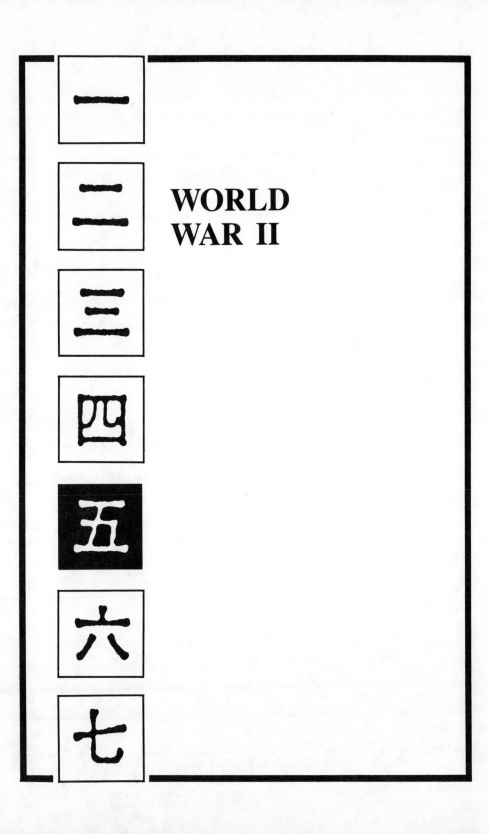

WORLD
WAR II

A. GENERAL

O. Tanin & E. Yohan, *When Japan Goes to War*, New York, The Vanguard Press, 1936.

The Sino-Japanese Conflict and Financial Resources, The Foreign Affairs Association of Japan, 1937.

Kate L. Mitchell, *Industrialization of the Western Pacific*, New York, Institute of Pacific Relations, 1942.

Fritz Sternberg, "Japan's Economic Imperialism," *Social Research* 12:3 (Sept 1945), 328-49.

Terutomo Makino, "Japan's Wartime Economy," *CJ* 8:10 (Dec 1939), 1188-1201.

Kamekichi Takahashi, "The 1940-41 Budget and Japan's Wartime Economy," *CJ* 9:4 (Apr 1940), 413-24.

"The European War and its Effects," *CJ* 9:8 (Aug 1940), 964-74.

Thomas A. Bisson, *Japan's War Economy*, New York, Institute of Pacific Relations, 1945.

Jerome Cohen, *Japan's Economy in War and Reconstruction*, University of Minnesota Press, 1949. (reprint: Greenwood Press, 1973).

Saburo Shiomi, *Japan's Finance and Taxation, 1940-1956*, Columbia University Press, 1957.

Shigeto Tsuru, *Essays on Japanese Economy*, Tokyo, Kinokuniya, 1958, esp. 154-236, "Japan's Economy under the Strain of the China Incident."

Peter Duus, ed. *The Cambridge History of Japan*, vol. VI, *The Twentieth Century*, Cambridge University Press, 1989, including:
Takafusa Nakamura, "Depression, Recovery, and War, 1918-1945."
Yutaka Kosai, "The Postwar Japanese Economy, 1945-1973."

B. ECONOMIC PLANNING AND CONTROL

Michael A. Barnhart, *Japan's Prepares for Total War: The Search for Economic Security, 1919-1941*, Cornell University Press, 1987.

Elizabeth B. Schumpeter, "Industrial Development and Government Policy, 1936-1940," in Schumpeter, ed. *The Industrialization of Japan and Manchukuo, 1930-1940: Population, Raw Materials and Industry*, New York, Macmillan, 1940, 787-861.

Shintaro Ryu, "Domestic Commodity Prices," *CJ* 6:2 (Sept 1937), 248-56.

Mitsuharu Ito, "Munitions Unlimited: The Controlled Economy," *Japan Interpreter* 7:3&4 (Sum-Aut 1972), 353-63.

Shintaro Ryu, "Economic Development of Modern Japan," in Hiro Sassa & Shintaro Ryu, *Recent Political and Economic Developments in Japan*, Tokyo, Japan Council, Institute of Pacific Relations, 1941, 120-60.

Makoto Takahashi, "The Development of War-Time Economic Controls," *DE* 5:4 (Dec 1967), 648-65.

Yohiji Minobe, "The Principles of the New Economic Structure," *CJ* 10:2 (Feb 1941), 161-70.

Shuko Shirayanagi, "Economic Self-defense," *CJ* 10:3 (March 1941), 295-309.

H.T. Oshima, "Japan's 'New Economic Structure'," *Pacific Affairs* 15 (1942), 261-79.

T.A. Bisson, "Problems of Production Control in Japan," *Pacific Affairs* 16 (1943), 301-10.

Kazuo Nonomura, "The Development of Wartime Reproduction Theories in Japan," *Annals of the Hitotsubashi Academy* 3:2 (Apr 1953), 179-90.

Kanae Hatano, "From Semi-wartime to Wartime Control of the Iron and Steel Industry," in Secretariat, Institute of Pacific Relations, ed. *Industrial Japan: Aspects of Recent Economic Changes as Viewed by Japanese Writers*, New York, Institute of Pacific Relations, 1941, 114-31.

Richard Rice, "Economic Mobilization in Wartime Japan: Business, Bureaucracy and the Military in Conflict," *Journal of Asian Studies* 38:4 (Aug 1979), 689-706.

Dan Kurzman, *Kishi and Japan: The Search for the Sun*, New York, Ivan Obolensky, 1960. (scattered comments on economic policy).

Chalmers Johnson, *MITI and the Japanese Miracle: The Growth of Industrial Policy, 1925-1975*, Stanford University Press, 1982.

Jerome Cohen, *Japan's Economy in War and Reconstruction*, University of Minnesota Press, 1949. (reprint: Greenwood Press, 1973).

Takafusa Nakamura, *The Postwar Japanese Economy: Its Development and Structure*, University of Tokyo Press, 1981.

C. DOMESTIC ECONOMIC INSTITUTIONS

Industry

Richard B. Rice, "Hitachi: Japanese Industry in an Era of Militarism, 1937-1945," Ph.D. dissertation, Harvard University, 1974 [Archives call no. HU 90/10838/10].

Tomoyoshi Murayama, "The Wartime Publishing Industry," *CJ* 9:5 (May 1940), 595-605.

Kamekichi Takahashi, "The Situation of Small & Middle Industries," *CJ* 10:7 (July 1941), 889-96.

Alvin Barber, "Steel in Japan's War Economy," *Amerasia* 5 (Aug 1941), 256-65.

T.A. Bisson, "Increase of *Zaibatsu* Predominance in Wartime Japan," *Pacific Affairs* 18 (1945), 55-61.

T.A. Bisson, "The *Zaibatsu*'s Wartime Role," *Pacific Affairs* 18 (1945), 355-68.

The United States Strategic Bombing Survey, Nakajima Aircraft Company. Ltd., Corporation Report No. 11, Aircraft Division, June 1947.

Labor & Social Conditions

Ernest J. Notar, "Japan's Wartime Labor Policy: A Search for Method," *Journal of Asian Studies* 44:2 (Feb 1985), 311-28.

Tayeko Watanabe, "Wartime Industry and Female Labour," *CJ* 8:3 (May 1939), 363-70.

B.F. Johnston et al, *Japanese Food Management in World War II*, Stanford University Press, 1957.

Kaichiro Oishi & Yoshiaki Nishida, "Food Supply and Reorganization of Rural Community in Japan, 1937-1945," *Annals of the Institute of Social Science* 27 (1985), 80-99.

Thomas Havens, *Valley of Darkness: The Japanese People and World War Two*, New York, W.W. Norton, 1978.

D. ECONOMIC DIPLOMACY AND WAR

Lloyd C. Gardner, *Economic Aspects of New Deal Diplomacy*, Boston, Beacon Press, 1971 (orig. pub., 1964), esp. 133-51.

John C. de Wilde, "Can Japan Be Quarantined?" *Foreign Policy Reports* (Foreign Policy Association) 13:18 (Dec 1, 1937).

Elizabeth Boody Schumpeter, "The Problems of Sanctions in the Far East," *Pacific Affairs* 12 (1939), 245-62.

Shinjiro Nagaoka, "Economic Demands on the Dutch East Indies," in James W. Morley, ed. *The Fateful Choice: Japan's Advance into Southeast Asia, 1939-1941*, Columbia University Press, 1980, 125-53.

Katausaburo Sasaki, "The Economic Pact with French Indo-China," *CJ* 10:5 (May 1941), 758-67.

Jonathan Utley, "Upstairs, Downstairs at Foggy Bottom: Oil Exports and Japan, 1940-1941," *Prologue: The Journal of the National Archives* 8:1 (1976), 17-28.

Robert Goralski & Russell W. Freeburg, *Oil & War: How the Deadly Struggle for Fuel in WWII Meant Victory or Defeat*, New York, William Morrow, 1987.

E. WARTIME POLICY & ASIA

Manchuria

Hideo Yamamoto, "Profile of an Asian Minded Man III: Shiraki Tachibana," *DE* 4:3 (Sept 1966), 381-403.

Yukio Cho, "An Inquiry into the Problem of Importing American Capital into Manchuria: A Note on Japanese-American Relations, 1931-1941," in Dorothy Borg & Shumpei Okamoto, eds. *Pearl Harbor as History: Japanese-American Relations, 1931-1941, Columbia University Press, 1973, 377-410.*

China

T.K. Koo, "Some Economic Documents Relating to the Genesis of the Japanese-Sponsored Regime in North China," *Far Eastern Quarterly* 6:1 (Nov 1946), 65-77.

Burke Inlow, "Japan's Special Trade' in North China, 1935-37," *Far Eastern Quarterly* 6:2 (Feb 1947), 139-67.

Takafusa Nakamura, "Japan's Economic Thrust into North China, 1933-1938: Formation of the North China Development Corporation," in Akira Iriye, ed. *The Chinese and the Japanese: Essays in Political and Cultural Interactions*, Princeton University Press, 1980, 220-53.

Shintaro Ryu, "Problems of North China Development," *CJ* 7:2 (Sept 1938), 259-68.

Chuan-hua Lowe, *Japan's Economic Offensive in China*, London, Allen & Unwin, 1939.

D.K. Lieu, "The Sino-Japanese Currency War," *Pacific Affairs* 12 (1939), 413-26.

Nobutaro Kawashima, "Economic Background of the Sino-Japanese Conflict," *CJ* 9:4 (Apr 1940), 413-24.

Lincoln Li, *The Japanese Army in North China, 1937-1941: Problems of Political and Economic Control*, Tokyo, Oxford University Press, 1975, esp. 122-86.

Arthur N. Young, *China's Wartime Finance & Inflation, 1937-1945*, Harvard University Press, 1965.

Co-Prosperity Sphere

Kamekichi Takahashi, "World Economy and the Monroe Doctrine," *CJ* 9:9 (Sept 1940), 1120-30.

Kamekichi Takahashi, "Economic Significance of the East Asiatic Co-Prosperity Sphere," *CJ* 10:1 (Jan 1941), 39-49.

Nobutaro Kawashima, "Our Past Foreign Trade Policy and the New Order," *CJ* 10:2 (Feb 1941), 161-70.

Fumio Yamada, "Economic Basis of our Southward Development," *CJ* 10:7 (July 1941), 871-82.

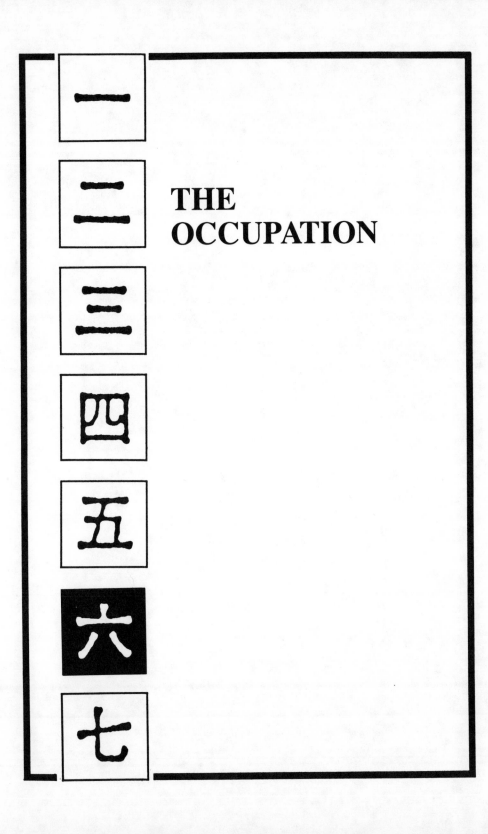

一
二
三
四
五
六
七

THE OCCUPATION

A. GENERAL

Reference

Robert Ward & Frank Shulman, eds. *The Allied Occupation of Japan, 1945-1952: An Annotated Bibliography of Western-Language Materials*, Chicago, American Library Association, 1974.

"Occupied Japan & the Cold War in Asia," in John W. Dower, *Japanese History & Culture From Ancient To Modern Times: Seven Basic Bibliographies*, New York, Markus Wiener, 1986, 199-222. (See especially the list of SCAP Monographs, pp. 207-08).

The Financial History of Japan: The Allied Occupation Period, 1945-1952, vol. 20, *English Documents*, ed. by Ikuhiko Hata & William Wray for Japanese Ministry of Finance, Tokyo, Toyo Keizai Shimposha, 1982 [Japanese title: *Showa zaiseishi: Shusen kara kowa made*], contains major documents on all topics listed below. Abbreviated in this section as *Financial History*.

U.S. Department of State, *Foreign Relations of the United States*, Japan Volume, 1945-early 1950s.

Jon Livingston, et al., comp. *Postwar Japan: 1945 to the Present*, New York, Pantheon, 1973.

Surveys

Pre-Surrender Planning, in *Financial History*, 79-149.

Kazuo Kawai, *Japan's American Interlude*, University of Chicago Press, 1960.

Hugh T. Patrick, "The Phoenix Risen from the Ashes: Postwar Japan," in James B. Crowley, ed. *Modern East Asia: Essays in Interpretation*, New York, Harcourt, Brace & World, 1970, 298-336.

Yonosuke Nagai & Akira Iriye, eds. *The Origins of the Cold War in Asia*, University of Tokyo Press, 1977.

J.W. Dower, *Empire and Aftermath: Yoshida Shigeru and the Japanese Experience, 1878-1954*, Harvard University Press, 1979.

Lawrence H. Redford, *The Occupation of Japan: Economic Policy and Reform*, Norfolk, The MacArthur Memorial, 1980.

Takafusa Nakamura, *The Postwar Japanese Economy: Its Development and Structure*, University of Tokyo Press, 1981.

Yutaka Kosai, *The Era of High-Speed Growth: Notes on the Postwar Japanese Economy*, University of Tokyo Press, 1986.

Nisuke Ando, "Surrender, Occupation, and Private Property in International Law: An Evaluation of Some United States Practices during the Occupation of Surrendered Japan," *Kobe International Law Review* (1) 20 (1986), 1-60; (2) 21 (1987), 9-78.

Robert E. Ward & Yoshikazu Sakamoto, eds. *Democratizing Japan: The Allied Occupation*, University Press of Hawaii, 1987.

Yutaka Kosai, "The Postwar Japanese Economy, 1945-1973," in Peter Duus, ed. *The Cambridge History of Japan*, vol. VI, *The Twentieth Century*, Cambridge University Press, 1989.

Contemporary Accounts

The Yoshida Memoirs: The Story of Japan in Crisis, trans. Kenichi Yoshida, Boston, Houghton Mifflin, 1962.

U.S. Department of State, *Occupation of Japan: Policy and Progress*, Washington, D.C., Government Printing Office, 1946 (Greenwood Press reprint, 1969), esp. 37-46.

Robert W. Barnett, "Occupied Japan: The Economic Aspect," in Seymour E. Harris, ed. *Foreign Economic Policy for the United States*, Harvard University Press, 1948, 104-33.

Edwin M. Martin, *Allied Occupation of Japan*, New York, Institute of Pacific Relations, 1948.

Jerome B. Cohen, "Japan's Economy on the Road Back," *Pacific Affairs* 21 (1948), 264-79.

Jerome B. Cohen, "Reform versus Recovery," *Far Eastern Survey* 17:12 (June 23, 1948), 137-42.

Shigeto Tsuru, "Toward Economic Stability in Japan," *Pacific Affairs* 22:4 (Dec 1949), 357-66.

T.A. Bisson, *Prospects for Democracy in Japan*, New York, Macmillan, 1949, esp. 94-122.

Robert A. Fearey, *The Occupation of Japan: Second Phase, 1948-50*, New York, Macmillan, 1950.

William Adams Brown, Jr. & Redvers Opie, *American Foreign Assistance*, Washington, D.C., The Brookings Institution, 1953, (352-70, "Japan").

Theodore Cohen, *Remaking Japan: The American Occupation as New Deal*, ed. by Herbert Passin, New York, The Free Press, 1987.

B. GOVERNMENT CONTROLS

"Economic Disarmament and Reparations," in *Financial History*, 430-88.

Edwin W. Pauley, *Report on Japanese Assets in Manchuria to the President of the United States*, Washington, D.C., 1946.

Edwin W. Pauley, *Report on Japanese Reparations to the President of the United States, November 1945 to April 1946*, Department of State Publication 3174, Far Eastern Series 25 ("Pauley Report").

T.A. Bisson, "The Economic Purge in Japan," *Far Eastern Quarterly* 12 (May 1953), 279-99.

Yoshiya Ariyoshi, *Half a Century in Shipping*, Tokyo News Service, 1977.

Leon Hollerman, "International Economic Controls in Occupied Japan," *Journal of Asian Studies* 38:4 (Aug 1979), 707-19.

C. ZAIBATSU DISSOLUTION

Zaibatsu

Report on the Mission on Japanese Combines, Part I: Analytical and Technical Data (A Report to the Dept. of State and the War Dept., March 1946), Department of State Publication 2628, Far Eastern Series 14, Washington, U.S. Government Printing Office. (See also the formerly secret Part II).

C.D. Edwards, "The Dissolution of Zaibatsu Combines," *Pacific Affairs* 19:3 (Sept 1946), 227-40.

Eleanor M. Hadley, "Trust Busting in Japan," *Harvard Business Review* 27:4 (July 4, 1948), 425-40.

The Holding Company Liquidation Commission, ed. *Laws, Rules and Regulations Concerning the Reconstruction and Democratization of Japanese Economy*, Tokyo, Kaiguchi Publishing Co., 1949.

Thomas A. Bisson, *Zaibatsu Dissolution in Japan*, University of California Press, 1954.

Mitsubishi Economic Research Institute, *Mitsui-Mitsubishi-Sumitomo: Present Status of the Former Zaibatsu Enterprises*, 1955.

Kazuo Kawai, *Japan's American Interlude*, University of Chicago Press, 1960, 133-59.

Kazuo Shibagaki, "Dissolution of Zaibatsu and Deconcentration of Economic Power," *Annals of the Institute of Social Science* 20 (1979), 1-60.

Konosuke Matsushita, *Quest for Prosperity: The Life of a Japanese Industrialist*, Kyoto, PHP Institute, 1988, 241-57.

Industrial Organization

Eleanor M. Hadley, "Japan: Competition or Private Collectivism?" *Far Eastern Survey* 18:25 (Dec 14, 1949), 289-94.

Kozo Yamamura, "An Observation on the Post-war Japanese Anti-monopoly Policy," *Indian Journal of Economics* 45 (July 1964), 31-68.

Kozo Yamamura, *Economic Policy in Postwar Japan: Growth versus Economic Democracy*, University of California Press, 1967.

Eleanor M. Hadley, *Antitrust in Japan*, Princeton University Press, 1970.

Masu Uekusa, "Effects of the Deconcentration Measures in Japan," *Antitrust Bulletin* 22 (Fall 1977), 687-715.

U.S. Policy Formation

"Economic Reform," in *Financial History*, 320-429.

Joyce & Gabriel Kolko, *The Limits of Power: The World and United States Foreign Policy, 1945-1954*, New York, Harper & Row, 1972, esp. 300-25 & 510-33.

Howard Schonberger, "Zaibatsu Dissolution and the American Restoration of Japan," *Bulletin of Concerned Asian Scholars* 5:2 (Sept 1973), 16-31.

Howard Schonberger, "The Japan Lobby in American Diplomacy, 1947-1952," *Pacific Historical Review* 46:3 (Aug 1977), 327-59.

John G. Roberts, "The 'Japan Crowd' and the Zaibatsu Restoration," *Japan Interpreter* 12:3-4 (Sum 1979), 384-415.

Eleanor M. Hadley, "From Deconcentration to Reverse Course," in Robert Wolfe, ed. *Americans as Proconsuls*, Southern Illinois University Press, 1984, 138-54.

Michael Schaller, *The American Occupation of Japan: The Origins of the Cold War in Asia*, New York, Oxford University Press, 1985.

Michael Schaller, "MacArthur's Japan: The View from Washington," *Diplomatic History* 10:1 (Win 1986), 1-23.

D. JAPANESE MANAGEMENT & LABOR

Hideo Otake, "The *Zaikai* under the Occupation: The Formation and Transformation of Managerial Councils," in Robert E. Ward & Yoshikazu Sakamoto, eds. *Democratizing Japan: The Allied Occupation*, University Press of Hawaii, 1987, 366-91.

Ichiro Nakayama, "Facts about Japan's Unemployment," *CJ* 18 (July-Sept 1949), 292-308.

Miriam S. Farley, *Aspects of Japan's Labor Problems*, John Day, 1950.

Robert B. Textor, *Failure in Japan: With Keystones for a Positive Policy*, New York, The John Day Co., 1951, 126-48.

Kanae Iida, "The Origin of the Enterprise Union in the Post-War Labour Movement of Japan," *Keio Economic Studies* 7:1 (1970), 46-63.

Chalmers Johnson, *Conspiracy at Matsukawa*, University of California, 1972.

Kiyoshi Yamamoto, "'The Production Control Struggle' in the Period of Postwar Crisis," *Annals of the Institute of Social Science* 13 (1972), 63-73.

Yoshio Sugimoto, "Labor Reform and Industrial Turbulence: The Case of the American Occupation of Japan," *Pacific Sociological Review* 20 (Oct 1977), 492-513.

Howard Schonberger, "American Labor's Cold War in Occupied Japan," *Diplomatic History* 3:3 (Sum 1979), 249-72.

Joe Moore, *Japanese Workers and the Struggle for Power, 1945-1947*, University of Wisconsin Press, 1983.

Sheldon M. Garon, "The Imperial Bureaucracy and Labor Policy in Postwar Japan," *Journal of Asian Studies* 43:3 (May 1984), 441-57.

Koshi Endo, "Reflections on the Turnabout in Labor Relations Policy in Occupied Japan," *Annals of the Institute of Social Science* 26 (1984), 78-101.

Joe Moore, "Production Control: Workers' Control in Early Postwar Japan," *Bulletin of Concerned Asian Scholars* 17:4 (Oct-Dec 1985), 2-26.

Andrew Gordon, *The Evolution of Labor Relations in Japan: Heavy Industry, 1853-1955*, Harvard University Press, 1985.

Koji Taira, "Economic Development, Labor Markets, and Industrial Relations in Japan, 1905-1955," in Peter Duus, ed. *The Cambridge History of Japan*, vol. VI, *The Twentieth Century*, Cambridge University Press, 1989.

E. LAND REFORM

On Land Reform, documents #6-5, 6-11, 6-34, and 6-46, in *Financial History*.

Nochi kaikaku shiryo hensan iinkai, ed. *Nochi kaikaku shiryo shusei* [Collected Materials on the Land Reform], vol. 14, *GHQ/SCAP shiryo hen* [GHQ/SCAP Document Volume], Tokyo, Nosei Chosakai, 1982, 913pp. (English document volume, with Japanese introduction).

"Retrospect on and Documents of Land Reform in Japan," *DE* 4:2 (June 1966), 195-219.

Tsutomu Takizawa, "Historical Background of Agricultural Land Reform in Japan," *DE* 10:3 (1972), 290-310.

W.N. Gilmartin & W.I. Ladejinsky, "Promise of Agrarian Reform in Japan," *Foreign Affairs* 26:2 (Jan 1948), 312-24.

Lawrence I. Hewes, *Japan: Land and Men—An Account of the Japanese Land Reform Program, 1945-51*, Ames, Iowa State College Press, 1955.

Ronald Dore, *Land Reform in Japan*, Oxford University Press, 1959.

Wolf I. Ladejinsky, "Agrarian Revolution in Japan," *Foreign Affairs* 38 (Oct 1959), 95-109.

Tsutomu Ouchi, "The Japanese Land Reform: Its Efficacy and Limitations," *DE* 4:2 (June 1966), 129-50.

Masaru Kajita, "Land Policy after Land Reform in Japan," *DE* 3:1 (March 1965), 88-105.

Shigeto Kawano, "Economic Significance of the Land Reform in Japan," *DE* 3:2 (June 1965), 139-57.

Tsutomu Takigawa, "A Note on the Comparative Analysis of Agrarian Reform," *DE* 4:2 (June 1966), 245-55.

Hiromitsu Kaneda, "Structural Change and Policy Response in Japanese Agriculture after the Land Reform," in Lawrence H. Reford, ed. *The Occupation of Japan: Economic Policy and Reform*, Norfolk, The MacArthur Memorial, 1980, 91-160.

Ann Waswo, "The Transformation of Rural Society, 1900-1950," in Peter Duus, ed. *The Cambridge History of Japan*, vol. VI, *The Twentieth Century*, Cambridge University Press, 1989.

Richard K. Beardsley, John W. Hall, & Robert E. Ward, *Village Japan*, University of Chicago Press, 1959.

F. TAXATION

"Finance," in *Financial History*, 674-731.

Martin Bronfenbrenner, "The Japanese Value-added Sales Tax," *National Tax Journal* 3 (Dec 1950), 298-313.

The following articles from *Annals of the Hitotsubashi Academy*:
Hanya Ito, "The Value-added Tax in Japan," 1:1 (Oct 1950), 43-59.
Chotaro Takahashi, "The Income Tax Burden: A Japanese Experiment," 1:1 (Oct 1950), 60-79.
Motokazu Kimura, "Taxation and Capital Accumulation," 4:1 (Oct 1953), 15-39.
Motokazu Kimura, "An Unrealized Plan: The Value-Added Tax in Japan," 8:2 (Apr 1958), 113-26.

Hanya Ito, "Direct Taxes in Japan and the Shoup Report," *Public Finance* 8:4 (1953), 357-83.

M. Bronfenbrenner & K. Kogiku, "The Aftermath of the Shoup Tax Reforms, Part I and Part II," *National Tax Journal* 10 (Sept 1957), 236-54; 10 (Dec 1957), 345-60.

G. FINANCIAL & INDUSTRIAL POLICIES

Domestic Policies

Financial History, including:
"Economic Control and Planning," 489-581.
"The Dodge Line," 732-97.
"Money and Banking," 798-824.

Ichiro Katano, "Business Income during the Inflation in Japan," *Annals of the Hitotsubashi Academy* 4:2 (Apr 1954), 98-111.

Ichiro Katano, "Accounting Theory for Determining the Amount of Compensation for War Damage to Shares Owned by Allied Nationals under Post-War Inflationary Condition in Japan," *Hitotsubashi Journal of Commerce and Management* 1:1 (March 1961), 21-35.

Hyoe Ouchi, *Financial and Monetary Situation in Post-War Japan*, Institute of Pacific Relations, 1947.

Ryokichi Minobe, "The Economic Stabilization Program for Japan," *CJ* 18 (Jan-March 1949), 20-33.

Martin Bronfenbrenner, "Four Positions on Japanese Finance," *Journal of Political Economy* 58:4 (1950), 281-88.

T.F.M. Adams, *Japanese Securities Markets: A Historical Survey*, Tokyo, Seihei Okuyama, 1953.

Edna E. Ehrlich & Frank M. Tamagna, "Japan," in Benjamin Haggott Beckhart, ed. *Banking Systems*, Columbia University Press, 1954, 517-71.

Saburo Shiomi, *Japan's Finance and Taxation, 1940-1956*, Columbia University Press, 1957.

Sherwood M. Fine, "Japan's Postwar Industrial Recovery," *CJ* 21 (1952), 165-216.

Sherwood M. Fine, *Japan's Postwar Industrial Recovery*, Foreign Affairs Association of Japan, 1953.

Tsunesaburo Tokoyama, "Economic Recovery and Public Finance in Post-War Japan," *Public Finance* 8:3 (1953), 283-216.

Martin Bronfenbrenner, "Inflation Theories of the SCAP Period," *History of Political Economy* 7:2 (1975), 137-55.

Chalmers Johnson, *Japan's Public Policy Companies*, Washington, American Enterprise Institute, 1978.

Chalmers Johnson, *MITI and the Japanese Miracle: The Growth of Industrial Policy, 1925-1975*, Stanford University Press, 1982.

Ryoichi Miwa, "Government and the Japanese Shipping Industry, 1945-64," *Journal of Transport History* 9:1 (March 1988), 37-49.

International & Geopolitical Issues

Leon Hollerman, "Japan and Far Eastern Development," *Pacific Affairs* 24 (1951), 372-97.

Henry F. Angus, *Canada and the Far East, 1940-53*, University of Toronto Press, 1953.

Mitsuru Yamamoto, "The Cold War and U.S.-Japan Economic Cooperation," in Yonosuke Nagai & Akira Iriye, eds. *The Origins of the Cold War in Asia*, University of Tokyo Press, 1977, 408-25.

Lawrence H. Reford, ed. *The Occupation of Japan: Economic Policy and Reform*, Norfolk, The MacArthur Memorial, 1980, 269-316, including:
Roger W. Buckley, "The British Foreign Office and Economic Policy for Japan."
Leon Hollerman, "The Formation of International Economic Policy during the Occupation of Japan."

Michael Schaller, "Securing the Great Crescent: Occupied Japan and the Origins of Containment in Southeast Asia," *Journal of American History* 69:2 (Sept 1982), 392-414.

William S. Borden, *The Pacific Alliance: United States Foreign Economic Policy and Japanese Trade Recovery, 1947-1955*, University of Wisconsin Press, 1984.

Michael Schaller, *The American Occupation of Japan: The Origins of the Cold War in Asia*, New York, Oxford University Press, 1985.

Robert A. Pollard, *Economic Security and the Origins of the Cold War, 1945-1950*, Columbia University Press, 1985, esp. 168-96.

Howard B. Schonberger, "The Cold War and the American Empire in Asia," *Radical History Review* 33 (1985), 139-54.

H.W. Brands, Jr., "The United States and the Reemergence of Independent Japan," *Pacific Affairs* 59:3 (Fall 1986), 387-401.

Alan Rix, *The Politics of Australia's Trade with Japan, 1945-1957*, Sydney, 1986.

H. TRADE & FOREIGN EXCHANGE

"Aid and Trade," in *Financial History*, 582-673.

Frank M. Tamagna, "The Fixing of Foreign Exchange Rates," *Journal of Political Economy* 53:1 (March 1945), 57-72.

Saburo Miyakawa, ed. *Japan's Export Industries, 1949*, Tokyo, Oriental Economist, 1948.

Masahiro Fujita, "The Exchange Control Policy in Post-war Japan," *Kobe Economic and Business Review* 1 (1953), 65-91.

Shigeru Fujii, "Recovery and Development of Foreign Trade Firms in Kobe after the War," *Kobe University Economic Review* 3 (1957), 25-52. (re: trading companies).

Fukuo Kawata, "Trade Controls in Occupied Japan (1945-1949)," *Kobe Economic and Business Review* 13 (1966), 9-22.

Leon Hollerman, "Interventionism and Foreign Trade Statistics in Occupied Japan," in Hollerman, ed. *Japan and the United States: Economic and Political Adversaries*, Boulder, Westview Press, 1979, 1-12.

I. SOCIAL ISSUES

Irene B. Taeuber, "Japan's Increasing People: Facts, Problems and Policies," *Pacific Affairs* 23 (1950), 271-93.

Tokijiro Minoguchi, "The Over-Population Problem in Post-war Japan," *Annals of the Hitotsubashi Academy* 1:2 (Apr 1951), 111-19.

Kazushi Ohkawa, "Measurements of Standards of Living of the Working Classes in Japan," *Annals of the Hitotsubashi Academy* 1:2 (Apr 1951), 120-37.

Tomitaro Hirata, "International Social Security and Japanese Social Insurance Systems," *Waseda Economic Papers* 2 (1958), 28-46.

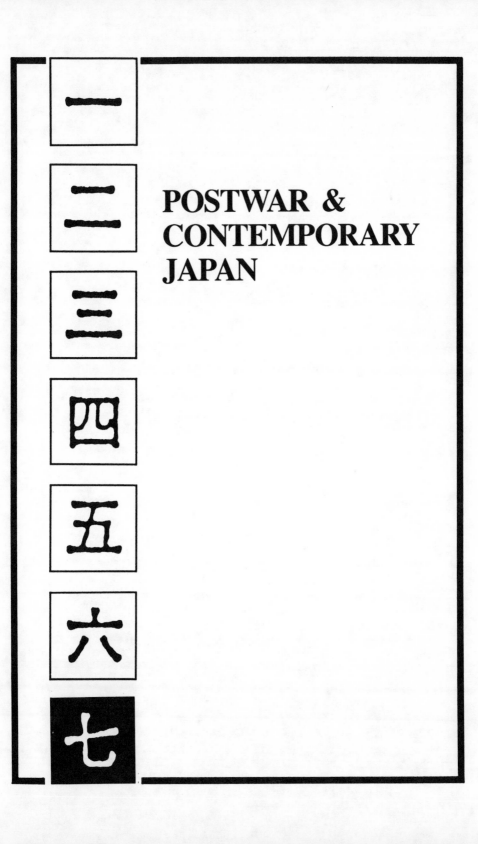

一
二
三
四
五
六
七

POSTWAR & CONTEMPORARY JAPAN

1. GENERAL

A. OVERVIEWS & GENERAL ISSUES

Reference

Japan, Economic Planning Agency, *Economic Survey of Japan*, annual.

Oriental Economist, *Japan Company Handbook*, 1st and 2nd Half, annual.

Keizai Koho Center (Japan Institute for Social and Economic Affairs), *Japan 19xx: An International Comparison* (annual).

OECD, *Economic Surveys, Japan*, Paris.

Yasukichi Yasuba, "Modern Economists' Views on the Japanese Economy: A Survey," *JES* 1:2 (Win 1972-73), 3-46.

Kazuo Sato, "The State of Economic Studies in Japan," *JES* 4:3 (Spr 1976), 90-100.

Yasukichi Yasuba, "Economists and Society in Postwar Japan," *JES* 5:3 (Spr 1977), 96-104.

"The Communist View of the Japanese Economy," *JES* 7:2 (Win 1978-79), proposals by the Japan Communist Party.

Historical Surveys

Jerome B. Cohen, *Japan's Postwar Economy*, Bloomington, Indiana University Press, 1958.

Yutaka Matsumura, *Japan's Economic Growth, 1945-60*, Tokyo, Tokyo News Service, 1961.

Hugh T. Patrick, "The Phoenix Risen from the Ashes: Postwar Japan," in James B. Crowley, ed. *Modern East Asia: Essays in Interpretation*, New York, Harcourt, Brace & World, 1970, 298-336.

Andrea Boltho, *Japan: An Economic Survey, 1953-1973*, Oxford University Press, 1975.

Hugh Patrick and Henry Rosovsky, "Japan's Economic Performance: An Overview," in Hugh Patrick & Henry Rosovsky, eds. *Asia's New Giant: How the Japanese Economy Works*, Brookings Institution, 1976, 1-61.

Takafusa Nakamura, *The Postwar Japanese Economy: Its Development and Structure*, University of Tokyo Press, 1981.

Tatsuro Uchino, *Japan's Postwar Economy*, Tokyo, Kodansha, 1982.

Gianni Fodella, ed. *Japan's Economy in a Comparative Perspective*, Tenterden, U.K., Norbury, 1983.

Yutaka Kosai, *The Era of High-Speed Growth: Notes on the Postwar Japanese Economy*, University of Tokyo Press, 1986.

Martin Bronfenbrenner, "Japan and Two World Economic Depressions," in Ronald Dore & Radha Sinha, eds. *Japan and the World Depression, Then and Now: Essays in Memory of E.F. Penrose*, London, Macmillan, 1987, 32-51.

Edwin O. Reischauer, *The Japanese Today: Change and Continuity*, Harvard University Press, 1988, esp. 295-412.

Yutaka Kosai, "The Postwar Japanese Economy, 1945–1973," in Peter Duus, ed. *The Cambridge History of Japan*, vol. VI, *The Twentieth Century*, Cambridge University Press, 1989.

Structural Analyses

Miyohei Shinohara, "Inventory Cycles in Post-War Japan," *Annals of the Hitotsubashi Academy* 9:2 (Apr 1959), 218-32.

William W. Lockwood, "Japan's 'New Capitalism'," in Lockwood, ed. *The State and Economic Enterprise in Japan*, Princeton University Press, 1965, 447-522.

Ken Bieda, *The Structure and Organization of the Japanese Economy*, Sydney, Wiley, 1970.

Kazuo Sato, "Growth and Technical Change in Japan's Nonprimary Economy, 1930-1967," *JES* 1:4 (Sum 1973), 63-103.

Gianni Fodella, *Social Structure and Economic Dynamics in Japan up to 1980*, Milan, Luigi Bocconi University, 1975.

Kanji Haitani, *The Japanese Economic System: An Institutional Overview*, Lexington, Heath, 1976.

Hugh Patrick & Henry Rosovsky, eds. *Asia's New Giant: How the Japanese Economy Works*, Brookings Institution, 1976.

Lewis Austin, ed. *Japan: The Paradox of Progress*, Yale University Press, 1976.

Tadashi Kawata, "The Japanese Economic Disequilibrium," *DE* 14:1 (March 1976), 3-20.

Special Issue: "Econometric Studies on the Structure of the Japanese Economy," *Keio Economic Studies* 15:1 (1978).

Hideichiro Nakamura, "Japan, Incorporated and Postwar Democracy," *JES* 6:3-4 (Spr-Sum 1978), 68-109.

Hyoe Murakami & Johannes Hirschmeier, eds. *Politics and Economics in Contemporary Japan*, Tokyo, Japan Culture Institute, 1979.

William V. Rapp & Robert A. Feldman, "Japan's Economic Strategy and Prospects," in William J. Barnds, ed. *Japan and the United States: Challenges and Opportunities*, Council on Foreign Relations, New York University Press, 1979, 86-154.

Kazuo Sato, ed. *Industry and Business in Japan*, White Plains, N.Y., M.E. Sharpe, 1980.

William V. Rapp & Robert A. Feldman, "Japan's Economic Strategy and Prospects," in William J. Barnds, ed. *Japan and the United States: Challenges and Opportunities*, London, Macmillan, 1980, 86-154.

Bradley M. Richardson & Taizo Ueda, *Business and Society in Japan: Fundamentals for Businessmen*, New York, Praeger, 1981.

G.C. Allen, *The Japanese Economy*, London, Weidenfeld and Nicolson, 1981.

Y. Nakagawa & N. Ota, *The Japanese Economic System: A New Balance Between Intervention and Freedom*, Tokyo, Foreign Press Centre, 1981.

Yasusuke Murakami, "Toward a Socioinstitutional Explanation of Japan's Economic Performance," in Kozo Yamamura, ed. *Policy and Trade Issues of the Japanese Economy: American and Japanese Perspectives*, University of Washington Press, 1982, 3-46.

Daniel I. Okimoto, ed. *Japan's Economy: Coping with Change in the International Environment*, Boulder, Westview Press, 1982.

Rob Steven, *Classes in Contemporary Japan*, Cambridge University Press, 1983.

Hideichiro Nakamura, "Is Japan's Economic Strength Fortuitous?" *JES* 11:3 (Spr 1983), 48-74.

Ronald Dore, "Goodwill and the Spirit of Market Capitalism," *The British Journal of Sociology* 34:4 (1983), 459-81.

Yutaka Kosai & Yoshitaro Ogino, *The Contemporary Japanese Economy*, London, Macmillan, 1984.

Thomas Pepper, Merit E. Janow, & Jimmy W. Wheeler, *The Competition: Dealing with Japan*, New York, Praeger, 1985.

Economic Views from Japan: Selections from Economic Eye, Tokyo, Keizai Koho Center, 1986.

T.J. Pempel, *Japan: The Dilemmas of Success*, New York, Foreign Policy Association, 1986.

Tessa Morris-Suzuki & Takuro Seiyama, *Japanese Capitalism since 1945: Critical Perspectives*, London, Athlone, 1987.

Kimio Uno, *Japanese Industrial Performance*, Amsterdam, North Holland, 1987.

Kozo Yamamura & Yasukichi Yasuba, eds. *The Political Economy of Japan*, vol. 1, *The Domestic Transformation*, Stanford University Press, 1987.

Bruce Babcock, "The Japanese Economy After Endaka," *Journal of Northeast Asian Studies* 6:3 (Fall 1987), 51-67.

"The Economic Miracle in Perspective," in E. Patricia Tsurumi (for the *Bulletin of Concerned Asian Scholars*), ed. *The Other Japan: Postwar Realities*, Armonk, N.Y., M.E. Sharpe, 1988, 78-162.

Edward J. Lincoln, *Japan: Facing Economic Maturity*, Washington, D.C., The Brookings Institution, 1988.

Daniel Okimoto & Thomas P. Rohlen, eds. *Inside the Japanese System: Readings on Contemporary Society and Political Economy*, Stanford University Press, 1988.

David Friedman, *The Misunderstood Miracle: Industrial Development and Political Change in Japan*, Cornell University Press, 1988.

Growth

M. Bronfenbrenner, "Notes on the Productivity Campaign in Japan," *Studies on Asia* 1 (1960), 63-78.

Kiyoshi Kojima, "Economic Development and Import Dependence in Japan," *Hitotsubashi Journal of Economics* 1:1 (Oct 1960), 29-51.

Saburo Okita, "Economic Growth of Postwar Japan," *DE* preliminary issue 2 (1962).

Kazushi Ohkawa & Henry Rosovsky, "Recent Japanese Growth in Historical Perspective," *American Economic Review* 53:2 (May 1963), 578-88.

Leon Hollerman, "Japan's Place in the Scale of Economic Development," *Economic Development and Cultural Change* 12:2 (Jan 1964), 139-57.

Miyohei Shinohara, "Factors in Japan's Economic Growth," *Hitotsubashi Journal of Economics* 4:1&2 (Feb 1964), 21-36.

Martin Bronfenbrenner, ""Economic Miracles and Japan's Income-Doubling Plan," in William W. Lockwood, ed. *The State and Economic Enterprise in Japan*, Princeton University Press, 1965, 523-53.

Ryutaro Komiya, ed. *Postwar Economic Growth in Japan*, University of California Press, 1966.

Kozo Yamamura, "Growth vs. Economic Democracy in Japan—1945-1965," *Journal of Asian Studies* 25:4 (Aug 1966), 713-28.

Yoshikazu Miyazaki, "Rapid Economic Growth in Post-War Japan: With Special Reference to 'Excessive Competition and the Formation of *Keiretsu*'," *DE* 5:2 (June 1967), 329-50.

William V. Rapp, "Theory of Changing Trade Patterns Under Economic Growth: Tested for Japan," *Yale Economic Essays* 7:2 (Fall 1967), 69-135.

Kazushi Ohkawa & Henry Rosovsky, "Postwar Japanese Growth in Historical Perspective: A Second Look," in Lawrence Klein & Kazushi Ohkawa, eds. *Economic Growth: The Japanese Experience since the Meiji Era*, Yale Economic Growth Series, Homewood, Ill., Richard D. Irwin, 1968, 3-34.

Miyohei Shinohara, "Causes and Patterns in the Postwar Growth," *DE* 8:4 (1970), 349-68.

Kenneth K. Kurihara, *The Growth Potential of the Japanese Economy*, Baltimore, Johns Hopkins University Press, 1971.

Hisao Kanamori, "What Accounts for Japan's High Rate of Growth," *Review of Income and Wealth* 18:2 (June 1972), 155-71.

Hisao Kanamori, "What Makes Japan's Economic Growth Rate High," *JES* 1:1 (Fall 1972), 31-48.

Tuvia Blumenthal, "Exports and Economic Growth in Postwar Japan," *Quarterly Journal of Economics* 86 (Nov 1972), 617-31.

Special Issue: "Japanese Economy at the Crossroads," *DE* 10:4 (Dec 1972), including:
Ichiro Nakayama, "Future Direction of Economic Growth," 329-39.

Kazuo Sato, "Growth and Technical Change in Japan's Nonprimary Economy, 1930-1967," *JES* 1 (Sum 1973), 63-103.

Richard Kosobud, "Measured Productivity Growth in Japan, 1952-1968," *JES* 2:3 (Spr 1974), 80-118.

Nobuko Nosse, "National Income and Expenditure at Factor Cost in Japan, 1955-1970: A Macro-Accounting for Growing Economy," *Kobe Economic and Business Review* 21 (1975), 23-38.

Takafusa Nakamura, "The Tarnished Phoenix," *Japan Interpreter* 9:4 (Spr 1975), 403-19.

Edward F. Denison & William K. Chung, "Economic Growth and Its Sources," in Hugh Patrick & Henry Rosovsky, eds. *Asia's New Giant: How the Japanese Economy Works*, Brookings Institution, 1976, 63-151.

Hugh Patrick, "Japanese Growth in Alternative 1980 World Economic Environments," in Lewis Austin, ed. *Japan: The Paradox of Progress*, Yale University Press, 1976, 89-140.

Kamekichi Takahashi, "Japan's Changing Growth Factors and its Future Prospects," *JES* 4:4 (Sum 1976), 3-43.

Tsuneo Iida, "The Lineage of Japanese Economics," *JES* 4:4 (Sum 1976), 63-80 (re: attitudes toward growth).

Iwao Ozaki, "The Effects of Technological Changes on the Economic Growth of Japan, 1955-1970," in K.R. Polenski & J.V. Skolka, eds. *Advances in Input-Output Analysis*, Cambridge, Ballinger, 1976.

Edward Denison & William Chung, *How Japan's Economy Grew So Fast: The Sources of Postwar Expansion*, Brookings Institution, 1976.

Masaru Yoshitomi, "The Recent Japanese Economy: The Oil Crisis and the Transition to Medium Growth Path," *DE* 14:4 (Dec 1976), 319-40.

Dale W. Jorgenson & Mieko Nishimizu, "U.S. and Japanese Economic Growth, 1952-1974: An International Comparison," *Economic Journal* 88:352 (Dec 1978).

Yoichi Shinkai, "Patterns of American and Japanese Growth and Productivity: A Japanese Perspective," *Japan Quarterly* 27:3 (July-Sept 1980), 357-75.

Takafusa Nakamura, "An Economy in Search of Stable Growth: Japan Since the Oil Crisis," *Journal of Japanese Studies* 6:1 (Win 1980), 155-78.

Kazuo Sato, "A Survey of Macroeconometric Forecasting Models of Japan: Development and Current State," *JES* 9:3 (Spr 1981), 3-60.

Seiji Shimpo, "Stagflation in Japan," *JES* 10:2 (Win 1981-82), 3-24.

Takao Komine, "The Japanese Economy's Resiliency since the Oil Crisis," *JES* 10:2 (Win 1981-82), 25-48.

Isamu Miyazaki, "The Real Reason for Japan's Success in Economic Growth," *JES* 10:3 (Spr 1982), 86-107.

Harry T. Oshima, "Reinterpreting Japan's Postwar Growth," *Economic Development and Cultural Change* 31:1 (Oct 1982), 1-43.

Hajime Imamura, "Sources of Quality Changes in Labor Input and Economic Growth in Japan, 1960-1979," *Keio Economic Studies* 19:2 (1982), 71-94.

Takashi Shiraishi, "Technological Innovation and Management Problems in Japan's Economic Growth: Its Past and Future," *Keio Business Review* 20 (1983), 117-38.

J.R. Norsworthy & H.D. Malmquist, "Input Measurement and Productivity Growth in Japanese and U.S. Manufacturing," *American Economic Review* 73 (1983), 947-66.

Tim Lee, "The Changing Composition of Economic Growth," *Asian Monetary Monitor* 7:6 (Nov-Dec 1983), 38-47.

Ryutaro Komiya & Kazuo Yasui, "Japan's Macroeconomic Performance Since the First Oil Crisis: Review and Appraisal," Carnegie-Rochester Conference Series on Public Policy, No. 20 (1984), 69-114.

Takamitsu Sawa, "The Paradigm of the High-Growth Period," *Japan Echo* 11:4 (Win 1984), 37-47.

Akiyoshi Horiuchi, "The Low Interest Rate Policy' and Economic Growth in Postwar Japan," *DE* 22:4 (Dec 1984), 349-71.

Kozo Yamamura, "The Cost of Rapid Growth and Capitalist Democracy in Japan," in Leon Lindberg & Charles Maier, eds. *The Politics of Inflation and Economic Stagnation*, Washington, The Brookings Institution, 1985, 467-508.

Kazuo Sato, "Externalization of Domestic Macroeconomic Performance: Export-Led Growth or Growth-Led Export?" in Michele Schmiegelow, ed. *Japan's Response to Crisis and Change in the World Economy*, New York, M.E. Sharpe, 1986, 181-208.

Dale W. Jorgenson, "The Oil Price Decline and Economic Growth in Japan and the U.S.," *Keio Economic Studies* 23:1 (1986), 1-19.

Dale W. Jorgenson, Masahiro Kuroda & Mieko Nishimizu, "Japan-U.S. Industry-Level Productivity Comparisons, 1960-1979," *Journal of the Japanese and International Economies* 1:1 (March 1987), 1-30.

Harry T. Oshima, *Economic Growth in Monsoon Asia: A Comparative Survey*, University of Tokyo Press, 1987, esp. 101-36, "Contrasting the Economic Growth of Prewar and Postwar Japan."

Contemporary Surveys

The Economist, *Consider Japan*, London, Gerald Duckworth & Co., Ltd., 1963.

Lee W. Farnsworth, "Japan: The Year of the Shock," *Asian Survey* 12:1 (Jan 1972), 46-55.

"Japanese Industry—Its Present & Future," *Oriental Economist*, May 1972, 37-90.

Hirofumi Uzawa, "Japan's Isolation in the International Arena—Over the New Stage of Currency Adjustment," *JES* 1:1 (Fall 1972), 7-30.

"A Special Strength: A Survey of Japan," *The Economist* March 31-April 6, 1973.

Hugh Patrick & Henry Rosovsky, "Prospects for the Future and Some Other Considerations," in Hugh Patrick & Henry Rosovsky, eds. *Asia's New Giant: How the Japanese Economy Works*, Brookings Institution, 1976, 897-923.

D.J. Daly, "Japanese Economic Developments, 1970-1976," in Shigeto Tsuru, ed. *Growth and Resources Problems Related to Japan*: Proceedings of Session VI of the Fifth Congress of the International Economic Association, Tokyo, Asahi Evening News, 1978, 315-36.

Manfred Pohl. ed. *Japan 1980/81: Politics and Economy*, Singapore, Maruzen Asia, 1981.

Symposium: "Japan," *Current History* 82:487 (Nov 1983), 353-95.

Jon Woronoff. *The Japan Syndrome: Symptoms, Ailments, and Remedies*, New Brunswick, Transaction Books, 1986.

Ronald Dore, "How Fragile a Super State?" in Ronald Dore & Radha Sinha, eds. *Japan and the World Depression, Then and Now: Essays in Memory of E.F. Penrose*, London, Macmillan, 1987, 83-110.

Peter Tasker, *Inside Japan: Wealth, Work and Power in the New Japanese Empire*, London, Sidgwick & Jackson, 1987.

Shotaro Ishinomori, *Japan, Inc.: Introduction to Japanese Economics (The Comic Book)*, University of California Press, 1988 (introduction by Peter Duus).

"Japan, 1988," *Current History* 87:528 (Apr 1988).

Views: Japan as a Model

Herman Kahn, *The Emerging Japanese Superstate: Challenge and Response*, Englewood Cliffs, N.J., Prentice-Hall, 1970.

V.K. Wickramasinghe, "Japan—The Emerging Superstate? Some Thoughts on Herman Kahn," *DE* 11:2 (June 1973), 196-210.

Ezra Vogel, *Japan as Number One: Lessons for America*, Harvard University Press, 1979.

Frank Meissner, "U.S. Export Trading Companies: Is the Japanese Success Story Reproducible, Adaptable, or Improvable?" in Michael R. Czinkota & George Tesar, eds. *Export Policy: A Global Assessment*, New York, Praeger, 1982, 131-45.

Ronald Dore, *Taking Japan Seriously: A Confucian Perspective on Leading Economic Issues*, Stanford University Press, 1987.

Susumu Awanohara, "Look East'—The Japan Model," *Asian-Pacific Economic Literature* 1:1 (May 1987), 75-89.

Peter J. Katzenstein, "Japan: Switzerland of the Far East?" in Takashi Inoguchi & Daniel Okimoto, eds. *The Political Economy of Japan*, vol. 2, *The Changing International Context*, Stanford University Press, 1988, 275-304.

B. SPECIFIC MACROECONOMIC ISSUES

Consumer Issues & Inflation

Robert S. Ozaki, "Japan's 'Price-Doubling' Plan," *Asian Survey* 5:10 (Oct 1965), 515-21.

Hiroshi Kawaguchi, "Nature and Causes of Contemporary Inflation," *DE* 10:4 (Dec 1972), 410-30.

Frank Baldwin, "The Idioms of Contemporary Japan, VI: *Kaishime*," *Japan Interpreter* 8:3 (Aut 1973), 396-409.

Maurine A. Kirkpatrick, "Consumerism and Japan's New Citizen Policies," *Asian Survey* 15 (March 1975), 234-46.

Yoichi Shinkai, "Is Stabilization Policy Possible in Japan," *JES* 5:4 (Sum 1977), 71-86.

Yoshio Suzuki, "The Inflation Debate in Japan: A Historical Survey," *JES* 11:1 (Fall 1982), 3-36.

Ching-yuan Lin, *Japanese and U.S. Inflation: A Comparative Analysis*, Lexington Books, 1984.

Hidekazu Nomura, "Consumer Co-operatives in Japan," *Kyoto University Economic Review* 56:2 (Oct 1986), 1-21.

"The Changing Japanese Consumer," Japan Economic Institute, Report No. 45A, December 2, 1988

Savings

Miyohei Shinohara, "The Structure of Savings and Consumption in Postwar Japan," *Journal of Political Economy* 67 (Oct 1959), 589-603.

R. Komiya, "The Supply of Personal Savings," Komiya, ed. *Postwar Economic Growth Japan*, University of California Press, 1966, 157-81.

T. Blumenthal, *Saving in Postwar Japan*, Harvard University Press, 1970.

Toshiyuki Mizoguchi, "High Personal Saving Rate and Changes in the Consumption Pattern in Postwar Japan," *DE* 8:4 (1970), 407-26.

Toshiyuki Mizoguchi, *Personal Savings and Consumption in Postwar Japan*, Tokyo, Kinokuniya, 1970.

Kunio Yoshihara, "The Growth Rate as a Determinant of the Saving Ratio," *Hitotsubashi Journal of Economics* 12:1 (Feb 1972), 60-72.

Tsunehiko Yui, "The Japanese Propensity for Saving," *Japan Interpreter* 8:4 (Win 1974), 478-83.

Toshimasa Shiba, "The Personal Savings Function of Urban Worker Households in Japan," *Review of Economics and Statistics* 61:2 (May 1979), 206-13.

Kazuo Sato, "Japan's Savings and Internal and External Macroeconomic Balance," in Kozo Yamamura, ed. *Policy and Trade Issues of the Japanese Economy: American and Japanese Perspectives*, University of Washington Press, 1982, 143-72.

Kazuo Sato, "Economic Laws and the Household Economy in Japan: Lags in Policy Response to Economic Changes," in Gary Saxonhouse & Kozo Yamamura, eds. *Law and Trade Issues of the Japanese Economy: American and Japanese Perspectives*, University of Washington Press, 1986,, 3-55.

Miyohei Shinohara, "The Determinants of Postwar Savings Behavior in Japan," in F. Modigliani et al., eds. *The Determinants of National Saving and Wealth*, New York, St. Martin's Press, 1983, 201-18.

Tsuneo Ishikawa & Kazuo Ueda, "The Bonus Payment System and Japanese Personal Savings," in Masahiko Aoki, ed. *The Economic Analysis of the Japanese Firm*, Amsterdam, North Holland, 1984, 133-92.

Charles Yuji Horioka, "The Applicability of the Life-Cycle Hypothesis of Saving to Japan," *Kyoto University Economic Review* 54:2 (Oct 1984), 31-56.

Charles Yuji Horioka, "The Importance of Saving for Education in Japan," *Kyoto University Economic Review* 55:1 (Apr 1985), 41-78.

Charles Y. Horioka, "Household Saving in Japan: The Importance of Target Saving for Education and Housing," Ph.D. diss., Harvard University, 1985.

Kazuo Sato, "Saving and Investment," in Kozo Yamamura & Yasukichi Yasuba, eds. *The Political Economy of Japan*, vol. 1, *The Domestic Transformation*, Stanford University Press, 1987, 137-85.

Journal of The Japanese and International Economies 2:3 (Sept 1988), the following:
Fumio Hayashi, Takatoshi Ito, & Joel Slemrod, "Housing Finance Imperfections, Taxation, and Private Saving: A Comparative Simulation Analysis of the United States and Japan," 215-38.
Kazuo Sato, "The Role of the IS Balance and Its Macroeconomic Implications: The Case of Japan," 239-58.
Philip Turner, "Savings and Investment, Exchange Rates, and International Imbalances: a Comparison of the United States, Japan, and Germany," 259-85.
Jeffrey Sachs & Peter Boone, "Japanese Structural Adjustment and the Balance of Payments," 286-327.

Susan M. Collins, "Savings and Growth Experiences of Korea and Japan," 328-50.
Charles Yuji Horioka, "Saving for Housing Purchase in Japan," 351-84.

Social Security

Tomitaro Hirata, "The National Pension System of Japan and its Problems," *Waseda Economic Papers* 7 (1962), 3-25.

Tomitaro Hirata, "Problems of Adjustment Between Public Pension and Enterprise Pension in Japan," *Waseda Economic Papers* 10 (1967), 1-27.

Masafumi Nakamura, "Drastic Revision of Medical Insurance Laws and Policies of Medical Care Cost in Japan," *Kobe University Economic Review* 18 (1972), 7-16.

Shigeyoshi Jinushi, "Social Security in Transition," *DE* 10:4 (Dec 1972), 496-515.

Satoshi Kawamoto, "Japan's Social Welfare and Public Investment in International Context," *DE* 10:4 (Dec 1972), 516-37.

Shigemi Jinushi, "Welfare: Social Security, Social Overhead Capital, and Pollution," *JES* 4:2 (Win 1975-76), 59-82.

Koichi Emi, "Financing of Health Care in Japan," *Hitotsubashi Journal of Economics* 17:1 (June 1976), 9-19.

Shigeyoshi Jinushi, "Towards Life Cycle Planning for Social Welfare in Postwar Japan," *DE* 14:4 (Dec 1976), 449-67.

Yatsuhiro Nakagawa, "Japan, the Welfare Super-Power," *Journal of Japanese Studies* 5:1 (Win 1979), 5-51.

Naomi Maruo, "The Levels of Living and Welfare in Japan Reexamined," *JES* 8:1 (Fall 1979), 42-93.

John Creighton Campbell, "The Old People Boom and Japanese Policy Making," *Journal of Japanese Studies* 5:2 (Sum 1979), 321-57.

Social Insurance Agency, *Outline of Social Insurance in Japan*, 1981, Tokyo, Yoshida Finance and Social Security Law Institute, 1981.

Yukio Noguchi, "Problem of Public Pensions in Japan," *Hitotsubashi Journal of Economics* 24:1 (June 1983), 43-68.

Taxation & Fiscal Policy

Chotaro Takahashi, "Public Investment in Postwar Japan," *Annals of the Hitotsubashi Academy* 8:2 (Apr 1958), 101-12.

Hanya Ito, "New Facts and Figures on Japanese Public Finance," *Annals of the Hitotsubashi Academy* 10:1 (Aug 1959), 1-20.

Morio Uematsu, "Computation of Income in Japanese Income Taxation: A Study in the Adjustment of Theory to Reality," in Arthur T. von Mehren, ed. *Law in Japan: The Legal Order in a Changing Society*, Harvard University Press, 1963, 567-621.

Hugh T. Patrick, ed. "Cyclical Instability and Fiscal-Monetary Policy in Postwar Japan," in William W. Lockwood, ed. *The State and Economic Enterprise in Japan*, Princeton University Press, 1965, 555-618.

Seiji Furuta, "Shifting of the Japanese Corporation Income Tax and the Differential Tax Burdens on Corporations by Size-Groups," *Keio Economic Studies* 3 (1965), 65-121.

R. Komiya, "Japan," in E. Gordon Keith, ed. *Foreign Tax Policies and Economic Growth*, New York, National Bureau of Economic Research, 1966.

Susumu Sato, "Japan's Fiscal System: An International Comparison," *JES* 4:2 (Win 1975-76), 3-26.

Sei Fujita, "Fiscal Policy in Postwar Japan," *JES* 4:2 (Win 1975-76), 27-58.

Hiromitsu Ishi, "The Stabilization of Tax Structures," *JES* 4:3 (Spr 1976), 3-27.

Mari Nishino, "Inequity in Distribution of the Corporate Tax Burden," *JES* 4:3 (Spr 1976), 28-67.

Hugh Patrick & Henry Rosovsky, eds. *Asia's New Giant: How the Japanese Economy Works*, Brookings Institution, 1976, including:
Gardner Ackley & Hiromitsu Ishi, "Fiscal, Monetary, and Related Policies," 153-247.
Joseph A. Pechman & Keimei Kaizuka, "Taxation," 317-82.

Rosser Brockman, "Japanese Taxation of the Foreign Income of Japanese Corporations," *Hastings International and Comparative Law Review* 2:1 (Spr 1979), 73-104.

Yukio Noguchi, "Decision Rules in the Japanese Budgetary Process," *JES* 7:4 (Sum 1979), 51-75.

Hiromitsu Ishi, "Effects of Taxation on the Distribution of Income and Wealth in Japan," *Hitotsubashi Journal of Economics* 21:1 (June 1980), 27-47.

Hiromitsu Ishi, "Inflation Adjustment for Individual Income Tax in Japan," *Hitotsubashi Journal of Economics* 21:2 (Feb 1981), 19-32.

Kazuo Nakamura, "The Present Financial State of Japanese Government and the Prospect of the Escape from Financial Crisis," *Kobe University Economic Review* 27 (1981), 15-28.

Yukio Noguchi, "The Government-Business Relationship in Japan: The Changing Role of Fiscal Resources," in Kozo Yamamura, ed. *Policy and Trade Issues of the Japanese Economy: American and Japanese Perspectives*, University of Washington Press, 1982, 123-42.

Tadao Uchida, "The Reform of Japan's Public Administration and Finance: A Critical Assessment," *JES* 10:3 (Spr 1982), 3-52.

Yukio Noguchi, "Japan's Fiscal Crisis," *JES* 10:3 (Spr 1982), 53-85.

Richard H. Pettway, "Interest Rates of Japanese Long-Term National Bonds: Have Interest Rates been Liberalized?" *Keio Economic Studies* 19:1 (1982), 91-100.

Hiromitsu Ishi, "An Overview of Postwar Tax Policies in Japan," *Hitotsubashi Journal of Economics* 23:2 (Feb 1983), 21-39.

Frank Gould, "Public Expenditure in Japan: A Comparative View," *Hitotsubashi Journal of Economics* 23:2 (Feb 1983), 57-67.

Hiromitsu Ishi, "International Tax Evasion and Avoidance in Japan," *Hitotsubashi Journal of Economics* 25:1 (June 1984), 21-29.

Yukio Ikemoto et al., "On the Fiscal Incentives for Investment: The Case of Postwar Japan," *DE* 22:4 (Dec 1984), 372-95.

Kazuo Sato, "Supply-Side Economics: A Comparison of the U.S. and Japan," *Journal of Japanese Studies* ll:l (Win 1985), 105-128.

Edward J. Lincoln, "Infrastrutural Deficiencies, Budget Policy, and Capital Flows," in Michele Schmiegelow, ed. *Japan's Response to Crisis and Change in the World Economy*, New York, M.E. Sharpe, 1986, 153-180.

Tokue Shibata, ed. *Public Finance in Japan*, University of Tokyo Press, 1986.

Michael G. Rukstad, "Fiscal Policy and Business-Government Relations," in Thomas K. McCraw, ed. *America versus Japan*, Boston, Harvard Business School Press, 1986, 299-336.

Hiromitsu Ishi, "Overview of Fiscal Deficits in Japan: With Special Reference to the Fiscal Policy Debate," *Hitotsubashi Journal of Economics* 27:2 (Dec 1986), 133-48.

Tatsuya Yasukochi, "The Underground Economy in Japan," *JES* 15:2 (Win 1986-87), 66-89.

Yukio Noguchi, "Public Finance," in Kozo Yamamura & Yasukichi Yasuba, eds. *The Political Economy of Japan*, vol. 1, *The Domestic Transformation*, Stanford University Press, 1987, 186-222.

Naohiro Yashiro, "Japan's Fiscal Policy: An International Comparison," *JES* 16:1 (Fall 1987), 34-59.

Masataka Nakamura, "Japan's Public Debt Management: New Developments," *JES* 16:1 (Fall 1987), 78-99.

Seiritsu Ogura & Naoyuki Yoshino, "The Tax System and the Fiscal Investment and Loan Program," in Ryutaro Komiya, Masahiro Okuno, & Kotaro Suzumura, eds., *Industrial Policy of Japan*, Academic Press, 1988, 121-53.

Osamu Ichioka, "The Value-Added Tax in Japan: A Numerical General Equilibrium Evaluation," *Journal of the Japanese and International Economies* 2:1 (March 1988), 11-41.

Income Distribution, Lifestyles & Living Standards

John W. Bennett, "Japanese Economic Growth: Background for Social Change," in Ronald Dore, ed. *Aspects of Social Change in Modern Japan*, Princeton University Press, 1967, 411-53.

Tadao Ishizaki, "The Income Distribution in Japan," *DE* 5:2 (June 1967), 351-70.

Naomichi Nakanishi, "Changes in Living Patterns Brought About by Television," *DE* 7:4 (Dec 1969), 572-89.

Toshiyuki Mizoguchi, "An Analysis of Consumption Pattern in Post-War Japan," *Hitotsubashi Journal of Economics* 11:1 (June 1970), 30-57.

Satish M. Kansal, "A Comparison of the Cost of Living in India and Japan," *DE* 9:2 (June 1971), 197-217.

Takemi Yasunaga, "Patterns of Living in a Changing Society," *DE* 10:4 (Dec 1972), 431-50.

Ross Mouer, "Income Distribution in Japan: An Examination of the Fies Data, 1963-1971," *Keio Economic Studies* (l) 10:1 (1973), 87-109; (2) 11:1 (1974), 9-28; (3) 11:2 (1974), 21-40.

Hugh Patrick, ed. *Japanese Industrialization and its Social Consequences*, University of California Press, 1973, including:
Akira Ono & Tsunehiko Watanabe, "Changes in Income Inequality in the Japanese Economy," 363-89.
John W. Bennett & Solomon B. Levine, "Industrialization and Social Deprivation: Welfare, Environment, and the Postindustrial Society in Japan," 439-92.

Kiichi Miyazawa, "Income Redistribution: Prescription for a Welfare Society," *Japan Interpreter* 9:3 (Win 1975), 257-75.

Special Issue: "Poverty in Japan," *JES* 5:1 (Fall 1976).

Hisao Kanamori, "Japanese Economic Growth and Economic Welfare," in Shigeto Tsuru, ed. *Growth and Resources Problems Related to Japan*: Proceedings of Session VI of the Fifth Congress of the International Economic Association, Tokyo, Asahi Evening News, 1978, 129-48.

Ryutaro Komiya, " 'Monopoly Capital' and Income Redistribution Policy," Kazuo Sato, ed. *Industry and Business in Japan*, White Plains, N.Y., M.E. Sharpe, 1980, 3-21.

Toshiyuki Mizoguchi et al., "Over-time Changes in the Size Distribution of Household Income under Rapid Economic Growth: The Japanese Experience," in Kazushi Ohkawa & Bernard Key, eds. *Asian Socioeconomic Development: A National Accounts Approach*, University Press of Hawaii, 1980, 233-66.

Noriyuki Takayama & Mitsutaka Togashi, "A Note on Wealth Distribution in Japan," *Philippine Economic Journal* 19:1 (July 1980), 163-88.

Noriyuki Takayama, "The Distribution of Assets in Japan," *JES* 9:3 (Spr 1981), 87-113.

Christiaan Grootaert, "Patterns of Final Demand, Demand Linkages between Socio-Economic Groups and Income Distribution: The Case of Japan," *Hitotsubashi Journal of Economics* 23:1 (June 1982), 68-84.

Toshiyuki Mizoguchi & Noriyuki Takayama, *Equity and Poverty under Rapid Economic Growth: The Japanese Experience*, Tokyo, Kinokuniya, 1984.

Toshiyuki Mizoguchi, "Economic Development Policy and Income Distribution: The Experience in East and Southeast Asia," *DE* 23:4 (Dec 1985), 307-24.

JES 14:2 (Win 1985-86), the following articles:
Toshio Sanuki, "Changing Fortunes of Occupations in Japan," 3-29.
Tadao Ishizaki, "Is Japan's Income Distribution Equal? An International Comparison," 30-55.
Masazo Ozawa, "Myths of Affluence and Equality," 56-99.

Kuniko Inoguchi, "Prosperity Without the Amenities," *Journal of Japanese Studies* 13:1 (Win 1987), 125-34.

Martin Bronfenbrenner & Yasukichi Yasuba, "Economic Welfare," in Kozo Yamamura & Yasukichi Yasuba, eds. *The Political Economy of Japan*, vol. 1, *The Domestic Transformation*, Stanford University Press, 1987, 93-136.

"Japanese Income Distribution," Japan Economic Institute, Report No. 33A, August 28, 1987.

Satoshi Daigo, "Income Distributive Consequences of the Accounting for the Privatization of the Nippon Telegraph and Telephone Public Corporation," *Kyoto University Economic Review* 57:2 (Oct 1987), 40-53.

2. GOVERNMENT & BUSINESS

A. GENERAL & POLITICAL ECONOMY

Philip H. Trezise, "Politics, Government, and Economic Growth in Japan," in Hugh Patrick & Henry Rosovsky, eds. *Asia's New Giant: How the Japanese Economy Works*, Brookings Institution, 1976, 753-811.

T.J.Pempel, ed. *Policymaking in Contemporary Japan*, Cornell University Press, 1977.

Ezra F. Vogel, "Guided Free Enterprise in Japan," *Harvard Business Review* (May-June 1978), 161-70.

T.J. Pempel, *Policy and Politics in Japan: Creative Conservatism*, Philadelphia, Temple University Press, 1981.

John Zysman, *Governments, Markets, and Growth*, Cornell University Press, 1983, 234-51.

Masaaki Kotabe, "Changing Roles of the Sogo Shoshas, the Manufacturing Firms, and the MITI in the Context of the Japanese 'Trade or Die' Mentality," *Columbia Journal of World Business* 19:3 (Fall 1984), 33-42.

Toshio Shishido & Ryuzo Sato, *Economic Policy and Development: New Perspectives*, Dover, Mass., Auburn House, 1985.

T.J. Pempel, "The Unbundling of 'Japan, Inc.': The Changing Dynamics of Japanese Policy Formation," *Journal of Japanese Studies* 13:2 (Sum 1987), 271-306.

Michio Muramatsu, "In Search of National Identity: The Politics and Policies of the Nakasone Administration," *Journal of Japanese Studies* 13:2 (Sum 1987), 307-42.

Yasusuke Murakami, "The Japanese Model of Political Economy," in Kozo Yamamura & Yasukichi Yasuba, eds. *The Political Economy of Japan*, vol. 1, *The Domestic Transformation*, Stanford University Press, 1987, 33-90.

Chalmers Johnson, "Political Institutions and Economic Performance: THe Government-Business Relationship in Japan, South Korea, and Taiwan," in Frederic C. Deyo, ed. *The Political Economy of the New Asian Industrialism*, Ithaca, Cornell University Press, 1987, 136-64.

Chalmers Johnson, "Studies of Japanese Political Economy: A Crisis in Theory," in The Japan Foundation, *Japanese Studies in the United States: Part I: History and Present Condition*, Association for Asian Studies, 1988, 95-113.

Kent Calder, *Crisis and Compensation*, Princeton University Press, 1988.

B. THE BUREAUCRACY & BUSINESS

Daiichi Ito, "The Bureaucracy: Its Attitudes and Behavior," *DE* 6:4 (Dec 1968), 446-67.

Ehud Harari, "Japanese Politics of Advise in Comparative Perspective: A Framework for Analysis and a Case Study," *Public Policy* 22:4 (Fall 1974), 537-77.

Chalmers Johnson, "The Reemployment of Retired Government Bureaucrats in Japanese Big Business," *Asian Survey* 14:11 (Nov 1974), 953-65.

Yoshihisa Ojimi, "A Government Ministry: The Case of the Ministry of International Trade and Industry," in Ezra F. Vogel, ed. *Modern Japanese Organization and Decision-Making*, University of California Press, 1975, 101-12.

Chalmers Johnson, "Japan: Who Governs? An Essay on Official Bureaucracy," *Journal of Japanese Studies* 2:1 (Aut 1975), 1-28.

William E. Bryant, *Japanese Private Economic Diplomacy: An Analysis of Business-Government Linkages*, New York, Praeger, 1975.

Yukio Noguchi & Eisuke Sakakibara, "Dissecting the Finance Ministry-Bank of Japan Dynasty," *Japan Echo* 4:4 (Win 1977), 98-123.

Haruhiro Fukui, "The GATT Tokyo Round: The Bureaucratic Politics of Multilateral Diplomacy," in Michael Blaker, ed. *The Politics of Trade: U.S. and Japanese Policymaking for the GATT Negotiations*, Occasional Papers of the East Asian Institute, Columbia University, 1979, 75-169.

Richard P. Suttmeier, "The *Gikan* Question in Japanese Government: Bureaucratic Curiosity or Institutional Failure?" *Asian Survey* 18:10 (Oct 1978), 1046-66.

Ryutaro Komiya & Kozo Yamamoto, "Japan: The Officer in Charge," *History of Political Economy* 13:3 (Fall 1981), 600-28.

Ehud Harari, "Turnover and Autonomy in Japanese Permanent Public Advisory Bodies," *Journal of Asian and African Studies* (Leiden) 17:3&4 (1982), 235-49.

James Elliott, "The 1981 Administrative Reform in Japan," *Asian Survey* 23:6 (June 1983), 765-79.

Shumpei Kumon, "Japan Faces its Future: The Political-Economics of Administrative Reform," *Journal of Japanese Studies* 10:1 (Win 1984), 143-65.

Tuvia Blumenthal, "The Practice of Amakudari Within the Japanese Employment System," *Asian Survey* 25:3 (March 1985), 310-21.

Yung H. Park, *Bureaucrats and Ministers in Contemporary Japanese Government*, Berkeley, University of California, Institute of East Asian Studies, 1986.

Ehud Harari, *Policy Concentration in Japan*, Occasional Papers No. 58/59, East Asian Institute, Free University Berlin, Verlag Ute Schiller, 1986.

John O. Haley, "Governance by Negotiation: A Reappraisal of Bureaucratic Power in Japan," *Journal of Japanese Studies* 13:2 (Sum 1987), 343-57.

Haruhiro Fukui, "Too Many Captains in Japan's Internationalization: Travails at the Foreign Ministry," *Journal of Japanese Studies* 13:2 (Sum 1987), 359-81.

C. PUBLIC CORPORATIONS

Chalmers Johnson, *Japan's Public Policy Companies*, Washington, American Enterprise Institute, 1978.

Masu Uekusa, "Japan," in Prahlad K. Basu & Alec Nove, eds. *Public Enterprise Policy on Investment, Pricing and Returns*, Kuala Lumpur, Asian and Pacific Development Administration Center, 1979, 331-74.

Kenneth A. Skinner, "Conflict and Command in a Public Corporation in Japan," *Journal of Japanese Studies* 6:2 (Sum 1980), 301-29.

D. BUSINESS & POLITICS

Frank C. Langdon, "Organized Interests in Japan and Their Influence on Political Parties," *Pacific Affairs* 34:3 (Fall 1961), 271-78.

Frank C. Langdon, "Big Business Lobbying in Japan: The Case of Central Bank Reform," *American Political Science Review* 55:3 (Sept 1961), 527-38.

James R. Soukup, "Business Political Participation in Japan: Continuity and Change," *Studies on Asia* 6 (1965), 163-78.

Chitoshi Yanaga, *Big Business in Japanese Politics*, Yale University Press, 1968.

Haruhiro Fukui, *Party in Power: The Japanese Liberal Democrats and Policymaking*, University of California, 1970, 144-70.

Yung Ho Park, "The Governmental Advisory Commission System in Japan," *Journal of Comparative Administration* 3:4 (Feb 1972), 435-67.

Gerald L. Curtis, "Big Business and Political Influence," in Ezra F. Vogel, ed. *Modern Japanese Organization and Decision-Making*, University of California Press, 1975, 33-70.

Yung Ho Park, " 'Big Business' and Education Policy in Japan," *Asian Survey* 22:3 (March 1982), 315-36.

Kozo Yamamura & Yasukichi Yasuba, eds. *The Political Economy of Japan*, vol. 1, *The Domestic Transformation*, Stanford University Press, 1987, including:
Michio Muramatsu & Ellis S. Krauss, "The Conservative Policy Line and the Development of Patterned Pluralism," 516-54.
Yutaka Kosai, "The Politics of Economic Management," 555-92.

Yujiro Shinoda, "Japan's Management Associations," *Sophia University Socio-Economic Institute Bulletin* 15 (1967), 1-27.

Gerald L. Curtis, "Organizational Leadership in Japan's Economic Community," *Journal of International Affairs* 26:2 (1972), 179-85.

Yujiro Shinoda, "Economic Organizations and Business Leaders in Postwar Japan," *Sophia University Socio-Economic Institute Bulletin* 43 (1973) 2-22.

Gary D. Allinson, "Japan's Keidanren and its New Leadership," *Pacific Affairs* 60:3 (Fall 1987), 385-407.

Leonard H. Lynn & Timothy J. McKeown, *Organizing Business: Trade Associations in America and Japan*, Washington, D.C., American Enterprise Institute for Public Policy Research, 1988.

E. BUDGETS, FINANCIAL POLICY MAKING & ECONOMIC PLANS

Yuzo Yamada, "On the Five Year Economic Plan in Japan," *Annals of the Hitotsubashi Academy* 7:1 (Oct 1956), 33-45.

Yuzo Yamada, "On the Method of the Economic Plan (1958-62) of Japan," *Annals of the Hitotsubashi Academy* 10:1 (Aug 1959), 21-36.

Saichi Nakamura, "Importance of Financial Policies in Japanese Economy: Studies of Japan's Deflationary Policy in 1956-57," *Waseda Economic Papers* 3 (1959), 1-29.

Yasuhiko Shima, "The Income-Doubling Program and Public Investment," *Kyoto University Economic Review* 31:1 (Apr 1961), 14-52.

M. Fujioka, "Appraisal of Japan's Plan to Double Income," *IMF Staff Papers* 10:1 (1963), 150-85.

Martin Bronfenbrenner, ""Economic Miracles and Japan's Income-Doubling Plan," in William W. Lockwood, ed. *The State and Economic Enterprise in Japan*, Princeton University Press, 1965, 523-53.

Konosuke Yamada, "Economic Planning in Japan Critically Examined," *Keio Economic Studies* 3 (1965), 159-72.

Isamu Miyazaki, "Economic Planning in Postwar Japan," *DE* 8:4 (1970), 369-85.

Haruhiro Fukui, "Economic Planning in Postwar Japan: A Case Study in Policy Making," *Asian Survey* 12:4 (April 1972), 327-48.

John Creighton Campbell, "Japanese Budget *Baransu*," in Ezra F. Vogel, ed. *Modern Japanese Organization and Decision-Making*, University of California Press, 1975, 71-100.

Victor D. Lippit, "Economic Planning in Japan," *Journal of Economic Issues* 9:1 (March 1975), 39-58.

John C. Campbell, *Contemporary Japanese Budget Politics*, University of California Press, 1977.

Y. Noguchi, "Decision Rules in the Japanese Budgetary Process," *JES* 7:4 (1979), 51-75.

Kent E. Calder, "Politics and the Market: The Dynamics of Japanese Credit Allocation, 1946-1978," Ph.D. diss., Harvard University, 1979. [Harvard Archives: call no. HU 90.11306.05].

Walter Arnold, "The Politics of Economic Planning in Postwar Japan: A Study in Political Economy," Ph.D. diss., University of California, Berkeley, 1984.

Saburo Okita, "Economic Planning in Japan," in Lester C. Thurow, ed. *The Management Challenge: Japanese Views*, MIT Press, 1985, 191-217.

3. MANAGEMENT

A. GENERAL

Surveys of Business

T.F.M. Adams & N. Kobayashi, *The World of Japanese Business: An Authoritative Analysis*, Tokyo, Kodansha International, 1969.

James C. Abegglen, ed. *Business Strategies for Japan*, Sophia University Press, 1970.

Kimpei Shiba & Kenzo Nozue, *What Makes Japan Tick: Successful Big Businessmen*, Asahi Evening News, 1971.

Hugh Patrick, "New Studies on Japanese Business," *Journal of Japanese Studies* 4:2 (Sum 1978), 413-27 (review article).

Moriaki Tsuchiya, "The Japanese Business as a 'Capsule'," *JES* 8:1 (Fall 1979), 8-41.

Paul Norbury & Geoffrey Bownas, eds. *Business in Japan: A Guide to Japanese Practice and Procedure*, rev. ed. Boulder, Westview Press, 1980.

Takatoshi Nakamura, "Japan's Giant Enterprises: Their Power and Influence," *JES* 12:4 (Sum 1984), 50-90.

Kazuo Sato & Yasuo Hoshino, eds. *The Anatomy of Japanese Business*, Armonk, N.Y., M.E. Sharpe, 1984.

Akira Esaka, "The Malaise in the Japanese Corporation," *Japan Echo* 11:3 (Aut 1984), 35-43.

Mansel G. Blackford, *The Rise of Modern Business in Great Britain, the United States, and Japan*, Chapel Hill, The University of North Carolina Press, 1988, 115-72.

Accounts of Japanese-Style Management

Susumu Takamiya, "Characteristics of Management in Japanese Enterprise," *Annals of the Hitotsubashi Academy* 10:2 (Dec 1959), 181-93.

Shunzo Arai, *An Intersection of East and West: Japanese Business Management*, Tokyo, Rikugei Publishing, 1971.

Peter F. Drucker, "What We Can Learn from Japanese Management," *Harvard Business Review*, 49 (March-April 1971), 110-22.

Tai K. Oh, "Japanese Management: A Critical Review," *The Academy of Management Review* (Jan 1976), 14-25.

Yoshi Tsurumi, *Japanese Business: A Research Guide with Annotated Bibliography*, New York, Praeger, 1978.

Richard Tanner Pascale & Anthony G. Athos, *The Art of Japanese Management: Applications for American Executives*, New York, Simon & Schuster, 1981.

William Ouchi, *Theory Z: How American Business Can Meet the Japanese Challenge*, Reading, Mass., Addison-Wesley, 1981.

Boye De Mente, *The Japanese Way of Doing Business: The Psychology of Management in Japan*, Englewood Cliffs, Prentice-Hall, 1981.

Ken'ichi Ohmae, *The Mind of the Strategist: The Art of Japanese Business*, New York, McGraw-Hill, 1982.

Naoto Sasaki, *Management & Industrial Structure in Japan*, Oxford, Pergamon Press, 1981.

Robert B. Reich, "The Profession of Management," *The New Republic*, June 27, 1981, 27-32 [review article].

John L. Graham, "A Hidden Cause of America's Trade Deficit with Japan," *Columbia Journal of World Business* 16:3 (Fall 1981), 5-15.

Ryushi Iwata, *Japanese-Style Management: Its Foundations and Prospects*, Tokyo, Asian Productivity Organization, 1982.

William Ouchi, *The M-Form Society: How American Teamwork can Recapture the Competitive Edge*, Reading, Mass., Addison-Wesley, 1984 (re: computers, 93-123).

S. Prakash Sethi, Nobuaki Namiki, & Carl L. Swanson, *The False Promise of the Japanese Miracle: Illusions and Realities of the Japanese Management System*, Boston, Pitman, 1984.

Carl Pegels, *Japan vs. the West: Implications for Management*, Boston, Kluwer-Nijhoff, 1984.

Rosalie L. Tung, *Key to Japan's Economic Strength: Human Power*, Lexington Books, Heath, 1984.

Leonard Nadler, "What Japan Learned from the U.S.—That We Forgot to Remember," *California Management Review* 26:4 (Sum 1984), 46-61.

Lester Thurow, ed., *The Management Challenge: Japanese Views*, MIT Press, 1985.

Tomoko Hamada, "Corporation, Culture, and Environment: The Japanese Model," *Asian Survey* 25:12 (Dec 1985), 1214-28.

K. John Fukuda, "What Can We Really Learn from Japanese Management?" *Journal of General Management* 11:3 (Spr 1986), 16-26.

Kunio Odaka, *Japanese Management: A Forward-Looking Analysis*, Tokyo, Asian Productivity Organization, 1986.

Masaaki Imai, *Kaizen (Ky'zen): The Key to Japan's Competitive Success*, New York, Random House, 1986.

Shuji Hayashi, *Culture and Management in Japan*, University of Tokyo Press, 1986.

Khalid R. Mehtabdin, *Comparative Management: Business Styles in Japan and the United States*, Lewiston, New York, Edwin Mellen Press, 1986.

Jon P. Alston, *The American Samurai: Blending American and Japanese Managerial Practices*, Berlin, Walter de Gruyter, 1986.

Boye De Mente, *Japanese Etiquette & Ethics in Business*, Lincolnwood, Illinois, NTC Business Books, 1987.

Strategy & Management Systems

M.Y. Yoshino, *Japan's Managerial System: Tradition and Innovation*, MIT Press, 1968.

Peter F. Drucker, "Economic Realities and Enterprise Strategy," in Ezra F. Vogel, ed. *Modern Japanese Organization and Decision-Making*, University of California Press, 1975, 228-48 (with comment by Hugh Patrick).

Masumi Tsuda, "Japanese-Style Management: Principle and System," *JES* 7:4 (Sum 1979), 3-32.

Kuniyoshi Urabe, "A Critique of Theories of the Japanese-Style Management System," *JES* 7:4 (Sum 1979), 33-50.

D.J. Daly, "Corporate Strategies and Productivity Performance in Japan's Manufacturing Industries," in Keith A.J. Hay, ed. *Canadian Perspectives on Economic Relations with Japan*, Montreal, Institute for Research on Public Policy, 1980, 317-36.

A. Goto, "Statistical Evidence on the Diversification of Japanese Large Firms," *Journal of Industrial Economies* 29:3 (March 1981).

Sang M. Lee & Gary Schwendiman, eds., *Management by Japanese Systems*, New York, Praeger, 1982.

Masanori Moritani, *Japanese Technology: Getting the Best for the Least*, Tokyo, Simul Press, 1982.

Tadao Kagono et al., "Strategic Adaptation to Environment: Japanese and U.S. Firms Compared," *JES* 12:2 (Win 1983-84), 33-80.

JES 12:3 (Spr 1984), the following:
Kohzo Nishida, "Social Relations and Japanese-Style Management: Internal and External *Ittaika*-Mode Relations of Japanese Enterprises," 21-63.
Naohito Suzuki, "Japanese-Style Management and its Transferability, 64-79.

Hajime Eto & Konomu Matsui, eds. *R&D Management Systems in Japanese Industry*, Amsterdam, North Holland, 1984.

James C. Abegglen, *The Strategy of Japanese Business*, Cambridge, Ballinger, 1984.

Toyohiro Kono, *Strategy & Structure of Japanese Enterprises*, Armonk, N.Y., M.E. Sharpe, 1984.

Kazuo Sato & Yasuo Hoshino, eds. *The Anatomy of Japanese Business*, Armonk, N.Y., M.E. Sharpe, 1984, including the following articles:
Tadao Kagono et al., "Mechanistic vs. Organic Management Systems: A Comparative Study of Adaptive Patterns of American and Japanese Firms," 27-69.
Yasuo Okamoto, "The Grand Strategy of Japanese Business," 277-318 [re: Matsushita and Hitachi].
Hiroyuki Itami et al., "Diversification Strategies and Economic Performance," 319-51.

Hideki Yoshihara, "Diversification of Large Japanese Manufacturing Firms," *Kobe Economic and Business Review* 30 (1984), 61-71.

Rosalie L. Tung, *Strategic Management in the United States and Japan: A Comparative Analysis*, Cambridge, Ballinger, 1986.

Noboru Makino, *Decline and Prosperity: Corporate Innovation in Japan*, Tokyo, Kodansha, 1987.

Mitsuru Misawa, "New Japanese-Style Management in a Changing Era," *Columbia Journal of World Business* 22:4 (Win 1987), 9-17.

Ikujiro Nonaka, "Self-renewal of the Japanese Firm and the Human Resource Strategy," *Human Resource Management* 27:1 (Spr 1988), 45-62.

Hiroshi Tanaka, *The Human Side of Japanese Enterprise*, University of Pennsylvania Press, 1988.

Hideki Yoshihara, "Strategic Corporate Innovation and Japanese Management," *Kobe Economic & Business Review* 33 (1988), 9-22.

Robert S. Ozaki, "The Humanistic Enterprise System in Japan," *Asian Survey* 28:8 (Aug 1988), 830-48.

Production Management

Tadao Miyakawa, "Nakada Machinery Company, Ltd.: A Case in Production Control," *Hitotsubashi Journal of Commerce and Management* 1:1 (March 1961), 36-49.

Jeremy Main, "The Battle for Quality Begins," *Fortune*, December 29, 1980, 28-33.

N. Hatvany & V. Pucik, "Japanese Management Practices and Productivity," *Organizational Dynamics* (Spr 1981), 5-21.

J.M. Juran, "Japanese and Western Quality: A Contrast in Methods and Results," *Management Review* 67:1 (1978), 27-45.

Hirotaka Takeuchi, "Productivity: Learning from the Japanese," *California Management Review* 23:4 (Sum 1981), 5-19.

Tatsuki Mikami, *Management and Productivity Improvement in Japan*, Tokyo, Japan Management Association, 1982.

Richard Schonberger, *Japanese Manufacturing Techniques: Nine Hidden Lessons in Simplicity*, New York, The Free Press, 1982.

Yoshiaki Shimabukuro, *Consensus Management in Japanese Industry*, Tokyo, I.S.S., 2nd ed., 1983.

Charles J. McMillan, "Production Planning in Japan," *Journal of General Management* 8:4 (Sum 1983), 44-72.

Kazuo Sato & Yasuo Hoshino, eds. *The Anatomy of Japanese Business*, Armonk, N.Y., M.E. Sharpe, 1984, including the following:
Yotaro Kobayashi, "Quality Control in Japan: The Case of Fuji Xerox," 197-215.
Japanese External Trade Organization, "Productivity and Quality Control: Case Studies," 246-74.

Eiji Ogawa, *Modern Production Management: A Japanese Experience*, Tokyo, Asian Productivity Organization, 1984.

Quality Control Circles At Work: Cases From Japan's Manufacturing and Service Sectors, Tokyo, Asian Productivity Organization, 1984.

Robert H. Hayes & Steven C. Wheelwright, *Restoring our Competitive Edge: Competing Through Manufacturing*, New York, John Wiley & Sons, 1984, 352-74.

David A. Garvin, "Japanese Quality Management," *Columbia Journal of World Business* 19:3 (Fall 1984), 3-12.

Innovations in Management: The Japanese Corporation, ed. by Yasuhiro Monden et al., Atlanta, Industrial Engineering and Management Press, 1985.

Ken'ichi Imai, Ikujiro Nonaka & Hirotaka Takeuchi, "Managing the New Product Development Process: How Japanese Companies Learn and Unlearn," in Kim B. Clark, Robert H. Hayes, & Christopher Lorenz, eds. *The Uneasy*

Alliance: Managing the Productivity-Technology Dilemma, Boston, Harvard Business School Press, 1985, 337-75.

Kaoru Ishikawa, *What is Total Quality Control? The Japanese Way*, trans. by David J. Lu, Englewood Cliffs, NJ, Prentice Hall, 1985.

David J. Lu, *Inside Corporate Japan: The Art of Fumble-Free Management*, Cambridge, Mass., Productivity Press, 1987.

Harris Jack Shapiro & Teresa Cosenza, *Reviving Industry in America: Japanese Influences on Manufacturing and the Service Sector*, Cambridge, Ballinger, 1987.

Martin Kenney & Richard Florida, "Beyond Mass Production: Production and the Labor Process in Japan," *Politics & Society* 16:1 (March 1988), 121-58.

B. COMPANY ORGANIZATION

General

Yasuo Kotaka, "Survey of Top Executives' Views on Business Organization," *Keio Business Review* 3 (1964), 1-31.

Norio Yanagihara, "The Strategy and Structure of Japanese Industrial Corporations," *KSU Economic and Business Review* (Kyoto Sangyo University) 1 (May 1974), 24-45.

Ryuei Shimizu, "A Positive Study of Organization and Other Related Matters: Referring Mainly to a Survey of Organizational Effectiveness on 260 Firms of Japan," *Keio Business Review* 15 (1978), 17-105.

Rodney Clark, *The Japanese Company*, Yale University Press, 1979.

Tadao Kagono et al., "Mechanistic vs. Organic Management Systems: A Comparative Study of Adaptive Patterns of U.S. and Japanese Firms," *Annals of the School of Business Administration* (Kobe University) 25 (1981), 115-45.

William V. Ruch, *Corporate Communications: A Comparison of Japanese and American Practices*, Westport, Quorum Books, 1984.

Masahiro Aoki, "Aspects of the Japanese Firm," in Masahiko Aoki, ed. *The Economic Analysis of the Japanese Firm*, Amsterdam, North Holland, 1984, 3-43.

Kiyoshi Okada et al., *Corporate Strategies in Japan*, London, Longman Professional Intelligence Reports, 1985.

Stewart R. Clegg, Dexter C. Dunphy & S. Gordon Redding, *The Enterprise and Management in East Asia*, Center of Asian Studies, University of Hong Kong, 1986.

Masahiko Aoki, "The Japanese Firm in Transition," in Kozo Yamamura & Yasukichi Yasuba, eds. *The Political Economy of Japan*, vol. 1, *The Domestic Transformation*, Stanford University Press, 1987, 263-88.

Organization & Decision Making

Susumu Takamiya, "Decision-Making and Reorganization in Japanese Enterprises," in Robert K. Paus, ed. *Business in Japan Workshop*, vol. 1, Tokyo, Sophia Univesity Press, 1966, 71-81.

Matsutaro Wadaki et al., "Decision-Making by Top-Management and Business Performance in Firms of Japan: From an Interview Research to the Presidents of Sixty Four Electrical Machinery Companies Listed," *Keio Business Review* 11 (1972), 1-27.

Kazuo Noda, "Big Business Organization," in Ezra F. Vogel, ed. *Modern Japanese Organization and Decision-Making*, University of California Press, 1975, 115-45.

Masumi Tsuda, "Study of Japanese Management Development Practices," *Hitotsubashi Journal of Arts & Sciences* 18:1 (September 1977), 1-19.

Lee Smith, "Japan's Autocratic Managers," *Fortune*, January 7, 1985, 56-65.

James C. Abegglen & George Stalk, *Kaisha: The Japanese Corporation*, New York, Basic Books, 1985.

M.Y. Yoshino & Thomas B. Lifson, *The Invisible Link: Japan's Sogo Shosha and the Organization of Trade*, MIT Press, 1986.

Mayumi Otsubo, "A Guide to Japanese Business Practices," *California Management Review* 28:3 (Spr 1986), 28-42.

Ryuei Shimizu, "Top Management's Decision Making in Japanese Companies," *Keio Business Review* 23 (1986), 1-15.

Management Characteristics

Masahiko Oda, *Compensation and Promotion: The Plight of Middle Managers*, Tokyo, Sophia University, Institute of Comparative Culture, 1983.

Alfred D. Chandler, Jr., "The Emergence of Managerial Capitalism," *Business History Review* 58:4 (Winter 1984), 473-503.

Ryuei Shimizu, "The Growth of Firms in Japan: An Empirical Study of Chief Executives," in Kazuo Sato & Yasuo Hoshino, eds. *The Anatomy of Japanese Business*, Armonk, N.Y., M.E. Sharpe, 1984, 70-100.

Ryuei Shimizu, *Top Management in Japanese Firms*, Tokyo, Chikura Shobo, 1986.

Masahiko Aoki, "Innovative Adaptation Through the Quasi-Tree Structure: An Emerging Aspect of Japanese Entrepreneurship," *Zeitschrift fur Nationalokonomie*, supplement 4 (1984), 177-98.

Wanda Anasz, Hirofumi Ueda & Kiyoshi Yamamoto, "Industrial Structures in Japan: Pyramidal Organization in the Automobile and Electrical/Electronic Industries," *Annals of the Institute of Social Science* 28 (1986), 31-64.

Ikujiro Nonaka, "Creating Organizational Order Out of Chaos: Self-Renewal in Japanese Firms," *California Management Review* 30:3 (Spr 1988), 57-73.

Frank Baldwin, "The Idioms of Contemporary Japan, VII: *Sokaiya*," *Japan Interpreter* 8:4 (Win 1974), 502-09.

C. COMPANY FINANCE

Ownership & Stockholding

Makoto Yazawa, "The Legal Structure for Corporate Enterprise: Shareholder-Management Relations Under Japanese Law," Arthur T. von Mehren, ed. *Law in Japan: The Legal Order in a Changing Society*, Harvard University Press, 1963, 547-66.

Yoshikazu Miyazaki, "The Japanese-type Structure of Big Business," in Kazuo Sato, ed. *Industry and Business in Japan*, White Plains, N.Y., M.E. Sharpe, 1980, 285-343.

Mitsuhiro Hirata, "Realities of General Meetings of Shareholders in Japan," *Hitotsubashi Journal of Commerce and Management* 16:1 (Oct 1981), 17-26.

Tadonori Nishiyama, "The Structure of Managerial Control: Who Owns and Controls Japanese Businesses?" in Kazuo Sato & Yasuo Hoshino, eds. *The Anatomy of Japanese Business*, Armonk, N.Y., M.E. Sharpe, 1984, 123-63.

Lawrence Repeta, "Declining Public Ownership of Japanese Industry: A Case of Regulatory Failure," *Law in Japan* 17 (1984), 153-84.

Finances of the Firm

Eiichi Furukawa, "The Business Audit System in Japan," *Annals of the Hitot-subashi Academy* 1:2 (Apr 1951), 138-46.

Yasuo Kotaka, "Survey of Top Business Executives's Views on Rationalization of Business Finance," in *Keio Business Review* 2 (1963), 1-25.

Ryuei Shimizu, "A Study on the Capital Costs in the Japanese Enterprises for Long-Range Planning," *Keio Business Review* 4 (1965), 177-208.

Hidekazu Nomura, "The Window Dressing of Accounts at the Present Stage and the Accumulation of Capital in Japan," *Kyoto University Economic Review* 38:2 (Oct 1968), 46-68.

Hiroshi Kawaguchi, " 'Over-Loan' and the Investment Behavior of Firms," *DE* 8:4 (1970), 386-406.

Shigeru Tamura, "The Business Demand for Cash in Japan and its Characteristics by Industry," *Keio Business Review* 10 (1971), 83-96.

Hiroyuki Itami, "A Japanese-American Comparison of Management Productivity," *JES* 7:1 (Fall 1978), 3-41.

Iwao Kuroda & Yoshiharu Oritani, "A Reexamination of the Unique Features of Japan's Corporate Financial Structure: A Comparison of Corporate Balance Sheets in Japan and the United States," *JES* 8:4 (Sum 1980), 82-117.

Hidekazu Nomura, "Capital Accumulation by Large Enterprises in Japan," *Kyoto University Economic Review* 54:1 (Apr 1984), 11-39.

Masahiko Aoki, ed. *The Economic Analysis of the Japanese Firm*, Amsterdam, North Holland, 1984, [see the review by Kozo Yamamura, *JJS* 11:2 (Sum 1985), 493-504], including the following article:
Masahiko Aoki, "Shareholders' Non-unanimity on Investment Financing: Banks vs. Individual Investors," 193-224.

Takaaki Wakasugi, "Capital and Finance of Japanese Business," *JES* 12:4 (Sum 1984), 3-49.

Ilari Tyrni, *The Rate of Return, Risk and the Financial Behaviour of the Japanese Industrial Firms*, Helsinki, Finnish Society of Sciences and Letters, 1984.

Yasuo Hoshino, "General Comparison of Financial Characteristics between Merging and Nonmerging Firms in Japan," in Kazuo Sato & Yasuo Hoshino, eds. *The Anatomy of Japanese Business*, Armonk, N.Y., M.E. Sharpe, 1984, 352-69.

Hiroyuki Itami, "The Firm and the Market in Japan," Lester C. Thurow, ed. *The Management Challenge: Japanese Views*, MIT Press, 1985, 69-81.

Yoshi Tsurumi & Hiroki Tsurumi, "Value-Added Maximizing Behavior of Japanese Firms and Roles of Corporate Investment and Finance," *Columbia Journal of World Business* 20:1 (Spr 1985), 29-36.

James E. Hodder & Adrian E. Tschoegl, "Some Aspects of Japanese Corporate Finance," *Journal of Financial and Quantitative Analysis* 20:2 (1985), 173-91.

Akihiro Yoshikawa & Brian Woodall, "Venture Boom' and Japanese Industrial Policy: Promoting the Neglected Winners," *Asian Survey* 25:6 (June 1985), 692-714.

Michael A. Rappa, "Capital Financing Strategies of the Japanese Semiconductor Industry," *California Management Review* 27:2 (Win 1985), 85-99.

Hiroyuki Itami & Thomas W. Roehl, *Mobilizing Invisible Assets*, Harvard University Press, 1987.

Rodney Clark, *Venture Capital in Britain, America and Japan*, London, Croom Helm, 1987, 27-64.

Robert J. Ballon & Iwao Tomita, *The Financial Behavior of Japanese Corporations*, New York, Kodansha, 1988.

Kazayuki Suzuki & Tsutomu Miyakawa, "Replacement Investment and International Competitiveness of Firms," *JES* 17:1 (Fall 1988), 36-64.

Accounting

Masao Matsumoto, "The Development of Managerial Accounting in Japan," *Annals of the Hitotsubashi Academy* 4:1 (Oct 1953), 40-54.

Toshio Iino, "The Accounting Regulations in the Revised Japanese Commercial Code," *Hitotsubashi Journal of Commerce and Management* 4:1 (Nov 1966), 3-17.

Gerhard G. Mueller & Hiroshi Yoshida, *Accounting Practices in Japan*, University of Washington, Graduate School of Business Administration, International Business Series, No. 6, 1968.

Tadahiro Yamamasu, "Feature of the Japan's Audit System," *Keio Business Review* 12 (1973), 1-12.

Tadashi Nakamura, "Corporate Financial Reporting in Japan," *Hitotsubashi Journal of Commerce and Management* 8:1 (July 1973), 36-51.

Robert J. Ballon, Iwao Tomita & Hajime Usami, *Financial Reporting in Japan*, Tokyo, Kodansha International, 1976.

Susumu Katsuyama, "Recent Problems of the Financial Accounting System in Japan," *International Journal of Accounting* 12:1 (1976), 121-31.

Frederick D.S. Choi & Kazuo Hiramitsu, eds. *Accounting and Financial Reporting in Japan: Current Issues and Future Prospects in a World Economy*, Wokingham, Berkshire, Van Nostrand Reinhold, 1987

Toshiro Hiromoto, "Another Hidden Edge: Japanese Management Accounting," *Harvard Business Review* 88:4 (July-Aug 1988), 22-26.

Securities

Toyoji Kotake, "Unyo-Azukari' Loan and the Yamaichi-Securities Scare," *Keio Business Review* 5 (1966), 1-20.

K. Hashidate, *Financing Corporations with Convertible Debentures in the USA and Japan*, Tokyo, Kinokuniya, 1977.

John B. Bennett & Norman Doelling, *Investing in Japanese Securities*, Tokyo, Tuttle, 1972.

Misao Tatsuta, *Securities Regulation in Japan*, University of Washington Press, 1972.

Mitsuko Akabori-Shibuya, "A Study of the Shareholders' Position in Public Issue Corporations," *Law in Japan* 10 (1977), 101-11.

D. POSTWAR ENTERPRISE GROUPS

Tadakatsu Inoue, "Notes on the ZAIBATSU Combines," *Kobe Economic & Business Review* 3 (1956), 125-34.

Tasuku Noguchi, "A Theory on the Business Concentration in Japan," *Keio Business Review* 2 (1963), 53-77.

Kozo Yamamura, "Zaibatsu, Pre-War and Zaibatsu, Postwar," *Journal of Asian Studies* 23:4 (Aug 1964), 539-54.

Yoshikazu Miyazaki, "Rapid Economic Growth in Post-War Japan: With Special Reference to 'Excessive Competition and the Formation of *Keiretsu*'," *DE* 5:2 (June 1967), 329-50.

"Zaibatsu Banking Groups," *Oriental Economist*, series in 1971.

Mitsubishi Group, ed. by Mainichi Daily News, Tokyo, 1970.

Mitsui Group, ed. by Mainichi Daily News, Tokyo, 1971.

Yoshikazu Miyazaki, "Big Corporations and Business Groups in Postwar Japan," *DE* 14:4 (Dec 1976), 381-401.

Kazuo Sato, ed. *Industry and Business in Japan*, White Plains, N.Y., M.E. Sharpe, 1980, including:
Yoshikazu Miyazaki, "Excessive Competition and the Formation of *Keiretsu*," 53-73.
Tadao Kiyonari and Hideichiro Nakamura, "The Establishment of the Big Business System," 247-84.
Yoshikazu Miyazaki, "The Japanese-type Structure of Big Business," 285-343.
Yusaku Futatsugi, "The Measurement of Interfirm Relationships," 344-71.

"Sumitomo Group: Its New Global Strategy," *Oriental Economist*, October 1981, 12-40.

Hirohiko Yasuki, "Internal Organization and Corporation Groupings in Japan," *Kansai University Review of Economics and Business* 11:2 (Dec 1982), 29-48.

Dodwell Marketing Consultants, *Industrial Groupings in Japan: 1982/1983*, rev. ed. New York, International Publications Service, 1982.

Masahiko Aoki, ed, *The Economic Analysis of the Japanese Firm*, Amsterdam, North Holland, 1984, including:
Iwao Nakatani, "The Economic Role of Financial Corporate Grouping in Japan," 227-58.
Masahiko Aoki, "Risk Sharing in the Corporate Group," 259-64.
Eleanor Hadley, "Counterpoint on Business Groupings and Government-Industry Relations in Automobiles," 319-27.

Hiroshi Okumura, "Interfirm Relations in an Enterprise Group: The Case of Mitsubishi," in Kazuo Sato & Yasuo Hoshino, eds., *The Anatomy of Japanese Business*, Armonk, N.Y., M.E. Sharpe, 1984, 164-93.

Hiroshi Okumura, "Enteprise Groups in Japan," *Shoken keizai* 147 (March 1984), 160-89.

Munemichi Inoue, "Competition and Cooperation among Japanese Corporations," in Lester C. Thurow, ed. *The Management Challenge: Japanese Views*, MIT Press, 1985, 139-59.

Paul Sheard, "Main Banks and Structural Adjustment in Japan," *Pacific Economic Papers* (Australia-Japan Research Centre) 129 (1985), 1-93.

Paul Sheard, "Intercorporate Shareholdings and Structural Adjustment in Japan," *Pacific Economic Papers* (Australia-Japan Research Centre) 137 (1986), 1-65.

Yoshiaki Ueda, "Intercorporate Networks in Japan: A Study of Interlocking Directorates in Modern Large Corporations," *Shoken keizai* 157 (Sept 1986), 236-53.

Paul Sheard, "Main Banks and Internal Capital Markets in Japan," *Shoken keizai* 157 (Sept 1986), 255-85.

Gary G. Hamilton, Marco Orru, & Nicole Woolsey Biggart, "Enterprise Groups in East Asia: An Organizational Analysis," *Shoken keizai* 161 (Sept 1987), 78-106.

Michael Gerlach, "Business Alliances and the Strategy of the Japanese Firm," *California Management Review* 30:1 (Fall 1987), 126-42.

Ken'ichi Imai, "The Corporate Network in Japan," *JES* 16:2 (Win 1987-88), 3-37.

Akiyoshi Horiuchi, Frank Packer, & Shin'ichi Fukuda, "What Role has the 'Main Bank' Played in Japan," *Journal of the Japanese and International Economies* 2:2 (June 1988), 159-80.

E. GENERAL TRADING COMPANIES (SOGO SHOSHA)

"Trading Houses [Firms] in Japan," *Oriental Economist*, annual study since the 1960s, usually in January or April issue.

Morihisa Emori, "Japanese General Trading Companies: Their Functions and Roles," in Pierre Uri, ed. *Trade and Investment Policies for the Seventies: New Challenges for the Atlantic Area and Japan*, New York, Praeger, 1971.

Chujiro Fujino, "The Role of General Trading Company in the Industrialization of Developing Countries," *Management Japan* 5:2 (1971), 9-13.

"The Giant Trading Companies: Japan's Secret Weapon?" *Forbes*, May 1972.

Saburo Kojima & Koichiro Hirata, "Growth and Organization in Business: Empirical Study on Six High-Rank Trading Companies (Sogo-Shosha)," *Keio Business Review* 12 (1973), 99-132.

Kozo Yamamura, "General Trading Companies in Japan: Their Origins and Growth," in Hugh Patrick, ed. *Japanese Industrialization and its Social Consequences*, University of California Press, 1973, 161-99.

R. Kikuiri, "Shosha: Organizers of the World Economy," *Japan Interpreter* 8:3 (Aut 1973), 353-73.

A. Kapoor, ed. *Asian Business and Environment in Transition: Selected Readings and Essays*, Princeton, Darwin Press, 1976, the following:
Alexander K. Young, "Internationalization of the Japanese General Trading Companies," 231-43.
Terutomo Ozawa, "Japan's Mid-East Diplomacy," 479-90.

Eisuke Daido, "Why are They 'General Trading Firms'?" *JES* 4:4 (Sum 1976), 44-62.

M.Y. Yoshino, *Japan's Multinational Enterprises*, Harvard University Press, 1976.

Yoshi Tsurumi, *The Japanese Are Coming: A Multinational Interaction of Firms and Politics*, Cambridge, Ballinger, 1976.

Nagahide Shioda, "The Sogo Shosha and its Functions in Direct Foreign Investment," *DE* 14:4 (Dec 1976), 402-18.

Marubeni, The Unique World of the Sogo Shosha, 1978.

Japan Quarterly 25:2 (1978), the following articles:
Nagahide Shioda, "The *Sogo Shosha* at the Turning Point," 152-60.
Yasuo Oki, "Inside View of the *Sogo Shosha*," 161-68.
Hiroshi Hasegawa, "A Drama of Ataka & Co.'s Collapse," 169-77.

Saburo Zushi, "The Ataka Affair: How to Go Bankrupt and Still Stay Afloat," in Hyoe Murakami & Johannes Hirschmeier, eds. *Politics and Economics in Contemporary Japan*, Tokyo, Japan Culture Institute, 1979, 204-21.

Alexander Young, *The Sogo Shosha: Japan's Multinational Trading Companies*, Boulder, Westview Press, 1979.

"Mitsubishi Shoji: A Century-old Conglomerate Goes Transnational," *Ampo* 11:1 (1979), 59-69.

Takeo Tsuchiya, "MITSUI: Japan's Advance Guard in the Third World," *Ampo* 12:1 (1980), 54-65.

Yoshi Tsurumi, *Sogoshosha: Engines of Export-Based Growth*, Toronto, The Institute for Research on Public Policy, 1980.

Hideki Yoshihara, "Research on Japan's General Trading Firms: An Overview," *JES* 9:3 (Spr 1981), 61-86.

"The General Trading Companies of Japan and the Export-led Industrialisation," in Eddy Lee, ed. *Export-led Industrialisation & Development*, Asian Employment Programme, 1981, 179-204.

The Japanese Edge: The Real Story behind a Sogo Shosha, Tokyo, Marubeni, 1981.

Kunio Yoshihara, *Sogo Shosha: The Vanguard of the Japanese Economy*, Tokyo, Oxford University Press, 1982.

Ku-Hyun Jung, "The Sogo Shosha: Can it be Exported (Imported)?" in Michael R. Czinkota, ed. *Export Promotion: The Public and Private Sector Interaction*, New York, Praeger, 1983, 66-88.

Thomas Roehl, "A Transactions Cost Approach to International Trading Structures: The Case of the Japanese General Trading Companies," *Hitotsubashi Journal of Economics* 24:2 (Dec 1983), 119-35.

Kiyoshi Kojima & Terutomo Ozawa, *Japan's General Trading Companies: Merchants of Economic Development*, Paris, Development Centre of the OECD, 1984.

Vladimir Pucik, "Promotion Patterns in a Japanese Trading Company," *Columbia Journal of World Business* 20:3 (Fall 1985), 73-79.

M.Y. Yoshino & Thomas B. Lifson, *The Invisible Link: Japan's Sogo Shosha and the Organization of Trade*, MIT Press, 1986.

Paul Sheard, "General Trading Companies and Structural Adjustment in Japan," *Pacific Economic Papers* (Australia-Japan Research Centre), 132 (1986), 1-55.

F. COMMERCIAL LAW

Seiji Tanaka, "The 1950 Amendment Act of the Business Corporation Law," *Annals of the Hitotsubashi Academy* 1:2 (Apr 1951), 163-80.

Kaichiro Bamba, "Commercial Law Provisions and Accounting for Capital Stock," *Annals of the Hitotsubashi Academy* 5:1 (Oct 1954), 60-71.

Arthur T. von Mehren, ed. *Law in Japan: The Legal Order in a Changing Society*, Harvard University Press, 1963, including:
Shinichiro Michida, "The Legal Structure for Economic Enterprise: Some Aspects of Japanese Commercial Law," 507-46.
Makoto Yazawa, "The Legal Structure for Corporate Enterprise: Shareholder-Management Relations Under Japanese Law," 547-66.

Takenori Kawashima, "The Legal Consciousness of Contracts in Japan," *Law in Japan* 7 (1974), 1-21.

Teruo Doi, "Industrial Property Law," in Akira Kawamura, ed. *Law and Business in Japan*, Tokyo, Japan-Australia Business Cooperation Committee, 1982, 170-95.

Shin Ushijima, "The Internationalization of the Japanese Economy and Corporate Reorganization Procedures: The Iwazawa Group and Sapporo Toyopet Failures," *Law in Japan* 18 (1985), 27-54.

Robert W. Dziubla, "Enforcing Corporate Responsibility: Japanese Corporate Directors' Liability to Third Parties for Failure to Supervise," *Law in Japan* 18 (1985), 55-75.

Yasuhei Taniguchi, "International Bankruptcy and Japanese Law," *Stanford Journal of International Law* 23:2 (Sum 1987), 449-75.

4. LABOR & EMPLOYMENT

A. REFERENCE

Kazutoshi Koshiro, "Japanese Studies in Labor Economics," *JES* 8:4 (Sum 1980), 42-81.

Taishiro Shirai, ed. *Contemporary Industrial Relations in Japan*, University of Wisconsin Press, 1983, the following:
Haruo Shimada, "Japanese Industrial Relations: A New General Model? A Survey of the English-Language Literature," 3-27.
Shigeyoshi Tokunaga, "A Marxist Interpretation of Japanese Industrial Relations, with Special Reference to Large Private Enterprises," 313-29.

B. EMPLOYING LABOR

Labor-Management Relations: General

Solomon B. Levine, "Management and Industrial Relations in Postwar Japan," *Far Eastern Quarterly* 15 (Nov 1955), 57-75.

James C. Abegglen, *The Japanese Factory: Aspects of its Social Organization*, Glencoe, Illinois, The Free Press, 1958.

Solomon B. Levine, *Industrial Relations in Postwar Japan*, Urbana, University of Illinois Press, 1958.

Ichiro Nakayama, "Fifteen Years in Labor-Management Mediation," *CJ* 26:4 (Nov 1960), 757-61.

John W. Bennett & Iwao Ishino, *Paternalism in the Japanese Economy: Anthropological Studies of Oyabun-Kobun Patterns*, University of Minnesota Press, 1963.

Robert J. Ballon, ed. *The Japanese Employee*, The Voyagers' Press, 1969.

James Abegglen, *Management and Worker: The Japanese Solution*, Sophia University Press, 1973.

Kazuo Okochi, Bernard Karsh & Solomon E. Levine, eds. *Workers and Employers in Japan*, Princeton University Press, 1973.

Kunio Odaka, *Toward Industrial Democracy: Management and Workers in Modern Japan*, Harvard University Press, 1975.

OECD, *The Development of Industrial Relations Systems: Some Implications of Japanese Experience*, Paris, 1977.

Hiroshi Hazama, "Characteristics of Japanese-Style Management," *JES* 6:3-4 (Spr-Sum 1978), 110-73.

Kazuo Koike, "Japan's Industrial Relations: Characteristics and Problems," *JES* 7:1 (Fall 1978), 42-90.

Ryu Kazama, "Problems of Workers' Participation in Management in Japan," *Kanto Gakuin University Economic Review* 1 (1978), 42-56.

Tadashi Hanami, *Labor Relations in Japan Today*, Tokyo, Kodansha International, 1979.

T.J. Pempel & K. Tsunekawa, "Corporatism without Labor? The Japanese Anomaly," in P.C. Schmitter & G. Lembruch, eds. *Trends Toward Corporatist Intermediation*, Beverly Hills, Sage, 1979.

Medium-term Labor Policy Discussion Group, "Recommendations on Japan's Labor Policy," *JES* 8:2 (Win 1979-80), 5-47.

Ken'ichi Furuya, "Labor-Management Relations in Postwar Japan: Their Reality and Change," *Japan Quarterly* 27:1 (Jan-Mar 1980), 30-38.

Labour Market Information for Decision-Making: The Case of Japan, Geneva, International Labour Office, 1980.

Yoshio Sugimoto, Haruo Shimada & Solomon B. Levine, *Industrial Relations in Japan*, Melbourne, Monash University, Papers of the Japanese Studies Centre, 4, 1982.

Haruo Shimada, "Perceptions and the Reality of Japanese Industrial Relations: Role in Japan's Postwar Industrial Success," *Keio Economic Studies* 19:2 (1982), 1-22. (See also Shimada's "The Perceptions and the Reality of Japanese Industrial Relations," in Lester C. Thurow, ed. *The Management Challenge: Japanese Views*, MIT Press, 1985, 42-68).

Taishiro Shirai, ed. *Contemporary Industrial Relations in Japan*, University of Wisconsin Press, 1983, including:
Taishiro Shirai, "A Supplement: Characteristics of Japanese Managements and Their Personnel Practices," 369-82.

Solomon B. Levine, "Employers Associations in Japan," in John P. Windmuller & Alan Gladstone, eds. *Employers Associations and Industrial Relations: A Comparative Study*, New York, Oxford University Press, 1984, 318-56.

Yoshihiro Tsurumi, "Labor Relations and Industrial Adjustment in Japan and the United States: A Comparative Analysis," *Yale Law & Policy Review* 2:2 (1984), 256-71.

Masahiko Aoki, "The Japanese Firm in Transition," in Kozo Yamamura & Yasukichi Yasuba, eds. *The Political Economy of Japan*, vol. 1, *The Domestic Transformation*, Stanford University Press, 1987, 263-88.

Sheldon Garon, *The State and Labor in Modern Japan*, University of California Press, 1987.

Ikuo Kume, "Changing Relations among the Government, Labor, and Business in Japan after the Oil Crisis," *International Organization* 42:4 (Aut 1988), 659-87.

Labor-Management Relations: Specific Industries

Shin Aochi, "Coal Miners in Northern Kyushu," *CJ* 26:2 (Dec 1959), 339-42.

Takeo Yamasaki, "The Forestry Labour of Japan," *Kyoto University Economic Review* 31:2 (Oct 1961), 17-41.

Hiromasa Yamamoto, articles on shipping labor, *Kobe Economic and Business Review*, 1960s to 1970s.

Annals of the Institute of Social Science 21 (1980), the following:
Kiyoshi Yamamoto, "Labor-Management Relations at Nissan Motor Co., Ltd. (Datsun)," 24-44.
Tadashi Matsuzaki, "Japanese Steel Industry and its Labor-Management Relations," 45-68.

S. Takezawa et al., *Improvements in the Quality of Working Life in Three Japanese Industries*, Geneva, International Labour Office, 1982.

Andrew Gordon, *The Evolution of Labor Relations in Japan: Heavy Industry, 1853-1955*, Harvard University Press, 1985.

Ronald Dore, *Flexible Rigidities: Industrial Policy and Structural Adjustment in the Japanese Economy, 1970-80*, Stanford University Press, 1986, 87-119, 253-65.

Permanent Employment, Enterprise Unions, & Wages

Ken'ichi Kobayashi, "The Employment and Wage Systems in Postwar Japan," *DE* 7:2 (June 1969), 187-219.

Yoshio Kaneko, "Employment and Wages," *DE* 8:4 (1970), 445-74.

Robert E. Cole, "The Theory of Institutionalization: Permanent Employment and Tradition in Japan," *Economic Development and Cultural Change* 20:1 (Oct 1971), 47-70.

Robert M. Marsh & Hiroshi Mannari, "A New Look at Lifetime Commitment' in Japanese Industry," *Economic Development and Cultural Change* 20:4 (July 1972), 611-30, (also in A. Kapoor, ed. *Asian Business and Environment in Transition: Selected Readings and Essays*, Princeton, Darwin Press, 1976, 195-214).

Robert E. Cole, "Permanent Employment in Japan: Facts and Fantasies," *Industrial and Labor Relations Review* 26:1 (Oct 1972), 615-30.

Isao Akaoka, "Control of Amount of Employment in Japanese Companies under the Life-Time Employment," *Kyoto University Economic Review* 44:1-2 (Apr-Oct 1974), 59-78.

R.C. Clark, "Union-Management Conflict in a Japanese Company," in W.G. Beasley, ed. *Modern Japan: Aspects of History, Literature & Society*, London, Allen & Unwin, 1975, 209-26.

Mikio Sumiya, "Japanese Industrial Relations Revisited: A Discussion of the *Nenko* System," *JES* 5:3 (Spr 1977), 3-47.

Yoko Sano, "Seniority-Based Wages in Japan: A Survey," *JES* 5:3 (Spr 1977), 48-65.

R.J. Gordon, "Why U.S. Wage and Employment Behaviour Differs from that in Britain and Japan," *The Economic Journal* 92:365 (March 1982), 13-44.

Kanji Haitani, "Changing Characteristics of the Japanese Employment System," *Asian Survey* 18:10 (Oct 1978), 1029-45.

Ryohei Magota, "The End of the Seniority-Related (*Nenko*) Wage System," *JES* 7:3 (Spr 1979), 71-125.

Kazuo Koike, "Employment in Japan, a Superdeveloped Country," *Japan Echo* 4:2 (Sum 1979), 34-47.

Thomas P. Rohlen, " 'Permanent Employment' Faces Recession, Slow Growth, and an Aging Work Force," *Journal of Japanese Studies* 5:2 (Sum 1979), 235-72.

Masanori Hashimoto, "Bonus Payments, On-the-job Training, and Lifetime Employment in Japan," *Journal of Political Economy* 87.Pt. 1:5 (Oct 1979), 1086-1104.

Osamu Mano, "Recent Research on the Japanese Personnel Management System in Japan: A Comparative Perspective," *Hokudai Economic Papers* 9 (1979-1980), 1-23.

Shojiro Ujihara, "Enterprise-Based Labor Unions in Japan," *Annals of the Institute of Social Science* 21 (1980), 1-23.

Veljko Rus, Akihiro Ishikawa & Thomas Woodhouse, *Employment and Participation: Industrial Democarcy in Crisis*, Tokyo, Chuo University Press, 1982, 135-235.

Toshiaki Tachibana, "Further Results on Japanese Wage Differentials: Nenko Wages, Hierarchical Position, Bonuses and Working Hours," *International Economic Review* 23:2 (June 1982), 447-61.

Akira Kubota, "Japanese Employment System and Japanese Social Structure," *Asia Pacific Community* 15 (Win 1982), 96-120.

Taishiro Shirai, ed. *Contemporary Industrial Relations in Japan*, University of Wisconsin Press, 1983, including the following:
Kazuo Koike, "Internal Labor Markets: Workers in Large Firms," 29-61.
Taishiro Shirai, "A Theory of Enterprise Unionism," 117-43.

Vladimir Pucik, "Promotion Patterns in a Japanese Trading Company," *Columbia Journal of World Business* 20:3 (Fall 1985), 73-79.

JES 15:3 (Spr 1987), the following:
Eiko Shinozuka, "Employment Adjustment in Japanese Manufacturing," 3-28.
Kuramitsu Muramatsu, "The Effect of Wages on Employment in Japan," 29-57.

Richard B. Freeman & Martin L. Weitzman, "Bonuses and Employment in Japan," *Journal of the Japanese and International Economies* 1:2 (June 1987), 168-94.

White Collar

Koya Azumi, *Higher Education and Business Recruitment in Japan*, New York, Columbia University, Teachers College Press, 1969.

Shigeru Susato, "The White-Collar Strata in Postwar Japan," *DE* 7:4 (Dec 1969), 451-70.

Thomas P. Rohlen, "Spiritual Education in a Japanese Bank," *American Anthropologist* 35:5 (1973), 1542-62.

Thomas P. Rohlen, *For Harmony and Strength: Japanese White-Collar Organization in Anthropological Perspective*, University of California Press, 1974.

Ehud Harari & Yoram Zeira, "Training Expatriates for Managerial Assignments in Japan," *California Management Review* 20:4 (Sum 1978), 56-62.

Vladimir Pucik, "White Collar Human Resource Management: A Comparison of the US and Japanese Automobile Industries," *Columbia Journal of World Business* 19:3 (Fall 1984), 87-94.

Kiyonori Sakakibara & D. Eleanor Westney, "Comparative Study of the Training, Careers and Organization of Engineers in the Computer Industry in the United States and Japan," *Hitotsubashi Journal of Commerce & Management* 20:1 (Dec 1985), 1-20.

Public Enterprises

Ehud Harari, "The Public Sector in Japan: Industrial Relations and Politics," *Journal of Asian and African Studies* (Haifa) 18:1 (March 1984), 87-110.

Taishiro Shirai, ed. *Contemporary Industrial Relations in Japan*, University of Wisconsin Press, 1983, including the following:
Kazutoshi Koshiro, "Labor Relations in Public Enterprises," 259-93.
Koichiro Yamaguchi, "The Public Sector: Civil Servants," 295-312.

Labor Law

Kichiemon Ishikawa, "The Regulation of the Employer-Employee Relationship: Japanese Labor-Relations Law," in Arthur T. von Mehren, ed. *Law in Japan: The Legal Order in a Changing Society*, Harvard University Press, 1963, 439-79.

Ehud Harari, *The Politics of Labor Legislation in Japan: National-International Interaction*, University of California Press, 1973.

Tadashi Hanami, *Labor Law and Industrial Relations in Japan*, Deventer, Netherlands, Kluwer, 1979.

Tadashi A. Hanami, "The Function of the Law in Japanese Industrial Relations," in Taishiro Shirai, ed. *Contemporary Industrial Relations in Japan*, University of Wisconsin Press, 1983, 161-77.

Tadashi Hanami, "Conflict and Its Resolution in Industrial Relations and Labor Law," in Ellis S. Krauss, Thomas C. Rohlen, & Patricia G. Steinhoff, eds. *Conflict in Japan*, University Press of Hawaii, 1984, 107-35.

Masahiro Ken Kuwahara, "Japanese Industrial Relations and Law with Reference to Introduction of High Tech Affecting Unemployment," *Hosei Riron* 17:1&2 (Sept 1984), 267-90 ("backward" pagination).

William B. Gould, *Japan's Reshaping of American Labor Law*, MIT Press, 1984.

Fujio Hamada, "The Gist of Labor Relations Law in Japan: Its Universalities and Peculiarities," Kobe University Law Review 21 (1987), 79-96.

C. WORK & LABOR

Factory Analyses

Robert E. Cole, Japanese Blue Collar: The Changing Tradition, University of California Press, 1971.

Ronald P. Dore, *British Factory-Japanese Factory, The Origins of National Diversity in Employment Relations*, University of California Press, 1973.

Thomas P. Rohlen, "The Company Work Group," in Ezra F. Vogel, ed. *Modern Japanese Organization and Decision-Making*, University of California Press, 1975, 185-209.

Robert Marsh & Hiroshi Manari, *Modernization and the Japanese Factory*, Princeton University Press, 1976.

John C. Pelzel, "Factory Life in Japan and China Today," in Albert M. Craig, ed. *Japan: A Comparative View*, Princeton University Press, 1979, 371-432.

Masatoshi Yorimitsu, "A Note on the Working Conditions of Subcontracting Establishments in the Iron and Steel Industry," *Hitotsubashi Journal of Social Studies* 12:1 (Nov 1980), 47-66.

Satoshi Kamata, *Japan in the Passing Lane: An Insider's Account of Life in a Japanese Auto Factory*, Pantheon, 1982.

Kazutoshi Koshiro, "The Quality of Working Life in Japanese Factories," in Taishiro Shirai, ed. *Contemporary Industrial Relations in Japan*, University of Wisconsin Press, 1983, 63-87.

Koya Azumi et al., "Structural Uniformity and Cultural Diversity in Organizations: A Comparative Study of Factories in Britain, Japan, and Sweden," in Kazuo Sato & Yasuo Hoshino, eds. *The Anatomy of Japanese Business*, Armonk, N.Y., M.E. Sharpe, 1984, 101-20.

Unions & Strikes

Solomon B. Levine, "Postwar Trade Unionism, Collective Bargaining, and Japanese Social Structure," in Ronald Dore, ed. *Aspects of Social Change in Modern Japan*, Princeton University Press, 1967, 245-85.

Alice H. Cook, *An Introduction to Japanese Trade Unionism*, Cornell University Press, 1966.

Alice H. Cook, "Political Action and Trade Unions: A Case Study of the Coal Miners in Japan," *Monumenta Nipponica* 22:1&2 (1967), 103-21.

Eitaro Kishimoto, "Labour-Management Relations and the Trade Unions in Post-War Japan," *Kobe University Economic Review* 38:1 (Apr 1968), 1-35.

John Price, "Labour Relations in Japan's Postwar Coal Industry: The 1960 Miike Lockout," M.A. thesis, University of British Columbia, 1987.

Haruo Shimada, "Japanese Labour's Spring Wage Offensive and Wage Spillover," *Keio Economic Studies* 7:2 (1970), 33-61.

Frank Baldwin, "Junpo-toso [Work-to-rule slowdown tactic]," *Japan Interpreter* 9:2 (Sum-Aut 1974), 227-37.

Taishiro Shirai, "Decision-Making in Japanese Labor Unions," in Ezra F. Vogel, ed. *Modern Japanese Organization and Decision-Making*, University of California Press, 1975, 167-84.

Gary Dean Allinson, "The Moderation of Organized Labor in Postwar Japan," *Journal of Japanese Studies* 1:2 (Spr 1975), 409-36.

J. Victor Koschmann, "Sutoken suto [Right-to-strike strike]," *Japan Interpreter* 11:1 (Spr 1976), 85-96.

Kaichi Maekawa, "Labour Union Movements and 'Shun-to' (Spring Campaign) in Japan," *Kyoto University Economic Review* 49:1-2 (Apr-Oct 1979), 1-12.

Solomon B. Levine & Koji Taira, "Interpreting Industrial Conflict: The Case of Japan," in Benjamin Martin & Everett Kassalaw, eds. *Labor Relations in Advanced Industrial Societies: Issues and Problems*, Washington, D.C., Carnegie Endowment for International Peace, 1980.

Kazutoshi Koshiro, "Japan's Wage Determination Reexamined," *JES* 10:2 (Win 1981-82), 49-78.

Taishiro Shirai, ed. *Contemporary Industrial Relations in Japan*, University of Wisconsin Press, 1983, the following articles:
Norikuni Naito, "Trade Union Finance and Adminstration," 145-59.
Yasuhiko Matsuda, "Conflict Resolution in Japanese Industrial Relations," 179-203.
Kazutoshi Koshiro, "Development of Collective Bargaining in Postwar Japan," 205-57.
Taishiro Shirai, "Japanese Labor Unions and Politics," 331-52.

Michael A. Cusumano, *The Japanese Automobile Industry: Technology and Management at Nissan and Toyota*, Harvard University Press, 1985, 137-85.

V. Fedyainov, "Japan's Trade Unions at Crossroads," *Far Eastern Affairs* 61:5 (1988), 45-53.

Work Ethic, Attitudes and Skills

Iwao Ishizaka, "Problems of Industrial Training in Japan," *Keio Business Review* 4 (1965), 29-55.

Kazutoshi Koshiro, "Perceptions of Work and Living Attitudes of the Japanese," *Japan Quarterly* 27:1 (Jan-Mar 1980), 46-55.

Soloman Levine & Hisashi Kawada, *Human Resources in Japanese Industrial Development*, Princeton University Press, 1980.

Isao Akaoka, "Motivation of Employees in Japan," *Kyoto University Economic Review* 53:1-2 (Apr-Oct 1983), 25-50.

Jon Woronoff, *Japan's Wasted Workers*, Totowa, New Jersey, Allenheld, Osmun & Co., 1983.

David W. Plath, ed. *Work and Lifecourse in Japan*, State University of New York, 1983.

Kazuo Koike, "The Formation of Worker Skill in Small Japanese Firms," *JES* 11:4 (Sum 1983), 3-57.

Koji Okubayashi, "The Impacts of Industrial Robots on Working Life in Japan," *Journal of General Management* 11:4 (Sum 1986), 22-34.

Kazuo Koike, "Human Resource Development and Labor-Management Relations," in Kozo Yamamura & Yasukichi Yasuba, eds. *The Political Economy of Japan*, vol. 1, *The Domestic Transformation*, Stanford University Press, 1987, 289-330.

Kazuo Koike, *Understanding Industrial Relations in Modern Japan*, London, Macmillan, 1988.

D. INTERNATIONAL DIMENSIONS

International Comparisons

Bernard Karsh & Robert E. Cole, "Industrialization and the Convergence Hypothesis: Some Aspects of Contemporary Japan," *Journal of Social Issues* 24:4 (1968), 45-64.

Arthur Whitehall & Shin'ichi Takezawa, *The Other Worker: A Comparative Study of Industrial Relations in the United States and Japan*, The University Press of Hawaii, 1969.

Ronald Dore, "Industrial Relations in Japan and Elsewhere," in Albert M. Craig, ed. *Japan: A Comparative View*, Princeton University Press, 1979, 324-70.

Robert E. Cole, *Work, Mobility and Participation: A Comparative Study of American and Japanese Industry*, University of California Press, 1979.

Takao Nishioka, "Industrial Relations in Japan: An International Comparison and Description of its Characteristics," *Kansai University Review of Economics and Business* 8:1 (June 1979), 11-20.

Charles J. McMillan, "Human Resource Policies, Labour Markets, and Unions: Canada-Japan Comparisons," in Keith A.J. Hay, ed. *Canadian Perspectives on Economic Relations with Japan*, Montreal, Institute for Research on Public Policy, 1980, 141-58.

Shin-ichi Takezawa & Arthur M. Whitehall, *Work Ways: Japan and America*, The Japan Institute of Labour, 1981.

Kazuo Koike, "Skill Formation in the U.S. and Japan: A Comparative Study," in Masahiko Aoki, ed. *The Economic Analysis of the Japanese Firm*, Amsterdam, North Holland, 1984, 47-75.

Tamotsu Sengoku, *Willing Workers: The Work Ethics in Japan, England, and the United States*, Westport, Quorum Books, 1985.

Multinationals & Japanese Systems Abroad

Tadashi A. Hanami, "The Multinational Corporation and Japanese Industrial Relations," in Duane Kujawa, ed. *International Labor and Multinational Enterprise*, New York, Praeger, 1976, 173-86.

Ehud Harari & Yoram Zeira, "Attitudes of Japanese and Non-Japanese Employees: A Cross-National Comparison in Uninational and Multinational Corporations," *International Journal of Comparative Sociology* 18:3&4 (Sept-Dec 1977), 228-41.

Thomas J. Nevins, *Labor Pains and the Gaijin Boss: Hiring, Managing and Hiring the Japanese*, Tokyo, The Japan Times, 1984.

Michael White and Malcolm Trevor, *Under Japanese Management: The Experience of British Workers*, London, Heinemann, 1983.

Francine McNulty, "Employment Rights of Japanese-American Joint Ventures in the United States under the U.S.-Japan Treaty of Friendship, Commerce and Navigation," *Law & Policy in International Business* 16:4 (1984), 1225-48.

Vivian Lin, "Productivity First: Japanese Management Methods in Singapore," *Bulletin of Concerned Asian Scholars* 16:4 (Oct-Dec 1984), 12-25.

Yasuo Kuwahara, *Decision-Making Structures and Processes in Multinationals in Japan*, Geneva, International Labour Organization, 1985.

Wolf Reitsperger, "Japanese Management: Coping with British Industrial Relations," *Journal of Management Studies* 23:1 (Jan 1986), 72-87

Wolf Reitsperger, "British Employees: Responding to Japanese Management Philosophies," *Journal of Management Studies* 23:5 (Sept 1986), 563-86.

Harris Jack Shapiro & Teresa Cosenza, *Reviving Industry in America: Japanese Influences on Manufacturing and the Service Sector*, Cambridge, Ballinger, 1987.

Peter Wickens, *The Road to Nissan: Flexibility Quality Teamwork*, London, Macmillan, 1987 (re: Nissan in Britain).

Hem C. Jain, "The Japanese System of Human Resource Management: Transferability to the Indian Industrial Environment," *Asian Survey* 27:9 (Sept 1987), 1023-35.

Robert E. Cole & Donald R. Deskins, Jr., "Racial Factors in Site Location and Employment Patterns of Japanese Auto Firms in America," *California Management Review* 31:1 (Fall 1988), 9-22.

Mitsunobu Sugiyama, "Should Foreign Workers Be Welcomed?" *Japan Quarterly* 35:3 (July-Sept 1988), 260-65.

E. MACROECONOMIC ISSUES

Labor Market

Tokijiro Minoguchi, "The Employment Problem in Japan in Next Ten Years," *Annals of the Hitotsubashi Academy* 8:2 (Apr 1958), 169-75.

Mataji Umemura, "An Analysis of Employment Structure in Japan," *Hitotsubashi Journal of Economics* 2:2 (March 1962), 16-29.

Solomon B. Levine, "Labor Markets and Collective Bargaining in Japan," William W. Lockwood, ed. *The State and Economic Enterprise in Japan*, Princeton University Press, 1965, 633-67.

Ryoichi Suzuki, "A US-Japan Comparison of Wages-Price Structure," *Keio Business Review* 7 (1968), 1-15.

Yoko Sano, "A Quantitative Analysis of Wage-Determination in Japan," *Keio Business Review* 7 (1968), 65-89.

Tuvia Blumenthal, "Scarcity of Labor and Wage Differentials in the Japanese Economy, 1958-64," *Economic Development and Cultural Change* 17:1 (Oct 1968), 15-32.

Kang Chao, "Labor Institutions in Japan and Her Economic Growth," Journal of Asian Studies 28:1 (Nov 1968), 5-17.

Mataji Umemura, "Regional Differences in the Distribution of Industrial Employment in Japan," *DE* 7:2 (June 1969), 117-32.

Koichi Emi, "Employment Structure in the Service Industries," *DE* 7:2 (June 1969), 133-57.

Koji Taira, *Economic Development and the Labor Market in Japan*, Columbia University Press, 1970.

Kaichi Maekawa, "Changes of Government Employment Policy in the Face of Economic Growth in Japan since World War II," *Kyoto University Economic Review* 40:2 (Oct 1970), 44-54.

Robert Evans, *The Labor Economies of Japan and the United States*, New York, Praeger, 1971.

Robert E. Cole & Ken'ichi Tominaga, "Japan's Changing Occupational Structure and its Significance," in Hugh Patrick, ed. *Japanese Industrialization and its Social Consequences*, University of California Press, 1973, 53-95.

Ken'ichi Tominaga, "Social Mobility in Japan: Prewar and Postwar Patterns," *Japan Interpreter* 8:3 (Aut 1973), 374-86.

Shunsaku Nishikawa & Haruo Shimada, "Employment and Unemployment: 1970-1975," *Keio Business Review* 13 (1974), 43-58.

Masanori Nozawa & Kiyofumi Kawaguchi, "Capital Accumulation and Changes in the Structure of the Laboring Classes in Japan since 1960," *Kyoto University Economic Review* 44:1-2 (Apr-Oct 1974), 19-58.

Walter Galenson, "The Japanese Labor Market," in Hugh Patrick & Henry Rosovsky, eds. *Asia's New Giant: How the Japanese Economy Works*, Brookings Institution, 1976, 587-671.

Iwao Ozaki, "Industrial Structure and Employment: The Experiences in Japanese Economic Development, 1955-68," *DE* 14:4 (Dec 1976), 341-65.

Solomon B. Levine & Koji Taira, "Labor Markets, Trade Unions and Social Justice: Japanese Failures?" *JES* 5:3 (Spr 1977), 66-95.

Haruo Shimada, "The Japanese Labor Market after the Oil Crisis: A Factual Report," *Keio Economic Studies* (1) 14:1 (1977), 49-66; (2) 14:2 (1977), 37-60.

Shin'ichi Yoshioka, "A Study on Wage Distribution in Korea and Japan," *DE* 16:1 (March 1978), 97-110.

Taishiro Shirai & Haruo Shimada, "Japan," in John T. Dunlop & Walter Galenson, eds. *Labor in the Twentieth Century*, New York, Academic Press, 1978, 241-322.

Haruo Shimada & Shunsaku Nishikawa, "An Analysis of Japanese Employment System and Youth Labor Markets," *Keio Economic Studies* 16:1-2 (1979), 1-16.

Ernest van Helvoort, *The Japanese Working Man: What Choice? What Reward?*, University of British Columbia Press, 1979.

Shunsaku Nishikawa, ed. *The Labor Market in Japan*, trans. by Ross Mouer, University of Tokyo Press, 1980.

Soloman B. Levine & Hisashi Kawada, *Human Resources in Japanese Industrial Development*, Princeton University Press, 1980.

Yoko Sano, "Development of the Internal Labor Market among Firms of Employment Growing Sectors," *Keio Business Review* 19 (1982), 1-20.

Special Issue: "The Japanese Labor Market: A Survey," *JES* 11:2 (Win 1982-83).

Isao Ohashi, "A Comparison of the Labor Market in Japan and the United States," *JES* 11:4 (Sum 1983), 58-84.

William Paul Sterling, "Comparative Studies of American and Japanese Labor Markets," Ph.D. diss., Harvard University, 1984.

Toshio Sanuki, "Waxing and Waning Job Markets," *Japan Echo* 11:1 (Spr 1984), 19-26.

Asao Mizuno, "Wage Flexibility and Employment Changes," *JES* 16:2 (Win 1987-88), 38-73.

Giorgio Brunello, "Transfers of Employees in Japan between Japanese Manufacturing Enterprises: Some Results from an Enquiry on a Small Sample of Large Firms," *British Journal of Industrial Relations* 26:1 (March 1988), 119-32.

Jacob Mincer & Yoshio Higuchi, "Wage Structures and Labor Turnover in the United States and Japan," *Journal of the Japanese and International Economies* 2:2 (June 1988), 97-133.

Hiroshi Osano & Touru Inoue, "Implicit Contracts in the Japanese Labor Market," *Journal of the Japanese and International Economies* 2:2 (June 1988), 181-98.

Norma Chalmers, *Industrial Relations in Japan: The Peripheral Sector*, New York, Routledge, 1988.

195

Productivity

Kenzo Yukizawa, "A Comparison of Labour Productivity in Japanese and American Manufacturing Industry," *Kyoto University Economic Review* 38:1 (Apr 1968), 36-56.

Hugh Patrick, "The Future of the Japanese Economy: Output and Labor Productivity," *Journal of Japanese Studies* 3:2 (Sum 1977), 219-49.

Kenzo Yukizawa, "Relative Productivity of Labor in American and Japanese Industry and its Change, 1958-1972," in Shigeto Tsuru, ed. *Growth and Resources Problems Related to Japan*: Proceedings of Session VI of the Fifth Congress of the International Economic Association, Tokyo, Asahi Evening News, 1978, 61-88.

Women

Etsuko Kaji, "The Invisible Proletariat: Working Women in Japan," *Ampo* 18 (Aut 1973), 48-58.

Hazel J. Jones, "Japanese Women and the Dual-Track Employment System," *Pacific Affairs* 49 (1976), 589-606.

Alice H. Cook & Hiroko Hayashi, *Working Women in Japan: Discrimination, Resistance and Reform*, Cornell University, New York State School of Labor & Industrial Relations, 1980.

Special Issue: "Female Labor-Force Participation," *JES* 9:2 (Win 1980-81), including:
Kazuo Koike, "A Japan-Europe Composition of Female Labor-Force Participation and Male-Female Wage Differentials," 3-27.
Naohiro Yashiro, "Male-Female Wage Differentials in Japan: A Rational Explanation," 28-61.
Shunsaku Nishikawa & Yoshio Higuchi, "Determinants of Female Labor-Force Participation," 62-87.

Yuriko Saisho, *Women Executives in Japan*, Yuri International, 1981.

Makoto Sakurabayashi, "The Wage of Woman Part-time Employees in Today's Japan," *Sophia Economic Review* 28:2 (Dec 1981), 14-46.

Kazuo Koike, "Workers in Small Firms and Women in Industry," in Taishiro Shirai, ed. *Contemporary Industrial Relations in Japan*, University of Wisconsin Press, 1983, 89-115.

Eiko Shinotsuka, "Female Workers as Described in a Help-Wanted Information Magazine," *JES* 12:3 (Spr 1984), 3-20.

Paul Lansing & Kathryn Ready, "Hiring Women Managers in Japan: An Alternative for Foreign Employers," *California Management Review* 30:3 (Spr 1988), 112-27.

Machiko Osawa, "Working Mothers: Changing Patterns of Employment and Fertility in Japan," *Economic Development and Cultural Change* 36:4 (July 1988), 623-50.

Bulletin of Concerned Asian Scholars 20:3 (July-Sept 1988), the following:
Kuniko Fujita, "Women Workers, State Policy, and the International Division of Labor: The Case of Silicon Island in Japan," 42-53.
Reiko Atsumi, "Dilemmas and Accommodations of Married Japanese Women in White-Collar Employment, 54-62.

Population

Minoru Tachi & Yoichi Okazaki, "Japan's Postwar Population and Labor Force," *DE* 7:2 (June 1969), 170-86.

Shinichi Takahashi, "Recent Fertility Patterns in Metropolitan Regions of Japan," *Kobe University Economic Review* 21 (1975), 91-105.

Carl Mosk, "The Decline of Marital Fertility in Japan," *Population Studies* 33 (March 1979), 19-38.

Hiroshi Ohbuchi, "The Aging of Population and Economic Growth in Japan," *JES* 7:3 (Spr 1979), 3-29.

Yasukichi Yasuba, "Policy-Induced Growth and the Older Generation," *JES* 7:3 (Spr 1979), 30-70.

Hiroshi Hazama, "The Maturation of Society and Labor-Management Relations," *JES* 8:2 (Win 1979-80), 48-82.

Hirohide Tanaka, "Low Growth and Aging Labor Force," *Japan Quarterly* 27:1 (Jan-Mar 1980), 39-45.

Masatoshi Yorimitsu, "A Review of Recent Population Changes in Japan," *Hitotsubashi Journal of Social Studies* 19:1 (Apr 1987), 15-30.

Randall S. Jones, "The Economic Implications of Japan's Aging Population," *Asian Survey* 28:9 (Sept 1988), 958-69.

Unemployment and Social Insurance

Kaichi Maekawa, "Unemployment Relief Work in Japan," *Kyoto University Economic Review* 33:1 (Apr 1963), 27-41.

Ehud Harari, "Unemployment in Japan: Policy and Politics," *Asian Survey* 18:10 (Oct 1978), 1013-28.

Koji Taira, "Japan's Low Employment: An Economic Miracle or Statistical Artifact," *Monthly Labour Review* 106:7 (July 1983), 3-10.

Special Issue on "Japan's Unemployment Rate," *JES* 14:1 (Fall 1985), the following:
Sadanori Nagayama, "Is Japan's Unemployment Rate too Low?" 34-61.
Kenji Tominomori, "Unemployment Rates of Japan and the United States," 62-73.
Akira Ono, "On Recent Studies of Unemployment in Japan," 74-100.

C. Arthur Williams, Jr., "Workmen's Accident Compensation Insurance: Japan's Lesser Known Social Insurance Scheme," *Keio Business Review* 22 (1985), 67-89.

Koji Taira, "The Labor Force Survey and Unemployment: A Philosophical Note," *JES* 14:1 (Fall 1985) 3-33.

5. INDUSTRIAL ORGANIZATION

A. HISTORICAL SURVEYS

Martin Bronfenbrenner, " 'Excessive Competition' in Japanese Business," *Monumenta Nipponica* 21 (1966), 114-24.

Masahiro Hattori, "Market Competition and Public Policy in Japan," *KSU Economic and Business Review* (Kyoto Sangyo University) 2 (May 1975), 48-60.

Masu Uekusa, "Effects of the Deconcentration Measures in Japan," *Antitrust Bulletin* 22 (Fall 1977), 687-715.

B. INDUSTRIAL ORGANIZATION & THE ANTI-MONOPOLY LAW

Economic Analyses

Tasuku Noguchi, "A Theory on the Business Concentration in Japan," *Keio Business Review* 2 (1963), 53-77.

Eugene Rotwein, "Economic Concentration and Monopoly in Japan," *Journal of Political Economy* (June 1964), 262-77.

Kozo Yamamura, "An Observation on the Post-war Japanese Anti-monopoly Policy," *Indian Journal of Economics* 45 (July 1964), 31-68.

Kozo Yamamura, "Market Concentration and Growth in Postwar Japan," *Southern Economic Journal* (April 1966), 451-64.

Kozo Yamamura, *Economic Policy in Postwar Japan: Growth versus Economic Democracy*, University of California Press, 1967.

Koujiro Niino, "Industrial Organization Policy and Economic Growth in Postwar Japan," *Kobe University Economic Review* 14 (1968), 29-42.

Eleanor M. Hadley, *Antitrust in Japan*, Princeton University Press, 1970.

Robert S. Ozaki, "Japanese Views on Industrial Organization," *Asian Survey* 10 (Oct 1970), 872-89.

Martin Bronfenbrenner, "Japan's Galbraithian Economy," *The Public Interest* 21 (Fall 1970), 149-57.

James C. Abegglen & William V. Rapp, "Japanese Managerial Behavior and 'Excessive Competition'," *DE* 8:4 (Dec 1970), 427-44.

Jiro Ono, "The Characteristics of Recent Corporate Mergers in Japan," *Kobe Economic & Business Review* 17 (1970), 53-67.

Yoshihige Higuchi & Kazuo Watanabe, "General Concentration in Japan: Status and Trends," *JES* 2:4 (Sum 1974), 3-61.

Yoshio Sato & Koichi Ito, "A Theory of Oligopolistic Core and Competitive Fringe: Japan's Wheat Flour Milling Industry," *Keio Business Review* 13 (1974), 17-42.

Kozo Yamamura, "Structure is Behavior: An Appraisal of Japanese Economic Policy, 1960-1972," in Isaiah Frank, ed. *The Japanese Economy in International Perspective*, Baltimore, Johns Hopkins University Press, 1975, 67-100.

Richard Caves & Masu Uekusa, "Industrial Organization," in Hugh Patrick & Henry Rosovsky, eds. *Asia's New Giant: How the Japanese Economy Works*, Brookings Institution, 1976, 459-523.

Richard E. Caves & Masu Uekusa, *Industrial Organization in Japan*, Brookings Institution, 1976.

Eleanor M. Hadley, " 'Industrial Organization' by Caves and Uekusa: A Review Essay," *JES* 5:2 (Win 1976-77), 64-82.

Eugene Rotwein, "Economic Concentration and Monopoly in Japan—A Second View," *Journal of Asian Studies* 36:1 (Nov 1976), 57-77.

Ken'ichi Imai & Masu Uekusa, "Industrial Organization and Economic Growth in Japan," in Shigeto Tsuru, ed. *Growth and Resources Problems Related to Japan*: Proceedings of Session VI of the Fifth Congress of the International Economic Association, Tokyo, Asahi Evening News, 1978, 91-112.

Kazuo Sato, ed. *Industry and Business in Japan*, White Plains, N.Y., M.E. Sharpe, 1980, including:
Ken'ichi Imai, "Japan's Industrial Organization," 74-135.
Kazunori Echigo, "Japanese Studies of Industrial Organization," 450-63.

Naohiro Amaya, "Harmony and the Antimonopoly Law," *Japan Echo* 1 (1981), 85-102.

Kozo Yamamura, "Success that Soured: Administrative Guidance and Cartels in Japan," in Kozo Yamamura, ed. *Policy and Trade Issues of the Japanese Economy: American and Japanese Perspectives*, University of Washington Press, 1982, 77-112.

Takatoshi Nakamura, "Japan's Giant Enterprises: Their Power and Influence," *JES* 12:4 (Sum 1984), 50-90.

Ken'ichi Imai & H. Itami, "Interpenetration of Organization and Market: Japan's Firm and Market in Comparison with the U.S.," *International Journal of Industrial Organization* 2 (1984), 285-310.

James C. Abegglen & George Stalk, Jr., "The Japanese Corporation as Competitor," *California Management Review* 28:3 (Spr 1986), 9-27.

Harry First, "Japan's Antitrust Policy: Impact on Import Competition," in Thomas A. Pugel, ed. *Fragile Interdependence: Economic Issues in U.S.-Japanese Trade and Investment*, Lexington, Heath, 1986, 63-90.

Hiroshi Iyori, "Antitrust and Industrial Policy in Japan: Competition and Cooperation," in Gary Saxonhouse & Kozo Yamamura, eds. *Law and Trade Issues of the Japanese Economy: American and Japanese Perspectives*, University of Washington Press, 1986, 56-82.

Thomas K. McCraw & Patricia A. O'Brien, "Production and Distribution: Competition Policy and Industry," in Thomas K. McCraw, ed. *America versus Japan*, Boston, Harvard Business School Press, 1986, 77-116.

Akinori Uesugi, "Japan's Cartel System and Its Impact on International Trade," *Harvard International Law Journal* 27: Special Issue (1986), 389-424.

Masu Uekusa, "Industrial Organization: The 1970s to the Present," in Kozo Yamamura & Yasukichi Yasuba, eds. *The Political Economy of Japan*, vol. 1, *The Domestic Transformation*, Stanford University Press, 1987, 469-515.

Ryutaro Komiya, Masahiro Okuno, & Kotaro Suzumura, eds., *Industrial Policy of Japan*, Academic Press, 1988, the following:
Yoshiro Miwa, "Coordination Within Industry: Output, Price, and Investment," 475-96.
Akira Iwasaki, "Mergers and Reorganizations," 497-511.

Legal Issues & Administrative Policy

Yoshio Kanazawa, "The Regulation of Corporate Enterprise: The Law of Unfair Competition and the Control of Monopoly Power," in Arthur T. von Mehren, ed. *Law in Japan: The Legal Order in a Changing Society*, Harvard University Press, 1963, 480-506.

Yoriaki Narita, "Administrative Guidance," *Law in Japan* 2 (1968), 45-79.

Ichiro Ogawa, "Judicial Review of Administrative Actions in Japan," *Washington Law Review* 43 (1968), 1075-94.

"Japanese Fair Trade Commission—Decision on the Yawata-Fuji Steel Merger," *Antitrust Bulletin* 15 (1970), 803-27.

Kazuo Yamanouchi, "Administrative Guidance and the Rule of Law," *Law in Japan* 7 (1974), 22-33.

"Administrative Guidance," in Hideo Tanaka, ed., assisted by Malcolm D.H. Smith, *The Japanese Legal System: Introductory Cases and Materials*, University of Tokyo Press, 1976, 353-404.

Michiko Ariga, "Efforts to Revise the Japanese Antimonopoly Act," *Antitrust Bulletin* 21 (Win 1976), 703-25.

Kenji Sanekata, "Administrative Guidance and the Antimonopoly Law," *Law in Japan* 10 (1977), 65-80.

Antimonopoly Legislation of Japan, ed. by Counselor's Office of Fair Trade Commission, Tokyo, Kosei Torihiki Kyokai, 1977.

John O. Haley, "Marketing and Antitrust in Japan," *Hastings International and Comparative Law Review* 2:1 (Spr 1979), 51-72.

James Sameth & John O. Haley, "Guidelines Concerning the Activities of Trade Associations under the Antimonopoly Law," *Law in Japan* 12 (1979), 118-52.

Mitsuo Matsushita, "Export Control and Export Cartels in Japan," *Harvard International Law Journal* 20:1 (Win 1979), 103-25.

"Trustbusting in Japan: Cartels and Government-Business Cooperation," *Harvard Law Review* 94:5 (March 1981), 1064-84.

J. Amanda Covey, "Vertical Restraints Under Japanese Law: The Antimonopoly Law Study Group Report," *Law in Japan* 14 (1981), 49-81.

J. Mark Ramseyer, "Japanese Antitrust Enforcement after the Oil Embargo," *American Journal of Comparative Law* 31:3 (Sum 1982), 395-430.

Law in Japan 15 (1982), including:
John O. Haley, "The Oil Cartel Cases: The End of an Era," 1-11.
Wolfgang Pape, "*Gyosei Shido* and the Antimonopoly Law," 12-23.
Larry Repeta, "The Limits of Administrative Authority in Japan: A Report on the Petroleum Cartel Decisions and the Reaction of MITI and the Fair Trade Commission," 24-56.
J. Mark Ramseyer, "The Oil Cartel Criminal Cases: Translations and Postscript," 57-78.
Mitsuo Matsushita, "Problems and Analysis of the Oil Cartel Case Decisions," 79-94.

Hiroshi Iyori & Akinori Uesugi, *The Antimonopoly Laws of Japan*, Washington, Federal Legal Publications, 1983.

Akira Shoda, "Antimonopoly Law Violations and Compensatory Damages," *Law in Japan* 16 (1983), 1-20.

Makoto Matsuo, "Mergers and Acquisitions under Japanese Law," *Antitrust Law Journal* 52:4 (1983), 1011-16.

Michael K. Young, "Administrative Guidance in the Courts: A Case Study in Doctrinal Adaptation," *Law in Japan* 17 (1984), 120-52.

Michael Young, "Judicial Review of Administrative Guidance: Governmentally Encouraged Consensual Dispute Resolution in Japan," *Columbia Law Review* 84:4 (1984), 923-83.

J. Mark Ramseyer, "The Costs of the Consensual Myth: Antitrust Enforcement and Institutional Barriers to Litigation in Japan," *Yale Law Journal* 94:3 (Jan 1985), 604-45.

Thomas R. Radcliffe, "Exclusive Dealing Arrangements under Japanese Antimonopoly Law: The *Toyo Seimaiki* Case," *Law in Japan* 18 (1985), 76-107.

Frank K. Upham, "Legal and Institutional Dynamics in Japan's Cartel Policy," in Michele Schmiegelow, ed. *Japan's Response to Crisis and Change in the World Economy*, New York, M.E. Sharpe, 1986, 278-303.

Frank K. Upham, *Law and Social Change in Postwar Japan*, Harvard University Press, 1987, 166-204.

C. DUAL STRUCTURE & SMALL BUSINESS

Tokutaro Yamanaka, "Prerequisites for Japanese Economy and Small-Medium Industry," *Annals of the Hitotsubashi Academy* 7:2 (Apr 1957), 91-114.

Miyohei Shinohara, "Inventory Cycles and the Dual Structure," *Hitotsubashi Journal of Economics* 2:2 (March 1962), 30-39.

Yoshio Sato, "A Recent Trend of the Small Business Problem in Japan: An Analytical Viewpoint," *Keio Business Review* 3 (1964), 77-94.

Seymour Broadbridge, *Industrial Dualism in Japan: A Problem of Economic Growth and Structural Change*, Chicago, Aldine Publishing Co., 1967.

Miyohei Shinohara, "A Survey of the Japanese Literature on Small Industry," in Bert F. Hoselitz, ed. *The Role of Small Industry in the Process of Economic Growth*, New York, Humanities Press, 1968, 1-114.

Hiroshi Wagatsuma & George De Vos, "The Entrepreneurial Mentality of Lower-Class Urban Japanese in Manufacturing Industries," in George De Vos, *Socialization for Achievement*, University of California Press, 1973,

Naoki Kobayashi, "The Small and Medium-Sized Enterprises Organization Law," in Hiroshi Itoh, ed. *Japanese Politics: An Inside View*, Cornell University Press, 1973, 49-67.

Ryoshin Minami & Akiri Ono, "Price Changes in a Dual Economy," *JES* 3:3 (Spr 1975), 32-58.

Lawrence Repeta, "The Small and Medium Enterprise Domain Protection Law of 1977: Its Operation and Likely Effect," *Law in Japan* 10 (1977), 140-51.

Tadao Kiyonari, "Small Businesses," in Hyoe Murakami & Johannes Hirschmeier, eds. *Politics and Economics in Contemporary Japan*, Tokyo, Japan Culture Institute, 1979, 157-83.

Ken'ichi Miyazawa, "The Dual Structure of the Japanese Economy and Its Growth Pattern," in Kazuo Sato, ed. *Industry and Business in Japan*, White Plains, N.Y., M.E. Sharpe, 1980, 22-52.

Mitsuru Yamazaki, *Japan's Community-Based Industries: A Case Study of Small Industry*, Tokyo, Asian Productivity Organization, 1980.

David Harold Stark, "The Yakuza: Japanese Crime Incorporated," Ph.D. diss., University of Michigan, 1981.

Felix Twaalfhoven & Tomohisa Hattori, *The Supporting Role of Small Japanese Enterprises*, Schiphol, Netherlands, N.V. Indivers Research, 1982.

Dorinne Kay Kondo, "Work, Family and Self: A Cultural Analysis of Japanese Family Enterprise," Ph.D. diss., Harvard University, 1982.

Yoshio Sato, "The Subcontracting Production (*Shitauke*) System in Japan," *Keio Business Review* 21:1 (1983),

Japan, MITI, *Small and Medium Enterprise Agency, Outline of Small and Medium-Scale Enterprise Policies of the Japanese Government*, Tokyo, 1984.

Special Issue: "*Keiretsu* and Subcontracting in Japan's Automobile Industry," *JES* 13:4 (Spr 1985).

Sueo Sekiguchi, "Industrial Policy in Japan: Interactions Between Policies and Dualist Structure," in Michele Schmiegelow, ed. *Japan's Response to Crisis and Change in the World Economy*, New York, M.E. Sharpe, 1986, 230-56.

Hideichiro Nakamura, "The Challenge of Japanese Small Business," *JES* 15:1 (Fall 1986), 76-101.

Hiroshi Takeuchi, "The Balance Sheet of the Yakuza Business," *JES* 15:2 (Win 1986-87), 49-65.

Hugh T. Patrick & Thomas P. Rohlen, "Small-Scale Family Enterprises," in Kozo Yamamura & Yasukichi Yasuba, eds. *The Political Economy of Japan*, vol. 1, *The Domestic Transformation*, Stanford University Press, 1987, 331-84.

Takashi Yokokura, "Small and Medium Enterprises," Ryutaro Komiya, Masahiro Okuno, & Kotaro Suzumura, eds., *Industrial Policy of Japan*, Academic Press, 1988, 513-39.

6. INDUSTRIAL STRUCTURE & INDUSTRIAL POLICY

A. GENERAL

Industrial Structure

Iwao Ozaki, "Recent Changes in the Structure of Japanese Production and Trade," *JES* 1:4 (Sum 1973), 3-32.

Iwao Ozaki, "Industrial Structure and Employment: The Experiences in Japanese Economic Development, 1955-68," *DE* 14:4 (Dec 1976), 341-65.

Special Issue: "Changing Industrial Structure in International Perspective," *DE* 18:4 (Dec 1980), including:
Yukio Kaneko, "Changes in Japan's Industrial Structure since the Oil Crisis," 484-501.
Nobuyoshi Namiki, "The Industrial Structure of Japan in the 1980s," 502-21.

Yoko Sazanami, "Possibilities of Expanding Intra-Industry Trade in Japan," *Keio Economic Studies* 18:2 (1981), 27-43.

William V. Rapp, "Industrial Structure and Japanese Trade Friction," *Journal of International Affairs* 37:1 (Sum 1983), 67-79.

Industrial Policy

R. Takahashi, "Trade Policies and the New Japan," *Foreign Affairs* 30 (1952), 289-97.

Leon Hollerman, "Industrial Structure and Economic Planning in Japan," *Pacific Affairs* 33 (1960), 219-26.

M.Y. Yoshino, *Japan's Managerial System: Tradition and Innovation,* MIT Press, 1968.

Robert S. Ozaki, "Japanese Views on Industrial Organization," *Asian Survey* 10 (Oct 1970), 872-89.

Ryutaro Komiya, "Planning in Japan," in Morris Bornstein, ed. *Economic Planning, East and West,* Ballinger, 1975, 189-235.

William V. Rapp, "Japan's Industrial Policy," in Isaiah Frank, ed. *The Japanese Economy in International Perspective,* Baltimore, Johns Hopkins University Press, 1975, 37-66.

Ippei Yamazawa, "Trade Policy and Changes in Japan's Trade Structure: With Special Reference to Labor-Intensive Manufactures," *DE* 13:4 (Dec 1975), 374-99.

Miyohei Shinohara, "MITI's Industrial Policy and Japanese Industrial Organization: A Retrospective Evaluation," *DE* 14:4 (Dec 1976), 366-80.

Chalmers Johnson, "MITI and Japanese International Economic Policy," in Robert A. Scalapino, ed. *The Foreign Policy of Modern Japan,* University of California Press, 1977, 227-79.

William V. Rapp, "Japan: Its Industrial Policies and Corporate Behavior," *Columbia Journal of World Business* (Spr 1977), 38-48.

Hiroya Ueno, "The Conception and Evaluation of Japanese Industrial Policy," in Kazuo Sato, ed. *Industry and Business in Japan,* White Plains, N.Y., M.E. Sharpe, 1980, 375-434.

Ira C. Magaziner & Thomas M. Hout, *Japanese Industrial Policy,* Berkeley, Institute of International Studies, University of California, 1980.

Dezso Horvath & Charles McMillan, "Industrial Planning in Japan," *California Management Review* 23:1 (Fall 1980), 11-21.

Chalmers Johnson, *MITI and the Japanese Miracle: The Growth of Industrial Policy, 1925-1975,* Stanford University Press, 1982.

Miyohei Shinohara, *Industrial Growth, Trade, and Dynamic Patterns in the Japanese Economy,* University of Tokyo Press, 1982.

Kozo Yamamura, "Success that Soured: Administrative Guidance and Cartels in Japan," in Kozo Yamamura, ed. *Policy and Trade Issues of the Japanese Economy: American and Japanese Perspectives,* University of Washington Press, 1982, 77-112.

F. Gerard Adams & Shinichi Ichimura, "Industrial Policy in Japan," in F.G. Adams & Lawrence R. Klein, eds. *Industrial Policies for Growth and Competitiveness: An Economic Perspective,* Lexington, Mass., D.C. Heath, Lexington Books, 1983, 307-30.

Edward Lincoln, *Japan's Industrial Policies,* Washington, Japan Economic Institute of America, 1984.

Julian Gresser, *Partners in Prosperity: Strategic Industries for the U.S. & Japan,* New York, McGraw-Hill, 1984.

Robert S. Ozaki, "How Japanese Industrial Policy Works," in Chalmers Johnson, ed. *The Industrial Policy Debate,* San Francisco, Institute for Comparative Studies Press, 1984, 47-70.

"Japanese Industrial Policies," in Thomas Pepper, Merit E. Janow, & Jimmy W. Wheeler, *The Competition: Dealing with Japan,* New York, Praeger, 1985, 69-142.

Michele Schmiegelow, "Cutting Across Doctrines: Positive Adjustment in Japan," *International Organization* 39:2 (Spr. 1985), 261-96.

Sueo Sekiguchi & Toshihiro Horiuchi, "Myth and Reality of Japan's Industrial Policies," *The World Economy* 8:4 (Dec 1985), 373-91.

Masaaki Kotabe, "The Roles of Japanese Industrial Policy for Export Success: A Theoretical Perspective," *Columbia Journal of World Business* 20:3 (Fall 1985), 59-64.

Ezra Vogel, *Comeback—Case by Case: Building the Resurgence of American Business,* New York, Simon & Schuster, 1985.

Toshimasa Tsuruta, "Japan's Industrial Policy," in Lester C. Thurow, ed. *The Management Challenge: Japanese Views,* MIT Press, 1985, 160-90.

Ryutaro Komiya, "Industrial Policy in Japan," *JES* 14:4 (Sum 1986), 51-81.

Sueo Sekiguchi, "Industrial Policy in Japan: Interactions Between Policies and Dualist Structure," in Michele Schmiegelow, ed. *Japan's Response to Crisis and Change in the World Economy,* New York, M.E. Sharpe, 1986, 230-56.

Chalmers Johnson, "The Institutional Foundations of Japanese Industrial Policy," *California Management Review* 27:4 (Sum 1985), 59-69, included in Claude E. Barfield & William A. Schambra, eds. *The Politics of Industrial Policy,* Washington, American Enterprise Institute, 1986, 187-205.

Hiroshi Iyori, "Antitrust and Industrial Policy in Japan: Competition and Cooperation," in Gary Saxonhouse & Kozo Yamamura, eds. *Law and Trade Issues of the Japanese Economy: American and Japanese Perspectives,* University of Washington Press, 1986, 56-82.

Daniel I. Okimoto, "Regime Characteristics of Japanese Industrial Policy," in Hugh Patrick, ed. *Japan's High Technology Industries: Lessons and Limitations of Industrial Policy,* University of Washington Press, 1986, 35–95.

Hiromichi Mutoh, Sueo Sekiguchi, Kotaro Suzumura & Ippei Yamazawa, eds. *Industrial Policies for Pacific Economic Growth,* Sydney, Allen & Unwin, 1986, including the following articles:

Masahiro Okuno & Kotaro Suzumura, "The Economic Analysis of Industrial Policy: A Conceptual Framework through the Japanese Experience," 23-41.

Masu Uekusa & Hideki Ide, "Industrial Policy in Japan," 147-69.

Takashi Wakiyama, "The Nature and Tools of Japan's Industrial Policy," *Harvard International Law Journal* 27: Special Issue (1986), 467-98.

George C. Eads & Kozo Yamamura, "The Future of Industrial Policy," in Kozo Yamamura & Yasukichi Yasuba, eds. *The Political Economy of Japan,* vol. 1, *The Domestic Transformation,* Stanford University Press, 1987, 423-68.

John Shoven, ed. *Government Policy Toward Industry in the United States and Japan,* New York, Cambridge University Press, 1987.

Kotaro Suzumura & Masahiro Okuno-Fujiwara, "Industrial Policy in Japan: Overview and Evaluation," in Ryuzo Sato & Paul Wachtel, eds. *Trade Friction and Economic Policy: Problems and Prospects for Japan and the United States,* Cambridge University Press, 1987, 50-85.

Ryutaro Komiya, Masahiro Okuno, & Kotaro Suzumura, eds., *Industrial Policy of Japan,* Academic Press, 1988, including:

Ryutaro Komiya, "Introduction," 1-22.

Yutaka Kosai, "The Reconstruction Period," 25-48.

Toshimasa Tsuruta, "The Rapid Growth Era," 49-87.

Masu Uekusa, "The Oil Crisis and After," 89-117.

Motoshige Itoh et al., "Industrial Policy as a Corrective to Market Failures," 233-55.

Motoshige Itoh et al., "Industry Promotion and Trade," 257-78.

Chalmers Johnson, "MITI, MPT, and the Telecom Wars: How Japan Makes Policy for High Technology," in Berkeley Roundtable on the International Economy (BRIE), ed. *Creating Advantage: American and Japanese Strategies for Adjusting to Change in a New World Economy,* Berkeley, University of California, forthcoming.

Daniel I. Okimoto, *Between MITI and the Market: Japanese Industrial Policy for High Technology,* Stanford University Press, *forthcoming.*

Administrative Guidance

Kenji Sanekata, "Administrative Guidance and the Antimonopoly Law," *Law in Japan* 10 (1977), 65-80.

Malcolm D.H. Smith, "Prices and Petroleum in Japan: 1973-1974—A Study of Administrative Guidance," *Law in Japan* 10 (1977), 81-100.

John O. Haley, "Administrative Guidance versus Formal Regulation: Resolving the Paradox of Industrial Policy," in Gary Saxonhouse & Kozo Yamamura, eds. *Law and Trade Issues of the Japanese Economy: American and Japanese Perspectives,* University of Washington Press, 1986, 107-28.

Frank K. Upham, *Law and Social Change in Postwar Japan,* Harvard University Press, 1987, 166-204.

Allan D. Smith, "The Japanese Foreign Exchange and Foreign Trade Control Law and Administrative Guidance: The Labyrinth and the Castle," *Law & Policy in International Business* 16:2 (1984), 417-76.

Reports

Japan in World Economy: Japan's Foreign Economic Policy for the 1970s, Report of the Industrial Structure Council, MITI, 1972.

Eugene Kaplan, *Japan: The Government-Business Relationship: A Guide for the American Businessman,* U.S. Department of Commerce, Bureau of International Commerce, Washington, U.S. Government Printing Office, 1972.

Organization for Economic Co-operation and Development, *The Industrial Policy of Japan,* Paris, 1972.

MITI, *Japan's Industrial Structure: A Long Range Vision, 1978,* Tokyo, MITI Information Office, 1978.

MITI, *The Industrial Structure of Japan in the 1980s: Future Outlook and Tasks,* Tokyo, MITI Information Office (BI-44), 1981.

Comptroller General of the United States, *Industrial Policy: Japan's Flexible Approach,* Report to the Chariman, Joint Economic Committee United States Congress, Washington, D.C., General Accounting Office, 1982.

U.S. General Accounting Office, *Industrial Policy: Case Studies in the Japanese Experience,* Report to the Chairman, Joint Economic Committee, U.S. Congress, Washington, GAO, 1982.

U.S. International Trade Commission, *Foreign Industrial Targeting and its Effects on U.S. Industries: Japan,* Washington, USITC Publication #1437, 1983.

Ronald P. Dore, *A Case Study in Technology Forecasting: The Japanese Next Generation Base Technologies Programme,* London, Technical Change Centre, 1983.

The Industrial Policy Debate

Robert B. Reich, "Making Industrial Policy," *Foreign Affairs* 60:2 (Spr 1982), 852-81.

Philip H. Trezise, "Industrial Policy in Japan," in Margaret E. Dewer, ed. *Industrial Vitalization: Toward a National Industrial Policy*, New York, Pergamon Press, 1982, 177-95.

Jimmy W. Wheeler, Merit E. Janow & Thomas Pepper, *Japanese Industrial Development Policies in the 1980s: Implications for U.S. Trade and Investment*, Croton-on-Hudson, Hudson Institute, 1982.

Charles Schultze, "Industrial Policy: A Solution in Search of a Problem," *California Management Review* 25:4 (Sum 1983), 5-26.

The Public Interest 72 (Sum 1973), the following articles:
George Gilder, "A Supply-side Economics of the Left," 29-43.
Amitai Etzioni, "The MITIzation of America?" 44-51.
—and in reply:
Robert B. Reich, "An Industrial Policy of the Right," *The Public Interest* 73 (Fall 1983), 3-17.

Robert B. Reich, "High Tech Industrial Policy: Comparing the U.S. with Other Advanced Industrial Nations," *Journal of Japanese Trade and Industry* 2:4 (1983), 28-33.

Paul Krugman, "Targeted Industrial Policies: Theory and Evidence," in Federal Reserve Bank of Kansas City, ed. *Industrial Change and Public Policy*, Kansas City, 1983, 123-56.

Robert B. Reich, *The Next American Frontier*, New York, Times Books, 1983, 235-82.

Alan M. Kantrow, "The Political Realities of Industrial Policy," *Harvard Business Review* 61:5 (1983), 79-86.

Gary R. Saxonhouse, "What is All This About 'Industrial Targeting' in Japan?" *The World Economy* 6:3 (Sept 1983), 253-74.

Naohiro Amaya, "Refuting the Critics of Japan's Industrial Policy," *Japan Echo* 10:4 (Win 1983), 38-43.

Kevin P. Phillips, *Staying On Top: The Business Case for a National Industrial Strategy*, New York, Random House, 1984.

Chalmers Johnson, ed. *The Industrial Policy Debate,* San Francisco, Institute for Comparative Studies Press, 1984, including the editor's "Introduction: The Idea of Industrial Policy," 3-26, reprinted as "The Industrial Policy Debate Re-examined," in *California Management Review* 27:1 (Fall 1984), 71-89.

Kenan Patrick Jarboe, "A Reader's Guide to the Industrial Policy Debate," *California Management Review* 27:4 (Sum 1985), 198-219 (review article).

Chalmers Johnson, "Studies of Japanese Political Economy: A Crisis in Theory," in The Japan Foundation, *Japanese Studies in the United States: Part I: History and Present Condition,* Association for Asian Studies, 1988, 95-113.

Structural Depression & Adjustment

Gary R. Saxonhouse, "Industrial Restructuring in Japan," *Journal of Japanese Studies* 5:2 (Sum 1979), 273-320.

J. Mark Ramseyer, "Letting Obsolete Firms Die: Trade Adjustment Assistance in the United States and Japan," *Harvard International Law Journal* 22:3 (Fall 1981), 595-619.

Ippei Yamazawa, "Adjusting to the ADCs in Face of Structurally Depressed Industries: The Case of Japan," in Wontack Hong & Lawrence B. Krause, eds. *Trade and Growth of the Advanced Developing Countries in the Pacific Basin,* Seoul, Korea Development Institute, 1981, 435-475.

Edward Boyer, "How Japan Manages Declining Industries," *Fortune,* January 10, 1983, 58-68.

Sueo Sekiguchi, "Industrial Adjustment in East Asia's Resource-Poor Economies," *The World Economy* 6:2 (June 1983), 147-58.

Robert M. Uriu, "The Declining Industries in Japan: Adjustment and Reallocation," *Journal of International Affairs* 38 (1984), 99-111.

Yoshihiro Tsurumi, "Labor Relations and Industrial Adjustment in Japan and the United States: A Comparative Analysis," *Yale Law & Policy Review* 2:2 (1984), 256-71.

"Japan's Declining Industries," in Thomas Pepper, Merit E. Janow, & Jimmy W. Wheeler, *The Competition: Dealing with Japan,* New York, Praeger, 1985, 247-87.

"Japan's Policies for Declining Industries: An Overview," Japan Economic Institute, Report No. 34A, September 6, 1985.

Paul Sheard, "Main Banks and Structural Adjustment in Japan," *Pacific Economic Papers* (Australia-Japan Research Centre) 129 (1985), 1-93.

Paul Sheard, "General Trading Companies and Structural Adjustment in Japan," *Pacific Economic Papers* (Australia-Japan Research Centre), 132 (1986), 1-55.

Paul Sheard, "Intercorporate Shareholdings and Structural Adjustment in Japan," *Pacific Economic Papers* (Australia-Japan Research Centre) 137 (1986), 1-65.

Michael K. Young, "Structurally Depressed and Declining Industries in Japan: A Case Study in Minimally Intrusive Industrial Policy," in Joint Economic Committee, *Japan's Economy and Trade with the United States*, Washington, U.S. Government Printing Office, 1986.

R.P. Dore, with contributions by K. Taira, *Structural Adjustment in Japan, 1970-82*, Geneva, International Labour Office, 1986.

Douglas D. Anderson, "Managing Retreat: Disinvestment Policy," in Thomas K. McCraw, ed. *America versus Japan*, Boston, Harvard Business School Press, 1986, 337-72.

Harvard International Law Journal 27: Special Issue (1986), including:
Akinori Uesugi, "Japan's Cartel System and Its Impact on International Trade," 389-424.
Frank K. Upham, "The Legal Framework of Japan's Declining Industries Policy: The Problem of Transparency in Administrative Processes," 425-66.

Merton J. Peck, Richard C. Levin, & Akira Goto, "Picking Losers: Public Policy Toward Declining Industries in Japan," *Journal of Japanese Studies* 13:1 (Win 1987), 79-123.

Sueo Sekiguchi & Toshihiro Horiuchi, "Trade and Adjustment Assistance," in Ryutaro Komiya, Masahiro Okuno, & Kotaro Suzumura, eds., *Industrial Policy of Japan*, Academic Press, 1988, 369-93.

Domestic Demand & Restructuring

Ken'ichi Imai, "The Possibilities and Pitfalls of Information Society," *Japan Echo* 11:2 (Sum 1984), 70-79.

Special Issue on Asset-Doubling Proposals, *Japan Echo* 11:4 (Win 1984), 11-36.

Ryuichiro Tachi, "The 'Softization' of the Japanese Economy," *JES* 13:3 (Spr 1985), 67-104.

Akihiro Yoshikawa & Brian Woodall, " 'Venture Boom' and Japanese Industrial Policy; Promoting the Neglected Winners," *Asian Survey* 25:6 (June 1985), 692-714.

T.J. Lee, "The Markings of a Resurgence in the Domestic Economy," *Asian Monetary Monitor* 10:2 (Mar-Apr 1986), 12-18.

Tim Lee, "A Stronger Domestic Economy Will Follow Further Deregulation," *Asian Monetary Monitor* 10:5 (Sept-Oct 1986), 15-26.

"Economic Growth and Industrial Restructuring in Japan," Japan Economic Institute, Report No. 46A, December 19, 1986.

Kozo Yamamura, "Shedding the Shackles of Success: Saving Less for Japan's Future," *Journal of Japanese Studies* 13:2 (Sum 1987), 429-56.

"Economic Restructuring in Japan," Japan Economic Institute, Report No. 37A, October 2, 1987.

Hiroshi Kato, "Expanding Domestic Demand in Japan," *Japan Review of International Affairs* 1:2 (Fall/Win 1987), 170-85.

Gary Saxonhouse, "Comparative Advantage, Structural Adaptation, and Japanese Performance," in Takashi Inoguchi & Daniel Okimoto, eds. *The Political Economy of Japan,* vol. 2, *The Changing International Context,* Stanford University Press, 1988, 225-48.

"The Maekawa Reports: Reality or Rhetoric," Japan Economic Institute, Report No. 39A, October 14, 1988 (includes text of reports).

Technology

Akira Uchino, "Technological Innovation in Postwar Japan," *DE* 7:4 (Dec 1969), 406-27.

Ryoichi Iwauchi, "Adaptation to Technological Change," *DE* 7:4 (Dec 1969), 428-50.

T. Dixon Long, "Technology and Power: Japan Catches Up," in Lewis Austin, ed. *Japan: The Paradox of Progress,* Yale University Press, 1976, 141-64.

Merton J. Peck, "Technology," in Hugh Patrick & Henry Rosovsky, eds. *Asia's New Giant: How the Japanese Economy Works,* Brookings Institution, 1976, 525-85.

Tuvia Blumenthal, "Japan's Technological Strategy," *Journal of Development Economics* 3 (Sept 1976), 245-55.

Mieko Nishimizu, "Technological Superiority: A Milestone in the Postwar Japanese Growth," Leon Hollerman, ed. *Japan and the United States: Economic and Political Adversaries,* Boulder, Westview Press, 1979, 13-37.

Reinosuke Hara, *Management of R&D in Japan,* Tokyo, Institute of Comparative Culture, Sophia University, 1982.

Leonard Lynn, "Japan Adopts a New Technology: The Roles of Government, Trading Firms and Suppliers," *Columbia Journal of World Business* 19:4 (Win 1984), 39-46.

William H. Davidson, *The Amazing Race: Winning the Technorivalry with Japan,* New York, John Wiley & Sons, 1984.

Alun M. Anderson, *Science and Technology in Japan,* Harlow, Essex, Longman, 1984.

Shigeru Kimura, *Japan's Science Edge,* Lanham, MD., University Press of America, 1985.

Masanori Yoshikai, "R & D and Technology Policy in Japan," *JES* 14:4 (Sum 1986), 3-50.

Thomas A. Pugel, ed. *Fragile Interdependence: Economic Issues in U.S.-Japanese Trade and Investment,* Lexington, Heath, 1986, including:
Thomas A. Pugel, "Industrial Policy in Japan: Implications for Technological Catch-up and Leadership," 209-35.
Ryuzo Sato, "Japan's Challenge to Technological Competition and Its Limitations," 237-61.

Hugh Patrick, ed. *Japan's High Technology Industries: Lessons and Limitations of Industrial Policy,* University of Washington Press, 1986, including;
Hugh Patrick, "Japanese High Technology Industrial Policy in Comparative Context," 3-33.
Ken-ichi Imai, "Japan's Industrial Policy for High Technology Industry," 137-69.
Yasusuke Murakami, "Technology in Transition: Two Perspectives on Industrial Policy," 211-41.

Christopher Freeman, *Technology Policy and Economic Performance: Lessons from Japan,* London, Pinter, 1987.

"Update on Japanese Research and Development: Superconductors," Japan Economic Institute, Report No. 43A, Nov. 13, 1987.

The following articles from Ryutaro Komiya, Masahiro Okuno, & Kotaro Suzumura, eds., *Industrial Policy of Japan,* Academic Press, 1988:

Akira Goto & Ryuhei Wakasugi, "Technology Policy," 183-204.

Ken'ichi Imai, "Industrial Policy and Technological Innovation," 205-29.

William G. Ouchi & Michele Kremen Bolton, "The Logic of Joint Research and Development," *California Management Review* 30:3 (Spr 1988), 9-33.

Thomas R. Howell, William A. Noellert, Janet H. MacLaughlin, & Alan Wm. Wolff, *The Microelectronics Race: The Impact of Government Policy on International Competition,* Boulder, Westview Press, 1988, esp. 35-144, "The Japanese Challenge."

George Gamota & Wendy Frieman, *Gaining Ground: Japan's Strides in Science & Technology,* Cambridge, Ballinger, 1988.

B. SPECIFIC INDUSTRIES

Brian Ike, "The Japanese Textile Industry: Structural Adjustment and Government Policy," *Asian Survey* 20:5 (May 1980), 532-51.

Ippei Yamazawa, "Increasing Imports and Structural Adjustment of the Japanese Textile Industry," *DE* 18:4 (Dec 1980), 441-62.

Ronald Dore (with Koji Taira), "Flexible Rigidities: Industrial Policy and Structural Adjustment in the Japanese Economy, 1970-80," *World Employment Programme Research,* WP24, Geneva, ILO, July 1983 (esp. textiles & electronics).

Ronald Dore, *Flexible Rigidities: Industrial Policy and Structural Adjustment in the Japanese Economy, 1970-80,* Stanford University Press, 1986.

Ippei Yamazawa, "The Textile Industry," in Ryutaro Komiya, Masahiro Okuno, & Kotaro Suzumura, eds., *Industrial Policy of Japan,* Academic Press, 1988, 395-423.

Leonard H. Lynn, *How Japan Innovates: A Comparison with the U.S. in the Case of Oxygen Steelmaking,* Boulder, Westview Press, 1982.

Hideki Yamawaki, "The Steel Industry," In Ryutaro Komiya, Masahiro Okuno, & Kotaro Suzumura, eds., *Industrial Policy of Japan,* Academic Press, 1988, 281-305.

Richard J. Samuels, "The Industrial Destructuring of the Japanese Aluminum Industry," *Pacific Affairs* 56:3 (Fall 1983), 495-509.

Naoki Tanaka, "Aluminum Refining Industry," in Ryutaro Komiya, Masahiro Okuno, & Kotaro Suzumura, eds., *Industrial Policy of Japan,* Academic Press, 1988, 451-71.

"Shipbuilding: High Priority Basic Industry," in Ezra Vogel, *Comeback—Case by Case: Building the Resurgence of American Business,* New York, Simon & Schuster, 1985, 27-57.

George O. Totten, "The Reconstruction of the Japanese Shipbuilding Industry," in Robert L. Friedheim, et al., *Japan and the New Ocean Regime,* Westview Press, 1984, 130-72.

Yoshie Yonezawa, "The Shipbuilding Industry," in Ryutaro Komiya, Masahiro Okuno, & Kotaro Suzumura, eds., *Industrial Policy of Japan,* Academic Press, 1988, 425-49.

Hiromichi Mutoh, "The Automotive Industry," in Ryutaro Komiya, Masahiro Okuno, & Kotaro Suzumura, eds., *Industrial Policy of Japan,* Academic Press, 1988, 307-31.

Gary R. Saxonhouse, "Industrial Policy and Factor Markets: Biotechnology in Japan and the United States," in Hugh Patrick, ed. *Japan's High Technology Industries: Lessons and Limitations of Industrial Policy,* University of Washington Press, 1986, 97-135.

Mark D. Dibner, "Biotechnology in Pharmaceuticals: The Japanese Challenge," *Science* 47:229 (Sept 1985), 1230-35.
"Developing Advanced Television: Industrial Policy Revisited," Japan Economic Institute, Report No. 2A, January 13, 1989.

Koji Shinjo, "The Computer Industry," in Ryutaro Komiya, Masahiro Okuno, & Kotaro Suzumura, eds., *Industrial Policy of Japan,* Academic Press, 1988, 333-65.

Marie Anchordoguy, "Mastering the Market: Japanese Government Targeting of the Computer Industry," *International Organization* 42:3 (Sum 1988), 509-43.

Youichi Ito, "Telecommunications and Industrial Policies in Japan: Recent Developments," in Marcellus S. Snow, *Marketplace for Telecommunications: Regulation and Deregulation in Industrialized Democracies,* London, Longman, 1986, 201-30.

C. REGIONAL IMPACT

Pollution

Minoru Beika, "Environmental Pollution Problems from the View Point of Business Management," *Kobe Economic and Business Review* 18 (1971), 1-11.

Yukimoto Iwata, "Environmental Pollution in a Rapidly Growing Economy," *DE* 10:4 (Dec 1972), 479-95.

Yasuo Shimazu & Kozo Sugiyama, "Limits to Growth by Pollution," *JES* 2:3 (Spr 1974), 53-79.

Hideo Nakanishi & Tsutomu Yamaguchi, "Pollution," *JES* 2:4 (Sum 1974), 62-91.

Sueo Sekiguchi, "Environmental Regulations and Japan's Industry and International Trade," *JES* 3:4 (Sum 1975), 83-126.

Shosuke Tanaka, "Japan's Anti-Pollution Measures and Their Results," *DE* 14:4 (Dec 1976), 468-87.

Hikaru Shoji & Kenichi Miyamoto, "Environmental Pollution in Japan," *JES* 5:4 (Sum 1977), 3-40.

The following articles from Shigeto Tsuru, ed. *Growth and Resources Problems Related to Japan:* Proceedings of Session VI of the Fifth Congress of the International Economic Association, Tokyo, Asahi Evening News, 1978:
Remy Prud'homme, "Appraisal of Environmental Policies in Japan," 193-208.
Ken'ichi Miyamoto, "The Environmental Protection Policy in Japan," 209-27.

Nobuko Iijima, ed. *Pollution Japan: Historical Chronology,* Tokyo, Asahi Evening News, 1979.

Susan J. Pharr & Joseph L. Badaracco, Jr., "Coping with Crisis: Environmental Regulation," in Thomas K. McCraw, ed. *American versus Japan,* Boston, Harvard Business School Press, 1986, 229-60.

Regional Issues & Decentralization

Saburo Okita, "Regional Planning in Japan Today," in William W. Lockwood, ed. *The State and Economic Enterprise in Japan,* Princeton University Press, 1965, 619-31.

Minoru Beika, "Problems of Regional Industrial Development Relating to National Planning in Japan," *Kobe Economic and Business Review* 14 (1967), 11-20.

Mataji Umemura, "Regional Differences in the Distribution of Industrial Employment in Japan," *DE* 7:2 (June 1969), 117-32.

Atsushi Shimokobe, "Concepts and Methodology of Regional Development," *DE* 8:4 (Dec 1970), 497-511.

Kakuei Tanaka, *Building a New Japan: A Plan for Remodeling the Japanese Archipelago,* Tokyo, Simul, 1973.

John Sargent, "Regional Development Policy in Japan: Some Aspects of the Plan for Remodelling the Japanese Archipelago," in W.G. Beasley, ed. *Modern Japan: Aspects of History, Literature & Society*, London, Allen & Unwin, 1975, 227-43.

Minoru Beika, "Regional Development Policies of Japan in Recent Quarter of the Twentieth Century," *Kobe Economic and Business Review* 21 (1975), 1-22.

Tsuneo Unno, "Problems of Overpopulation and Depopulation," *JES* 3:3 (Spr 1975), 59-87.

"Kyushu without Coal Mining: Managing Decline and Regional Renaissance," in Ezra Vogel, *Comeback—Case by Case: Building the Resurgence of American Business*, New York, Simon & Schuster, 1985, 96-124.

Sheridan Tatsuno, *The Technopolis Strategy: Japan's High Technology and the Control of the 21st Century*, New York, Prentice Hall Press, Brady Book, 1986.

Tatsuhiko Kawashima & Makoto Taketoshi, "Regional Economic Policies: Through Development of High Technology Oriented Industries," *Keizai ronshu* (Gakushuin University) 23:4 (March 1987), 13-37.

Kuniko Fujita, "Women Workers, State Policy, and the International Division of Labor: The Case of Silicon Island in Japan," *Bulletin of Concerned Asian Scholars* 20:3 (July-Sept 1988), 42-53.

7. MANUFACTURING

A. GENERAL

Fukuo Kawata, "Patterns of the Japanese Engineering Trade (1951-1970)," *Kobe Economic and Business Review* 18 (1971), 13-36.

Hachiro Fukazawa, "Salient Features of Rubber Consumption in Japan," *DE* 15:3 (Sept 1977), 360-73.

Toshimasa Tsuruta, "Industry Studies of Japan: A Survey," in Kazuo Sato, ed. *Industry and Business in Japan*, White Plains, N.Y., M.E. Sharpe, 1980, 437-49.

Kiyoji Murata, ed. *An Industrial Geography of Japan*, London, Bell & Hyman, 1980.

B. TEXTILES

Keizo Seki, *The Cotton Industry of Japan*, Tokyo, Japan Society for the Promotion of Science, 1956.

Richard F. Hough, "Impact of the Decline in Raw Silk on the Suwa Basin of Japan," *Economic Geography* 44:2 (Apr 1968), 95-116.

John Lynch, *Toward an Orderly Market: An Intensive Study of Japan's Voluntary Quota in Cotton Textile Exports*, Tokyo, Sophia University Press, 1968.

Kisou Tasugi, "Modernization of the Functions of the Assemblers in Each Local Producing Area in Japan," *Kyoto University Economic Review* 41:1 (Apr 1971), 1-28.

Yoshi Sato, "The Silk-Reeling Industry of Japan and the Catch-up Case," *Keio Business Review* 11 (1972), 63-78.

Ki Do Woo, "Wages and Labor Productivity in the Cotton Spinning Industries of Japan, Korea, and Taiwan," *DE* 19:2 (June 1978), 182-98.

Ippei Yamazawa, "Increasing Imports and Structural Adjustment of the Japanese Textile Industry," *DE* 18:4 (Dec 1980), 441-62.

Vinod K. Aggarwal, "The Politics of Protection in the U.S. Textile and Apparel Industries," in John Zysman and Laura Tyson, eds. *American Industry in International Competition: Government Policies and Corporate Strategies*, Cornell University Press, 1983, 249-312.

Ronald Dore, *Flexible Rigidities: Industrial Policy and Structural Adjustment in the Japanese Economy, 1970-80*, Stanford University Press, 1986, 153-243.

Ippei Yamazawa, "The Textile Industry," in Ryutaro Komiya, Masahiro Okuno, & Kotaro Suzumura, eds., *Industrial Policy of Japan*, Academic Press, 1988, 395-423.

C. STEEL

Yoshihiro Inayama, "Present and Future of Japan's Steel Industry," *Keidanren Review* 9 (Oct 1968), 25-31.

Yoshihiro Inayama, "The Iron and Steel Industry Today," *CJ* 29:1 (Sept 1968), 22-47.

"Japanese Fair Trade Commission—Decision on the Yawata-Fuji Steel Merger," *Antitrust Bulletin* 15 (1970), 803-27.

Kiyoshi Kawahito, *The Japanese Steel Industry: With an Analysis of the US Steel Import Program*, New York, Praeger, 1971.

Ken'ichi Imai, "Iron and Steel," in Kazuo Sato, ed. *Industry and Business in Japan*, White Plains, N.Y., M.E. Sharpe, 1980, 191-244.

Luc Kiers, *The American Steel Industry*, Boulder, Westview Press, 1980 (chapter on Japan).

Leonard H. Lynn, *How Japan Innovates: A Comparison with the U.S. in the Case of Oxygen Steelmaking*, Boulder, Westview Press, 1982.

Seiichiro Yonekura, "Kawasaki Steel and its Innovative Behavior in post-World War II Period," in *A Study on the Growth Pattern of Firms in an International Perspective*, ed. by Institute of Business Research, Hitotsubashi University, 1984.

Kiyoshi Kawahito, "Relative Profitability of the US Japanese Steel Industries," *Columbia Journal of World Business* 19:3 (Fall 1984), 13-17.

Fumio Kondo, "Sales System of the Steel Industry," *Kyoto University Economic Review* 56:1 (Apr 1986), 23-49.

Hirohisa Kohama & Hirokazu Kajiwara, "Structural Change in Steel Trade and International Industrial Adjustment," *DE* 24:2 (June 1986), 109-30.

Marvin Berkowitz & Krishna Mohan, "The Role of Global Procurement in the Value Chain of Japanese Steel," *Columbia Journal of World Business* 22:4 (Win 1987), 97-110.

Hideki Yamawaki, "The Steel Industry," in Ryutaro Komiya, Masahiro Okuno, & Kotaro Suzumura, eds., *Industrial Policy of Japan*, Academic Press, 1988, 281-305.

D. SHIPBUILDING

Kazunori Echigo, "Development of Postwar Japanese Shipbuilding Industry and Revival of Monopoly: Particularly, Problems of Rationalization and Grouping in the Industry," *Kyoto University Economic Review* 28 (Oct 1958), 35-58.

Hajime Yamada, "Shipbuilding Industry Today," *CJ* 28:4 (May 1967), 706-37.

Tuvia Blumenthal, "The Japanese Shipbuilding Industry," in Hugh Patrick, ed. *Japanese Industrialization and its Social Consequences*, University of California Press, 1973, 129-60.

Goro Murata, "IHI—A Fake 'Kingdom of Shipbuilding'," *Ampo* 17 (Sum 1973), 38-56.

Ezra Vogel, "Shipbuilding: High Priority Basic Industry," in Vogel, *Comeback— Case by Case: Building the Resurgence of American Business*, New York, Simon & Schuster, 1985, 27-57.

George O. Totten, "The Reconstruction of the Japanese Shipbuilding Industry," in Robert L. Friedheim, et al., *Japan and the New Ocean Regime*, Boulder, Westview Press, 1984, 130-72.

Dong Sung Cho & Michael E. Porter, "Changing Global Industry Leadership: The Case of Shipbuilding," in Michael E. Porter, ed. *Competition in Global Industries*, Boston, Harvard Business School Press, 1986, 539-67.

Yoshie Yonezawa, "The Shipbuilding Industry," in Ryutaro Komiya, Masahiro Okuno, & Kotaro Suzumura, eds., *Industrial Policy of Japan*, Academic Press, 1988, 425-49.

E. THE AUTO INDUSTRY

General

Yutaka Tsuji, "Japan's Automobile Industry," *Japan Quarterly* 6 (1959), 364-72.

Mitsuhiro Hirata, "Changes in Shareownership in Japanese Automotive Industry: Toyota Motor Co., Ltd. and Nissan Motor Co., Ltd.," *Hitotsubashi Journal of Commerce and Management* 12:1 (June 1977), 17-32.

Hiroya Ueno & Hiromichi Muto, "The Automobile Industry of Japan," in Kazuo Sato, ed. *Industry and Business in Japan*, White Plains, N.Y., M.E. Sharpe, 1980, 139-90.

Krish Bhaskar, *The Future of the World Motor Industry*, New York, Nichols, 1980, 211-46, "Japan."

Robert E. Cole, ed. *The Japanese Automobile Industry: Model and Challenge For the Future?* University of Michigan, Center for Japanese Studies, 1981.

David Friedman, "Beyond the Age of Ford: The Strategic Basis of the Japanese Success in Automobiles," in John Zysman and Laura Tyson, eds. *American Industry in International Competition: Government Policies and Corporate Strategies*, Cornell University Press, 1983, 350-90.

Robert Cole & Taizo Yakushiji, *The Japanese and American Automotive Industry in Transition*, University of Michigan, Center for Japanese Studies, 1984.

Special Issue: *"Keiretsu and Subcontracting in Japan's Automobile Industry," JES* 13:4 (Sum 1985), the following:
Koichi Shimokawa, "Japan's *Keiretsu* System: The Case of the Automobile Industry," 3-31.
Banri Asanuma, "The Organization of Parts Purchases in the Japanese Automotive Industry," 32-53.
Banri Asanuma, "The Contractual Framework for Parts Supply in the Japanese Automotive Industry," 54-78.

John C. Campbell, ed., *Entrepreneurship in a "Mature Industry,"* University of Michigan, Center for Japanese Studies, 1986.

Koichi Shimokawa, "Marketing and Sales Financing in the Automobile Industry: U.S. and Japan," in *Marketing and Finance in the Course of Industrialization*, vol. 3 of *International Conference on Business History*, ed. by Keiichiro Nakagawa, University of Tokyo Press, 1978, 121-42.

Masaru Udagawa, "Japan's Automobile Marketing: Its Introduction, Consolidation, Development and Characteristics," in *Development of Mass Marketing: The Automobile and Retailing Industries*, vol. 7 of *International Conference on Business History*, ed. by Akio Okochi & Koichi Shimokawa, University of Tokyo Press, 1981, 163-87.

Taizo Yakushiji, "The Government in a Spiral Dilemma: Dynamic Policy Interventions Vis-a-Vis Auto Firms, C.1900-C.1960," in Masahiko Aoki, ed. *The Economic Analysis of the Japanese Firm*, Amsterdam, North Holland, 1984, 265-310.

Hiromichi Mutoh, "The Automotive Industry," in Ryutaro Komiya, Masahiro Okuno, & Kotaro Suzumura, eds., *Industrial Policy of Japan*, Academic Press, 1988, 307-31.

Specific Companies

Yasuhiro Monden, "What Makes the Toyota Production System Really Tick?" *Industrial Engineering* 13 (January 1981), 36-46.

Satoshi Kamata, *Japan in the Passing Lane: An Insider's Account of Life in a Japanese Auto Factory*, Pantheon, 1982.

Yasuhiro Monden, *Toyota Production System: Practical Approach to Production Management*, Norcross, Georgia, Industrial Engineering and Management Press, 1983.

Taiichi Ohno, "How the Toyota Production System Was Created," in Kazuo Sato & Yasuo Hoshino, eds. *The Anatomy of Japanese Business*, Armonk, N.Y., M.E. Sharpe, 1984, 197-215.

Michael A. Cusumano, *The Japanese Automobile Industry: Technology and Management at Nissan and Toyota*, Harvard University Press, 1985.

Kanban: Just-in-Time at Toyota, Management Begins at the Workplace, ed. by Japan Management Association, Stamford, Conn., Productivity Press, 1986.

Eiji Toyoda, *Toyota: Fifty Years in Motion*, Tokyo, Kodansha International, 1987.

Stephen E. Weiss, "Creating the GM-Toyota Joint Venture: A Case of Complex Negotiation," *Columbia Journal of World Business* 22:2 (Sum 1987), 23-37.

David Halberstam, *The Reckoning*, New York, William Morrow, 1986 (mostly Nissan).

Richard Pascale & Thomas P. Rohlen, "The Mazda Turnaround," *Journal of Japanese Studies* 9:2 (Sum 1983), 219-63.

Sol Sanders, *Honda: The Man and His Machines*, Tokyo, Tuttle, 1975.

Tetsuo Sakiya, *Honda Motor: The Men, The Management, The Machines*, Kodansha, 1982.

Richard T. Pascale, "Perspectives on Strategy: The Real Story Behind Honda's Success," *California Management Review* 26:3 (Spr 1984), 47-72.

International Trade & Investment

William C. Duncan, *U.S.-Japan Automobile Diplomacy: A Study in Economic Confrontation*, Cambridge, Ballinger, 1973.

"Japan-U.S. Automobile Conflict," articles in *Japan Quarterly* 27:3 (July-Sept 1980), by Junjiro Hara and Shuichi Miyoshi, 341-50.

C. S. Chang, *The Japanese Auto Industry and the U.S. Market*, New York, Praeger, 1981.

Haruo Sono, "Japan's Automotive Capital and International Competition," *Ampo* 13:1 (1981), 60-69; and 13:2 (1981), 60-67.

John B. Rae, *Nissan/Datsun: A History of Nissan Motor Corporation in U.S.A., 1960-1980*, McGraw-Hill, 1982.

Brock Yates, *The Decline and Fall of the American Automobile Industry* (chapters on Japan), Random House, 1984.

Robert Sobel, *Car Wars*, New York, Dutton, 1984.

Paul Ingrassia and Damon Darlin, "Japanese Auto Makers Find the Going Tough," *Wall Street Journal*, December 15 & 16, 1986, pp. 1, 20 & 1, 23.

Konosuke Odaka, ed. *The Motor Vehicle Industry in Asia: A Study of Ancillary Firm Development*, Singapore University Press, 1983, re: Japan, 325-96.

David Marsden et al, *The Car Industry: Labour Relations and Industrial Adjustment*, London, Tavistock Publications, 1985.

F. THE ELECTRICAL INDUSTRY

Specific Companies

Sheba Togo, *Konosuke Matsushita: Portrait of a Japanese Business Magnate*, Tokyo, Rengo Press, 1969.

Rowland Gould, *The Matsushita Phenomenon*, Daimondo sha, 1970.

Bernard Wysocki, Jr., "Matsushita is Moving Beyond Appliances," *Wall Street Journal*, March 26, 1986, p. 32.

Konosuke Matsushita, *Quest for Prosperity: The Life of a Japanese Industrialist*, Kyoto, PHP Institute, 1988.

Nick Lyons, *The Sony Vision*, Crown, 1976.

James Bartholomew, "The Running Walkmen [Sony]," *Far Eastern Economic Review*, January 15, 1982, 38-43.

Akio Morita, *Made in Japan: Akio Morita and Sony*, New York, E.P. Dutton, 1986.

NEC Corporation: The First 80 Years, NEC Corporation, 1984.

E.S. Browning, "Battered Invader [NEC]," *Wall Street Journal*, March 25, 1985, pp. 1, 22.

Robert Steinberg, "*NEC v. Intel*: The Battle over Copyright Protection for Microcode," *Jurimetrics* 27:2 (Win 1987), 173-99.

Takashi Kiuchi, "Strategy for Overseas Markets," in Lester C. Thurow, ed. *The Management Challenge: Japanese Views*, MIT Press, 1985, 122-38 [re: Mitsubishi Electric].

General Accounts

Japan Electronics Almanac, Tokyo, Dempa Publications, 1981.

Yasuo Okamoto, "The Grand Strategy of Japanese Business," in Kazuo Sato & Yasuo Hoshino, eds. *The Anatomy of Japanese Business*, Armonk, New York, M. E. Sharpe, 1984, 277-318 [re: Matsushita and Hitachi].

Makoto Kikuchi, *Japanese Electronics: A Worm's Eye View of its Evolution*, Tokyo, Simul, 1985.

Gene Gregory, *Japanese Electronics Technology: Enterprise and Innovation*, New York, John Wiley & Sons, 1986.

Products

James E. Millstein, "Decline in an Expanding Industry: Japanese Competition in Color Television," in John Zysman and Laura Tyson, eds. *American Industry in International Competition: Government Policies and Corporate Strategies*, Cornell University Press, 1983, 106-141.

Kozo Yamamura & Jan VanDenBerg, "Japan's Rapid-Growth Policy on Trial: The Television Case," in Gary Saxonhouse & Kozo Yamamura, eds. *Law and Trade Issues of the Japanese Economy: American and Japanese Perspectives*, University of Washington Press, 1986, 238-83.

"Developing Advanced Television: Industrial Policy Revisited," Japan Economic Institute, Report No. 2A, January 13, 1989.

Yotaro Kobayashi, "Quality Control in Japan: The Case of Fuji Xerox," in Kazuo Sato & Yasuo Hoshino, eds. *The Anatomy of Japanese Business*, Armonk, N.Y., M.E. Sharpe, 1984, 216-45.

Gary Jacobson & John Hillkirk, *Xerox: American Samurai*, New York, Macmillan, 1986.

Richard S. Rosenbloom & Michael A. Cusumano, "Technological Pioneering and Competitive Advantage: The Birth of the VCR Industry," *California Management Review* 29:4 (Sum 1987), 51-76.

James Lardner, *Fast Forward: Hollywood, The Japanese, and the VCR Wars*, New York, W.W. Norton, 1987.

Overseas Investment

Taku Oshima, "Problems of Present Japanese Direct Foreign Investment in the Electric Equipment Industry," *Osaka City University Economic Review* 18 (1982), 9-27.

Tetsuo Abo, "U.S. Subsidiaries of Japanese Electronic Companies Enter a New Phase of Activities: A Report of On-the-Spot Observations," *Annals of the Institute of Social Science* 26 (1984), 1-32.

G. SEMICONDUCTORS & COMPUTERS

Semiconductors

Daniel I. Okimoto, Takuo Sugano, & Franklin B. Weinstein, eds. *Competitive Edge: The Semiconductor Industry in the U.S. and Japan*, Stanford University Press, 1984.

Michael A. Rappa, "Capital Financing Strategies of the Japanese Semiconductor Industry," *California Management Review* 27:2 (Win 1985), 85-99.

United States International Trade Commission, *Competitive Factors Influencing World Trade in Integrated Circuits*, Washington, Government Printing Office, 1979.

Michael Borrus, James Millstein & John Zysman, *U.S.-Japanese Competition in the Semiconductor Industry: A Study in International Trade and Technological Development*, Institute of International Studies, University of California, Berkeley, [1982].

Michael Borrus, James Millstein & John Zysman, "Trade and Development in the Semiconductor Industry: Japanese Challenge and American Response," in John Zysman and Laura Tyson, eds. *American Industry in International Competition: Government Policies and Corporate Strategies*, Cornell University Press, 1983, 142-248. (similar to above).

T. Howell, W. Davis, & J. Greenwald, *The Effects of Government Targeting on World Semiconductor Competition*, Cupertino, Calif., Semiconductor Industry Association, 1983.

Warren E. Davis & Daryl G. Hatano, "The American Semiconductor Industry and the Ascendancy of East Asia," *California Management Review* 27:4 (Sum 1985), 128-43.

Brenton R. Schlender & Stephen Kreider Yoder, "Falling Chips (1)," *Wall Street Journal*, February 12, 1987, pp. 1, 10; Peter Waldman & Brenton R. Schlender, "Falling Chips (2)," *Wall Street Journal*, February 17, 1987, pp. 1, 24.

Documentary Case Studies in International Trade. Study I: The Japan-U.S. Semiconductor Cases, Frederick, Md., University Publications of America, 1987 (microfiche with printed guide).

Thomas A. Pugel, "Limits of Trade Policy toward High Technology Industries: The Case of Semiconductors," in Ryuzo Sato & Paul Wachtel, eds. *Trade Friction and Economic Policy: Problems and Prospects for Japan and the United States*, Cambridge University Press, 1987, 184-237.

Kuniko Fujita, "Women Workers, State Policy, and the International Division of Labor: The Case of Silicon Island in Japan," *Bulletin of Concerned Asian Scholars* 20:3 (July-Sept 1988), 42-53.

Thomas R. Howell, William A. Noellert, Janet H. MacLaughlin, & Alan Wm. Wolff, *The Microelectronics Race: The Impact of Government Policy on International Competition*, Boulder, Westview Press, 1988, esp. 35-144, "The Japanese Challenge."

Ryuhei Wakasugi, "Research and Development and Innovations in High Technology Industry: The Case of the Semiconductor Industry," *JES* 17:1 (Fall 1988), 3-35.

Computers

Koji Kobayashi, *Computers and Communications: A Vision of C&C*, MIT Press, 1986. [Kobayashi was the chairman of NEC].

Robert Sobel, *IBM vs. Japan: The Struggle for the Future*, New York, Stein and Day, 1986 (more on IBM than on Japan).

Koji Shinjo, "The Computer Industry," in Ryutaro Komiya, Masahiro Okuno, & Kotaro Suzumura, eds., *Industrial Policy of Japan*, Academic Press, 1988, 333-65.

Marie Anchordoguy, "Mastering the Market: Japanese Government Targeting of the Computer Industry," *International Organization* 42:3 (Sum 1988), 509-43.

K.H. Kim, "A Look at Japan's Development of Software Engineering Technology," *Computer*, May 1983, 26-37.

Noburu Takagi & John Branch, eds. *CAD/CAM and MIS in Japan: Computer Applications in Japanese Industry*, New York, Academic Press, 1986.

Marshall N. Margolis, "Hi-Tech Creativity: The IBM/Fujitsu Arbitration," *Review of International Business Law* 2:1 (March 1988), 59-66.

Information Networks

William H. Davidson, *The Amazing Race: Winning the Technorivalry with Japan*, New York, John Wiley & Sons, 1984.

"The Information Revolution: National Transformation," Ezra Vogel, *Comeback—Case by Case: Building the Resurgence of American Business*, New York, Simon & Schuster, 1985, 125-67.

"Japan's New Industries," in Thomas Pepper, Merit E. Janow, & Jimmy W. Wheeler, *The Competition: Dealing with Japan*, New York, Praeger, 1985, 187-246.

Artificial Intelligence

Edward A. Feigenbaum & Pamela McCorduck, *The Fifth Generation: Artificial Intelligence and Japan's Computer Challenge to the World*, Addison-Wesley, 1983, revised and updated ed., Signet, 1984.

J. Marshall Unger, *The Fifth Generation Fallacy: Why Japan is Betting Its Future on Artificial Intelligence*, Oxford University Press, 1987.

H. ROBOTS

Kuni Sadamoto, *Robots in the Japanese Economy: The Third Industrial Revolution*, Tokyo, Survey Japan, 1981.

Masahiro Mori, *The Buddha in the Robot*, Tokyo, Kosei Publishing, 1981.

Jack Baranson, *Robots in Manufacturing: Key to International Competitiveness*, Mt. Airy, Md., Lomond Publications, 1983.

"Machine Tools and Robots: Auxiliary Industry," Ezra Vogel, *Comeback—Case by Case: Building the Resurgence of American Business*, New York, Simon & Schuster, 1985, 58-95.

Koji Okubayashi, "The Impacts of Industrial Robots on Working Life in Japan," *Journal of General Maangement* 11:4 (Sum 1986), 22-34.

Frederik L. Schodt, *Inside the Robot Kingdom: Japan, Mechatronics, and the Coming Robotopia*, New York, Kodansha International, 1987.

V. Daniel Hunt, *Mechatronics: Japan's Newest Threat*, New York, Chapman & Hall, 1988.

I. DEFENSE INDUSTRIES, PROCUREMENT, AND COMMERCIAL AIRCRAFT

Publications on space enterprise appear under the section on SERVICES, RE-SOURCES, AND COMMUNICATIONS.

Masao Kihara, "The Militarisation of the Japanese Economy," *Kyoto University Economic Review* 38:2 (Oct 1968), 26-45.

Herbert P. Bix, "The Security Treaty Sustem and the Japanese Military-Industrial Complex," *Bulletin of Concerned Asian Scholars* 2:2 (Jan 1970), 30-53.

Masao Kihara, "Production of Weapons in Postwar Japan and its Characteristics," *Kyoto University Economic Review* 47:1-2 (Apr-Oct), 1-26.

Anthony Sampson, *The Arms Bazaar: The Companies, The Dealers, The Bribes: From Vickers to Lockheed*, London, Hodder and Stoughton, 1977, esp. 222-40, "Japan: Behind the Black Curtain."

Kazuo Tomiyama, "The Future of Japan's Defense-Related Industries," *Japan Quarterly* 25 (1978), 407-12.

Sungjoo Han, "Japan's 'PXL' Decision: The Politics of Weapons Procurement," *Asian Survey* 18:8 (Aug 1978), 769-84.

Kazuo Tomiyama, "Revival and Growth of Japan's Defense Industry," *JES* 9:4 (Sum 1981), 3-51.

Daniel I. Okimoto, "Arms Transfers: The Japanese Calculus," in John Barton & Ryukichi Imai, eds. *Arms Control II*, Cambridge, Mass., Oelgeschlager, Gunn & Hain. 1981, 273-317.

Daniel I. Okimoto, "The Economics of National Defense," in Daniel I. Okimoto, ed. *Japan's Economy: Coping with Change in the International Environment*, Boulder, Westview Press, 1982, 231-83.

Kazuo Tomiyama, "Weapon Manufacturers Continue to Grow," *Japan Quarterly* 29:3 (July-Sept 1982), 335-45.

Kazuo Tomiyama, "The Defence Industry of Japan," *Pacific Casements* (Linfield College and Kanto Gakuin University) 1:1 (Oct 1982), 26-40.

Neil W. Davis, "Is Japan Ready for Missile Independence?" *Aerospace America*, March 1986, 32-47 [article and interviews].

Reinhard Drifte, *Arms Production in Japan: The Military Applications of Civilian Technology*, Westview, 1986.

David Mowery & Nathan Rosenberg. "Commercial Aircraft: Cooperation and Competition Between the U.S. and Japan," *California Management Review* 27:4 (Sum 1985), 70-92.

Marie Soderberg, *Japan's Military Export Policy*, University of Stockholm, 1986.

J. OTHER

"Case Material: The Sankyo Company Limited," *Keio Business Review* 1 (1962), 101-26 (plus charts).

Asahi Shimbun Staff, "Unique Enterprises," *Japan Quarterly* 27:1 (Jan-Mar 1980), 60-74.

David Landes, *Revolution in Time: Clocks and the Making of the Modern World*, Harvard University Press, 1983, 338-360.

Ichiro Hattori, "Product Diversification," in Lester C. Thurow, ed. *The Management Challenge: Japanese Views*, MIT Press, 1985, 103-21 [re: Seiko].

Naoki Tanaka, "Aluminum Refining Industry," in Ryutaro Komiya, Masahiro Okuno, & Kotaro Suzumura, eds., *Industrial Policy of Japan*, Academic Press, 1988, 451-71.

Akira Goto, "The Aluminum Industry in Japan," in M.J. Peck, ed. *The World Aluminum Industry in an Era of Changing Energy Prices*, Washington, Resources for the Future, forthcoming.

Fumio Hasegawa & the Shimizu Group FS, *Built by Japan: Competitive Strategies of the Japanese Construction Industry*, John Wiley & Sons, 1988.

8. SERVICES, RESOURCES, COMMUNICATIONS

A. THE SERVICE ECONOMY

Koichi Emi, "Employment Structure in the Service Industries," *DE* 7:2 (June 1969), 133-57.

Gary Saxonhouse, "Service in the Japanese Economy," in Robert P. Inman, ed. *Managing the Service Economy: Prospects and Problems*, Cambridge University Press, 1984, 53-83.

Kyoko Sheridan, "Softnomisation: The Growth of the Service Sector in Japan," *Journal of Contemporary Asia* 14:4 (1984), 430-41.

B. BANKING AND FINANCE

The Financial System

Hiroshi Kawaguchi, "The 'Dual Structure' of Finance in Post-War Japan," *DE* 5:2 (June 1967), 301-28.

Yutaka Maekawa, "The Structure of Nonlife Insurance Market of Japan," *Keio Business Review* 7 (1968), 91-102.

T.F.M. Adams & Hoshii Iwao, *A Financial History of the New Japan*, Tokyo, Kodansha International, 1972.

Shoichi Royama, "The Financial Mechanism of Japan: Survey and Synthesis of Major Issues," *JES* 3:3 (Spr 1975), 3-31.

Andreas R. Prindl, *Japanese Finance: A Guide to Banking in Japan*, New York, John Wiley & Sons, 1981.

Hiromitsu Ishi, "Financial Institutions and Markets in Japan," in Michael T. Skully, ed. *Financial Institutions and Markets in the Far East: A Study of China, Hong Kong, Japan, South Korea and Taiwan*, New York, St. Martin's Press, 1982, 84-129.

Stephen Bronte, *Japanese Finance: Markets and Institutions*, London, Euromoney, 1982.

Eisuke Sakakibara, Robert Feldman, & Yuzo Harada, *The Japanese Financial System in Comparative Perspectives*, Washington, D.C., U.S. Government Printing Office, 1982.

Shoichi Royama, "The Japanese Financial System: Past, Present, and Future," *JES* 12:2 (Win 1983-84), 3-32, (also in Lester C. Thurow, ed. *The Management Challenge: Japanese Views*, MIT Press, 1985, 82-102).

James Horne, *Japan's Financial Markets: Conflict and Consensus in Policymaking*, Sydney, Allen & Unwin, 1985.

"The Japanese Financial System," in Thomas Pepper, Merit E. Janow, & Jimmy W. Wheeler, *The Competition: Dealing with Japan*, New York, Praeger, 1985, 143-85.

Robert A. Feldman, *Japanese Financial Markets: Deficits, Dilemmas, and Deregulation,* MIT Press, 1986.

Kazuhito Ikeo, "A Micro-Theoretic Analysis of Japanese Financial System," *Kyoto University Economic Review* 56:2 (Oct 1986), 23-36.

Juro Teranishi, "Economic Growth and Regulation of Financial Markets: Japanese Experience during Postwar High Growth Period," *Hitotsubashi Journal of Eonomics* 27:2 (Dec 1986), 149-65.

Helen Troughton, *Japanese Finance: The Impact of Deregulation*, London, Euromoney Publications, 1986.

Koichi Hamada & Akiyoshi Horiuchi, "The Political Economy of the Financial Market," in Kozo Yamamura & Yasukichi Yasuba, eds. *The Political Economy of Japan*, vol. 1, *The Domestic Transformation*, Stanford University Press, 1987, 223-60.

Kazuhito Ikeo, "Japan's Financial System: A Micro Approach," *JES* 16:1 (Fall 1987), 60-77.

Yoshi Suzuki, ed. *The Japanese Financial System*, Oxford University Press, 1987.

Hiroya Ueno, "Deregulation and Reorganization of Japan's Financial System," *JES* 16:3 (Spr 1988), 39-75.

Royama Shoichi, "The Financial System of Japan: A New View," *JES* 16:3 (Spr 1988), 76-97.

"Japanese Insurance Companies," Japan Economic Institute, Report No. 31A, August 12, 1988.

Thomas F. Cargill, "Competition and the Transition of Finance in Japan and the United States," *Journal of Comparative Economics* 12:3 (Sept 1988), 380-400.

The Banking System

Edna E. Ehrlich & Frank M. Tamagna, "Japan," in Benjamin Haggott Beckhart, ed. *Banking Systems*, Columbia University Press, 1954, 517-71.

Hubert F. Schiffer, *The Modern Japanese Banking System*, New York, University Publishers, 1962.

The Bank of Japan: Economic Research Department, *Money and Banking in Japan*, 1964 (contains prewar summary).

Jiro Yao, "The Commercial Banking and Mixed Banking Principles in Japan," *Kobe University Economic Review* 14 (1968), 1-28.

L.S. Pressnell, ed. *Money and Banking in Japan*, Bank of Japan, Economic Research Department, 1973.

Shunsaku Nishikawa, "The Banking System: Competition and Control," *JES* 2:3 (Spr 1974), 3-52.

Philip Thorn, ed. *Banking Structures and Sources of Finance in the Far East*, London, The Banker Research Unit, Financial Times, Nov., 1974, 1-22.

Henry C. Wallich and Mable I. Wallich, "Banking and Finance," in Hugh Patrick & Henry Rosovsky, eds. *Asia's New Giant: How the Japanese Economy Works*, Brookings Institution, 1976, 317-82.

Special Issue: "Central Banking in Japan," *JES* 6:2 (Win 1977-78).

Michael T. Skully, *Merchant Banking in the Far East*, London, Financial Times Business Publishing, 2nd ed., 1980, 152-218.

Masahiro Fujita & Kenichi Ishigaki, "The Internationalization of Japanese Commercial Banking: Experiences in the '70s," *Kobe Economic and Business Review* 28 (1982), 1-28.

Masahiro Fujita et al., "Internationalization of Japanese Commercial Banking: The Recent Experience of City Banks," *Kobe Economic and Business Review* 30 (1984), 23-53.

Hiroshi Osano & Yoshiro Tsutsui, "Implicit Contracts in the Japanese Bank Loan Market," *Journal of Financial and Quantitative Analysis* 20:2 (1985), 211-29.

Brian W. Semkow, "Japanese Banking Law: Current Deregulation and Liberalization of Domestic and External Financial Transactions," *Law and Policy in International Business* 17:1 (1985), 81-156.

Colyer Crum & David M. Meerschwam, "From Relationship to Price Banking: The Loss of Regulatory Control," in Thomas K. McCraw, ed. *America versus Japan*, Boston, Harvard Business School Press, 1986, 261-98.

Paul Sheard, "Main Banks and Internal Capital Markets in Japan," *Shoken keizai* 157 (Sept 1986), 255-85.

Akiyoshi Horiuchi, Frank Packer, & Shin'ichi Fukuda, "What Role has the Main Bank' Played in Japan," *Journal of the Japanese and International Economies* 2:2 (June 1988), 159-80.

233

Access to Credit & Capital

Kojiro Niino, "Size of Firm and Credit Availability: With Special Reference to the Japanese Economy," *Kobe University Economic Review* 4 (1958), 19-28.

Akira Koizumi, "The Overloan' Problem: Characteristic Feature of the Banking System in Japan," *Hitotsubashi Journal of Commerce and Management* 2:1 (Nov 1962), 53-65.

Hidekazu Nomura, "The Window Dressing of Accounts at the Present Stage and the Accumulation of Capital in Japan," *Kyoto University Economic Review* 38:2 (Oct 1968), 46-68.

Toshihiko Kato, "High Growth and the Supply of Funds in the Postwar Japanese Economy," *Annals of the Institute of Social Science* 13 (1972), 1-15.

Yukio Rimbara & A.M. Santamero, "A Study of Credit Rationing in Japan," *International Economic Review* 17:3 (Oct 1976), 567-80.

Juro Teranishi, "A Model of the Relationship between Regulated and Unregulated Financial Markets: Credit Rationing in Japanese Context," *Hitotsubashi Journal of Economics* 22:2 (Feb 1982), 25-43.

Walter E. Hoadley, "Banking and Finance: The Cost of Capital in Japan and the United States," in Chalmers Johnson, ed. *The Industrial Policy Debate*, San Francisco, Institute for Comparative Studies Press, 1984, 173-93.

Albert Ando & Alan J. Auerbach, "The Cost of Capital in the United States and Japan: A Comparison," *Journal of the Japanese and International Economies* 2:2 (June 1988), 134-58.

Monetary Policy & Issues

Tsukumo Shionoya, *Problems Surrounding the Revision of the Bank of Japan Law: A Controversy on the Monetary Policy and the Central Banking System*, Nagoya, The Beckhart Foundation, 1962.

Hugh T. Patrick, *Monetary Policy and Central Banking in Contemporary Japan*, University of Bombay, 1962.

Hugh T. Patrick, ed. "Cyclical Instability and Fiscal-Monetary Policy in Postwar Japan," in William W. Lockwood, ed. *The State and Economic Enterprise in Japan*, Princeton University Press, 1965, 555-618.

OECD, *Monetary Policy in Japan*, 1972.

Ryoichi Mikitani, "Monetary Policy in Japan," in Karel Holbik, ed. *Monetary Policy in Twelve Industrial Countries*, Boston, Federal Reserve Bank of Boston, 1973, 246-81.

Tsuneo Ishikawa, "Some Reflections on the New Scheme for Monetary Control' by the Bank of Japan," *Kyoto University Economic Review* 43:1-2 (Apr-Oct 1973), 45-58.

T.R.G. Bingham, "Monetary Policy in Japan," *JES* 7:4 (Sum 1979), 76-88.

Yoshio Suzuki, *Money and Banking in Contemporary Japan*, Yale University Press, 1980.

Kazumasa Iwata & Koichi Hamada, "The Call Market and the Money Supply Process in Japan," *Internationales Asienforum* 11:3-4 (Nov 1980), 337-56.

John Greenwood, "Monetary Base Control in Action," *Asian Monetary Monitor* 7:4 (July-Aug 1983), 13-24.

John Greenwood, "The Japanese Experiment in Monetarism, 1974 to 1984," *Asian Monetary Monitor* 8:2 (March-Apr 1984), 2-8.

Koichi Hamada & Fumio Hayashi, "Monetary Policy in Postwar Japan," in Albert Ando et al., eds. *Monetary Policy in Our Time*, Cambridge, MIT Press, 1985, 83-121.

Yoshio Suzuki, *Money, Finance, and Macroeconomic Performance in Japan*, Yale University Press, 1986.

Yoshio Suzuki & Hiroshi Yomo, eds. *Financial Innovation and Monetary Policy: Asia and the West*, University of Tokyo Press, 1986.

Masaru Yoshitomi, "The External Safeguard of Domestic Monetary and Fiscal Policies," in Michele Schmiegelow, ed. *Japan's Response to Crisis and Change in the World Economy*, New York, M.E. Sharpe, 1986, 104-30.

Michael M. Hutchison, "Monetary Control with an Exchange Rate Objective: The Bank of Japan, 1973-86," *Journal of International Money and Finance* 7:3 (Sept 1988), 261-71.

Interest Rates

Hugh T. Patrick, "Japan's Interest Rates and the Grey' Financial Market," *Pacific Affairs* 38 (1965), 326-44.

Richard H. Pettway, "Interest Rates of Japanese Long-Term National Bonds: Have Interest Rates been Liberalized?" *Keio Economic Studies* 19:1 (1982), 91-100.

Akiyoshi Horiuchi, "The Low Interest Rate Policy' and Economic Growth in Postwar Japan," *DE* 22:4 (Dec 1984), 349-71.

Tim Lee, "The Effect of Rising Interest Rates on Institutional Flows of Funds," *Asian Monetary Monitor* 11:4 (July-Aug 1987), 17-25.

Money Markets, Securities, & The Stock Exchange

Robert F. Emery, *The Japanese Money Market*, Heath, Lexington Books, 1984.

Richard H. Pettway & T. Craig Tapley, "The Tokyo Stock Exchange: An Analysis of Stock Market Prices," *Keio Business Review* 21 (1984), 75-93.

Lawrence Repeta, "Declining Public Ownership of Japanese Industry: A Case of Regulatory Failure," *Law in Japan* 17 (1984), 153-84.

Richard H. Pettway & T. Craig Tapley, "Segmented versus Integrated Capital Markets: The Case of Dually Listed Stocks on the Tokyo and New York Stock Exchanges," *Keio Economic Studies* 22:2 (1985), 17-34.

Yasuhiro Yonezawa & Junko Maru, "Functions of the Japanese Stock Market," *JES* 15:1 (Fall 1986), 42-75.

"Japanese Equity Markets: An Overview," Japan Economic Institute, Report No. 38A, October 9, 1987.

Aron Viner, *Inside Japan's Financial Markets*, London, Economist Publications, 1987.

Securities in Japan 1988, Tokyo, Japan Securities Research Institute, 1988.

Megumu Sudo, "Competition in Japan's Securities Industry: A Historical Overview," *JES* 16:3 (Spr 1988), 3-38.

Shinji Takagi, "Recent Developments in Japan's Bond and Money Markets," *Journal of the Japanese and International Economies* 2:1 (March 1988), 63-91.

C. AGRICULTURE, FOOD, & LAND POLICY

Agriculture

Masaharu Yasukawa, "Position of Agriculture in Postwar Japanese Capitalism's Reproduction Structure," *Keio Economic Studies* 1 (1963), 89-133.

Takekazu Ogura, "Recent Agrarian Problems in Japan," *DE* 4:2 (June 1966), 151-70.

Bruce F. Johnston, *Agriculture and the Economic Development: The Relevance of the Japanese Experience*, Stanford Univerity Press, 1967.

Tohru Ishimitsu, "The Impact of Changing Food Habits on Imports and the Future Land Use Pattern in Japan," *Kobe University Economic Review* 14 (1968), 59-88.

DE 7:2 (June 1969), the following:
Masayoshi Namiki, "Active Agricultural Population in Postwar Japan, 158-69.
Seiki Nakayama, "Long-Term Changes in Food Consumption in Japan," 220-32.

Yuzuru Kato, "Sources of Loanable Funds of Agricultural Credit Institutions in Asia: Japan's Experience," *DE* 10:2 (June 1972), 126-40.

Shigeto Kawano, "Impeding Factors in the Adjustment of Japan's Agriculture," *DE* 11:1 (March 1973), 3-22.

Keizo Tsuchiya, *Productivity and Technological Progress in Japanese Agriculture*, University of Tokyo, 1976.

Keiichi Sakamoto, "Can Japanese Agriculture be Revived?" *JES* 4:3 (Spr 1976), 68-89.

Takekazu Ogura, "Implications of Japan's Declining Food Self-Sufficiency Ratio," *DE* 14:4 (Dec 1976), 419-48.

Yasuhiko Yuize, "Truth About Japanese Agriculture," *Japan Quarterly* 25 (1978), 264-97.

Susumu Yamaji, "Agriculture," in Hyoe Murakami & Johannes Hirschmeier, eds. *Politics and Economics in Contemporary Japan*, Tokyo, Japan Culture Institute, 1979, 184-203.

Takekazu Ogura, *Can Japanese Agriculture Survive? A Historical and Comparative Approach*, Tokyo, Argicultural Research Center, 1980.

Tadashi Fukutake, *Rural Society in Japan*, University of Tokyo Press, 1980.

Bernard Bernier, "The Japanese Peasantry and Economic Growth Since the Land Reform of 1946-47," *Bulletin of Concerned Asian Scholars* 12:1 (Jan-March 1980), 40-52.

Osamu Tanaka, "Analysis of the Feasibility of Large-scale Owner-Tenancy in Japan," *Kobe University Economic Review* 28 (1982), 17-29.

James Simpson et al, *Technological Change in Japan's Beef Industry*, Boulder, Westview Press, 1985.

JES 13:3 (Spr 1985), the following:
Ikutsune Adachi, "Japanese Agriculture: Fallacy of the Revitalization Argument," 3-33.
Yoshikazu Kano, "Japanese Agriculture: It Can Be Revitalized," 34-66.

Richard H. Moore, *Japanese Agriculture: Patterns of Rural Development*, Boulder, Westview Press, 1988.

Policy & Trade

Haruhiro Fukui, *Party in Power: The Japanese Liberal Democrats and Policymaking*, University of California Press, 1970, 173-97.

Haruhiro Fukui, "The Japanese Farmer and Politics," in Isaiah Frank, ed. *The Japanese Economy in International Perspective*, Baltimore, Johns Hopkins University Press, 1975, 134-67.

Michael W. Donnelly, "The Political Economy of Food in Japan," in Barbara Huddleston & Jon McLin, eds. *Political Investments in Food Production*, Indiana University Press, 1979, 185-201.

Keith A.J. Hay & Michael W. Donnelly, "Canadian-Japanese Agricultural Trade," in Keith A.J. Hay, ed. *Canadian Perspectives on Economic Relations with Japan*, Montreal, Institute for Research on Public Policy, 1980, 341-76.

Takeshi Ishida & Aurelia D. George, "Nokyo: The Japanese Farmers' Representative," in Peter Drysdale & Hironobu Kitaoji, eds. *Japan & Australia: Two Societies and Their Interaction*, Canberra, Australian National University Press, 1981, 194-214.

Aurelia D. George, "The Japanese Farm Lobby and Agricultural Policymaking," *Pacific Affairs* 54:3 (Fall 1981), 409-30.

Hideo Sato & Michael W. Hodin, "Agricultural Trade: The Case of Beef and Citrus," in I.M. Destler & Hideo Sato, eds. *Coping with U.S.-Japanese Economic Conflicts*, Lexington, Mass., D.C. Heath, 1982, 121-83.

Emery N. Castle & Kenzo Hemmi, eds. *U.S.-Japanese Agricultural Trade Relations*, Washington, D.C., Resources for the Future, 1982, including:
Kenzo Hemmi, Agriculture and Politics in Japan," 219-68.
Fumio Egaitsu, "Japanese Agricultural Policy: Present Problems and Their Historical Background," 148-81.

John W. Longworth, *Beef in Japan: Politics, Production, Marketing and Trade*, St. Lucia, Queensland, University of Queensland Press, 1983.

Tim Sears, "Carrots, Sticks, and Rice: Japan's Quest for Food Security," *Journal of International Affairs* 37:1 (Sum 1983), 177-90.

Michael W. Donnelly, "Conflict over Government Authority and Markets: Japan's Rice Economy," in Ellis S. Krauss, Thomas C. Rohlen, & Patricia G. Steinhoff, eds. *Conflict in Japan*, University Press of Hawaii, 1984, 335-74.

Keijiro Otsuka and Yujiro Hayami, *Rice Policy in Japan: Its Costs and Distributional Consequences*, Canberra, Australian National University, Australia-Japan Research Centre, Pacific Economic Papers No. 114, 1984.

Kym Anderson & Yujiro Hayami, eds. *The Political Economy of Agricultural Protection; East Asia in International Perspective*, Winchester, Mass., Allen & Unwin, 1986.

Michael R. Reich, Yasuo Endo, & C. Peter Timmer, "Agriculture: The Political Economy of Structural Change," in Thomas K. McCraw, ed. *America versus Japan*, Boston, Harvard Business School Press, 1986, 151-92.

D. Gale Johnson, *Agricultural Issues in the US and Japan*, New York University Press, 1987.

James Fallows, "The Rice Plot," *The Atlantic* (Jan 1987), 22-26.

Kym Anderson & Rod Tyers, "Japan's Agricultural Policy in International Perspective," *Journal of the Japanese and International Economies* 1:2 (June 1987), 131-46.

"Japan, Agriculture and the MTN," Japan Economic Institute, Report No. 44A, November 20, 1987.

Jeffrey Sachs & Peter Boone, "Japanese Structural Adjustment and the Balance of Payments," *Journal of The Japanese and International Economies* 2:3 (Sept 1988), 286-327.

"Liberalization of Japan's Beef and Orange Markets: Winners and Losers," Japan Economic Institute, Report No. 42A, November 4, 1988.

Urban Land Policy

Susumu Kobe, "The Transport Problem of Tokyo," *Waseda Economic Papers* 8 (1963), 1-26.

Susumu Kurasawa, "Japanese City: A Study in Its Structural Changes," *DE* 7:4 (Dec 1969), 527-43.

Ryohei Kakumoto, "The Revolution in Commuter Transportation: A Proposal for Solving the Housing Shortage and Commuter Congestion in the Metropolis by a New Tokaido Line Type High Speed Railway," *DE* 7:4 (Dec 1969), 590-616.

Kikunosuke Ohno, "Rising Trend of Urban Land Value in Japan, 1955-1969," *Kobe University Economic Review* 16 (1970), 65-83.

Ei'ichi Isomura, "Urbanization and City Planning Policies," *DE* 10:4 (Dec 1972), 451-67.

Yuzuru Hanayama, "Urban Land Prices and the Housing Problem,"*DE* 10:4 (Dec 1972), 468-78.

Edwin S. Mills & Katsutoshi Ohta, "Urbanization and Urban Problems," in Hugh Patrick & Henry Rosovsky, eds. *Asia's New Giant: How the Japanese Economy Works*, Brookings Institution, 1976, 673-751.

Yuzuru Hanayama, "Urbanization and Land Prices: The Case of Tokyo," in Shigeto Tsuru, ed. *Growth and Resources Problems Related to Japan*: Proceedings of Session VI of the Fifth Congress of the International Economic Association, Tokyo, Asahi Evening News, 1978, 341-53.

Norman J. Glickman, *The Growth and Management of the Japanese Urban System*, New York, Academic Press, 1979.

Yuzuru Hanayama, "The Housing Land Shortage in Japan: A Myth," *JES* 11:3 (Spr 1983), 3-47.

Luciano Minerbi et al., eds. *Land Readjustment: The Japanese System*, Boston, Oelgeschlager, Gunn & Hain, 1986.

Frank G. Bennett, Jr., "Legal Protection of Solar Access under Japanese Law," *UCLA Pacific Basin Law Journal* 5:1&2 (Spr & Fall 1986), 107-31.

Ken'ichi Miyamoto, "Cities under Contemporary Japanese Capitalism," *JES* 16:1 (Fall 1987), 3-33.

D. ENERGY

General: Resources & Historical Background

Edward A. Ackerman, *Japan's Natural Resources and Their Relation to Japan's Economic Future*, University of Chicago Press, 1953.

J.J. Kaplan, "Raw Materials Policy: Japan and the United States," in Isaiah Frank, ed. *The Japanese Economy in International Perspective*, Baltimore, Johns Hopkins University Press, 1975, 231-47.

Masao Sakisaka, "Japan's Energy Policy," *JES* 3:4 (Sum 1975), 4-37.

Masaru Saito, "Japan's Overseas Resource Development Policy," *JES* 3:4 (Sum 1975), 38-82.

Hiroaki Fukami, "Problems of Natural Resources and the Japanese Economy," *Keio Economic Studies* 15:2 (1978), 83-99.

Shigeto Tsuru, ed. *Growth and Resources Problems Related to Japan*: Proceedings of Session VI of the Fifth Congress of the International Economic Association, Tokyo, Asahi Evening News, 1978, including:
Yasukichi Yasuba, "Resources in Japan's Development," 229-53.
E. Stuart Kirby, "Resource Potentials of Continental East Asia and Japan's Material Needs," 257-84.
Masao Sakisaka, "Economic Growth in Japan and Energy," 285-95.
Jun Nishikawa, " 'Resource Constraints': A Problem of the Japanese Economy," 297-313.

Shigeto Tsuru, "The Energy Prospect for Japan," *Japan Quarterly* 27:1 (Jan-Mar 1980), 15-19.

Ronald Morse, ed. *The Politics of Japan's Energy Strategy*, Berkeley, University of California, Institute of East Asian Studies, 1981, including:
Peter A. Petri, "High-Cost Energy and Japan's International Economic Strategy," 15-36.

Herbert I. Goodman, "Japan and the World Energy Problem," in Daniel I. Okimoto, ed. *Japan's Economy: Coping with Change in the International Environment*, Boulder, Westview Press, 1982, 21-88.

Raymond Vernon, *Two Hungry Giants: The United States and Japan in the Quest for Oil and Ores*, Harvard University Press, 1982.

Daniel Yergin & Martin Hillenbrand, eds., *Global Insecurity: a Strategy for Energy & Economic Renewal*, Houghton Mifflin, 1982, including:

Joji Watanuki, "Japanese Society and the Limits of Growth," 168-99.
Teruyasu Murakami, "The Remarkable Adaptation of Japan's Economy," 138-67.

Peter Nemetz, et al., "Japan's Energy Strategy at the Crossroads," *Pacific Affairs* 57:4 (Win 1984-85), 553-76.

Richard H.K. Vietor, "Energy Markets and Policy," Thomas K. McCraw, ed. *America versus Japan*, Boston, Harvard Business School Press, 1986, 193-228.

Richard J. Samuels, *The Business of the Japanese State: Energy Markets in Comparative and Historical Perspective*, Cornell University Press, 1987.

"Japan's Energy Policy: 1986 Update," Japan Economic Institute, Report No. 3A, January 23, 1987.

S. Hayden Lesbirel, "The Political Economy of Substitution Policy: Japan's Response to Lower Oil Prices," *Pacific Affairs* 61:2 (Sum 1988), 285-302.

Coal

Nobuaki Hizume, "Some Aspects of Coal Mining Industry," *CJ* 26:2 (Dec 1959), 246-66.

Shin Aochi, "Coal Miners in Northern Kyushu," *CJ* 26:2 (Dec 1959), 339-42.

Joseph R. D'Cruz, "Quasi Integration in Raw Material Markets: The Overseas Procurement of Coking Coal by the Japanese Steel Industry," Harvard DBA thesis, 1979.

John Price, "Labour Relations in Japan's Postwar Coal Industry: The 1960 Miike Lockout," M.A. thesis, University of British Columbia, 1987.

Oil & Gas

Yoshikazu Miyazaki, "A New Price Revolution," *Japan Interpreter* 9:4 (Spr 1975), 420-50.

Yoshi Tsurumi, "Japan," in Raymond Vernon, ed. *The Oil Crisis*, New York, W.W. Norton, 1976, 113-27.

Tsunehiko Watanabe, "Japan," in Edward R. Fried and Charles L. Schultze, eds. *Higher Oil Prices and the World Economy*, Brookings Institution, 1976, 143-67.

Yuan-li Wu, *Japan's Search for Oil: A Case Study on Economic Nationalism and International Security*, Stanford, Hoover Institution, 1977.

Malcolm D.H. Smith, "Prices and Petroleum in Japan: 1973-1974—A Study of Administrative Guidance," *Law in Japan* 10 (1977), 81-100.

Selig S. Harrison, *China, Oil, and Asia: Conflict Ahead?*, Columbia University Press, 1977.

Yoshi Tsurumi, "The Case of Japan: Price Bargaining and Controls on Oil Products," *Journal of Comparative Economics* 2 (1978), 126-43.

Donald W. Klein, "Japan 1979: The Second Oil Crisis," *Asian Survey* 20:1 (Jan 1980), 42-52.

Masaru Yoshitomi, "Supply Management: The Economic Key to Survival in the 1980s," *Asian Survey* 20:7 (July 1980), 683-93.

Minoru Nishida, "Industrial Policy toward Petroleum in Japan since 1945," *Osaka City University Economic Review* 16 (1980), 33-54.

Martha A. Caldwell, "Petroleum Politics in Japan: State and Industry in a Changing Policy Context," Ph.D. diss., University of Wisconsin, 1981.

Martha Caldwell, "The Dilemmas of Japan's Oil Dependency," in Ronald Morse, ed. *The Politics of Japan's Energy Strategy*, Berkeley, University of California, Institute of East Asian Studies, 1981, 65-84.

Valerie Yorke, "Oil, the Middle East and Japan's Search for Security," *International Affairs* (London) 57:3 (Sum 1981), 428-48.

Yoichi Shinkai, "Oil Crises and Stagflation in Japan," in Kozo Yamamura, ed. *Policy and Trade Issues of the Japanese Economy: American and Japanese Perspectives*, University of Washington Press, 1982, 173-93.

Dale W. Jorgenson, "The Oil Price Decline and Economic Growth in Japan and the U.S.," *Keio Economic Studies* 23:1 (1986), 1-19.

Peter N. Nemetz & Ilan B. Vertinsky, "Japan and the International Market for LNG," *Columbia Journal of World Business* 19:1 (Spr 1984), 70-76.

Electric Power

Saburo Takahashi, "The Electric Power Industry," *Japan Quarterly* 6 (1959), 240-50.

Roger W. Gale, "Tokyo Electric Power Company: Its Role in Shaping Japan's Coal and LNG Policy," in Ronald Morse, ed. *The Politics of Japan's Energy Strategy*, Berkeley, University of California, Institute of East Asian Studies, 1981, 85-105.

Atomic Power

Susumu Nagai, "Going Ahead With Atomic Power: A Dangerous Choice," *Japan Quarterly* 25:1 (Jan-Mar 1978), 12-19.

Michael Blaker, ed. *Oil and the Atom: Issues in US-Japan Energy Relations*, Columbia University, East Asian Institute, 1980.

Richard A. Ruidl, "The Mutsu Malaise: Another Affliction of Japan's Nuclear Allergy?" *Asian Profile* 8:4 (August 1980), 311-28.

Richard P. Suttmeier, "The Japanese Nuclear Power Option: Technological Promise and Social Limitations," in Ronald Morse, ed. *The Politics of Japan's Energy Strategy*, Berkeley, University of California, Institute of East Asian Studies, 1981, 106-33.

Yuki Tanaka, "Nuclear Power Plant Gypsies in High-Tech Society," *Bulletin of Concerned Asian Scholars* 18:1 (Jan-Mar 1986), 2-22.

New Forms of Energy

Richard J. Samuels, "The Politics of Alternative Energy Research and Development in Japan," in Ronald Morse, ed. *The Politics of Japan's Energy Strategy*, Berkeley, University of California, Institute of East Asian Studies, 1981, 134-66.

Diplomacy of Resources

A. Kapoor, ed. *Asian Business and Environment in Transition: Selected Readings and Essays*, Princeton, Darwin Press, 1976, including:
Saburo Okita, "Natural Resource Dependency and Japanese Foreign Policy," 507-17, from *Foreign Affairs* (July 1974).
Terutomo Ozawa, "Japan's Mod-East Diplomacy," 479-90, from *Columbia Journal of World Business*.

Ronald A. Morse, "Energy and Japan's National Security Strategy," in Morse, ed. *The Politics of Japan's Energy Strategy*, Berkeley, University of California, Institute of East Asian Studies, 1981, 37-61.

Akao Nobutoshi, ed., *Japan's Economic Security: Resources as a Factor in Foreign Policy*, Hampshire, Gower Publishing, 1983.

Charles K. Ebinger & Ronald A. Morse, eds. *U.S.-Japanese Energy Relations: Cooperation and Competition*, Boulder, Westview Press, 1984.

Michael M. Yoshitsu, *Caught in the Middle East: Japan's Diplomacy in Transition*, Lexington Books, 1984.

Roger A. Sedjo, "United States-Japanese Solidwood Products Trade," *Columbia Journal of World Business* 19:1 (Spr 1984), 83-88.

Vaclav Smil, "China and Japan in the New Energy Era," in Peter N. Nemetz, ed. *The Pacific Rim: Investment, Development and Trade*, University of British Columbia Press, 1987, 223-33.

Roy Licklider, "The Power of Oil: The Arab Oil Weapon and the Netherlands, The United Kingdom, Canada, Japan, and the United States," *International Studies Quarterly 32:2 (June 1988), 205-26.*

E. TRANSPORT

Railways & Local Transport

Edward J. Lincoln, "Technical Change on the Japanese National Railways: 1949-1974," PhD diss., Yale University, 1978.

Katsumasa Harada, "Technological Independence and Progress of Standardization in the Japanese Railways," *DE* 19:3 (Sept 1980), 313-32.

The Shinkansen High-Speed Rail Network of Japan, eds. A Straszak & R. Tuch, Pergamon, 1980.

Shuhei Konno, "Strengths and Weaknesses of the Bullet Train," *Japan Echo* 11:3 (Aut 1984), 73-80.

Susumu Kobe, "The Transport Problem of Tokyo," *Waseda Economic Papers* 8 (1963), 1-26.

Hiroyuki Yamada, "Urban Transportation Problem in Contemporary Japan," *Kyoto University Economic Review* 38:1 (Apr 1968), 57-84.

Ushio Chujo, "On Management Systems of Rural Transport in Japan: Basic Policies for Improvement," *Keio Business Review* 17 (1980), 115-37.

"Case Material: Hakuyosha Company Ltd.," *Keio Business Review* 7 (1968), 103-26 (a cleaning service).

Shipping

Shipping and Trade News, Anniversary Supplements, Tokyo News Service.

Hiromasa Yamamoto, "The Recovery Method of the Japanese Shipping Industry in the Post-War World," *Kobe Economic and Business Review* 2 (1954), 89-108.

Ginjiro Shibata, "Present Status of Japan's Shipping," *Kobe Economic and Business Review* 3 (1956), 27-43.

Ginjiro Shibata, "Tramp Shipping Freights and International Trade," *Kobe Economic and Business Review* 4 (1957), 149-64

Hiromasa Yamamoto, "On the Regulating Policy of Japan Against the Shipping Conference—Especially in Relation to the Refusal of the Entry of New Comers," *Kobe Economic and Business Review* 4 (1957), 177-94.

Kenichi Masui, "Japan's Ocean Shipping Development Program and its Subsidy Problem," *Keio Business Review* 1 (1962), 49-62.

Seiji Sasaki, "Patterns of Domestic Shipping Services: Characteristics of Japanese Coastwise Shipping," *Kobe Economic and Business Review* 13 (1966), 23-34.

Hiromasa Yamamoto, articles on shipping labor, *Kobe Economic and Business Review*, 1960s to 1970s.

Ryoichi Furuta & Yoshikazu Hirai, *A Short History of Japanese Merchant Shipping*, trans. by Duncan MacFarlane, Tokyo News Service, 1967.

Hideo Suzuki, "Containerization in the Japanese Shipping Industry," *Management Japan* 5:2 (1971), 22-27.

Yoshiya Ariyoshi, *Half a Century in Shipping*, Tokyo News Service, 1977.

Japan Maritime Research Institute, comp. *World Containerization 1983: Analysis and Future Outlook on Containerization Developments*, Tokyo News Service, 1983.

Tomohei Chida, "The Development of Japan's Post-War Shipping Policy," *Journal of Transport History* 5:1 (March 1984), 82-90.

Ryoichi Miwa, "Government and the Japanese Shipping Industry, 1945-64," *Journal of Transport History* 9:1 (March 1988), 37-49.

F. TELECOMMUNICATIONS

T.J. Pempel, "Land Mobile Communication in Japan: Technical Development and International Trade," in Raymond Bowers et al., eds. *Communications for a Mobile Society*, Beverly Hills & Sage, 1978.

Ken'ichi Imai, "Some Proposals Concerning Japan's Telecommunications Policy," *Hitotsubashi Journal of Commerce and Management* 17:1 (1982), 1-24.

Edward Meadows, "Japan Runs into America, Inc.," *Fortune*, March 22, 1982, 56-61 [re: AT&T-Fujitsu controversy].

Peter E. Fuchs, "Regulatory Reform and Japan's Telecommunications Revolution," in *U.S.-Japan Relations: New Attitudes for a New Era*, 1983-84 Annual Review of the Program on U.S.-Japan Relations, Harvard University, Center for International Affairs, 1984, 123-41.

Mick McLean, ed. *The Information Explosion: The New Electronic Media in Japan & Europe*, London, Frances Pinter, 1985.

Michael Borrus, "Japanese Telecommunications: Reforms and Trade Implications," *California Management Review* 28:3 (Spr 1986), 43-61.

Chalmers Johnson, "MITI, MPT, and the Telecom Wars: How Japan Makes Policy for High Technology," in Berkeley Roundtable on the International Economy (BRIE), ed. *Creating Advantage: American and Japanese Strategies for Adjusting to Change in a New World Economy*, Berkeley, University of California, forthcoming.

G. SPACE ENTERPRISE

Space in Japan, Keidanren, annual.

G.R. Hall & R.E. Johnson, "Transfers of United States Aerospace Technology to Japan," in R. Vernon, ed. *The Technology Factor in International Trade*, Columbia University Press, 1970, 305-58.

"Situation of Space Development in Japan," *Science & Technology in Japan* 1:3 (July 1982), 4-15.

Alun M. Anderson, *Science and Technology in Japan*, Harlow, Essex, Longman, 1984, 194-217.

"Japan's Satellite Development Program," Japan Economic Institute, Report No. 11A, March 16, 1984.

"Japan's Aerospace Industry: An Interview with the Head of Mitsubishi Corp.'s Aerospace Department," Japan Economic Institute, Report No. 41A, October 26, 1984.

Neil W. Davis, "Japanese-US Space Issues: Communication Satellites and Launch Vehicle Technology," Program on Information Policy Resources, Harvard University, 1985.

Tsutomu Okada, "Satellite Broadcasting in Japan," in Mick McLean, ed. *The Information Explosion: The New Electronic Media in Japan & Europe*, London, Frances Pinter, 1985, 97-111.

Mick McLean, ed. *Astroelectronics: Japan and Europe in Space*, London, Frances Pinter, 1986.

Neil W. Davis, "Gearing Up for Business in Space," *Asian Technology Review*, May 1987, 29-37.

"Space," *Science & Technology in Japan* 6:23 (Aug 1987), 7-51.

Neil W. Davis, "Japan's Profits Motive Blasts into Orbit," *Far Eastern Economic Review*, August 13, 1987, 92-97.

"Japan Shoots for the Stars," Japan Economic Institute, Report No. 40A, October 23, 1987.

Takeshi Inagaki, "Rocket Readiness," *Japan Quarterly* 35:2 (April-June 1988), 146-51.

9. MARKET ACCESS

A. GENERAL

Chalmers Johnson, "The 'Internationalization' of the Japanese Economy," *California Management Review* 25:3 (Spr 1983), 5-26.

Harry First, "Japan's Antitrust Policy: Impact on Import Competition," in Thomas A. Pugel, ed. *Fragile Interdependence: Economic Issues in U.S.-Japanese Trade and Investment*, Lexington, Heath, 1986, 63-90.

B. FOREIGN INVESTMENT, LIBERALIZATION, & PROTECTIONISM

Protectionism: Imports

G.C. Allen, *Japan as a Market and Source of Supply*, Oxford, Pergamon Press, 1967.

Boye De Mente & Fred T. Perry, *The Japanese as Consumers: Asia's First Great Mass Market*, Tokyo, Weatherhill, 1967.

Yoichi Shinkai, "The Basic Doctrine of Japanese Commercial Policy," *JES* 1:3 (Spr 1973), 9-38.

Patricia Kuwayama, "Tariff Protection and Japanese Industry," *Keio Economic Studies* 11:1 (1974), 47-76.

A. Kapoor, ed. *Asian Business and Environment in Transition: Selected Readings and Essays*, Princeton, Darwin Press, 1976.

Lawrence B. Krause & Sueo Sekiguchi, "Japan and the World Economy," in Hugh Patrick & Henry Rosovsky, eds. *Asia's New Giant: How the Japanese Economy Works*, Brookings Institution, 1976, 383-458 (see esp. the appendix on chronology of trade policy, 451-58).

Frank A. Weil & Norman D. Glick, "Japan: Is the Market Open? A View of the Japanese Market Drawn from U.S. Corporate Experience," *Law and Policy in International Business* 11:3 (1979), 845-902.

Ippei Yamazawa, "Manufactured Exports from Thailand and the Japanese Market," *Hitotsubashi Journal of Economics* 20:2 (Feb 1980), 1-10.

Atsushi Murakami, "The Underlying Factors of Successful Penetration of the East Asian Countries' Products into Japanese Market," *Kobe University Economic Review* 26 (1980), 1-28.

Gary Saxonhouse, "Evolving Comparative Advantage and Japan's Imports of Manufactures," in Kozo Yamamura, ed. *Policy and Trade Issues of the Japanese Economy: American and Japanese Perspectives*, University of Washington Press, 1982, 239-69.

Kent E. Calder, "Opening Japan," *Foreign Policy* 47 (Sum 1982), 82-97.

Gary R. Saxonhouse, "The Micro- and Macroeconomics of Foreign Sales to Japan," in William R. Cline, ed. *Trade Policy in the 1980s*, Washington, Institute for International Economics, 1983, 259-304.

Timothy J. Curran, "The Politics of Trade Liberalization," *Journal of International Affairs* 37:1 (Sum 1983), 105-22.

Saburo Okita, "Role of the Trade Ombudsman in Liberalizing Japan's Market," *The World Economy* 7:3 (Sept 1984), 241-56.

Expanding your Market in Japan, Survey on Machinery Marketplace: Electric Measuring Equipment, Medical Electronic Equipment, Electronic Computers & Peripherals, Tokyo, Manufactured Imports Promotion Organization, March 1985.

Hirotaka Takeuchi, "The Changing Role of the Japanese Market and its Impact on Global Strategy," *Hitotsubashi Journal of Commerce & Management* 20:1 (Dec 1985), 49-61.

William V. Rapp, "Japan's Invisible Barriers to Trade," in Thomas A. Pugel, ed. *Fragile Interdependence: Economic Issues in U.S.-Japanese Trade and Investment*, Lexington, Heath, 1986, 21-62.

Akinori Uesugi, "Japan's Cartel System and Its Impact on International Trade," *Harvard International Law Journal* 27: Special Issue (1986), 389-424.

Daniel I. Okimoto, "Outsider Trading: Coping with Japanese Industrial Organization," *Journal of Japanese Studies* 13:2 (Sum 1987), 383-414, (relevant also to the next section on capital).

Peter B. Edelman, "Japanese Product Standards as Non-Tariff Barriers: When Regulatory Policy Becomes a Trade Issue," *Stanford Journal of International Law* 24:2 (Spr 1988), 389-446.

Shintaro Hagiwara, Yasuhiko Noguchi & Kazuhito Masui, "Anti-Dumping Laws in Japan," *Journal of World Trade Law* 22:4 (Aug 1988), 51-66.

John Quansheng Zhao, "The Making of Public Policy in Japan: Protectionism in Raw Silk Importation," *Asian Survey* 28:9 (Sept 1988), 926-44.

Protectionism: Capital

Leon Hollerman, *Japan's Dependence on the World Economy: The Approach Toward Economic Liberalization*, Princeton University Press, 1967.

Ryutaro Komiya, "Direct Foreign Investment in Postwar Japan," in Peter Drysdale, ed. *Direct Foreign Investment in Asia and the Pacific*, University of Toronto Press, 1970, 137-72.

N. Kobayashi, "Foreign Investment in Japan," in I.A. Litvak & C.J. Maule, eds. *Foreign Investment: The Experience of Host Countries*, New York, Praeger, 1970, 123-60.

Leon Hollerman, "Liberalization and Japanese Trade in the 1970s," *Asian Survey* 10:5 (May 1970), 427-37.

Robert S. Ozaki, "Japanese Views on Foreign Capital," *Asian Survey* 11:11 (Nov 1971), 1071-83.

Robert S. Ozaki, *The Control of Imports and Foreign Capital in Japan*, New York, Praeger, 1972 (includes documents).

Robert J. Ballon & Eugene H. Lee, eds., *Foreign Investment and Japan*, Tokyo, Kodansha, 1972.

Alfred K. Ho, *Japan's Trade Liberalization in the 1960s*, White Plains, New York, International Arts and Sciences Press, 1973.

Dan Fenno Henderson, *Foreign Enterprise in Japan: Laws & Policies*, Chapel Hill, University of North Carolina Press, 1973.

Dan F. Henderson, "Japan's Administration of Foreign Direct Investment," in Virginia Shook Cameron, ed. *Private Investment and International Transactions in Asian and South Pacific Countries*, New York, Matthew Bender, 1974, 321-71.

Richard W. Wright, "Joint Venture Problems in Japan," *Columbia Journal of World Business* 14:1 (Spr 1979), 25-31.

William F. Averyt, "Canadian and Japanese Foreign Investment Screening," *Columbia Journal of World Business* 21:4 (Win 1986), 47-54.

Thomas A. Pugel, ed. *Fragile Interdependence: Economic Issues in U.S.-Japanese Trade and Investment*, Lexington, Heath, 1986, including:
William H. Brown, "Opening Japanese Financial Markets: What Has Changed, What Will Change?" 115-39.
Terutomo Ozawa, "Japanese Policy toward Foreign Multinationals: Implications for Trade and Competitiveness," 141-74.

Harvard International Law Journal 27: Special Issue (1986), including:
Mitsuo Matsushita, "The Legal Framework of Trade and Investment in Japan," 361-88.
Walter L. Ames, "Buying a Piece of Japan, Inc.: Foreign Acquisitions in Japan," 541-69.

Dennis J. Encarnation, "Cross-Investment: A Second Front of Economic Rivalry," in Thomas K. McCraw, ed. *America versus Japan*, Boston, Harvard Business School Press, 1986, 117-50, also in *California Management Review* 29:2 (Win 1987), 20-48.

Leon Hollerman, *Japan Disincorporated: The Economic Liberalization Process*, Stanford, Hoover Institution Press, 1988.

Dominique Turpin, "Strategic Alliances with Small High-Tech Businesses in Japan," *Journal of Development Planning* 18 (1988), 153-63.

Protectionism: Services

Dan F. Henderson, "Access to the Japanese Market: Some Aspects of Foreign Exchange Controls and Banking Law," in Gary Saxonhouse & Kozo Yamamura, eds. *Law and Trade Issues of the Japanese Economy: American and Japanese Perspectives*, University of Washington Press, 1986, 131-56.

J. Mark Ramseyer, "Lawyers, Foreign Lawyers, and Lawyer-Substitutes: The Market for Regulation in Japan," *Harvard International Law Journal* 27: Special Issue (1986), 499-540.

John O. Haley, "The New Regulatory Regime for Foreign Lawyers in Japan," *UCLA Pacific Basin Law Journal* 5:1&2 (Spr & Fall 1986), 1-15.

Christopher Sheehey, "Japan's New Foreign Lawyer Law," *Law & Policy in International Business* 19:2 (1987), 361-83.

Louis Pauly, *Regulatory Politics in Japan: The Case of Foreign Banking*, Cornell University, East Asia Papers #45, 1988.

Chalmers Johnson, "MITI, MPT, and the Telecom Wars: How Japan Makes Policy for High Technology," in Berkeley Roundtable on the International Economy (BRIE), ed. *Creating Advantage: American and Japanese Strategies for Adjusting to Change in a New World Economy*, Berkeley, University of California, forthcoming.

Foreign Business in Japan

M.Y. Yoshino, "Japan as a Host to International Corporations," in Charles Kindleberger, ed. *The International Corporation*, MIT Press, 1971, 142-61.

Boye De Mente, *How Business is Done in Japan—A Personal View*, Tokyo, Simpson & Doyle, 1963.

Herbert Glazer, *The International Businessman in Japan*, Sophia University, 1968.

Robert Ballon, ed. *Doing Business in Japan*, Tokyo, Tuttle, 1968.

Special Report on Foreign Owned Firms in Japan, Business Intercommunications, Inc., 1969, 107pp.

Boye De Mente, *How to Do Business in Japan: A Guide for International Businessmen*, Los Angeles, Center for International Business, 1972.

Sueo Sekiguchi & Koji Matsuba, "Direct Foreign Investment in Japan," *JES* 4:1 (Fall 1975), 52-95.

Howard F. Van Zandt, "How to Negotiate in Japan," in A. Kapoor, ed. *Asian Business and Environment in Transition: Selected Readings and Essays*, Princeton, Darwin Press, 1976, 355-70, from *Harvard Business Review* (Nov-Dec 1970).

Robert J. Ballon, ed. *Japan's Market and Foreign Business*, Tokyo, Sophia University, 1971.

Yoshi Tsurumi, "Myths that Mislead U.S. Managers in Japan," *Harvard Business Review* 49:4 (July-Aug 1971), 118-27.

Louis Kraar, "Japan is Opening Up For *Gaijin* Who Know How," *Fortune*, March 1974, 146-57.

M.Y. Yoshino, "Japan as Host to the International Corporation," in Isaiah Frank, ed. *The Japanese Economy in International Perspective*, Baltimore, Johns Hopkins University Press, 1975, 273-90.

Max Boas & Steve Chain, *Big Mac: The Unauthorized Story of McDonald's*, New York, New American Library, 1976, 149-58.

A. Kapoor, ed. *Asian Business and Environment in Transition: Selected Readings and Essays*, Princeton, Darwin Press, 1976, including:
"Foreign Business in Japan," 35-56, from *The Japan Economic Journal*.
Robert A. Feldman, "American Businesses in Japan: A New Framework," 177-94.

Robert M. March, "Foreign Firms in Japan," *California Management Review* 22:3 (Spr 1980), 42-50.

Breaking the Barriers: True Accounts of Overseas Companies in Japan, Tokyo, Survey Japan, 1982.

McKinsey & Co. (for the United States Japan Trade Study Group), *Japan Business: Obstacles and Opportunities*, Tokyo, President Inc., 1983.

The Bank of Tokyo, comp. *Setting Up Enterprises in Japan*, JETRO, 1984.

Robert Christopher, *Second to None: American Companies in Japan*, New York, Crown Publishers, 1986.

Paul Lansing & Kathryn Ready, "Hiring Women Managers in Japan: An Alternative for Foreign Employers," *California Management Review* 30:3 (Spr 1988), 112-27.

C. DISTRIBUTION AND MARKETING

Shoji Murata, "Recent Changes in Japanese Distribution," *Keio Business Review* 5 (1966), 45-52.

Shigeto Konishi, "A Study on the Nature of Retail Competitive Structure," *Keio Business Review* 5 (1966), 67-85.

Koichi Tanouchi, "The Credit Card Business in Japan," *Hitotsubashi Journal of Commerce and Management* 5:1 (Apr 1968), 35-43.

M.Y. Yoshino, *The Japanese Marketing System: Adaptations and Innovations*, MIT Press, 1971.

Yoshihiro Tajima, *How Goods Are Distributed in Japan*, Tokyo, Walton-Ridgeway, 1971.

Kisou Tasugi, "Modernization of the Functions of the Assemblers in Each Local Producing Area in Japan," *Kyoto University Economic Review* 41:1 (Apr 1971), 1-28.

Koichi Tanouchi, "Voluntary Chains in Japan," *Hitotsubashi Journal of Commerce and Management* 8:1 (July 1973), 2-8.

C. Tait Ratcliffe, "Approaches to Distribution in Japan," in Isaiah Frank, ed. *The Japanese Economy in International Perspective*, Baltimore, Johns Hopkins University Press, 1975, 101-33.

Mitsuaki Shimaguchi & Larry J. Rosenberg, "Demystifying Japanese Distribution," *Columbia Journal of World Business* 14:1 (Spr 1979), 32-41.

Randolph E. Ross, "Marketing through the Japanese Distribution System," in Keith A.J. Hay, ed. *Canadian Perspectives on Economic Relations with Japan*, Montreal, Institute for Research on Public Policy, 1980, 269-307.

Kazutoshi Maeda, "The Evolution of Retailing Industries in Japan," in *Development of Mass Marketing: The Automobile and Retailing Industries*, vol. 7 of *International Conference on Business History*, ed. by Akio Okochi & Koichi Shimokawa, University of Tokyo Press, 1981, 265-89.

pp. 64-68 of Ken-ichi Imai, "Japan's Changing Industrial Structure and United States-Japan Industrial Relations," in Kozo Yamamura, ed. *Policy and*

Trade Issues of the Japanese Economy: American and Japanese Perspectives, University of Washington Press, 1982.

Takeshi Shimizu, "Advertising Performance in Japan," *Keio Business Review* 19 (1982), 27-50.

Kenichi Ohmae, "Breaking into Japan's Distribution System," *Wall Street Journal*, June 28, 1982, p. 14.

Hideto Ishida, "Anticompetitive Practices in the Distribution of Goods and Services in Japan: The Problem of Distribution *Keiretsu*," *Journal of Japanese Studies* 9:2 (Sum 1983), 317-34.

Shuji Ogawa, "The Distribution Industry in the 1980s," *Journal of Japanese Trade & Industry* 3 (March 1984), 12-21.

Michael R. Czinkota, "Distribution in Japan: Problems and Changes," *Columbia Journal of World Business* 20:3 (Fall 1985), 65-72.

Helmut Laumer, "The Distribution System: Its Social Function and Import Impeding Effects," in Michele Schmiegelow, ed. *Japan's Response to Crisis and Change in the World Economy*, New York, M.E. Sharpe, 1986, 257-77.

Michael R. Czinkota & Jon Woronoff, *Japan's Market: The Distribution System*, New York, Praeger, 1986.

Retail Distribution in Japan, Tokyo, Dodwell Marketing Consultants, 1986.

Mitsuo Wada, "Selling in Japan: Consumer Behavior and Distribution as Barriers to Imports," in Thomas A. Pugel, ed. *Fragile Interdependence: Economic Issues in U.S.-Japanese Trade and Investment*, Lexington, Heath, 1986, 91-113.

Christopher J. Chipello, "Mom-and-Pop Stores Lose Favor in Japan," *Wall Street Journal*, March 18, 1987, p. 26.

Charles Smith, "The Parallel Option: Japan's High Import Prices Come under Pressure," *Far Eastern Economic Review*, June 11, 1987, 102-03.

"The Japanese Distribution System," Japan Economic Institute, Report No. 28A, July 24, 1987.

10. INTERNATIONAL RELATIONS (by topic)

A. GENERAL

R. Takahashi, "Trade Policies and the New Japan," *Foreign Affairs* 30 (1952), 289-97.

Takashi Shiraishi, "Cyclical Movement in Export Market of Japan," *Keio Business Review* 1 (1962), 69-77.

Philip H. Trezise, "The Place of Japan in the Network of World Trade," *American Economic Review* 53:2 (May 1963), 589-98.

Fukuo Kawata, "Preserving Japan's Balance of Payments in an Open Economy," *DE* 3:1 (March 1965), 106-23.

Kiyoshi Ikemoto, "Japan's Export of Sundry Goods," *Kobe University Economic Review* 11 (1965), 59-76.

Noboru Kamakura, "Japanese Exports in the Nineteen-Fifties: Their Characteristics and Weaknesses," *Kyoto University Economic Review* 37:1 (Apr 1967), 15-29.

United States Tariff Commission, *Postwar Developments in Japan's Foreign Trade*, Washington, US Government Printing Office, 1958 (Greenwood Press reprint, 1969).

G.C. Allen, "Japan's Place in Trade Strategy," in Hugh Corbet, ed. *Trade Strategy and the Asian-Pacific Region*, London, Allen & Unwin, 1970, 43-106.

Nobuyoshi Namiki, "Growth of Japanese Exports," *DE* 8:4 (Dec 1970), 475-96.

"Japan in International Economic War," *Oriental Economist*, series on specific industries, 1971.

Fukuo Kawata, "Patterns of the Japanese Engineering Trade (1951-1970)," *Kobe Economic and Business Review* 18 (1971), 13-36.

T. Blumenthal, "Exports and Economic Growth in Postwar Japan," *Quarterly Journal of Economics* 86 (Nov 1972).

Hisao Kanamori, "Structure of Foreign Trade," *DE* 10:4 (Dec 1972), 359-84.

Hiroshi Kitamura, "What Posture should Japan Take in its Overseas Expansion?" *JES* 1:3 (Spr 1973), 39-55.

Thomas R. Kershner, *Japanese Foreign Trade*, Lexington, Heath, 1975.

Christopher Howe, "Japan's Policy Towards Foreign Trade: The Strategic Options," in W.G. Beasley, ed. *Modern Japan: Aspects of History, Literature & Society*, London, Allen & Unwin, 1975, 244-63.

William E. Bryant, *Japanese Private Economic Diplomacy: An Analysis of Business-Government Linkages*, New York, Praeger, 1975.

Isaiah Frank, ed. *The Japanese Economy in International Perspective*, Baltimore, Johns Hopkins University Press, 1975, including:
Leon Hollerman, "Foreign Trade in Japan's Economic Transition," 168-206.
Yoichi Okita, "Japan's Fiscal Incentives for Exports," 207-30.

Ippei Yamazawa, "Trade Policy and Changes in Japan's Trade Structure: With Special Reference to Labor-Intensive Manufactures," *DE* 13:4 (Dec 1975), 374-99.

A. Kapoor, ed. *Asian Business and Environment in Transition: Selected Readings and Essays*, Princeton, Darwin Press, 1976.

Lawrence B. Krause & Sueo Sekiguchi, "Japan and the World Economy," in Hugh Patrick & Henry Rosovsky, eds. *Asia's New Giant: How the Japanese Economy Works*, Brookings Institution, 1976, 383-458.

Robert A. Scalapino, ed. *The Foreign Policy of Modern Japan*, University of California Press, 1977, including:
Masataka Kosaka, "The International Economic Policy of Japan," 207-26.
Gary R. Saxonhouse, "The World Economy and Japanese Foreign Economic Policy," 281-318.

T.J. Pempel, "Japanese Foreign Economic Policy: The Domestic Bases for International Behavior," *International Organization* 31:3 (Aut 1977), 723-74, reprinted in Peter J. Katzenstein, ed. *Between Power and Plenty*, University of Wisconsin Press, 1978, 139-90.

Kazuichiro Ono, "Japanese Capitalism and Foreign Trade, 1945-1970," *Kyoto University Economic Review* (1) 47:1-2 (Apr-Oct 1977), 27-54; (2) 48:1-2 (Apr-Oct 1978), 1-21.

Hobart Birmingham, "Japanese Postwar Attitudes toward International Trade and Investment," *Hastings International and Comparative Law Review* 2:1 (Sept 1979), 1-20.

Mitsuo Matsushita, "Export Control and Export Cartels in Japan," *Harvard International Law Journal* 20:1 (Win 1979), 103-25.

Kazuo Nukazawa, "Whither Japan's Foreign Economic Policy? Straws in the Wind," *The World Economy* 2:4 (Feb 1980), 467-80.

Peter F. Drucker, "Japan Gets Ready for Tougher Times," *Fortune*, November 3, 1980, 108-14.

Kozo Yamamura, ed. *Policy and Trade Issues of the Japanese Economy: American and Japanese Perspectives*, University of Washington Press, 1982.

Hideo Kanemitsu, "Changes in the International Economic Environment," in Daniel I. Okimoto, ed. *Japan's Economy: Coping with Change in the International Environment*, Boulder, Westview Press, 1982, 7-20.

Masaru Yoshitomi, "An Appraisal of Japanese Financial Policies," *The World Economy* 6:1 (March 1983), 27-38.

Symposium: "Japan's New World Role," *Journal of International Affairs* 37:1 (Sum 1983), 1-190.

Chikara Higashi, *Japanese Trade Policy Formulation*, New York, Praeger, 1983.

Japan External Trade Organization, *A History of Japan's Postwar Export Policy*, Tokyo, JETRO, 1983.

Ravi Sarathy, "Export Activity and Realized Profit: Some Japanese Evidence," in Michael R. Czinkota, ed. *Export Promotion: The Public and Private Sector Interaction*, New York, Praeger, 1983, 210-26.

Toshio Watanabe & Hirokazu Kajiwara, "Pacific Manufactured Trade and Japan's Options," *DE* 21:4 (Dec 1983), 313-39.

Rosalie L. Tung, "How to Negotiate with the Japanese," *California Management Review* 26:4 (Sum 1984), 62-77.

Rosalie L. Tung, *Business Negotiations with the Japanese*, Heath, Lexington Books, 1984.

Robert S. Ozaki & Walter Arnold, eds., *Japan's Foreign Relations: A Global Search for Economic Security*, Boulder, Westview Press, 1985.

Philip Kotler, Somkid Jatusripitak, & Liam Fahey, "Strategic Global Marketing: Lessons from the Japanese," *Columbia Journal of World Business* 20:1 (Spr 1985), 47-54.

Michele Schmiegelow, ed. *Japan's Response to Crisis and Change in the World Economy*, New York, M.E. Sharpe, 1986, including:
Angelika Ernst, "Employment, Wages, and Export Competitiveness," 209-29.

David B. Yoffe, "Protecting World Markets," in Thomas K. McCraw, ed. *America versus Japan*, Boston, Harvard Business School Press, 1986, 35-76.

Mitsuo Matsushita, "The Legal Framework of Trade and Investment in Japan," *Harvard International Law Journal* 27: Special Issue (1986), 361-88.

Chikara Higashi & G. Peter Lauter, *The Internationalization of the Japanese Economy*, Boston, Klumer Academic Publishers, 1987.

Ali M. El-Agraa, *Japan's Trade Frictions: Realities or Misconceptions?* London, Macmillan, 1987.

Motoshige Itoh & Kazuharu Kiyono, "Foreign Trade and Direct Investment," in Ryutaro Komiya, Masahiro Okuno, & Kotaro Suzumura, eds., *Industrial Policy of Japan*, Academic Press, 1988, 155-81.

Kent E. Calder, "Japanese Foreign Economic Policy Formation: Explaining the Reactive State," *World Politics* 45:4 (July 1988), 517-41 (review article).

Bela Balassa & Marcus Noland, *Japan in the World Economy*, Washington, DC, Institute for International Economics, 1988.

Dominique Turpin, "Strategic Alliances with Small High-Tech Businesses in Japan," *Journal of Development Planning* 18 (1988), 153-63.

Takashi Inoguchi & Daniel Okimoto, eds. *The Political Economy of Japan*, vol. 2, *The Changing International Context*, Stanford University Press, 1988, including:
Takashi Inoguchi, "The Ideas and Structures of Foreign Policy: Looking Ahead with Caution," 23-63.
Ryutaro Komiya & Motoshige Itoh, "Japan's International Trade and Trade Policy, 1955-1984, 173-224."
Daniel I. Okimoto, "Political Inclusivity: The Domestic Structure of Trade, 305-44."

Koichi Hamada & Yoshiro Nakajo, "Trade Issues and Consumer Interests," in OECD, ed. *Proceedings of the Symposium on Consumer Policy and International Trade*, Paris, forthcoming.

B. FINANCE

General

Masao Fujioka, *Japan's International Finance: Today and Tomorrow*, Tokyo, The Japan Times, 1979.

Eric W. Hayden, "Internationalizing Japan's Financial System," in Daniel I. Okimoto, ed. *Japan's Economy: Coping with Change in the International Environment*, Boulder, Westview Press, 1982, 89-122.

Japan's Trade Finance: From Postwar Recovery to International Cooperation, JETRO, 1984.

J. Andrew Spingler, *The Politics of International Credit: Private Finance and Foreign Policy in Germany and Japan*, Washington, Brookings Institution, 1984.

Masaru Yoshitomi, "The External Safeguard of Domestic Monetary and Fiscal Policies," in Michele Schmiegelow, ed. *Japan's Response to Crisis and Change in the World Economy*, New York, M.E. Sharpe, 1986, 104-30.

Hugh T. Patrick & Ryuichiro Tachi, eds. *Japan and the United States Today: Exchange Rates, Macroeconomic Policies, and Financial Market Innovations*, New York, Columbia University, The Center on Japanese Economy and Business, 1987.

"Focus: Japan Banking and Finance," *Far Eastern Economic Review*, April 9, 1987, 47-106.

Richard W. Wright & Gunter A. Pauli, *The Second Wave: Japan's Global Assault on Financial Services*, London, Waterlow, 1987.

Roy C. Smith, "New Financial Aspects of the U.S.-Japanese Trade Relationship," in Ryuzo Sato & Paul Wachtel, eds. *Trade Friction and Economic Policy: Problems and Prospects for Japan and the United States*, Cambridge University Press, 1987, 110-26.

Yoichi Shinkai, "Internationalization of Finance in Japan," in Takashi Inoguchi & Daniel Okimoto, eds. *The Political Economy of Japan*, vol. 2, *The Changing International Context*, Stanford University Press, 1988, 249-71.

Foreign Exchange Control & Exchange Rates

Bank of Japan, *Outline of the Foreign Exchange Control in Japan*, Tokyo, Bank of Japan, Foreign Department, March 1981.

Allan D. Smith, "The Japanese Foreign Exchange and Foreign Trade Control Law and Administrative Guidance: The Labyrinth and the Castle," *Law & Policy in International Business* 16:2 (1984), 417-76.

Jeffrey A. Frankel, *The Yen/Dollar Agreement: Liberalizing Japanese Capital Markets*, Washington, Institute for International Economics, 1984.

Michele Schmiegelow, "The Reform of Japan's Foreign Exchange and Foreign Trade Control Law: A Case of Qualitative Economic Policy," in Michele Schmiegelow, ed. *Japan's Response to Crisis and Change in the World Economy*, New York, M.E. Sharpe, 1986, 1-27.

Takashi Murano, "International Currency Realignment and the Yen," *DE* 10:4 (Dec 1972), 340-58.

Toshiyuki Mizoguchi, "The New Official Exchange Rate From the Viewpoint of Effective Purchasing Power Parity," *JES* 1:3 (Spr 1973), 56-77.

Kenzo Yukizawa, "The Narrowing Japanese-United States Productivity Gap: As Related to the Yen Revaluation," *JES* 1:4 (Sum 1973), 48-62.

Kanji Haitani, "Japan's Trade Problem and the Yen," *Asian Survey* 13:8 (August 1973), 723-39.

Miyohei Shinohara, "On the Evaluation of the 360-Yen Exchange Rate," *JES* 4:1 (Fall 1975), 3-22.

Peter J. Quirk, "Exchange Rate Policy in Japan: Leaning Against the Wind," *IMF Staff Papers* 5:24 (Nov 1977), 642-64.

Akihiro Amano, "Flexible Exchange Rates and Macro-Economic Management: A Study of the Japanese Experience, 1973-78," *Annals of the School of Business Administration* (Kobe University) 24 (1980), 33-69.

Akihiro Amano, "The Yen-Dollar Exchange Rate and the Macro-Behavior of the Japanese Economy," *Annals of the School of Business Administration* (Kobe University) 25 (1981), 71-113.

Takeshi Moriyama, "The Fracas Over the Rising Yen: Have Business Leaders Been 'Crying Wolf'?" *Journal of Japanese Studies* 5:2 (Sum 1979), 359-83.

Kozo Yamamura, ed. *Policy and Trade Issues of the Japanese Economy: American and Japanese Perspectives*, University of Washington Press, 1982, including:
Koichi Hamada, "Policy Interactions and the United States-Japan Exchange Rate," 271-95.
John Makin, "Determinants of the Yen-Dollar Exchange Rate: The Course of the United States and Japanese Policies," 297-324.

Teizo Taya, "Effectiveness of Exchange Market Intervention in Moderating the Speed of Exchange Rate Movements: An Empirical Study of the Case of Japan," in David Bigman & Teizo Taya, eds. *Exchange Rates and Trade*

Instability: Causes, Consequences and Remedies, Cambridge, Ballinger, 1982, 217-55.

Michael W. Keran, "The Value of the Yen," in J.S. Dreyer, G. Haberler, & T.D. Willett, eds. *The International Monetary System: A Time of Turbulence*, American Enterprise Institute for Public Policy Research, 1982, 223-71.

Kazuo Nukazawa, "Political Arithmetic of Yen for Dollars," *The World Economy* 6:3 (Sept 1983), 275-90.

Miyohei Shinohara, "Real Exchange Rates and Patterns of Industrialization in East and Southeast Asia," *DE* 21:4 (Dec 1983), 357-75.

David C. Murchison & Ezra Solomon, "The Misalignment of the United States Dollar and the Japanese Yen: the Problem and Its Solution," *California Management Review* 27:1 (Fall 1984), 42-58.

Hugh Sloane, "The Yen-Dollar Exchange Rate and Complementary Developments in the Japanese and US Economies," *Asian Monetary Monitor* 9:2 (March-Apr 1985), 2-15.

Henrik Schmiegelow, "Japan's Exchange Rate Policy: Policy Targets, Nonpolicy Varieties, and Discretionary Adjustment," in Michele Schmiegelow, ed. *Japan's Response to Crisis and Change in the World Economy*, New York, M.E. Sharpe, 1986, 28-43.

"The Problem of U.S. Competitiveness in Manufacturing: A Study by Paul R. Krugman and George N. Hatsopoulos," Japan Economic Institute, Report No. 13A, April 3, 1987. (reprinted from Federal Reserve Bank of Boston, *New England Economic Review* (Jan-Feb 1987), re: exchange rate of dollar.

C. Randall Henning, *Macroeconomic Diplomacy in the 1980s: Domestic Politics and International Conflict among the United States, Japan, and Europe*, London, Croom Helm, Atlantic Paper No. 65, 1987.

Tim Lee, "The Influence of Japanese Institutional Investment Behaviour on the Yen-Dollar Rate," *Asian Monetary Monitor* 11:3 (May-June 1987), 1-12.

Journal of the Japanese and International Economies 1:3 (Sept 1987), the following:
Jeffrey A. Frankel & Kenneth A. Froot, "Short-Term and Long-Term Expectations of the Yen/Dollar Exchange Rate: Evidence from Survey Data," 249-74.
Takatoshi Ito, "The Intradaily Exchange Rate Dynamics and Monetary Policies after the Group of Five Agreement," 275-98.

Kazuo Ueda, "Japanese-U.S. Current Accounts and Exchange Rates before and after the G5 Agreement," in Ryuzo Sato & Paul Wachtel, eds. *Trade Friction and Economic Policy: Problems and Prospects for Japan and the United States*, Cambridge University Press, 1987, 127-56.

Yoichi Funabashi, *Managing the Dollar: From the Plaza to the Louvre*, Washington, DC, Institute for International Economics, 1988.

"The Yen Since the Plaza Accord," Japan Economic Institute, Report No. 40A, October 21, 1988.

Masaru Yoshitomi, "Dollar Decline Would Only Undo Hard-Won Gains," *Wall Street Journal*, December 29, 1988, p. A6.

International Money Markets & Japanese Surpluses

Masahiro Fujita, "International Liquidity Controversy in Japan," (1) *Kobe Economic and Business Review* 14 (1967), 73-86, and (2) 15 (1968), 47-56.

David W. Wise, "Corporate Debentures and the Internationalization of the Japanese Bond Market," *Columbia Journal of World Business* 17:3 (Fall 1982), 40-46.

Masahiro Fujita & Kenichi Ishigaki, "The Internationalization of Japanese Commercial Banking: Experiences in the '70s," *Kobe Economic and Business Review* 28 (1982), 1-28.

Masahiro Fujita et al., "Internationalization of Japanese Commercial Banking: The Recent Experience of City Banks," *Kobe Economic and Business Review* 30 (1984), 23-53.

Eisuke Sakakibara & Akira Kondoh, *Study on the Internationalization of Tokyo's Money Markets*, Tokyo, Japan Center for International Finance, 1984.

Brian W. Semkow, "Japanese Banking Law: Current Deregulation and Liberalization of Domestic and External Financial Transactions," *Law and Policy in International Business* 17:1 (1985), 81-156.

Michele Schmiegelow, ed. *Japan's Response to Crisis and Change in the World Economy*, New York, M.E. Sharpe, 1986, including:
Hirohiko Okumura, "The Internationalization of Japan's Financial Markets," 51-62.
Christiane Dosse, "The Position of Banks and Securities Companies in the Japanese Financial Market and its Effects on International Capital Flows," 131-52.

Adrian Hamilton, *The Financial Revolution: The Big Bang Worldwide*, New York, Viking, 1986.

Robert V. Roosa, *The United States and Japan in the International Monetary System, 1946-1985*, Occasional Papers No. 21, New York, Group of Thirty, 1986.

Richard S. Thorn, *The Rising Yen: The Impact of Japanese Financial Liberalization on World Capital Markets*, Singapore, Institute of Southeast Asian Studies, 1987.

V. Vance Roley, "US Money Announcements and Covered Interest Parity: The Case of Japan," *Journal of International Money and Finance* 6:1 (March 1987), 57-70.

William Guttman, "Japanese Capital Markets and Financial Liberalization," *Asian Survey* 27:12 (Dec 1987), 1256-67.

Koichi Hamada & Hugh T. Patrick, "Japan and the International Monetary Regime," in Takashi Inoguchi & Daniel Okimoto, eds. *The Political Economy of Japan*, vol. 2, *The Changing International Context*, Stanford University Press, 1988, 108-37.

Toshihiko Yoshino, " . . . Meanwhile Japan is Becoming a Major Exporter of Capital," *The World Economy* 2:4 (Feb 1980), 441-52.

Masaru Yoshitomi, "Japan's View of Current External Imbalances," in C. Fred Bergsten, ed. *Imbalances in the World Economy*, Washington, Institute for International Economics, 1985.

Masaru Yoshitomi, *Japan as Capital Exporter and the World Economy*, Occasional Papers 18, New York, Group of Thirty, 1985.

Kazuo Sato, "Externalization of Domestic Macroeconomic Performance: Export-Led Growth or Growth-Led Export?" in Michele Schmiegelow, ed. *Japan's Response to Crisis and Change in the World Economy*, New York, M.E. Sharpe, 1986, 181-208.

Tim Lee, "Will the Yen Appreciation Correct the Balance of Payments Disequilibrium?" *Asian Monetary Mirror* 10:3 (May-June 1986), 1-10.

Stephen E. Haynes et al., *Japanese Financial Policies and the U.S. Trade Deficit*, Dept. of Economics, Princeton University, 1986.

264

Juro Teranishi, "The Catch-up Process, Financial System, and Japan's Rise as a Capital Exporter," *Hitotsubashi Journal of Economics* 27: Special Issue (Oct 1986), 133-46.

"Japan's Role in World Financial Markets," Japan Economic Institute, Report No. 42A, November 14, 1986.

"Japan's Role as an International Creditor," Japan Economic Institute, Report No. 35A, September 16, 1988.

Jim Powell, *The Gnomes of Tokyo: Japanese Financial Power and its Impact on our Future*, Dodd, Mead & Co., 1988.

Foreign Aid

Hayato Ikeda, "Japan's Share in Economic Cooperation," *CJ* 26:1 (Aug 1959), 14-32.

Sukejiro Hasegawa, *Japanese Foreign Aid: Policy and Practice*, New York, Praeger, 1975.

Alan Rix, *Japan's Economic Aid: Policy-Making and Politics*, New York, St. Martin's Press, 1980.

Dennis T. Yasutomo, *Japan and the Asian Development Bank,* New York, Praeger, 1983.

William L. Brooks & Robert M. Orr, Jr., "Japan's Foreign Economic Assistance," *Asian Survey* 25:3 (March 1985), 322-40.

Kazuo Shibagaki, "Japan's Development Aid Policy as Motor for the Asia-Pacific Cooperation," *Annals of the Institute of Social Science* 27 (1985), 1-25.

Dennis T. Yasutomo, *The Manner of Giving: Strategic Aid and Japanese Foreign Policy*, Lexington, Heath, 1986.

Robert M. Orr, Jr., "The Rising Sun: Japan's Foreign Aid to ASEAN, the Pacific Basin and the Republic of Korea," *Journal of International Affairs* 41:1 (Sum/Fall 1987), 39-62.

"Japan's Foreign Aid Policy: 1987 Update," Japan Economic Institute, Report No. 41A, October 30, 1987.

Juichi Inada, "Japan's Aid Diplomacy: Increasing Role for Global Security," *Japan Review of International Affairs* 2:1 (Spr-Sum 1988), 91-112.

Robert M. Orr, Jr., "The Aid Factor in U.S.-Japan Relations," *Asian Survey* 28:7 (July 1988), 740-56.

"Japan's Foreign Aid Policy: 1988 Update," Japan Economic Institute, Report No. 43A, November 11, 1988.

C. OVERSEAS INVESTMENT & MULTINATIONALIZATION

General

Gregory Clark, "An Analysis of Japanese Direct Investment Overseas in Postwar Years," *DE* 9:1 (March 1971), 58-65.

Hiroshi Kitamura, "Foreign Aid and Investment: New Challenges to Japan," *DE* 10:4 (Dec 1972), 385-409.

Isaiah A. Litvak & Christopher J. Maule, "Japan's Overseas Investments," *Pacific Affairs* 46:2 (Sum 1973), 254-68.

M.Y. Yoshino, "Japanese Foreign Direct Investment," in Isaiah Frank, ed. *The Japanese Economy in International Perspective*, Baltimore, Johns Hopkins University Press, 1975, 248-72.

Kiyoshi Kojima, "Direct Foreign Investment between Advanced Industrialized Countries," *Hitotsubashi Journal of Economics* 18:1 (June 1977), 1-18.

Sueo Sekiguchi, *Japanese Direct Foreign Investment*, Montclair, N.J., Allanhead, Osmun & Co., 1979.

Richard W. Wright, "Foreign Investment Between Neighbours: Canada and Japan," in Keith A.J. Hay, ed. *Canadian Perspectives on Economic Relations with Japan*, Montreal, Institute for Research on Public Policy, 1980, 191-202.

Japanese Enterprises in Europe: A Survey Report on Management, Tokyo, Japan External Trade Organization, 1984.

Motoshige Itoh & Kazuharu Kiyono, "Japanese Foreign Direct Investment," in Michele Schmiegelow, ed. *Japan's Response to Crisis and Change in the World Economy*, New York, M.E. Sharpe, 1986, 63-84.

Dennis J. Encarnation, "Cross-Investment: A Second Front of Economic Rivalry," in Thomas K. McCraw, ed. *America versus Japan*, Boston, Harvard Business School Press, 1986, 117-50.

Shigeru Sugitani, "Japan's Direct Overseas Investment: Its Recent Trends," *Kwansei Gakuin University Annual Studies* 36 (Dec 1987), 215-30.

Specific Industries

Masayuki Yoshioka, "Overseas Investment by the Japanese Textile Industry," *DE* 17 (1979), 3-44.

Overseas Business Activities, vol. 9 of *International Conference on Business History*, ed. by Akio Okochi & Tadakatsu Inoue, University of Tokyo Press, 1984, including the following articles:
Yosuke Kinugasa, "Japanese Firms' Foreign Direct Investment in the U.S.: The Case of Matsushita and Others," 21-60.
Ken'ichi Yasumuro, "The Contribution of Sogo Shosha to the Multinationalization of Japanese Industrial Enterprises in Historical Perspective," 65-92.
Hideki Yoshihara, "Multinational Growth of Japanese Manufacturing Enterprises in the Postwar Period," 95-120.

Tetsuo Abo, "U.S. Subsidiaries of Japanese Electronic Companies Enter a New Phase of Activities: A Report of On-the-Spot Observations," *Annals of the Institute of Social Science* 26 (1984), 1-32.

Japanese Multinationalization

Yoshi Tsurumi, "Japanese Multinational Firms," *Journal of World Trade Law* 7:1 (Jan-Feb 1973), 74-90, reprinted in A. Kapoor, ed. *Asian Business and Environment in Transition: Selected Readings and Essays*, Princeton, Darwin Press, 1976, 403-19.

Masahiro Fujita, "International Money Flow and the Multinational Corporations," *Kobe Economic and Business Review* 20 (1973), 23-36.

M.Y. Yoshino, "The Multinational Spread of Japanese Manufacturing Investment since World War II," *Business History Review* 48:3 (Aut 1974), 357-81.

Hideki Yoshihara, "Japanese Business Abroad: Past, Present and Future," *Kobe Economic and Business Review* 21 (1975), 63-74.

M.Y. Yoshino, "Emerging Japanese Multinational Enterprises," in Ezra F. Vogel, ed. *Modern Japanese Organization and Decision-Making*, University of California Press, 1975, 146-66.

M.Y. Yoshino, *Japan's Multinational Enterprises*, Harvard University Press, 1976.

Yoshi Tsurumi, *The Japanese Are Coming: A Multinational Interaction of Firms and Politics*, Cambridge, Ballinger, 1976.

Norio Yanagihara, "Japanese Enterprises in the 'Multinational Era'," *KSU Economic and Business Review* (Kyoto Sangyo University) 3 (May 1976), 30-68.

Nagahide Shioda, "The Sogo Shosha and its Functions in Direct Foreign Investment," *DE* 14:4 (Dec 1976), 402-18.

Hideki Yoshihara, "Personnel Management of Japanese Companies in Thailand: A Field Paper," *Kobe Economic and Business Review* 23 (1977), 11-62.

Kiyoshi Yamazaki, Noritake Kobayashi, and Teruo Doi, "Toward Japanese-Type Multinational Corporations," *JES* 5:4 (Sum 1977), 41-70.

Kiyoshi Kojima, *Direct Foreign Investment: A Japanese Model of Multinational Business Operations*, London, Croom Helm, 1978. (Available also as *Japanese Direct Foreign Investment: A Model of Multinational Business Operations*, Tuttle, 1979).

Terutomo Ozawa, *Multinationalism, Japanese Style: The Political Economy of Outward Dependency*, Princeton University Press, 1979.

Hideki Yoshihara, "Japanese Multinational Enterprises: A View from Outside," *Kobe Economic and Business Review* 25 (1979), 15-35.

Atsushi Murakami, "Japanese Multinational Companies in Singapore," *Kobe University Economic Review* 25 (1979), 25-46.

Kichiro Hayashi, "The Role of the Multinational Enterprise in Canada-Japan Relations," in Keith A.J. Hay, ed. *Canadian Perspectives on Economic Relations with Japan*, Montreal, Institute for Research on Public Policy, 1980, 163-87.

Charles Brecher & Valdimir Pucik, "Foreign Banks in the U.S. Economy: The Japanese Example," *Columbia Journal of World Business* 15:1 (Spr 1980), 5-13.

T. Randall Emch, "Japanese Direct Foreign Investment in American Manufacturing," *Stanford Journal of International Law* 17:1 (Win 1981), 1-16.

Noritake Kobayashi, "The Present and Future of Japanese Multinational Enterprises: A Comparative Analysis of Japanese and U.S.-European Multinational Management," *International Studies of Management and Organization* 12:1 (Sept 1982), 38-58.

L.G. Franko, *The Threat of Japanese Multinationals: How the West Can Respond*, New York, Wiley, 1983.

Malcolm Trevor, "Does Japanese Management Work in Britain?" *Journal of General Management* 8:4 (Sum 1983), 28-43.

Francine McNulty, "Employment Rights of Japanese-American Joint Ventures in the United States under the U.S.-Japan Treaty of Friendship, Commerce and Navigation," *Law & Policy in International Business* 16:4 (1984), 1225-48.

John H. Dunning, *Japanese Participation in British Industry*, London, Croom Helm, 1986.

JES 14:3 (Spr 1986), the following:
Mitsuhiko Yamada, "A Study on Divestitures by Japanese Corporations in Foreign Countries," 3-51.
Kiyoshi Kojima, "Japanese-Style Direct Foreign Investment," 52-82.

Kichiro Hayashi, "Crosscultural Interface Management: The Case of Japanese Firms Abroad," *JES* 15:1 (Fall 1986), 3-41.

Kichiro Hayashi, "Expansion of Japanese Companies Abroad: The Management of Cross-cultural Interface," in Thomas A. Pugel, ed. *Fragile Interdependence: Economic Issues in U.S.-Japanese Trade and Investment*, Lexington, Heath, 1986, 175-203.

F.H. Saelens, "Japanese Foreign Direct Investment in Western Europe," in Michele Schmiegelow, ed. *Japan's Response to Crisis and Change in the World Economy*, New York, M.E. Sharpe, 1986, 85-103.

Barbara Ritomsky & Robert M. Jarvis, "Doing Business in America: The Unfinished Work of *Sumitomo Shoji America, Inc. v. Avagliano*," *Harvard International Law Journal* 27:1 (Win 1986), 193-225.

K. John Fukuda, "Japanese-Style Management in Hong Kong and Singapore," *Journal of General Management* 13:1 (Aut 1987), 69-81.

Malcolm Trevor, ed. *The Internationalization of Japanese Business: European and Japanese Perspectives*, Frankfurt am Main, Campus Verlag, 1987.

Mamoru Yoshida, *Japanese Direct Manufacturing Investment in the United States*, New York, Praeger, 1987.

Harry I. Chernotsky, "The American Connection: Motives for Japanese Foreign Direct Investment," *Columbia Journal of World Business* 22:4 (Win 1987), 47-54.

Management & Organization

Richard Tanner Johnson & William G. Ouchi, "Made in America (Under Japanese Management)," *Harvard Business Review* 52:1 (Sept-Oct 1974), 61-69, reprinted in A. Kapoor, ed. *Asian Business and Environment in Transition: Selected Readings and Essays*, Princeton, Darwin Press, 1976, 429-39.

Yoshi Tsurumi, *Multinational Management: Business Strategy and Government Policy*, Cambridge, Ballinger, 1976.

Richard T. Johnson, "Success and Failure of Japanese Subsidiaries in America," *Columbia Journal of World Business* 12:1 (Spr 1977), 30-37.

Matt M. Amano, "Organizational Changes of a Japanese Firm in America," *California Management Review* 21:3 (Spr 1979), 51-59.

H. Matsusaki, "Japanese Managers and Management in the Western World: A Canadian Experience," in A.R. Negandhi, ed. *Functioning of the Multinational Corporation: A Global Comparative Study*, New York, Pergamon Press, 1980, 226-54.

A.R. Negandhi & B.R. Baliga, *Tables are Turning: German and Japanese Multinational Companies in the United States*, Cambridge, Mass., Oelgeschlager, Gunn, and Hain Publishers, 1981.

Mitsuhiko Yamada, "Japanese-Style Management in America: Merits and Difficulties," *JES* 10:1 (Fall 1981), 1-30.

Hideo Ishida, "Human Resources Management in Overseas Japanese Firms," *JES* 10:1 (Fall 1981), 53-81.

Malcolm Trevor, *Japan's Reluctant Multinationals: Japanese Management at Home and Abroad*, London, Frances Pinter, 1983.

Michael White and Malcolm Trevor, *Under Japanese Management: The Experience of British Workers*, London, Heinemann, 1983.

Susumu Takamiya & Keith Thurley, eds. *Japan's Emerging Multinationals: An International Comparison of Policies and Practices*, University of Tokyo Press, 1985. (This book focuses on issues of personnel and organization).

Anant R. Negandhi, Golpira S. Eshghi & Edith C. Yuen, "The Management Practices of Japanese Subsidiaries Overseas," *California Management Review* 27:4 (Sum 1985), 93-105.

Duane Kujawa, *Japanese Multinationals in the United States: Case Studies*, New York, Praeger, 1986.

Malcolm Trevor, Jochen Schendel & Bernard Wilpert, *The Japanese Management Development System: Generalists and Specialists in Japanese Companies Abroad*, London, Frances Pinter, 1986.

Setsuo Miyazawa, "Legal Departments of Japanese Corporations in the United States: A Study on Organizational Adaptation to Multiple Environments," *Kobe University Law Review* 20 (1986), 97-162.

J.T. Yamaguchi, "Acculturation and Alienation of the Expatriate Managers of Japanese Firms in Australia," in Stewart R. Clegg, Dexter C. Dunphy & S. Gordon Redding, *The Enterprise and Management in East Asia*, Center of Asian Studies, University of Hong Kong, 1986, 413-41.

Rosalie L. Tung, *The New Expatriates: Managing Human Resources Abroad*, Ballinger, 1988, 33-47.

Merry I. White, *The Japanese Overseas: Can They Go Home Again?*, The Free Press, 1988, esp. 135-44.

Christopher Bartlett & Hideki Yoshihara, "New Challenges for Japanese Multinationals: Is Organization Adaptation Their Achilles Heel?" *Human Resource Management* 27:1 (Spr 1988), 19-43.

D. INTERNATIONAL AND COMPARATIVE LAW

Toshio Sawada, "International Commercial Arbitration: Practice of Arbitral Institutions in Japan," *The Japanese Annual of International Law* 30 (1987), 69-88.

Maritime Issues

William R. Feeney, "Dispute Settlement, the Emerging Law of the Sea, and East Asian Maritime Boundary Conflicts," *Asian Profile* 8:6 (Dec 1980), 573-95.

Douglas M. Johnston, "Impact of the New Law of the Sea on Japanese-Canadian Relations," in Keith A.J. Hay, ed. *Canadian Perspectives on Economic Relations with Japan*, Montreal, Institute for Research on Public Policy, 1980, 95-127.

Robert L. Friedheim et al., *Japan and the New Ocean Regime*, Boulder, Westview Press, 1984.

Tsuneo Akaha, *Japan in Global Ocean Politics*, University Press of Hawaii, 1986.

Choon-ho Park, *East Asia and the Law of the Sea*, University Press of Hawaii, 1986.

Sueo Ikehara, Akira Takakuwa & Masato Dogauchi, "Conflict of Laws on Admirality and Shipping Laws in Japan," *The Japanese Annual of International Law* 30 (1987), 1-17.

Products & Patents

Terui Doi & Warren Shattuck, *Patent Know-How Licensing in Japan and the United States*, University of Washington Press, 1977.

Victor Rowley, "Computer Technology Trades Secrets Protection in an International Setting," *Hastings International and Comparative Law Review* 2:1 (Sept 1979), 181-214.

Sampson Helfgott, "Statistical Study of the Japanese Patent Office's Handling of Foreign Patent Applications," *Patents and Licensing* 5:3 (Spr 1983).

Gary Saxonhouse & Kozo Yamamura, eds. *Law and Trade Issues of the Japanese Economy: American and Japanese Perspectives*, University of Washington Press, 1986, the following articles:
Koichi Hamada et al., "The Evolution and Economic Consequences of Product Liability Rules in Japan," 83-106.
Terui Doi, "The Role of Intellectual Property Law in Bilateral Licensing Transactions between Japan and the United States," 157-92.

Kozo Yamamura, "Joint Research and Antitrust: Japanese vs. American Strategies," in Hugh Patrick, ed. *Japan's High Technology Industries: Lessons and Limitations of Industrial Policy*, University of Washington Press, 1986, 171-209.

Robert Steinberg, "*NEC v. Intel*: The Battle over Copyright Protection for Microcode," *Jurimetrics* 27:2 (Win 1987), 173-99.

Earl H. Kinmonth, "Japanese Patents: Olympic Gold or Public Relations Brass," *Pacific Affairs* 60:2 (Sum 1987), 173-99.

Nobuo Monya, "International Protection of Intellectual Properties and Japanese Laws: in Particular, Patent Law," *The Japanese Annual of International Law* 30 (1987), 56-68.

Arthur Wineberg, "The Japanese Patent System: A Non-Tariff Barrier to Foreign Businesses?" *Journal of World Trade* 22:1 (1988), 11-22.

Marshall N. Margolis, "Hi-Tech Creativity: The IBM/Fujitsu Arbitration," *Review of International Business Law* 2:1 (March 1988), 59-66.

E. INTERNATIONAL COMPETITION

Robert Guillain, *The Japanese Challenge*, Philadelphia, Lippincott, 1970.

Terutomo Ozawa, *Japan's Technological Challenge to the West, 1950-1974: Motivation and Accomplishment*, MIT Press, 1974.

Herman Kahn & Thomas Pepper, *The Japanese Challenge: The Success and Failure of Economic Success*, New York, Thomas Y. Crowell, 1979.

Jack Baranson, *The Japanese Challenge to U.S. Industry*, Lexington Books, 1981.

Roy Hofheinz Jr. & Kent E. Calder, *The Eastasia Edge*, New York, Basic Books, 1982.

Edson W. Spencer, "Japan: Stimulus or Scapegoat?" *Foreign Affairs* 62:1 (Fall 1983), 123-37.

Marvin J. Wolf, *The Japanese Conspiracy: The Plot to Dominate Industry World Wide—And How to Deal With It*, New York, Empire Books, 1984.

Steven Schlossstein, *Trade War: Greed, Power, and Industrial Policy on Opposite Sides of the Pacific*, New York, Congdon & Weed, 1984.

Charles J. McMillan, *The Japanese Industrial System*, Berlin, Walter de Gruyter, 1984.

Jon Woronoff, *Japan's Commercial Empire*, Armonk, New York, M.E. Sharpe, 1984.

Jon Woronoff, *World Trade War*, New York, Praeger, 1984.

Kenichi Ohmae, *Triad Power: The Coming Shape of Global Competition*, New York, The Free Press, 1985.

Philip Kotter, Liam Fahey & S. Jatusriptak, *The New Competition: What Theory Z Didn't Tell You About Marketing*, Englewood Cliffs, Prentice Hall, 1985.

Staffan B. Linder, *The Pacific Century: Economic and Political Consequences of Asian-Pacific Dynamism*, Stanford University Press, 1986.

Peter F. Drucker, "Japan and Adversarial Trade," *Wall Street Journal*, April 1, 1986, p. 30.

Peter F. Drucker, *The Frontiers of Management*, New York, E.P. Dutton, 1986, chapter on "The Perils of Adversarial Trade."

Richard Rosecrance, *The Rise of the Trading State: Commerce and Conquest in the Modern World*, New York, Basic Books, 1986.

Paul M. Kennedy, *The Rise and Fall of the Great Powers: Economic Change and Military Conflict from 1500 to 2000*, New York, Random House, 1987, esp. 458-71.

James Laxer, *Decline of the Superpowers: Winners and Losers in Today's Global Economy*, Toronto, James Lorimer, 1987.

Peter F. Drucker, "Beyond the Japanese Export Boom," *Wall Street Journal*, January 6, 1987, p. 28.

Peter F. Drucker, "Japan's Choices," *Foreign Affairs* 65:5 (Sum 1987), 924-41.

Ronald A. Morse, "Japan's Drive to Pre-eminence," *Foreign Policy* 69 (Win 1987-88), 3-21.

F. WORLD ECONOMIC ORDER

Ryokichi Minobe, "Free Trade and Japanese People," *CJ* 26:3 (May 1960), 523-26.

Tadashi Kawata, "UNCTAD and Japan," *DE* 2:3 (Sept 1964), 290-301.

Kiyoshi Kojima, *Japan and a Pacific Free Trade Zone*, University of California, 1971.

Yonosuke Nagai, "Politics and Economics in the Multipolar Age: From Cold War Consensus to Post-nationalism," *Japan Interpreter* 8:4 (Win 1974), 450-66.

Kiyoshi Kojima, *Japan and a New World Economic Order*, Boulder, Westview Press, 1977.

Stephen D. Krasner, "The Tokyo Round: Interests and Prospects for Stability in the Global Trading System," *International Studies Quarterly* 23 (Dec 1979), 491-531.

Brian Hindley, "Voluntary Export Restraints and the GATT's Main Escape Clause," *The World Economy* 3:3 (Nov 1980), 313-41.

Hiroshi Kitamura, "International Division of Labor and Industrial Adjustment: Relevance of Theory to Policy Analysis," *DE* 18:4 (Dec 1980), 377-92.

Jeffrey J. Schott, "Protectionist Threat to Trade and Investments in Services," *The World Economy* 6:2 (June 1983), 195-214.

Robert B. Reich, "Beyond Free Trade," *Foreign Affairs* 61:4 (Spr 1983), 773-804.

Bela & Carol Balassa, "Industrial Protection in the Developed Countries," *The World Economy* 7:2 (June 1984), 179-96.

Moriyuki Motono, "World Trade Issues Require More than a Piecemeal Approach," *The World Economy* 7:3 (Sept 1984), 229-40.

Kent E. Calder, "The Emerging Politics of the Trans-Pacific Economy," *World Policy Journal* 2 (1985), 593-623.

Gilbert R. Winham, *International Trade and the Tokyo Round Negotiation*, Princeton University Press, 1986.

Yasusuke Murakami & Yutaka Kosai, eds. *Japan in the Global Community: Its Role and Contributions on the Eve of the 21st Century*, University of Tokyo Press, 1986.

Foreign Affairs 64:4 (Spr 1986), including:
Ezra Vogel, "Pax Nipponica," 752-67.
Peter F. Drucker, "The Changed World Economy," 768-91.

Iwao Nakatani, "Towards the New International Economic Order: The Role of Japan in the World Economy," *Hitotsubashi Journal of Economics* 27: Special Issue (Oct 1986), 121-32.

Yoshikazu Miyazaki, "Debtor America and Creditor Japan: Will There be a Hegemony Change?" *JES* 15:3 (Spr 1987), 58-96.

Kenichi Ohmae, *Beyond National Borders*, New York, Dow Jones-Irwin, 1987, partially excerpted as "Japan's Role in the World Economy: A New Appraisal," *California Management Review* 29:3 (Spr 1987), 42-58.

Robert Gilpin, *The Political Economy of International Relations*, Princeton University Press, 1987, esp. 328-40.

Toru Yanagihara, "Pacific Basin Economic Relations: Japan's New Role," *DE* 25:4 (Dec 1987), 403-20.

Ernst-Ulrich Petersmann, "Strengthening GATT Procedures for Settling Trade Disputes," *The World Economy* 11:1 (March 1988), 55-90.

"Japan Ponders Free Trade Pacts: Building Blocks or Road Blocks?" Japan Economic Institute, Report No. 44A, November 18, 1988.

Takashi Inoguchi & Daniel Okimoto, eds. *The Political Economy of Japan*, vol. 2, *The Changing International Context*, Stanford University Press, 1988, including:
Shumpei Kumon & Akihiko Tanaka, "From Prestige to Wealth to Knowledge," 64-82.
Bruce Russett, "U.S. Hegemony: Gone or Merely Diminished, and How Does it Matter?" 83-107.

G. TECHNOLOGY

G.R. Hall & R.E. Johnson, "Transfers of United States Aerospace Technology to Japan," in R. Vernon, ed. *The Technology Factor in International Trade*, Columbia University Press, 1970, 305-58.

Yoshi Tsurumi, *Technology Transfer and Foreign Trade: The Case of Japan, 1950-1966*, New York, Arno Press, 1980.

Duane W. Layton, "Japan and the Introduction of Foreign Technology: A Blueprint for Less Developed Countries?" *Stanford Journal of International Law* 18:1 (Spr 1982), 171-214.

Gerard K. O'Neill, *The Technology Edge: Opportunities for America in World Competition*, New York, Simon & Schuster, 1983.

Science and Technology Agency, ed. *Japan: Science & Technology Outlook*, 1983.

William H. Davidson, *The Amazing Race: Winning the Technorivalry with Japan*, New York, John Wiley & Sons, 1984.

Leonard H. Lynn, "Technology Transfer to Japan," in Nathan Rosenberg & Claudio Frisvhtak, eds. *International Technology Transfer: Concepts, Measures, and Comparisons*, New York, Praeger, 1985, 255-76.

Charles T. Stewart, Jr. "Comparing Japanese and U.S. Technology Transfer to Less-Developed Countries," *Journal of Northeast Asian Studies* 4:1 (Spr 1985), 3-19.

Ronald A. Morse & Richard J. Samuels, eds. *Getting America Ready for Japanese Science and Technology*, Lanham, MD, University Press of America, 1986.

Walter Arnold, "Japan's Technology Transfer to Advanced Industrial Countries," in John R. McIntyre & Daniel S.S. Papp, eds. *The Political Economy of International Technology Transfer*, Westport, Greenwood Press, 1986, 161-86.

Daniel I. Okimoto & Gary R. Saxonhouse, "Technology and the Future of the Economy," in Kozo Yamamura & Yasukichi Yasuba, eds. *The Political Economy of Japan*, vol. 1, *The Domestic Transformation*, Stanford University Press, 1987, 385-419.

Thomas L. Ilgen & T.J. Pempel, *Trading Technology: Europe and Japan in the Middle East*, New York, Praeger, 1987, esp. 122-42.

Keichi Oshima, "The High Technology Gap: A View from Japan," in Andrew J. Pierre, ed. *A High Technology Gap? Europe, America and Japan*, Council on Foreign Relations, New York University Press, 1987, 88-114.

Yoshiro Hoshino, "What Technology has Postwar Japan Learned from the U.S.?" *JES* 17:1 (Fall 1988), 65-92.

Gary Saxonhouse, ed. *Japanese Technology Transfer and Innovations*, Boulder, Westview Press, forthcoming.

11. INTERNATIONAL RELATIONS
(by area: THE UNITED STATES)

A. TRADE DISPUTES: SPECIFIC INDUSTRIES

Textiles

John Lynch, *Toward an Orderly Market: An Intensive Study of Japan's Voluntary Quota in Cotton Textile Exports*, Tokyo, Sophia University Press, 1968.

Thomas W. Zeiler, "Free-Trade Politics and Diplomacy: John F. Kennedy and Textiles," *Diplomatic History* 11:2 (Spr 1987), 127-42.

Gary Saxonhouse, "The Textile Confrontation," in Jerome B. Cohen, ed. *Pacific Partnership: United States-Japan Trade, Prospects and Recommendations for the Seventies*, Lexington, Mass., Heath, 1972, 177-97.

I.M. Destler, et al., eds. *Managing an Alliance: The Politics of U.S.-Japanese Relations*, Washington, Brookings Institution, 1976, 35-45. (re:textiles).

I.M. Destler, Haruhiro Fukui, & Hideo Sato, *The Textile Wrangle: Conflict in Japanese-American Relations*, Cornell University Press, 1978.

Special Issue: The Multifiber Arrangement, *Law and Policy in International Business* 19:1 (1987).

H. Richard Friman, "Rocks, Hard Places, and the New Protectionism: Textile Trade Policy choices in the United States and Japan," *International Organization* 42:4 (Aut 1988), 689-723.

Steel

Kiyoshi Kawahito, *The Japanese Steel Industry: With an Analysis of the US Steel Import Program*, New York, Praeger, 1971.

Kiyoshi Kawahito, "The Steel Dumping Issue in Recent U.S.-Japanese Relations," *Asian Survey* 20:10 (Oct 1980), 1038-47.

Kiyoshi Kawahito, "Japanese Steel in the American Market: Conflict and Causes," *The World Economy* 4:3 (Sept 1981), 229-50.

Hugh Patrick & Hideo Sato, "The Political Economy of United States-Japan Trade in Steel," in Kozo Yamamura, ed. *Policy and Trade Issues of the Japanese Economy: American and Japanese Perspectives*, University of Washington Press, 1982, 197-238.

Hideo Sato & Michael W. Hodin, "The U.S.-Japanese Steel Issue of 1977," in I.M. Destler & Hideo Sato, eds. *Coping with U.S.-Japanese Economic Conflicts*, Lexington, Mass., D.C. Heath, 1982, 27-72.

Michael Borrus, "The Politics of Competitive Erosion in the U.S. Steel Industry," in John Zysman and Laura Tyson, eds. *American Industry in International Competition: Government Policies and Corporate Strategies*, Cornell University Press, 1983, 60-105.

Kent Jones, "Trade in Steel: Another Turn in the Protectionist Spiral," *The World Economy* 8:4 (Dec 1985), 393-408.

David G. Tarr, "Costs and Benefits to the United States of The 1985 Steel Import Quota Program," in Ryuzo Sato & Paul Wachtel, eds. *Trade Friction and Economic Policy: Problems and Prospects for Japan and the United States*, Cambridge University Press, 1987, 159-83.

John A.C. Conybeare, *Trade Wars: The Theory and Practice of International Commercial Rivalry*, Columbia University Press, 1987, 203-30.

Richard Pomfret, "World Steel Trade at a Crossroads," *Journal of World Trade* 22:3 (June 1988), 81-89.

Television

Ronald J. Metzler, "Color-TV Sets and U.S.-Japanese Relations: Problems of Trade-Adjustment Policymaking," *Orbis* (Sum 1979), 421-46.

Phillips B. Keller, "*Zenith Radio Corp. v. Matsushita Electrical Industrial Co.*: Interpreting the Antidumping Act of 1916," *Hastings International and Comparative Law Review* 6:1 (Fall 1982), 133-59.

Vincent A. LaFrance, "The United States Television Receiver Industry: United States versus Japan, 1960-1980," Ph.D. diss., Pennsylvania State University, 1985.

Kozo Yamamura & Jan VanDenBerg, "Japan's Rapid-Growth Policy on Trial: The Television Case," in Gary Saxonhouse & Kozo Yamamura, eds. *Law and Trade Issues of the Japanese Economy: American and Japanese Perspectives*, University of Washington Press, 1986, 238-83.

Autos

William C. Duncan, *U.S.-Japan Automobile Diplomacy: A Study in Economic Confrontation*, Cambridge, Ballinger, 1973.

James Rader, *Penetrating the US Auto Market: German and Japanese Strategies, 1965-1976*, Ann Arbor, UMI Research Press, 1980.

"Japan-U.S. Automobile Conflict," articles in *Japan Quarterly* 27:3 (July-Sept 1980), by Junjiro Hara and Shuichi Miyoshi, 341-50.

Proceedings of the U.S.-Japan Automotive Industry conferences, University of Michigin, Center for Japanese Studies, including:
Robert E. Cole, ed. *The Japanese Automobile Industry: Model and Challenge For the Future?*, 1981.
Robert E. Cole, ed. *Industry at the Crossroads*, 1982.
Robert E. Cole, ed. *Automobiles and the Future: Competition, Cooperation, and Change*, 1983.
Robert E. Cole, ed. *The American Automobile Industry: Rebirth or Requiem?*, 1984.
Robert Cole & Taizo Yakushiji, *The Japanese and American Automotive Industry in Transition*, 1984. [The final report of the Automotive Study]. The conferences continued, as follows:
John C. Campbell, ed., *Entrepreneurship in a "Mature Industry,"* 1986.
Peter J. Arnesen, ed. *The Japanese Competition: Phase 2*, 1987.
Peter J. Arnesen, ed. *Is There Enough Business to Go Around? Overcapacity in the Auto Industry*, 1988.

Gilbert R. Winham & Ikuo Kabashima, "The Politics of U.S.-Japanese Auto Trade," in I.M. Destler & Hideo Sato, eds. *Coping with U.S.-Japanese Economic Conflicts*, Lexington, Mass., D.C. Heath, 1982, 73-119.

Liberty Mahshigian, "Orderly Marketing Agreements: Analysis of United States Automobile Industry Efforts to Obtain Import Relief," *Hastings International and Comparative Law Review* 6:1 (Fall 1982), 161-83.

Spencer Weber Waller, "Redefining the Foreign Compulsion Defense in U.S. Antitrust Law: The Japanese Auto Restraints and Beyond," *Law and Policy in International Business* 14:3 (1982), 747-817.

Arthur F. Laffer et al., "A High Road for the American Automobile Industry," *The World Economy* 8:3 (Sept 1985), 267-86.

Michael W. Lochmann, "The Japanese Voluntary Restraint on Automobile Exports: An Abandonment of the Free Trade Principles of the GATT and the Free Market Principles of United States Antitrust Laws," *Harvard International Law Journal* 27:1 (Win 1986), 99-157.

"The U.S Automotive Parts Market and Japanese Competition," Japan Economic Institute, Report No. 11A, March 20, 1987.

Charles Collyns & Steven Dunaway, "The Cost of Trade Restraints: The Case of Japanese Automobile Exports to the United States," *IMF Staff Papers* 34:1 (March 1987), 150-75.

James A. Dunn, Jr., "Automobiles in International Trade: Regime Change or Persistence?" *International Organization* 41:2 (Spr 1987), 225-52.

Robert C. Feenstra, "Quality Changes Under Trade Restraints in Japanese Autos," *The Quarterly Journal of Economics* 103:1 (Feb 1988), 131-46.

Semiconductors

Ken'ichi Imai & Akimitsu Sakuma, "An Analysis of Japan-U.S. Semiconductor Friction," *Economic Eye* 4:2 (1983), 13-18.

Toshio Tanaka, "Setting the Record Straight on Semiconductors," *Journal of Japanese Trade and Industry* 2:4 (1983), 18-22.

Kenneth Flamm, "Internationalization in the Semiconductor Industry," in Joseph Grunwald & Kenneth Flamm, *The Global Factory: Foreign Assembly in International Trade*, Washington, D.C., The Brookings Institution, 1985, 38-136.

"Semiconductor Agreement: A Product of Anti-Japanese Sentiment" and Interviews, *Tokyo Business Today*, February 1987, 44-49.

"U.S.-Japan Competition in Semiconductors: American Makers Rethink Strategies," Japan Economic Institute, Report No. 16A, April 24, 1987.

Thomas A. Pugel, "Limits of Trade Policy toward High Technology Industries: The Case of Semiconductors," in Ryuzo Sato & Paul Wachtel, eds. *Trade Friction and Economic Policy: Problems and Prospects for Japan and the United States*, Cambridge University Press, 1987, 184-237.

John Greenwald, "Protectionism and U.S. Economic Policy," *Stanford Journal of International Law* 23:1 (Spr 1987), 233-61 (deals partly with semiconductor agreement).

Documentary Case Studies in International Trade. Study I: The Japan-U.S. Semiconductor Cases, Frederick, Md., University Publications of America, 1987 (microfiche with printed guide).

James W. Prendergast, "The European Economic Community's Challenge to the U.S.-Japan Semiconductor Agreement," *Law & Policy in International Business* 19:3 (1987), 579-601.

Thomas R. Howell, William A. Noellert, Janet H. MacLaughlin, & Alan Wm. Wolff, *The Microelectronics Race: The Impact of Government Policy on International Competition*, Boulder, Westview Press, 1988, esp. 35-144, "The Japanese Challenge."

Telecommunications

Timothy J. Curran, "Politics and High Technology: The NTT Case," in I.M. Destler & Hideo Sato, eds. *Coping with U.S.-Japanese Economic Conflicts*, Lexington, Mass., D.C. Heath, 1982, 185-241.

Edward Meadows, "Japan Runs into America, Inc.," *Fortune*, March 22, 1982, 56-61 [re: AT&T-Fujitsu controversy].

"U.S. Telecommunications Exports to Japan: The Deregulated Difference," Japan Economic Institute, Report No. 45A, December 12, 1986.

Defense, Technology, & Aircraft

William T. Tow, "U.S.-Japan Military Technology Transfers: Collaboration or Conflict?" *Journal of Northeast Asian Studies* 2:4 (Dec 1983), 3-23.

David Mowery & Nathan Rosenberg. "Commercial Aircraft: Cooperation and Competition Between the U.S. and Japan," *California Management Review* 27:4 (Sum 1985), 70-92.

Toshiro Hirota, "Technology Development of American and Japanese Companies," *Kansai University Review of Economics and Business* 14:1-2 (March 1986), 43-87.

Justin L. Bloom, "A New Era for U.S.-Japan Technical Relations? Problems and Prospects," *Journal of Northeast Asian Studies* 6:2 (Sum 1987), 24-52.

Cecil H. Uyehara, ed. *U.S.-Japan Science and Technology Exchange: Patterns of Interdependence*, Boulder, Westview Press, 1988.

Joint-Ventures & Investment

Thomas K. McCraw, ed. *America versus Japan*, Boston, Harvard Business School Press, 1986, including:
Dennis J. Encarnation, "Cross-Investment: A Second Front of Economic Rivalry," 117-50.

Robert B. Reich & Eric D. Mankin, "Joint Ventures with Japan: Giving Away our Future," *Harvard Business Review* 86:2 (March-April 1986), 78-86.

Richard N. Osborn & C. Christopher Baughn, "New Patterns in the Formation of US/Japanese Cooperative Ventures: The Role of Technology," *Columbia Journal of World Business* 22:2 (Sum 1987), 57-65.

Kiyoshi Kojima, "Agreed Specialisation and Cross Direct Investment," *Hitotsubashi Journal of Economics* 28:2 (Dec 1987), 87-105.

Harry I. Chernotsky, "The American Connection: Motives for Japanese Foreign Direct Investment," *Columbia Journal of World Business* 22:4 (Win 1987), 47-54.

Daniel Burstein, *YEN! Japan's New Financial Empire and Its Threat to America*, New York, Simon & Schuster, 1988.

Tyzoon T. Tyebjee, "A Typology of Joint Ventures: Japanese Strategies in the United States," *California Management Review* 31:1 (Fall 1988), 75-86.

B. GENERAL

Postwar Period, 1947-1971

H.W. Brands, Jr., "The United States and the Reemergence of Independent Japan," *Pacific Affairs* 59:3 (Fall 1986), 387-401.

Herbert P. Bix, "The Security Treaty System and the Japanese Military-Industrial Complex," *Bulletin of Concerned Asian Scholars* 2:2 (Jan 1970), 30-53.

Warren S. Hunsberger, "Japanese Exports and the American Market," *Far Eastern Survey* 26 (Sept 1957), 129-40.

United States Tariff Commission, *Postwar Developments in Japan's Foreign Trade*, Washington, US Government Printing Office, 1958 (Greenwood Press reprint, 1969).

Warren Hunsberger, *Japan and the United States in World Trade*, New York, Harper, 1964.

Hugh T. Patrick, "Dollar, Dollar, Who Has the Dollar?—Relationship Between the Japanese and American Balance of Payments," *Asian Survey* 6:8 (Aug 1966), 434-47.

Thomas K. McCraw, "From Partners to Competitors: An Overview of the Period Since World War II," in Thomas K. McCraw, ed. *America versus Japan*, Boston, Harvard Business School Press, 1986, 1-34.

Recent History, 1971-1988

Martin Bronfenbrenner, "A Japanese-American Economic War?" *Keio Economic Studies* 8:1 (1971), 1-12.

Henry Rosovsky, ed. *Discord in the Pacific: Challenges to the Japanese-American Alliance*, Washington, D.C., Columbia Books, 1972, including:
Gary R. Saxonhouse, "Employment, Imports, the Yen, and the Dollar," 79-116.

Jerome B. Cohen, ed. *Pacific Partnership: United States-Japan Trade, Prospects and Recommendations for the Seventies*, Lexington, Mass., Heath, 1972.

Japan and the Atlantic World, ed. by Curt Gasteyger, The Atlantic Papers, no. 3, London, Saxon House, 1972.

Asahi Shimbun, *The Pacific Rivals: A Japanese View of Japanese-American Relations*, Tokyo, Weatherhill, 1972.

Gary R. Saxonhouse, "A Review of Recent U.S.-Japanese Economic Relations," *Asian Survey* 12:9 (Sept 1972), 726-52.

Koji Taira, "Power and Trade in U.S.-Japanese Relations," *Asian Survey* 12:11 (Nov 1972), 980-98.

Koji Taira, "Reflections on U.S.-Japan Economic Conflict," *Management Japan* 6:3 (Win 1973), 26-34.

Allen Taylor, ed. *Perspectives on U.S.-Japan Economic Relations*, Cambridge, Ballinger, 1973.

A. Kapoor, ed. *Asian Business and Environment in Transition: Selected Readings and Essays*, Princeton, Darwin Press, 1976, including:
Yoshi Tsurumi, "The Strategic Framework for Japanese Investment in the United States," 420-28, from *Columbia Journal of World Trade* (Win 1973).

Martin Bronfenbrenner, "Japanese-American Economic War? Some Further Reflections," 440-49, from *Quarterly Journal of Economics & Business* (Aut 1973); see also *Keio Economic Studies* 10:1 (1973).

Priscilla Clapp & Morton Halperin, eds. *United States-Japanese Relations: The 1970s,* Harvard University Press, 1974, essays by Hisao Kanamori, Henry Rosovsky, and Dwight Perkins.

John E. Roemer, *U.S.-Japanese Competition in International Markets: A Study of the Trade-Investment Cycle in Modern Capitalism,* University of California, Berkeley, Institute of International Studies, Research Series no. 22, 1975.

Jack A. Lucken, "Japan and the United States: Economic Policy and Interdependence," *DE* 13:4 (Dec 1975), 337-73.

Gary Saxonhouse & Hugh Patrick, "Japan and the United States: Bilateral Tensions and Multilateral Issues in the Economic Relationships," in Donald Hellman, ed. *China & Japan: A New Balance of Power,* Lexington, Mass., Heath, 1976, 95-157.

James C. Abegglen & Thomas M. Hout, "Facing up to the Trade Gap with Japan," *Foreign Affairs* 57:1 (1978), 146-68.

Comptroller General of the United States, *United States-Japan Trade: Issues and Problems,* Washington, U.S. General Accounting Office, 1979.

I.M. Destler, "U.S.-Japanese Relations and the American Trade Initiative of 1977: Was This Trip Necessary?" in William J. Barnds, ed. *Japan and the United States: Challenges and Opportunities,* Council on Foreign Relations, New York University Press, 1979, 190-230.

Leon Hollerman, ed. *Japan and the United States: Economic and Political Adversaries,* Boulder, Westview Press, 1979, including:
Takeo Sasagawa, "Japanese-U.S. Relations in Science and Technology," 39-56.
Leon Hollerman, "Locomotive Strategy and U.S. Protectionism: A Japanese View," 189-212.

Michael Blaker, ed. *The Politics of Trade: U.S. and Japanese Policymaking for the GATT Negotiations,* Occasional Papers of the East Asian Institute, Columbia University, 1979.

George J. Viksnins, "U.S.-Japanese Trade: Perceptions and Reality," *Asian Survey* 19:3 (March 1979), 205-29.

Diana Tasca, ed. *U.S.-Japanese Economic Relations,* New York, Pergamon Press, 1980, including the following articles:

James C. Abegglen, "Narrow Self-interest: Japan's Ultimate Vulnerability?" 21-31.
Ken'ichi Imai, "Convergence or Collision: Alternative Scenarios for U.S.-Japanese Economic Relations," 97-115.

Matthew J. Marks, "Recent Changes in American Law on Regulatory Trade Measures," *The World Economy* 2:4 (Feb 1980), 427-40.

Leon Hollerman, "Disintegrative versus Integrative Aspects of Interdependence: The Japanese Case," *Asian Survey* 20:3 (March 1980), 324-31.

Sadako Ogata. "Some Japanese Views on United States-Japanese Relations in the 1980s," *Asian Survey* 20:7 (July 1980), 694-706.

"Global Protectionism and ADCs' Trade Strategies," in Wontack Hong & Lawrence B. Krause, eds. *Trade and Growth of the Advanced Developing Countries in the Pacific Basin*, Seoul, Korea Development Institute, 1981, 515-594.

Eleanor M. Hadley, "Is the U.S.-Japan Trade Imbalance a Problem? Economists Answer 'No,' Politicians 'Yes'," *Journal of Northeast Asian Studies* 1:1 (March 1982), 35-56.

Stefanie A. Lenway, "The Politics of Protection, Expansion, and Escape: International Collaboration and Business Power in U.S. Foreign Trade Policy," Ph.D. diss., University of California, Berkeley, 1982. [re: autos and telecommunications].

Ken-ichi Imai, "Japan's Changing Industrial Structure and United States-Japan Industrial Relations," in Kozo Yamamura, ed. *Policy and Trade Issues of the Japanese Economy: American and Japanese Perspectives*, University of Washington Press, 1982, 47-75.

I.M. Destler & Hideo Sato, eds. *Coping with U.S.-Japanese Economic Conflicts*, Lexington, Mass., D.C. Heath, 1982, including the following articles:
I.M. Destler & Hisao Mitsuyu, "Locomotives on Different Tracks: Macroeconomic Diplomacy, 1977-1979," 243-69.
I.M. Destler & Hideo Sato, "Coping with Economic Conflicts," 271-93.
Other articles from this volume are listed under the industry to which they pertain—steel, autos, agriculture, and telecommunications.

C. Fred Bergsten, "What To Do About the U.S.-Japan Economic Conflict," *Foreign Affairs* 60:5 (Sum 1982), 1059-75.

Yoshi Tsurumi, "Japan's Challenge to the U.S.: Industrial Policies and Corporate Strategies," *Columbia Journal of World Business* 17:2 (Sum 1982), 87-95.

Daniel I. Okimoto, ed. *Japan's Economy: Coping with Change in the International Environment*, Boulder, Westview Press, 1982, including:

Gary R. Saxonhouse, "Cyclical and Macrostructural Issues in U.S.-Japan Economic Relations," 123-48.

Hugh T. Patrick, "The Economic Dimensions of the U.S.-Japan Alliance: An Overview," 149-96.

Ryutaro Komiya, "The U.S.-Japan Trade Conflict: An Economist's View from Japan," 197-230.

Kent E. Calder, "Forestalling a Trade War," *Asia Pacific Community* 15 (Win 1982), 1-14.

Frank Langdon, "Japan-United States Trade Friction: The Reciprocity Issue," *Asian Survey* 23:5 (May 1983), 653-66.

Susan C. Schwab, "Japan and the U.S. Congress," *Journal of International Affairs* 37:1 (Sum 1983), 123-39.

John Zysman and Laura Tyson, eds., *American Industry in International Competition: Government Policies and Corporate Strategies*, Cornell University Press, 1983.

McKinsey & Co. (for the United States Japan Trade Study Group), *Japan Business: Obstacles and Opportunities*, Tokyo, President Inc., 1983.

George Gilder, *The Spirit of Enterprise*, New York, Simon & Schuster, 1984, "Japan's Entrepreneurs," 175-201 and passim.

Peter A. Petri, *Modeling Japanese-American Trade: A Study of Asymmetric Interdependence*, Harvard University Press, 1984.

Hideo Sato, "Political Dynamics of U.S.-Japan Economic Conflicts," *Journal of Northeast Asian Studies* 3:1 (Spr 1984), 3-15.

Robert Ballance & Stuart Sinclair, "Re-industrialising America: Policy Makers and Interest Groups," *The World Economy* 7:2 (June 1984), 197-214.

Stephen D. Cohen, *Uneasy Partnership: Competition and Conflict in U.S.-Japanese Trade Relations*, Cambridge, Mass., Ballinger, 1985.

Rachel McCulloch, "Trade Deficits, Industrial Competitiveness, and the Japanese," *California Management Review* 27:2 (Win 1985), 140-56.

C. Fred Bergsten & William R. Cline, *The United States-Japan Economic Problem*, Washington, D.C., Institute for International Economics, 1985.

Herbert P. Bix, "The 'Japanese Challenge': US-Japan Relations at Mid-Decade," *Bulletin of Concerned Asian Scholars* 17:4 (Oct-Dec 1985), 27-33.

Hiroshi Kitamura, Ryohei Murata, & Hisahiko Okazaki, *Between Friends: Japanese Diplomats Look at Japan-U.S. Relations*, New York, Weatherhill, 1985, 95-141.

I.M. Destler, *American Trade Politics: System under Stress*, Washington, DC, Institute for International Economics, 1986.

Thomas A. Pugel, ed. *Fragile Interdependence: Economic Issues in U.S.-Japanese Trade and Investment*, Lexington, Heath, 1986.

Gary Saxonhouse, "Japan's Intractable Trade Surpluses in a New Era," *The World Economy* 9:3 (Sept 1986), 239-257.

Gary Saxonhouse & Kozo Yamamura, eds. *Law and Trade Issues of the Japanese Economy: American and Japanese Perspectives*, University of Washington Press, 1986, the following articles:
Gary Saxonhouse, "The National Security Clause of the Trade Expansion Act of 1962: Import Competition and the Machine Tool Industry," 218-37.
Paula Stern & Andrew Wechsler, "Escape Clause Relief and Recessions: An Economic and Legal Look at Section 20l," 195-217.

George C. Eads & Richard R. Nelson, "Japanese High Technology Policy: What Lessons for the United States?" in Hugh Patrick, ed. *Japan's High Technology Industries: Lessons and Limitations of Industrial Policy*, University of Washington Press, 1986, 243-69.

Daniel K. Tarullo, "Foreword: The Structure of U.S.-Japan Trade Relations," *Harvard International Law Journal* 27: Special Issue (1986), 343-60.

Thomas J. Schoenbaum, Mitsuo Matsushita & Dorinda G. Dallmeyer, eds. *Dynamics of Japanese-United States Trade Relations*, Athens, University of Georgia Law School, 1986.

Henrik Schmiegelow, "Global Dimensions in US-Japan Relations," *Aussen Politik* 37:3 (1986), 222-38.

Karel G. van Wolferen, "The Japan Problem," *Foreign Affairs* 65:2 (Win 1986/87), 288-303.

C. Fred Bergsten, "Economic Imbalances and World Politics," *Foreign Affairs* 65:4 (Spr 1987), 770-94.

Martin Feldstein, "Correcting the Trade Deficit," *Foreign Affairs* 65:4 (Spr 1987), 795-806.

John Greenwald, "Protectionism and U.S. Economic Policy," *Stanford Journal of International Law* 23:1 (Spr 1987), 233-61 (deals partly with semiconductor agreement).

Chalmers Johnson, "How to Think About Economic Cooperation From Japan," *Journal of Japanese Studies* 13:2 (Sum 1987), 415-27.

Kevin C. Kennedy, "Voluntary Restraint Agreements: A Threat to Representative Democracy," *Hastings International and Comparative Law Review* 11:1 (Fall 1987), 1-40.

Thomas F. Cargill, "A Perspective on Trade Imbalances and United States Policies Toward Japan," *Columbia Journal of World Business* 22:4 (Win 1987), 55-60.

Clyde V. Prestowitz, Jr., "U.S.-Japan Trade Friction: Creating a New Relationship," *California Management Review* 29:2 (Win 1987), 9-19.

Ellen L. Frost, *For Richer, For Poorer: The New U.S.-Japan Relationship*, Council on Foreign Relations, 1987.

Ryuzo Sato & Paul Wachtel, eds. *Trade Friction and Economic Policy: Problems and Prospects for Japan and the United States*, Cambridge University Press, 1987.

Clyde V. Prestowitz Jr., *Trading Places: How We Allowed Japan to Take the Lead*, New York, Basic Books, 1988.

Helen Milner, "Trading Places: Industries for Free Trade," World Politics 45:3 (Apr 1988), 350-76.

Kazuo Nukazawa, "Japan & the USA: Wrangling toward Reciprocity," *Harvard Business Review* 88:3 (May-June 1988), 42-50.

Robert M. Orr, Jr., "The Aid Factor in U.S.-Japan Relations," *Asian Survey* 28:7 (July 1988), 740-56.

"The 1988 Trade Act: An Overview," Japan Economic Institute, Report No. 38A, October 7, 1988.

Takashi Inoguchi & Daniel Okimoto, eds. *The Political Economy of Japan*, vol. 2, *The Changing International Context*, Stanford University Press, 1988, including:
Robert G. Gilpin, "Implications of the Changing Trade Regime for U.S.-Japanese Relations," 138-70.
Stephen D. Krasner, "Japan and the United States: Prospects for Stability," 381-413.

Yearbook of U.S.-Japan Economic Relations, series since the late 1970s, Washington, Japan Economic Institute.

12. INTERNATIONAL RELATIONS (by area: non-USA)

A. CANADA & AUSTRALIA

Keith A.J. Hay, *Japan: Challenge and Opportunity for Canadian Industry*, The Canadian Economic Policy Committee Private Planning Association of Canada, 1971.

Lorne J. Kavic, "Canada and Asia: Evolving Awareness and Deepening Links," *Pacific Affairs* 45:4 (Win 1972-73), 521-34.

K.A.J. Hay, *Friends or Acquaintances? Canada and Japan's Other Trading Partners in the Early 1980's*, Montreal, Institute for Research on Public Policy, Occasional Paper No. 6, 1979.

Keith Hay, *Canada as a Resource Supplier to the Japanese Economy*, Montreal, Institute for Research on Public Policy, 1980.

Keith A.J. Hay, ed. *Canadian Perspectives on Economic Relations with Japan*, Montreal, Institute for Research on Public Policy, 1980, including:
Frank Langdon, "Problems of Canada-Japan Economic Diplomacy in the 1960s and 1970s: The Third Option," 73-89.
R.A. Matthews & A.R. Moroz, "The Impact of Imports from Japan on Canadian Manufacturers," 207-65.
Keith A.J. Hay & Michael W. Donnelly, "Canadian-Japanese Agricultural Trade," 341-76.

Frank Langdon, *The Politics of Canadian-Japanese Economic Relations, 1952-1983*, University of British Columbia Press, 1983.

Wendy Dobson, ed. *Canadian-Japanese Economic Relations in a Triangular Perspective*, C.D. Howe Institute, Observation No. 30, Scarborough, Prentice-Hall, 1987, the following articles:
Wendy Dobson, "A Canadian Perspective," 1-35.
Hideo Sato, "A Japanese Perspective," 37-54.

Keith A.J. Hay, S.R. Hill, & S.S. Rahman, *Canadian Coal for Japan*, Ottawa, Econolynx International, 1982.

Christopher E. Catliff, "Japan's Government and Steel Industry Policies towards Coking Coal Procurement: The Implications of Industrial Restructuring for the Northeast Coal Project," MA thesis, University of Biritsh Columbia, 1985.

David L. Anderson, *An Analysis of Japanese Coking Coal Procurement Policies: The Canadian and Australian Experience*, Kingston, Queens University Press, 1987.

Albert D. Cohen, *The Entrepreneurs: The Story of Gendis, Inc.*, Toronto, Mc-Clelland & Stewart, 1985 (re: Sony distribution).

H. Matsusaki, "Japanese Managers and Management in the Western World: A Canadian Experience," in A.R. Negandhi, ed. *Functioning of the Multinational Corporation: A Global Comparative Study*, New York, Pergamon Press, 1980, 226-54.

Richard W. Wright, *Japanese Business in Canada: The Elusive Alliance*, Montreal, The Institute for Research on Public Policy, 1984.

Peter Drysdale, "Minerals and Metals in Japanese-Australian Trade," *DE* 8:2 (June 1970), 198-218.

J.T. Yamaguchi, "Acculturation and Alienation of the Expatriate Managers of Japanese Firms in Australia," in Stewart R. Clegg, Dexter C. Dunphy & S. Gordon Redding, *The Enterprise and Management in East Asia*, Center of Asian Studies, University of Hong Kong, 1986, 413-41.

B. EUROPE

Japan and the Atlantic World, ed. by Curt Gasteyger, The Atlantic Papers, no. 3, London, Saxon House, 1972.

M. Hanabusa, *Trade between Japan and Western Europe*, London, RIIA, 1979.

Geoffrey Shepard, "The Japanese Challenge to Western Europe's New Crisis Industries," *The World Economy* 4:4 (Dec 1981), 375-90.

Frank Langdon, "Japan versus the European Community: The Automobile Crisis," *Journal of European Integration* (Revue d'integration europeenne) 5:1 (1981), 80-98.

Loukas Tsoulakis & Maureen White, eds. *Japan and Western Europe*, London, Frances Pinter, 1982.

Albrecht Rothacher, *Economic Diplomacy between the European Community and Japan, 1959-1981*, Hampshire, Gower Publishing, 1983.

Kwan S. Kim, "East Asian Coping Strategies: The South Korean Case," in Lee A. Tavis, ed. *Rekindling Development: Multinational Firms and World Debt*, University of Notre Dame Press, 1988, 119-37.

Chung-In Moon, "The Demise of a Developmentalist State? Neoconservative Reforms and Political Consequences in South Korea," *Journal of Developing Societies* 4:1 (Jan-Apr 1988), 67-84.

Peter K. Kang, "Political and Corporate Group Interest in South Korea's Political Economy,," *Asian Profile* 16:3 (June 1988), 209-23.

Northeast Asia: General

Tzong-shian Yu, "The Development of Relations Between the Republic of China and Japan since 1972," *Asian Survey* 21:9 (June 1981), 632-44.

James M. Lutz, "Symbiosis in Manufactures Trade in East Asia," *Journal of Northeast Asian Studies* 5:3 (Fall 1986), 3-18.

"The Changing Pattern of Japanese Trade: Northeast Asia," Japan Economic Institute, Report No. 31A, August 14, 1987.

Frederic C. Deyo, ed. *The Political Economy of the New Asian Industrialism*, Ithaca, Cornell University Press, 1987, the following:
Bruce Cumings, "The Origins and Development of the Northeast Asian Political Economy: Industrial Sectors, Product Cycles, and Political Consequences," 44-83.
Chalmers Johnson, "Political Institutions and Economic Performance: The Government-Business Relationship in Japan, South Korea, and Taiwan," 136-64.

D. ASEAN, NICs & THE THIRD WORLD

General

Yoichi Itagaki, "Reparations and Southeast Asia," *Japan Quarterly* 6 (1959), 410-19.

Fukuo Kawata, "The Development of Japanese Trade with the British Commonwealth in Asia," *Kobe Economic and Business Review* 14 (1967), 21-40.

Yung-Hwan Jo, "Regional Cooperation in Southeast Asia and Japan's Role," *The Journal of Politics* 30:3 (Aug 1968), 780-97.

Hisashi Kawada, "Japanese International Technical Cooperation and Economic Development: East and South Asian Countries," *Keio Economic Studies* 6:2 (1969), 1-22.

Liang-Shing Fan, "Pulling Effects and the Capacity to Follow: The Case of Japan in East Asia," *DE* 8:2 (June 1970), 219-28.

Akira Onishi, "Japanese Interests in Southeast Asia: A Japanese View," *Asian Survey* 11:4 (Apr 1971), 413-21.

Tadashi Kawata, "The Asian Situation and Japan's Economic Relations with the Developing Countries," *DE* 9:2 (June 1971), 133-53.

Chujiro Fujino, "The Role of General Trading Company in the Industrialization of Developing Countries," *Management Japan* 5:2 (1971), 9-13.

Atsushi Murakami, "Economic Policies of Japan toward Developing Asian Countries: The Role of Japan in Economic Cooperation," *Kobe University Economic Review* 17 (1971), 29-53.

K.V. Kesavan, *Japan's Relations with Southeast Asia, 1952-60: With Particular Reference to the Philippines and Indonesia*, Bombay, Somaiya Publications, 1972, 73-106 (reparations), and 181-201 (reparations and trade).

Chie Nakane, "Social Background of Japanese in Southeast Asia," *DE* 10:2 (June 1972), 115-25.

Yuzuru Kato, "Sources of Loanable Funds of Agricultural Credit Institutions in Asia: Japan's Experience," *DE* 10:2 (June 1972), 126-40.

Kiyoshi Kojima, "Reorganization of North-South Trade: Japan's Foreign Economic Policy for the 1970s," *Hitotsubashi Journal of Economics* 13:2 (Feb 1973), 1-28.

T.W. Allen, *Direct Investment of Japanese Enterprises in Southeast Asia: A Study of Motivations, Characteristics and Attitudes*, Manila, Ecocen, 1973.

Jon Halliday & Gavan McCormick, *Japanese Imperialism Today: Co-Prosperity in Greater East Asia*, Penguin, 1973.

Special Issue: "Southeast Asia's Economy and Japan," *DE* 11:4 (Dec 1973).

Noritake Kobayashi, "Japan's Role in Southeast Asia," in A. Kapoor, ed. *Asian Business and Environment in Transition: Selected Readings and Essays*, Princeton, Darwin Press, 1976, 450-78.

Raul S. Manglapus, *Japan in Southeast Asia: Collision Course*, New York, Carnegie Endowment for International Peace, 1976.

Franklin B. Weinstein, "Multinational Corporations and the Third World: The Case of Japan and Southeast Asia," *International Organization* 30 (Sum 1976), 373-404.

Miyohei Shinohara, *The Japanese Economy and Southeast Asia*, Institute of Developing Economies, Occasional Papers Series, no. 15, 1977.

Hikojo Kitano, et al. *Japan's Direct Investment to ASEAN Countries*, Kobe, Research Institute for Economics and Business Administration, 1978.

Kunio Yoshihara, *Japanese Investments in Southeast Asia*, The University Press of Hawaii, 1978.

Ippei Yamazawa & Akira Hirata, "Industrialization and External Relations: Comparative Analysis of Japan's Historical Experience and Contemporary Developing Countries' Performance," *Hitotsubashi Journal of Economics* 18:2 (Feb 1978), 33-61.

Kiyoshi Kojima, "Direct Foreign Investment to Developing Countries: The Issue of Over-Presence," *Hitotsubashi Journal of Economics* 19:1-2 (Dec 1978), 1-15.

Saburo Okita, "ASEAN and Its Relations with Japan and the United States," in Leon Hollerman, ed. *Japan and the United States: Economic and Political Adversaries*, Boulder, Westview Press, 1979, 97-110.

Saburo Okita, *The Developing Economies and Japan*, University of Tokyo Press, 1980.

Shin'ichi Ichimura, "Japan and Southeast Asia," *Asian Survey* 20:7 (July 1980), 754-62.

J.A. Braveboy-Wagner, "Japan and the Third World: A Study of the Changing Attitudes of Japanese Businessmen Toward Developing Countries and Peoples," *Asian Profile* 8:4 (Aug 1980), 329-48.

Special Issue: "Changing Industrial Structure in International Perspective," *DE* 18:4 (Dec 1980), including:
Toshio Watanabe, "An Analysis of Economic Interdependence among the Asian NICs, the ASEAN Nations, and Japan, 393-411.
Takuo Tanaka, "The Patterns of International Specialization among Asian Countries and the Future of Japanese Industry," 412-440.
Seiichi Nakajo, "Japanese Direct Investment in Asian Newly Industrializing Countries and Intra-Firm Division of Labor," 463-83.

Ippei Yamazawa, "Development through Industrialization and Foreign Trade: Comparative Analysis of Japan and Asian Developing Countries," in Hongladarom Chira & Medhi Kronkaew, eds. *Comparative Development: Japan and Thailand*, Bangkok, Thammasat University Press, 1981, 192-220.

Akira Ono, "Borrowed Technology in the Iron and Steel Industry: A Comparison between Brazil, India and Japan," *Hitotsubashi Journal of Economics* 21:2 (Feb 1981), 1-18.

Shin'ichi Ichimura, "Japanese Firms in Asia," *JES* 10:1 (Fall 1981), 31-52.

Ryokichi Hirono, "Industrialization and Technology Transfer in Southeast Asia: Case of Japanese Subsidiaries Overseas," in Alex Kerr, ed. *The Indian Ocean Region: Resources and Development*, Nedlands, Western Australia, University of Western Australia Press and Boulder, Westview Press, 1981, 61-108.

Kiichiro Fukasaku, "The Effects of Japan's Liberalisation of Trade on the Promotion of Exports by Developing Countries," *Proceedings of the British Association for Japanese Studies* 6: Part 1 (1981), 152-67.

Ronald Dore, "Japan and the Third World: Coincidence or Divergence of Interests," in Robert Cassen, et al., eds. *Rich Country Interests and Third World Development*, London, Croom Helm, 1982.

Lee Farnsworth, "Japan and the Third World," in P. Taylor & G.A. Raymond, eds. *Third World Policies of Industrialized Nations*, Westport, Greenwood Press, 1982, 163-85.

Shigeko N. Fukai, "Japan's North-South Dialogue at the United Nations," *World Politics* 35:1 (Oct 1982), 73-105.

Ippei Yamazawa et al., "Trade and Industrial Adjustment in Pacific Asian Countries," *DE* 21:4 (Dec 1983), 281-312.

Alan Rix & Ross Mouer, eds. *Japan's Impact on the World*, Griffith University, Japanese Studies Association of Australia, 1984.

J.E. Everett et al., *South-East Asian Managers: Mutual Perceptions of Japanese and Local Counterparts*, Singapore, Eastern Universities Press, 1984.

Tessa Morris-Suzuki, "Japan's Role in the International Division of Labour: A Reassessment," *Journal of Contemporary Asia* 14:1 (1984), 62-81.

Kazushi Ohkawa & Gustav Ranis, eds., *Japan and the Developing Countries: A Comparative Analysis*, Oxford, Basil Blackwell, 1985.

Warren E. Davis & Daryl G. Hatano, "The American Semiconductor Industry and the Ascendancy of East Asia," *California Management Review* 27:4 (Sum 1985), 128-43.

Ulrich Menzel, "The Newly Industrializing Countries of East Asia: Imperialist Continuity or a Case of Catching Up?" in Wolfgang J. Mommsen & Jurgen Osterhammel, eds. *Imperialism and After: Continuities and Discontinuities*, London, Allen & Unwin, 1986, 247-63.

Chalmers Johnson, "The Nonsocialist NICS: East Asia," *International Organization* 40:2 (1986), 557-65.

Wontack Hong, "Trade, Growth and Economic Problems of Asian NICs," *Hitotsubashi Journal of Economics* 27: Special Issue (Oct 1986), 79-l00.

Jon Woronoff, *Asia's 'Miracle' Economies*, Tokyo, Lotus Press, 1986.

Special Issue: "Technology Transfer from Japan to Asian Developing Countries," *DE* 24:4 (Dec 1986), 309-420.

K.S. Nathan & M. Pathmanathan, eds. *Trilateralism in Asia: Problems and Prospects in U.S.-Japan-ASEAN Relations*, Kuala Lumpur, Antara Book Co., 1986.

Anant R. Negandhi, et al., "Localisation of Japanese Subsidiaries in Southeast Asia," *Asia Pacific Journal of Management* 5:1 (Sept 1987), 67-79.

Sueo Sudo, "From Fukuda to Takeshita: A Decade of Japan-ASEAN Relations," *Contemporary Southeast Asia* 10:2 (Sept 1988), 119-43.

Charles E. Morrison, "Japan and the ASEAN Countries: The Evolution of Japan's Regional Role," in Takashi Inoguchi & Daniel Okimoto, eds. *The Political Economy of Japan*, vol. 2, *The Changing International Context*, Stanford University Press, 1988, 414-45.

"Japan and Southeast Asia: An Update," Japan Economic Institute, Report No. 1A, January 6, 1989.

Specific Countries & Territories

Vivian Lin, "Productivity First: Japanese Management Methods in Singapore," *Bulletin of Concerned Asian Scholars* 16:4 (Oct-Dec 1984), 12-25.

Hafiz Mirza, *Multinationals and the Growth of the Singapore Economy*, London, Croom Helm, 1986.

John Milton-Smith, "Japanese Management Overseas: International Business Strategy and the Case of Singapore," in Stewart R. Clegg, Dexter C. Dunphy & S. Gordon Redding, *The Enterprise and Management in East Asia*, Center of Asian Studies, University of Hong Kong, 1986, 395-411.

C.P. Lim & L.P. Ping, *Japanese Investment in Malaysia*, Singapore, Institute of Southeast Asian Studies, 1979.

Khong Kim Hoong, "Malaysia-Japan Relations in the 1980s," *Asian Survey* 27:10 (Oct 1987), 1095-1108.

J. Panglaykim, "Business Relations Between Indonesia and Japan," *DE* 12:3 (Sept 1974), 281-303.

J. Panglaykim, *Indonesia's Economic and Business Relations with ASEAN and Japan*, Jakarta, Centre for Strategic and Economic Studies, 1977.

J. Panglaykim, "Economic Cooperation: Indonesian-Japanese Joint Ventures," *Asian Survey* 18:3 (March 1978), 247-60.

Alan G. Rix, "The Mitsugoro Project: Japanese Aid Policy and Indonesia," *Pacific Affairs* 52 (Spr 1979), 42-63.

Yoshinori Murai, "Japan—the View from Indonesia," *Japan Quarterly* 27:2 (Apr-June 1980), 204-14.

Toshihiko Kinoshita, "Japanese Investment in Indonesia: Problems and Prospects," *Bulletin of Indonesian Economic Studies* 22:1 (Apr 1986), 34-56.

Ruperto Alonzo, "Japan's Economic Impact on ASEAN Countries," *Indonesian Quarterly* 15 (July 1987), 472-87.

Ippei Yamazawa, "Manufactured Exports from Thailand and the Japanese Market," *Hitotsubashi Journal of Economics* 20:2 (Feb 1980), 1-10.

Koji Taira, "Colonialism in Foreign Subsidiaries: Lessons from Japanese Investment in Thailand," *Asian Survey* 20:4 (April 1980), 373-96.

Jean-Pierre Lehmann, "Variations on a Pan-Asianist Theme: The 'Special Relationship' between Japan and Thailand," in Ronald Dore & Radha Sinha, eds. *Japan and the World Depression, Then and Now: Essays in Memory of E.F. Penrose*, London, Macmillan, 1987, 178-201.

Romeo M. Bautista & Gwendolyn R. Tecson, "Philippine Export Trade with Japan and the United States: Responsiveness to Exchange Rate Changes," *DE* 13:4 (Dec 1975), 400-20.

A.D.V. de S. Indraratna, "Sri Lanka and Japan: A Case Study in Economic Cooperation," *Keio Business Review* 18 (1981), 97-147.

Yoshiaki Nishimukai, "Recent Changes in Japan's Trade with Latin America and Brazil," *Kobe Economic and Business Review* 15 (1968), 77-112.

C. Harvey Gardiner, *The Japanese and Peru, 1873-1973*, Albuquerque, University of New Mexico Press, 1975.

Yoko Kitazawa, "Development as Dependence: Japanese Inroads into the Brazilian Economy," *Ampo* 11:4 (1979), 42-51.

Charles H. Smith III, *Japanese Technology Transfer to Brazil*, Epping, Essex, England, Bowker, 1982.

Leon Hollerman, *Japan's Economic Strategy in Brazil: Challenge for the United States*, Lexington, D.C. Heath, 1988.

James R. Soukup, "Japanese-African Relations: Problems and Prospects," *Asian Survey* 5:7 (July 1965), 333-40.

Katsu Yanaihara, "Japanese Overseas Enterprises in Developing Countries under Indigenization Policy: The African Case," *JES* 4:1 (Fall 1975), 23-51.

E. CHINA

Yoko Yasuharu, "Japan, Communist China, and Export Controls in Asia, 1948-52," *Diplomatic History* 10:1 (Win 1986), 75-89.

Nancy B. Tucker, "American Policy toward Sino-Japanese Trade in the Postwar Years: Politics and Prosperity," *Diplomatic History* 8:3 (Sum 1984), 183-208.

Takeo Arai, "Post-War Relations between Japan and China," *DE* 5:1 (March 1967), 105-21.

Chae-Jin Lee, "The Politics of Sino-Japanese Trade Relations, 1963-68," *Pacific Affairs* 42 (1969), 129-44.

Haruhiro Fukui, *Party in Power: The Japanese Liberal Democrats and Policymaking*, University of California, 1970, 227-62.

Kenzo Uchida, "A Brief History of Postwar Japan-China Relations," *DE* 9:4 (Dec 1971), 538-54.

Sadako Ogata, "The Business Community and Japanese Foreign Policy: Normalization of Relations with the People's Republic of China," in Robert A. Scalapino, ed. *The Foreign Policy of Modern Japan*, University of California Press, 1977, 175-203.

Kaheita Okazaki, "New Hope and Confidence: The 1971 Memorandum Trade Negotiations," *Japan Interpreter* 7:2 (Spr 1972), 120-28.

David G. Brown, "Chinese Economic Leverage in Sino-Japanese Relations," *Asian Survey* 12:9 (Sept 1972), 753-71.

Gene T. Hsiao, "The Role of Trade in China's Diplomacy with Japan," in Jerome A. Cohen, ed. *The Dynamics of China's Foreign Relations*, Harvard University Press, 1973, 41-56.

Alvin Coox & Hilary Conroy, eds. *China and Japan: Search for Balance Since World War I*, Santa Barbara, ABC-Clio Press, 1978, including:
Yung H. Park, "The Roots of Detente," 353-84, and "The Tanaka Government and the Mechanics of the China Decision," 385-97.

Chalmers Johnson, "The Japanese Problem," in Donald Hellman, ed. *China & Japan: A New Balance of Power*, Lexington, Mass., Heath, 1976, 51-94.

Song Yook Hong, *The Sino-Japanese Fisheries Agreements of 1975: A Comparison with Other North-Pacific Fisheries Agreements*, University of Maryland, School of Law, Occasional Papers/Reprint Series in Contemporary Asian Studies, 1977.

Wolf Mendl, *Issues in Japan's China Policy*, London, Macmillan, 1978 (some documents).

R.K. Jain, *China and Japan, 1949-1976*, Atlantic Highlands, N.J., Humanities Press, 1978.

Shinkichi Eto, "Recent Developments in Sino-Japanese Relations," *Asian Survey* 20:7 (July 1980), 726-43.

Masanori Moritani, "Japan, China, and Korea: A Cross-Cultural Comparison of Industrial Technology," *JES* 9:4 (Sum 1981), 3-51.

David G. Brown, "Sino-Foreign Joint Ventures: Contemporary Developments and Historical Perspectives," *Journal of Northeast Asian Studies* 1:4 (Dec 1982), 25-55.

Kosaku Matsumoto, "External Elements of China's Economic Policy and Japan's Financial Assistance to China," *JES* 12:1 (Fall 1983), 71-85.

Chae-Jin Lee, *China and Japan: New Economic Diplomacy*, Stanford University Press, 1984.

Walter Arnold, "Japan and China," in Robert S. Ozaki & Walter Arnold, eds., *Japan's Foreign Relations: A Global Search for Economic Security*, Boulder, Westview Press, 1985, 102-16.

David G. Brown, *Partnership with China: Sino-Foreign Joint Ventures in Historical Perspective*, Boulder, Westview. Press, 1985.

Hong N. Kim and Richard K. Nanto, "Emerging Patterns of Sino-Japanese Economic Cooperation," *Journal of Northeast Asian Studies* 4:3 (Fall 1985), 29-47.

Jack F. Williams, "The Economies of Hong Kong and Taiwan and their Future Relationships with the P.R.C.," *Journal of Northeast Asian Studies* 4:3 (Spr 1985), 58-80.

Roy F. Grow, "Japanese and American Firms in China: Lessons of a New Market," *Columbia Journal of World Business* 21:1 (Spr 1986), 49-56.

Chalmers Johnson, "The Patterns of Japanese Relations with China, 1952-1982," *Pacific Affairs* 59:3 (Fall 1986), 402-28.

S. Gordon Redding and D.S. Pugh, "The Formal and the Informal: Japanese and Chinese Organization Structures," in Stewart R. Clegg, Dexter C. Dunphy & S. Gordon Redding, *The Enterprise and Management in East Asia*, Center of Asian Studies, University of Hong Kong, 1986, 153-67.

Vaclav Smil, "China and Japan in the New Energy Era," in Peter N. Nemetz, ed. *The Pacific Rim: Investment, Development and Trade*, University of British Columbia Press, 1987, 223-33.

Ryutaro Komiya, "Japanese Firms, Chinese Firms: Problems for Economic Reform in China," *Journal of the Japanese and International Economies* (1) 1:1 (March 1987), 31-61; (2) 1:2 (June 1987), 229-47.

Taifa Yu, "Progress, Problems, and Prospects of Sino-Japanese Economic Relations: Bilateral Trade and Technological Cooperation," *Asian Perspective* 11:2 (Fall-Win 1987), 218-47.

Penelope Francks, "Learning from Japan: Plant Imports and Technology Transfer in the Chinese Iron and Steel Industry," *Journal of the Japanese and International Economies* 2:1 (March 1988), 42-62.

John Quansheng Zhao, "The Making of Public Policy in Japan: Protectionism in Raw Silk Importation," *Asian Survey* 28:9 (Sept 1988), 926-44.

301

Laura Newby, *Sino-Japanese Relations: China's Perspective*, London, Routledge, 1988, esp. 5-47.

K. John Fukuda, *Japanese-Style Management Transferred: The Experience of East Asia*, London, Routledge, 1988.

F. SOVIET UNION

David I. Hitchcock, Jr. "Joint Development of Siberia: Decision-Making in Japanese-Soviet Relations," *Asian Survey* 11:3 (March 1971), 279-300.

Special Issue: "Soviet Views of the Japanese Economy," *JES* 2:2 (Win 1973-74).

Gerald L. Curtis, "The Tyumen Oil Development Project and Japanese Foreign Policy Decision-Making," in Robert A. Scalapino, ed. *The Foreign Policy of Modern Japan*, University of California Press, 1977, 147-73.

Raymond S. Mathieson, *Japan's Role in Soviet Economic Growth: Transfer of Technology since 1965*, Praeger, 1979.

Hiroshi Kimura, "Japan-Soviet Relations: Framework, Developments, Prospects," *Asian Survey* 20:7 (July 1980), 707-25.

Allen S. Whiting, *Siberian Development and East Asia: Threat or Promise?*, Stanford University Press, 1981.

Kazuo Ogawa, "Japan-Soviet Economic Relations: Present Status and Future Prospects," *Journal of Northeast Asian Studies* 2:1 (March 1983), 3-15.

JES 12:1 (Fall 1983), the following:
Kazuo Ogawa, "The USSR's External Economic Relations and Japan," 26-53.
Keisuke Suzuki & Ken'ichiro Yokowo, "Japan's Trade Mission to Moscow, February 1983: What Did It Accomplish?" 54-70.

"Japanese-Soviet Relations: Will 'Glasnost' Bring a Breakthrough," Japan Economic Institute, Report No. 36A, September 23, 1988.

G. REGIONAL

William W. Lockwood, "Asian Triangle: China, India, Japan," in A. Kapoor, ed. *Asian Business and Environment in Transition: Selected Readings and Essays*, Princeton, Darwin Press, 1976, 11-31.

Barbara Johnson & Frank Langdon, "Two Hundred Mile Zones: The Politics of North Pacific Fisheries," *Pacific Affairs* 49 (1976), 5-27.

Akira Ishii, " 'Three Chinas' and 'One Russia'," *JES* 12:1 (Fall 1983), 3-25.

Chalmers Johnson, "Japan's Role in Asia and the Pacific: Its Relation with the United States, China, and the USSR," in Robert Scalapino & Chen Qimao, eds. *Pacific-Asian Issues: American and Chinese Views*, University of California, Institute of East Asian Studies, 1986, 111-31.

Tsuneo Akaha, "Japan's Response to Threats of Shipping Disruptions in Southeast Asia and the Middle East," *Pacific Affairs* 59:2 (Sum 1986), 255-77.

Edward J. Lincoln, *Japan's Economic Role in Northeast Asia*, Lanham, Maryland, University Press of America, 1987.

Yoko Sazanami, "Japanese Trade in the Pacific Rim: The Relationship between Trade and Investment," in Peter N. Nemetz, ed. *The Pacific Rim: Investment, Development and Trade*, University of British Columbia Press, 1987, 53-73.

Robert A. Scalapino, *Major Power Relations in Northeast Asia*, Lanham, MD, 1987, 4-21.

Roy Kim & Hilary Conroy, *New Tides in the Pacific*, Westport, Greenwood Press, 1987, the following:
James William Morley, "The Genesis of the Pacific Basin Movement and Japan," 11-34.
Vladimir I. Ivanov, "The Pacific Economic Community: Unsettled Problems," 69-81.